Alice
Pike
Barney

Alice Pike Barney

HER LIFE AND ART

JEAN L. KLING

Introduction by WANDA M. CORN

NATIONAL MUSEUM OF AMERICAN ART
in association with
SMITHSONIAN INSTITUTION PRESS
WASHINGTON AND LONDON

Frontispiece: Alice Pike Barney at her easel in her west studio at Studio House, 1909

Library of Congress Catalog Card Number: 93-26425
ISBN: 1-56098-344-2

Printed in Hong Kong by
South China Printing Company (1988) Limited

Editor: Jane D. Marsching
Editorial Assistant: Deborah Thomas
Designed by Wendy Byrne

Kling, Jean L.
    Alice Pike Barney : Her Life and Art / Jean L. Kling : introduction by
Wanda Corn.
        p.   cm.
    Includes bibliographical references and index.
        1. Barney, Alice Pike, 1857-1931. 2. Women artists — United States —
Biography. 3. Women art patrons — United States — Biography.
    I. Title.
    N6537.B222K58 1994
    700'.92 — dc20   93-26425
    [B]   CIP

The National Museum of American Art, Smithsonian Institution, is dedicated to the preservation, exhibition, and study of the visual arts in America. The museum, whose publications program also includes the scholarly journal *American Art*, has extensive research resources: the databases of the Inventories of American Painting and Sculpture, several image archives, and a variety of fellowships for scholars. The Renwick Gallery, one of the nation's premier craft museums, is part of NMAA. For more information or a catalogue of publications, write: Office of Publications, National Museum of American Art, Smithsonian Institution, Washington, D.C. 20560.

Alice Pike Barney

HER LIFE AND ART

JEAN L. KLING

Introduction by WANDA M. CORN

NATIONAL MUSEUM OF AMERICAN ART
in association with
SMITHSONIAN INSTITUTION PRESS
WASHINGTON AND LONDON

Frontispiece: Alice Pike Barney at her easel in her west studio at Studio House, 1909

Library of Congress Catalog Card Number: 93-26425
ISBN: 1-56098-344-2

Printed in Hong Kong by
South China Printing Company (1988) Limited

Editor: Jane D. Marsching
Editorial Assistant: Deborah Thomas
Designed by Wendy Byrne

Kling, Jean L.
     Alice Pike Barney : Her Life and Art / Jean L. Kling : introduction by
Wanda Corn.
       p.   cm.
     Includes bibliographical references and index.
      1. Barney, Alice Pike, 1857-1931. 2. Women artists—United States—
Biography. 3. Women art patrons—United States—Biography.
I. Title.
N6537.B222K58 1994
700'.92—dc20   93-26425
[B]   CIP

The National Museum of American Art, Smithsonian Institution, is dedicated to the preservation, exhibition, and study of the visual arts in America. The museum, whose publications program also includes the scholarly journal *American Art*, has extensive research resources: the databases of the Inventories of American Painting and Sculpture, several image archives, and a variety of fellowships for scholars. The Renwick Gallery, one of the nation's premier craft museums, is part of NMAA. For more information or a catalogue of publications, write: Office of Publications, National Museum of American Art, Smithsonian Institution, Washington, D.C. 20560.

Contents

List of Works of Art by Alice Pike Barney

* There are 265 works of art by Alice Pike
Barney in the collection of the
National Museum of American Art,
Smithsonian Institution.

In memory of
Laura Dreyfus Barney and
William E. Huntington

Acknowledgments

This book would never have been possible without the help and encouragement of a great many people. Dr. Joshua Taylor, director of the NCFA, gave me the courage to start. It was, however, the constant prodding of his successors, Drs. Charles C. Eldredge and especially Elizabeth Broun, and present and former National Museum of American Art staff members, Dr. Virginia M. Mecklenburg, Robert W. Johnston, and Thomas W. Bower, who, in seeming collusion with the Barney Studio House docents, forced me to continue when I most wanted to give up. I am particularly appreciative of the challenges presented me by Steve Dietz, NMAA chief of publications, and my editor Jane D. Marsching as we worked through the editing process. I am also indebted to Wendy Byrne for her sensitive approach to the book's design and to Ruth Pontius for help with proofreading.

Special thanks are due Margaret Johnson Garrett for her unflagging devotion to Studio House and her immense help on this project. I also wish to thank François Chapon and Nicole Prévot of the Bibliothèque Littéraire Jacques Doucet in Paris, and Richard Hall, author of *Stanley, An Adventurer Explored*. Of great assistance were the staffs of the public libraries, historical societies, and various history and art museums in Cincinnati, Philadelphia, New York, Los Angeles, and Washington, D.C. In particular, I appreciated the help given me by the librarians of the music, manuscript, and periodical divisions at the Library of Congress who remained helpful and unflappable no matter how arcane the material I was attempting to track down. Finally, I wish to thank the Historical Society of Washington, D.C., and its dynamic leader, Kathryn S. Smith, for publishing my article on Alice Pike Barney in 1990 in *Washington History* and for extending permission to use portions of it for this book.

Eventually, however, the publication of *Alice Pike Barney* rests on a group of people who have challenged me over the long run: my sons Christopher and Victor Lewton; my friends Helen J. Davis, Lillian S. Jenney, Val E. Lewton, Robert L. Tate, and Maryanne Summers; and my mother, Helen Kling Carver, who did not live to see its completion. My final thanks, however, go to Samuel F. H. Smith, editor of Washington's *D.C. Gazette*. Without his patient editing of and confidence in my fledgling reportorial efforts in the early 1970s, I would never have begun to write.

Preface

The impetus for a biography of Alice Pike Barney originated in 1980 when her Studio House on Massachusetts Avenue in Washington, D.C., was opened to the public following renovation by the Smithsonian Institution's National Museum of American Art. The director of the NMAA (then called the National Collection of Fine Arts) was Dr. Joshua Taylor and it was his personal interest in the project that made it possible to reendow Studio House with the spirit of its original owner.

When Dr. Taylor first came to Washington in 1970, he stayed at Studio House for several weeks while looking for a home. At that time the Smithsonian used Studio House's bedrooms for visiting dignitaries. He was both bemused and appalled by how Studio House looked. As a former scene designer for the ballet, he appreciated what it had been and envisioned what it could be—a dramatically striking house built by a woman who wished to show others how to live artistically. Finally, in January 1980, Dr. Taylor's dream was realized and Studio House was opened to the public as an intimate house museum and cultural center.

From the moment the first visits (as tours were called) to Studio House began, people expressed as much interest in the life of Alice Pike Barney as they did in her home. The preliminary research into her life was conducted by Delight Hall and Donald McCelland and these earlier efforts piqued my curiosity. Once I began delving into scrapbooks, letters, catalogues, old newspapers, and magazines for references to Alice Pike Barney and Studio House, it became clear that a projected eight-page monograph could not do justice to either the house or this remarkable woman. What began as an assignment to write a short history of Studio House grew into a full-scale biography of its owner.

I have worked off and on amidst the ghosts of Studio House for almost thirty years. To my mind there is a special, unnameable atmosphere at Studio House. Once you enter the house proper, contemporary Washington vanishes and it is easy to appreciate how Studio House became the base for Alice Pike Barney's quite joyful manipulation of culture. If, in the process, she scandalized a few of her stuffier contemporaries, it didn't matter because at Studio House she was true to herself.

Alice Pike Barney was, however, not only a Washingtonian. Her personal stage was much larger. Cincinnati, New York, Paris, London, and Hollywood were as much a part of Alice's life as was the nation's capital. While much of her story sounds like a romantic Victorian novel, it was her gen-

Studio House was the second home built on Sheridan Circle. Its Spanish Mission facade was in sharp contrast to the conventional brick exteriors of Washington, D.C., rowhouses.

uine commitment to the arts enacted with great style and courage that saves it from being just another tale of a wealthy grande dame who raised some dust during her lifetime.

Alice Pike Barney was a woman who, in defiance of her times, took her life in hand and lived it with zest. She never apologized for her money, her talent, or the choices she made. Although she had regrets and made what she perceived as some rather grotesque mistakes of judgment, she always pushed them aside to pursue her artistic obsession of the moment. In her unpublished autobiography, *Stanley's "Lady" Alice by One Who Knew*, Alice Pike Barney defined the eclectic aesthetic that guided her life:

> [I] never sentimentalized about the past. [I] lived in the present and for the present, and lived at it intently with such application that [I] had absolutely no place for either past or future....It mattered not so much which art form [I] was dabbling in,...they were all the same; one should be able to turn from one to the other with joy,...so the more arts [I] got a footing in the greater would be [my] agility in any one of them.

She "dabbled and daubed" and let her enthusiasm and joie de vivre override any criticism as she left her contemporaries breathless in her wake. Even now, some sixty years later, I find I run to catch a glimpse of her shadow; and a merry chase it is.

Jean L. Kling
Washington, D.C., 1993

Introduction

Alice Pike Barney's ghost still lives in Barney Studio House, or so my husband and I were told when we moved into its upstairs bedrooms in 1987. We lived there for a year, joining a long line of scholars, artists, and museum curators, who at one time or another had made Barney Studio House their temporary home. The ghost, we were assured, was a friendly one. She was rarely seen, only heard, and music often accompanied her movements.

Perhaps it was a failure of imagination, but I never encountered Barney's ghost. I wanted to get to know Alice—and her daughters Natalie and Laura—but I preferred to meet them as historical presences, not apparitions. So as I lived in the rooms the Barney women once occupied, I read everything I could about them. I tried to envision Alice getting up in the morning and going to her large, lavishly wood-paneled studio to paint. I attempted to conjure up the noise and confusion of her parties and theatricals and to imagine the mental peregrinations she went through as she first built a proper, Gilded Age mansion, and then designed and built a highly unconventional studio house to showcase the arts.

To get a better grasp on this unusual woman, I followed Jean Kling, then curator of the house, as she led visitors on tours and made every room of Barney House come alive. What I learned suggested Alice Pike Barney had exercised her will in extravagant ways, that her creation of an urban studio in Barney House was an important piece of American artistic history, and that she, like James Corcoran and Duncan Phillips, had been an important person in the early cultural life of Washington, D.C. Furthermore, she had raised two daughters who were as dedicated to their causes as she was: Natalie Barney, who lived as an expatriate in Paris and was one of the first Americans to write openly as a lesbian; and Laura Barney, an early follower of Bahai and a leader in the international women's rights movement.

Now we have the story in full. Jean Kling's biography, based on years of careful research, and accompanied by marvelous vintage photographs, gives Alice Pike Barney a flesh and blood place in history and exorcises, once and for all, the ghost of Barney House. Ghosts evaporate when the fullness and complexity of a person's life is known and she can no longer be reduced to colorful legend. Alice's life was colorful—no doubt about that— but it also tortuously conformed to many of the conventions and routines demanded of wealthy society women. It is the combination of the wildly unconventional (we like this best about her) with the mundanely conventional (this we find silly) that makes her life provocative.

Distilled into a three-hundred-page book, Barney's life reads like a rollercoaster ride. She is a restless subject, constantly on the go, tirelessly social, always squeezing out time for one more charity or one more spurt of writing. She travels and changes residences several times a year. Readers, especially women, will probably experience the same incredulity and vertigo I did in imagining what her everyday life must have been like. For not many women practice or enjoy living in perpetual motion as did Alice: racing to take on new projects, building and buying houses, packing a trunk for Europe or Bar Harbor on a moment's notice, and dressing and doing her hair to be noticed, an activity that itself takes forethought and time.

Barney was wealthy, of course, and that increased her options. But the way she chose to exercise them was highly unusual. She dedicated herself to a two-fold mission: to be an artist and to bring the arts to her city. Her energy seemed limitless, and she gave much more of her time and resources to her causes than did other art lovers at the time. Furthermore, her tastes were unusually liberal. She supported modern as well as traditional forms of aesthetic expression, and she wanted to patronize and practice them all—painting, sculpture, drama, poetry, opera, music and the dance.

Part of what Barney wanted to do was to make Washington, D.C., home to the arts. In her estimate, and in the minds of many others, the country's capital was an embarrassing cultural backwater in the early twentieth century. Nothing short of an entire overhaul of the city's artistic consciousness would be necessary if the arts were ever to thrive in such a provincial place. Barney worked at her mission from every angle. She gave money; she acted as entrepreneur to bring traveling troupes to Washington; she organized salons where artists and highly placed Washingtonians would mix; and she was herself a deeply committed artist and a writer, showcasing her own work as exemplary of progressive thinking. She also built performance spaces, the likes of which Washington had never seen: the Sylvan Theater near the Washington Monument for outdoor performances and the more private Barney Studio House on Sheridan Circle where the public rooms were designed to be as open spaces for exhibiting paintings, hosting theatricals and concerts, and giving salons.

Because Barney was so willful and eclectic, people in her day often called her "eccentric," a term still used to explain her lack of conformity to so many conventions and mores. Barney's deviations from the norm, however, were never so radical or perverse that she fell from social grace. To the contrary, Barney remained on Washington's social register and her every activity was reported in the society pages of the Washington papers. It seems clear that upper crust Washingtonians enjoyed having Barney

among them because she was colorful and a good source of gossip. Much of
what she did was regular fare for wealthy women of her time: her work
with charities and with settlement houses, for example, or her extensive
stays in Europe and in a large summer home in Bar Harbor, and, of course,
serving as hostess for major entertainments and elegant parties. But, within
these patterns, Barney would do the unexpected and the unusual: marrying
a man thirty years her junior; performing in her own ballets and plays;
building a studio house on Massachusetts Avenue among traditional marble
mansions; and ultimately, moving to Los Angeles to become a playwright.

Every major American city seems to have had a few rich women
eccentrics in the 1880–1930 period. Born to money made in the Gilded Age
and expected to live as ladies of leisure, they were a new social type:
women who lived proper upper-class lives, but did not follow the rules,
using their wealth and privilege to buy themselves freedoms and to promote causes the rich did not customarily embrace. Barney was one of several who devoted themselves to the arts. In Boston, there was Isabelle
Stewart Gardner who built a major art collection and a combined museum-
mansion for herself. In New York, there was Mabel Dodge Luhan who
aspired to write and ran a salon in her Washington Square apartment and
then reinvented herself anew in Taos, attracting artists and intellectuals to
her Southwestern home. A few years later, Gertrude Vanderbilt Whitney
emerged as Manhattan's most public eccentric, using her wealth to set herself up as a sculptor and begin the Whitney Studio Club that eventually
became the Whitney Museum of American Art.

As we learn more about such women, collectively and historically, we
may interpret eccentricity as a lifestyle upper-class women invented to give
themselves new freedoms and control over their own lives while avoiding
social ostracism. The one route to freedom that began to open up for
women in the early twentieth century, that of becoming what was called the
"new woman" was not an appealing option to the rich and well-born who
had been socialized to be upright community citizens, civic leaders, and
philanthropists. For Alice Pike Barney to join the ranks of the young Turks
and bohemians who frequented Greenwich Village, for example, or to ride
bicycles, smoke in public, or advocate birth control, would have been to
sever herself from her own past and to abandon completely her class,
wealth, and social standing. Eccentricity, on the other hand, permitted
wealthy women to work within their customary social settings while, at the
same time, use their resources to push gently at the boundaries of the
acceptable. Without overly embarrassing or insulting their peers, these
women experimented with new kinds of self-fulfillment and, in the process,
invented the "eccentric" model for upper-class female behavior.

As we can see from Alice's inability to succeed as an artist, there were tradeoffs. To be a prominent society figure was a full-time job, and she found it hard, if not impossible, to focus for long periods of time on her own painting and writing. As a consequence, Alice seldom gave the time or cultivated the discipline she needed to deepen her work and guide it into more original channels. Yet Alice was better off than some well-to-do socialite artists for whom the strain took its toll psychologically; many upper-class American women who aspired to professional writing or painting in this period—one thinks of Edith Wharton—suffered serious bouts of depression and neurasthenia. Alice's temperament appears to have been so effervescent and buoyant that she easily countered adversity. Usually she set off on travels, an antidote to depression common in wealthy circles, but one which, in its own way, also interfered with the making of art.

Alice's legacy then is not so much that of a professional artist as that of a zealous mistress of the arts. For her, the arts were soul food and without soul, there was no beauty in life. Without beauty, life was dull and impoverished. So Barney spent her waking hours on an endless quest to aesthetize her domestic environments and her city. Born to a father who introduced her early on to the magic of the stage, and drawn to *fin de siècle* painting, and then to writing, Barney made the arts her daily liquor of life. She loved hosting spectacles. For her, the line between theater and life was a thin and permeable one.

Wanda M. Corn
Stanford University, 1993

Alice
Pike
Barney

I
Early
Years

I
Her Father's Daughter

I n the spring of 1926, sixty-nine-year-old Alice Pike Barney decided to start over again. To do so, she needed to close her former life and so she traveled one last time to Washington, D.C., from her new home in Hollywood, California. She had business to conduct in the city she had called home for almost forty years. She was going to put a few finishing touches on her play, *The Lighthouse*, which she planned to enter in a playwriting contest sponsored by the D.C. Chapter of the Drama League of America. Another purpose was to wade through various papers stored at Studio House for the purpose of writing her biography. Finally, she hoped to sell Studio House before she moved to California the following spring.

Ultimately two of the three projects were successful: *The Lighthouse* won the Drama League's award for best original full-length play of 1927, and she completed her novelized autobiography. No one, however, seemed interested in buying Studio House, Alice's idiosyncratic homage to artistic living, which was located on Massachusetts Avenue, N.W., on what became known as Embassy Row.

Alice's plan for her autobiography was to focus on her romance with the legendary Henry Morton Stanley, but it soon became much more than the story of a young girl's first love. As it grew in length, she was forced to seek a secretary to give order to the myriad pages of lined paper covered with her almost illegible scrawl.

Upon the recommendation of Viktor Flambeau, a teacher of oriental art at George Washington University, she hired a university sophomore, William E. Huntington, to produce the typescript. In return for his typing and spelling ability, as well as his willingness to be on call at all hours, Huntington received fifty dollars per month plus room and board at Studio House. Many years later, Huntington recalled that he was thrilled by the pay, bemused by the thought of living in such a peculiar house, and totally undone by the short, amply endowed woman with steel gray bobbed hair, layers of makeup, and an imperious theatrical persona.[1]

During the interview, which was held in Studio House's dimly lit first floor sitting room, Huntington's eye was drawn to a vivid pastel of a screaming Medusa, casually leaning against a wall covered with faded red damask. Noticing the direction of his glance, Mrs. Barney waved her diamond-bedecked hand in its direction and offhandedly said, "That's my daughter Laura." For a moment Huntington considered backing out, but

SAMUEL N. PIKE,
c. 1859
A multimillionaire whiskey distiller and consummate businessman, Pike was also a great lover of the arts. Pike is shown here around the time of the opening of his Cincinnati Opera House in 1859.

*Preceding pages:
Dining room, Studio House,
c. 1911*

wishing to appear worldly-wise, he merely nodded sagely and answered: "Oh, yes. Of course."

The next day, he returned with his luggage and was led to his room on the fourth floor by the aging East Indian handyman, chauffeur, and butler, Mr. Charles Only. He was informed that his narrow bedroom overlooking Sheridan Circle was called the Whistler room. The lower three-quarters of the walls were paneled with simple pine wainscotting stained an indeterminate gray-green. The plaster wall above was hand-stenciled with Art Nouveau designs. Pastel portraits of elegant women hung alongside nineteenth century watercolors of musketeers and prints of Versailles. Unlike the heavily carved, ebonized furniture that filled the lower floors, the bedroom suite was Louis XVI. On the other side of the room's closet was Alice's large study, also facing Sheridan Circle. A few feet down the hallway was the door to Alice's bedroom. The high windows in her bedroom looked out on the roof garden and the room itself was almost entirely filled by a gilded, canopied bed piled high with feather mattresses.

During his first night, Huntington was awakened by a tapping on the back wall of the closet in his bedroom and a voice calling: "My dear, my dear. Wake up. I have a chapter for you to type. Two carbons. It's on my desk. Goodnight, Mr. Huntington."

Huntington recalled that he stumbled into the closet, grabbed his robe, and, rubbing the sleep from his eyes, went next door to the study. He began to type the title of the first chapter: "So American." By the time Alice left for California in late January, he had produced 342 pages with two carbons.[2]

From Huntington's nineteen-year-old perspective, Alice's autobiography was most peculiar. He found it difficult to reconcile the elderly woman with whom he ate an early morning breakfast before class with the lovely, beautiful, and talented girl described in the autobiography—a story written idiosyncratically in third-person narrative. Nevertheless, he was fascinated by the people who had passed through her life: James McNeill Whistler, Sir Henry Morton Stanley, and Oscar Wilde among others. Equally interesting were people with less familiar names such as opera diva Emma Calvè or portrait painter Hubert Vos. Foremost among them was Alice's father, Samuel Pike. According to Alice, her life's accomplishments had their genesis in her father's devotion to the arts, his sense of responsibility for the underprivileged, and his belief that dreams were within the realm of possibility if you decided to make them so.

These qualities comprised a philosophy that Alice endorsed wholeheartedly throughout her life. Although her calm disposition came from her mother, in her very essence, Alice was her father's daughter: a person whose intense appreciation of the arts molded her life. "He was," Alice

wrote, "the only man who understood me. I have needed his love and guid-
ance and I shall never stop grieving for him." Thus to tell Alice Pike Barney's story, one begins with her father.

SAMUEL N. PIKE

Samuel Napthali Pike was a complex and fascinating man. The story of his
Horatio Alger rise to riches and power and his achievements as a patron of
the arts is found not only in Alice's autobiography, but in the writings of his
contemporaries and of later scholars.[3] He was born in New York City in
1822, the son of an immigrant German-Jewish father and a Dutch-Chris-
tian mother. At seventeen he left home to seek his fortune and for the next
five years he met varying success as he traveled from town to town and job
to job. When Pike arrived in Cincinnati, Ohio, on July 4, 1844, he was
twenty-two years old and not much wealthier than when he had left home.
His plan was to catch a coach to New York, but, due to the holiday, there
was a day's delay. As he disembarked from the boat he had taken from St.
Louis, he was met with the noise and disorder of the warehouses, factories,
and slums in the Cincinnati basin.

As Pike climbed upward to the hills where the merchant princes lived,
the misery and noise of the basin disappeared. Once he reached the top of
an adjacent mountain (as Cincinnatians call the hills upon which the city is
built), he looked down upon the natural amphitheater and saw what
Charles Dickens had described two years before: a city "risen out of the
forest like an Arabian night city . . . cheerful, thriving, and animated . . . a
place that commends itself so favorably and pleasantly to a stranger at the
first glance . . . with its clean houses of red and white, its well paved roads,
and foot-ways of bright tile. . . . The streets are broad and airy, the shops
extremely good, the private residences remarkable for their elegance and
neatness. . ."[4]

Pike often told his friends that he was so impressed by what he saw that
day that he "concluded to remain and try his fortune in this locality." To his
children he recounted a more romantic story. In it he recalled that as he
strolled along the city's main street, which was to be the Fourth of July
parade route, he happened to glance up at the second-story balcony of one
of the large homes lining the street. Seated there was a beautiful young
woman, but as he stepped back to get a better view, he ignominiously fell
into a coal pit. Slightly stunned, he found himself looking up at the selfsame
person, Ellen Miller, who proceeded to help him up. From that very
moment, Pike told his children, "I knew Ellen was the girl I would marry,
and so, I settled in the town."

It was a courtship of opposites. Ellen Miller was the daughter of one of
the town's wealthiest and most prominent citizens, the Honorable William

Miller, a retired Louisiana judge and land owner, while Pike had nothing to offer other than the potential he knew he possessed. Where Ellen was born to a life of leisure, Pike knew only hard work. Ellen was placid and self-absorbed; Pike was a man driven by dreams of wealth. She was Catholic; he professed no faith. Nevertheless, a year later Ellen and Pike were married in the Episcopal Church.

Having won the girl, Pike was determined to support her in the manner to which she was accustomed. He first opened a dry-goods store, but after three years of hard work he was forced to close. Liquidating his stock, he invested every penny in a rectifying plant with an adjacent grocery store. Shortly thereafter, he began distilling Magnolia brand whiskey, which was an instant success. He was finally on his way to accumulating the fortune of which he had always dreamed. By 1857, thirteen years from the day he first stepped onto the Cincinnati docks, Pike was a multimillionaire and the father of four children. Alice, born on January 14, 1857, was the youngest.

In 1856, in expectation of the birth of his fourth child, Pike built a home at 355 West Fourth Street. Ever the practical businessman, Pike purchased not only the lot on which to build his new home, but the rest of the block as well. As his own home went up, so did his neighbors'—all grand homes for the very wealthy. The brownstone fronts were in the New York style of the period, totally different from the classic brick facades found elsewhere in Cincinnati.

Left:
WILLIAM MILLER
Right:
URSULA MUELLION MILLER
Artist and whereabouts unknown
At twenty-two, a penniless Samuel Pike fell in love with Ellen Miller, the daughter of "Honest" Judge William Miller and his French Louisiana wife Ursula Muellion Miller.

The Pike household was a lively one. Lawrence, born in 1848, was the eldest. He idolized his father and for many years kept a scrapbook of clippings detailing Pike's every activity. He was not, however, cut from the same cloth as his father. He lacked Pike's drive and, as the only son in a house of women, was spoiled to the point that when an adult, he became more interested in his inheritance than in carrying on the family business. The next eldest, Jeannette, or Nettie as she was called, was born in 1851. She was outgoing, authoritative, and a master at organization. "She should have been a boy," was said over and over again. If born a boy, Nettie would have assumed Pike's mantle, but instead she turned her energies towards bossing her younger sisters and organizing the neighborhood children. Eventually Nettie grew into a formidable woman whose aim in life seemed to be to control others.

The third child, Hester, born in 1853, was the one who most resembled Ellen. Alice wrote that "she was younger than Nettie and always seemed older, being very prim about her precious self, and always thoroughly proper and conscientious." It was Hessie, not Nettie or Lawrence, who paid attention to Alice; they had little use for a toddler. Although totally different in personality, Alice and Hessie understood each other well and according to Alice, "nary a cross word did they ever exchange all their lives."

The new row of houses quickly became a local architectural landmark. The Pike mansion was the central attraction primarily because it was the first house in Cincinnati to have a fully plumbed bathtub. Alice Barney remembered that the tub was big enough to hold all three girls at the same time and that Cincinnatians would bring visitors to the Pike's front gate and point with pride to the house where the "precious object was known to exist." She also recalled that it was a huge, grotesque, awkward tin affair into which their Irish nanny would plunk them and watch as they scrubbed themselves while singing their own version of the "Anvil Chorus."

THE OPERA HOUSE

It was not, however, for architectural innovation, installation of the city's first bathtub, or single-handedly building a multimillion dollar distillery that Pike's name came to be written into Cincinnati's annals. Rather, it was the result of an event that occurred in 1851, six years before Alice was born. In that year P. T. Barnum brought Jenny Lind, known as the Swedish Nightingale, to Cincinnati. Lind's popularity was at its peak and a huge crowd awaited her arrival from New Orleans at the wharf at the foot of Main Street. Her concerts were performed at the grossly inadequate National Theater, but no matter how difficult tickets were to obtain, Pike managed to be at every performance. On the one hand, he was totally smitten by Lind's golden voice and on the other, he was fascinated by

Barnum's ability to sell his high-class artistic commodity to poor and rich alike.

With his dream of making a fortune a reality, Pike had begun to cast about for another challenge. He deduced that the capacity audiences that attended Jenny Lind's concerts were large enough to support a first-class opera house and concluded that his new purpose in life would be to build an opera house for Cincinnati. His rationale was twofold: it would provide a fitting gesture of thanks to the city that had so generously supported a young man passing by on the Fourth of July, and it would serve as the anchor for the rapidly developing business district where Pike had extensive land holdings linked by the city's new trolley system of which he was majority owner.

Unlike Barnum, whose brazen personality was part and parcel of his promotional skills, there was nothing about Pike's demeanor to suggest a person who would have even a fleeting interest in theatrical pursuits. But then, there was little about Pike's persona to suggest a shrewd and driving businessman either. He was an exceedingly modest man with a stoic facade that belied his intense drive for success. Of slender build, he looked more like a poet than a businessman. He dressed conservatively; the single diamond stud affixed to his waistcoat was his only outward concession to millionaire status. He was, in fact, a puzzle to those who knew him. "His was a strange composition. He was debonair, in touch with the poet, musician, painter, and soldier, and on the other side of him was the practical businessman, manufacturing and wholesaling whiskey for the South. This last to great profit, while he pondered upon the best means of beautifying and benefitting his favorite city."[5]

Pike the dreamer was always a man of action. Once he decided which of his lots was best suited for an opera house, the project began. Shortly after Alice's birth in 1857, excavation started on a large site located on Fourth Street between Vine and Walnut. Whereas Alice's birth was a cause for jubilation in the Pike household, the birth of what was to be the finest opera house west of Philadelphia went almost unremarked. The assumption was that Pike was adding another office building to Cincinnati's burgeoning downtown. Few people other than his banker and close friends even knew his intentions. As construction of the massive building continued throughout the summer, its purpose remained a closely guarded secret.

Shortly after the completion of the first two stories, all construction stopped as the Panic of '58 hit Cincinnati with full force. Even the seemingly panic proof liquor industry was hard hit, and Pike was forced to stop construction for a year.

For Cincinnatians the end of the Panic was exemplified not only by the reopening of the city's banks, but by resumption of work on Pike's Fourth

PIKE'S OPERA HOUSE,
C. 1859
*Pike built his opera house
as a gift to the city that had
welcomed and supported
him as a young man. Pike
hired some of the finest
designers and artisans of the
mid-nineteenth century to
create what became known
as the jewel in the Queen
City's crown.*

Street building. Almost before people realized it, the five-story building
was completed and crowned by a great arched roof. When the top ornamentation was put in place, Pike's secret was revealed; for there it stood —
the largest and most magnificent opera house west of the Alleghenies — the
gift of one man to his adopted city.

Pike was notoriously reticent about his finances, so no one knew for certain what the opera building cost him. Estimates printed in local newspapers placed the cost at close to half a million dollars. From every side, however, it was clear that he had spared no expense. Pike had provided the
jewel in the Queen City's crown that would allow it to boast not only of its
commercial vitality, but of its cultural life as well.

The New York architectural firm of H. White and John M. Trimble had
been instructed by Pike to base its design upon Milan's Teatro Alla Scala.
The five-story, gray-blue sandstone facade was elaborately ornamented

with statues representing music, poetry, agriculture, and astronomy. Bas-relief portraits of Mozart and Shakespeare flanked the central entrance door. Inside were reception rooms, a grand promenade, and an auditorium that seated three thousand with additional standing room.

Of special note was the octagonal dome that formed the auditorium's ceiling. It was covered by murals designed by G. Guidecini of New York City and painted under his personal supervision by Italian artisans imported from the East Coast. Around the perimeter of the dome were three hundred gas jets. The stage measured fifty-eight feet deep by ninety feet wide and could easily accommodate the most elaborate and scenically complex operas. In the space under the auditorium Pike installed the Do You Smile Saloon with provision for easy access to and from the auditorium.

The opening was held on Washington's birthday in 1859, a month after Alice turned two years old. There was a grand ball followed by a supper organized by some of Cincinnati's leading citizens. Two thousand people paid ten dollars to inspect the new opera house, and they were not disappointed. On stage was a grotto with a working fountain. Two orchestras alternately played "waltzes, quadrilles, schottisches, and polkas." The grand promenade opening the festivities processed to the pronounced rhythm of the "Anvil Chorus" from Verdi's *Il Trovatore*. An elegant catered dinner was served until two in the morning in the promenade hall.[6]

Not only was Pike reticent about money, he also did not talk about himself freely. Even his most intimate friends were ignorant of his Jewish heritage. They did know, however, that he had grown up in a household enriched not by money, but by culture. They also knew he wrote poetry and played the flute. His family knew only slightly more. He told them the romantic story of how his parents eloped because their families did not approve of the marriage and when they decided to come to America, the only things they brought with them were two Dutch Renaissance paintings, several pieces of family silver, and their abiding faith in the value of art, music, and literature. It was a part of him that he wished to share with his children, but of the four, Alice was the only kindred spirit. She alone among his family "touched everything with her exuberant fantasy and turned it to sheer joy."

If Alice was Pike's joy at home, his opera house was his joy at work. From the day it opened, Pike was intimately involved in the theater's operation. Only the best available opera would be allowed on his stage. For the inaugural season he engaged New York's leading grand opera company, the Italian Opera Company, led by Maurice Strakosch. It opened with Flotow's *Martha* and included productions of operas by Donizetti, Verdi, Bellini, Rossini, Mozart, and Meyerbeer.

In spite of dire pronouncements from some pulpits that attending an opera was an immoral act, 3,500 advance tickets were sold and the first season was a rousing success with receipts of over three thousand dollars per performance. Everyone who could attended, from the highest society in the dress circle to their servants in the top balconies. With the opening of Pike's Opera House, Cincinnati became the reigning cultural center of the Midwest. No longer did the principal touring operatic, symphonic, and theatrical companies bypass the city, and the opera house's financial and artistic success provided the impetus for Chicago, Saint Louis, and other smaller midwestern cities to follow suit. Only Cincinnati, however, could boast that its opera house was the gift of one man acting alone.

HOME LIFE

Alice's earliest memories of her father were of holding his hand while they watched concerts, plays and opera, dramatic spectacles, readings, and community fund-raisers at the opera house. She sat enraptured in the audience while her father played the flute or recited his poetry at benefit performances. One of Alice's most vivid recollections was seeing Lola Montez, a flamboyant leading lady, in *Mazeppa*. In one scene Montez, dressed in flesh colored tights and leotard, galloped across the stage bound to the back of a white horse.

When they returned home, Alice would reenact what they had seen for her father. She would transform herself into a ballerina or a singer, or pound the piano in imitation of the orchestra. He especially loved when she sang. She had a natural voice and perfect pitch. "Her father appreciated her voice," Alice told a friend much later, "but that none of the other members of the family gave a 'hang', one way or another."

All of this creativity stood Alice in good stead when, at the age of six, she was sent for a year to a convent school. Alice was no student, but she was a performer. She recalled that she excelled in improvisations in song, dance, and piano.

That she could not learn the multiplication table or remember the alphabet was kept a close guarded secret. Every time the nuns had visitors and wanted to show off the brilliance of their prodigies, little Alice was asked to perform. At the piano she improvised according to request. 'Be a butterfly' — and she was; she lit on roses, lilies, dandelions, and sunflowers with equal agility. 'Be a storm' — she thundered, roared, exploded, and crashed with a vengeance that should have brought forth terrific wrath. And dance? On one occasion, when a young nun was taking the veil, Alice danced all around the prostrated girl, strewing her with flowers.

Like many only or youngest children, Alice spent many hours in a world

she created from her own imagination. Not sur-
prisingly her imaginary world was set in a tiny
pin theater where she created productions that
were, to her, as opulent as any she saw at the
Opera House. The actors and actresses were
devised by her governess from pins topped by
colored beads and glued together to create various characters. The colored beads that represented each character were selected with all the naïve
symbolism a child could muster after watching
some of the melodramas at the Opera House: a
red pin was the temptress, black the villain. The
heroine and hero were pink and blue. The multihued, carpeted floor of her bedroom served
equally well for forest, palace, or lowly hut, and
the stories she devised were complex and full of
cliff-hanging adventures. Sometimes her miniature productions were plays, but most often they
were operas where Alice's ability to mimic and
her perfect pitch were combined in mangled, but
musically agreeable, versions of the operas she
saw on the stage of the Opera House.

Once Alice reached five, her sisters considered
her old enough to be included in their activities.
On Saturdays the three Pike girls and as many as
twenty assorted neighborhood friends, led by
"General" Jeannette, would march to Pike's
"Palace of Harmony," as they called it. When
Jeannette reached the front door, she would call
out nonchalantly, "Pike's children," as they passed by the ticket taker into
the auditorium.

Once inside Jeannette loudly enumerated the wonders of the place for
her army, airily ignoring the angry murmurs of the paying customers.
Jeannette habitually timed their arrival to just before curtain to be sure
that everyone could admire her troop as she pointed out the "P" on every
seat of the vast dress circle. As the curtain rose, the children broke ranks
and scuttled in all directions to find a place to see the show.

If her father was the focus of Alice's world, her mother was not. Each
was an enigma to the other. Ellen was hard put to understand this energetic, imaginative child, and Alice was equally puzzled by a woman who
seemed to take so little interest in anything, including the activities of her
husband and children. She set an example of gentility for the household,

NETTIE, HESTER, AND
ALICE PIKE, C. 1859
*At two years old, Alice was
still too young to play with
her older sisters, who enjoyed
getting all their friends in
free to performances at their
father's opera house.*

but it was a strange one. "She was always the first one up, dressed, and ready for the day's activity—first to see that the servants had their duties done, the meals ordered, and then she was ready for her novel-reading by nine in the morning. From this pattern she never varied." Alice knew her mother adored her husband and her children, but once she had completed her morning duties, her responsibility was ended. "[I] thought often of [my] mother's life," Alice wrote, "and vowed that [mine] should not grow into such an uneventful existence. Nothing aroused her interest."

If Ellen refused to share Pike's enthusiasm for the theater, Pike seemed untouched by it. He seldom missed a performance, standing quietly at the rear of the auditorium with an unlit cigar clenched between his teeth. In honor of his leading performers, he organized late-night dinners at his home, which sparkled with witty conversation and provided his stars with a refuge away from the crowds and hotel noise, thereby ensuring their return season after season. As a special treat, Alice was occasionally allowed to stay up late to attend. Pike introduced her as his hostess and proudly called upon her to perform. Seated at the dining table, perched on a thick book, Alice felt the queen of all she surveyed. She never questioned her mother's absence, because even as a small child she knew that her mother disliked entertaining.

It was a long-standing pattern that Ellen would remain in her room when Pike entertained. For her, social affairs were hardly worth the energy it took to dress. Her extraordinary placidity led her to seek domestic harmony at the price of all enthusiasm for the surprises of daily life. She wrapped herself in a comfortable cocoon of passivity and accepted as her due the wealth that made possible the ordered and effortless progression of her life. If people wished to see her, they could come to her.

On occasion, however, Pike would order Ellen to be his hostess, and, as if to confound her husband, she would do it with assiduous charm. As Alice remembered, Ellen would entertain with "a royal hand, once she put her mind to it. She was like that, when she did a thing she did it well and always illuminated her appearances with her ready wit." The arrival of the nineteen-year-old Prince of Wales (traveling anonymously under the name of Baron Renfrew) in Cincinnati in September 1860 was just such an event. The future Edward VII was to be publicly honored at a grand ball at Pike's Opera House. Ellen was assigned the role of leading the opening grand promenade on the prince's arm. That night, Ellen attracted the admiration of Cincinnati's finest. Dressed in white taffeta, her new diamond pendant tiara and tiered emerald and diamond earrings sparkled in the gaslight. The jewels were her reward from her husband for agreeing to play a prominent public role. Yet, once the role was played, she put the tiara and earrings in her jewelry box and never wore them again.

ELLEN PIKE'S EARRINGS, 1860
Diamonds and emeralds, white gold and silver,
4 x ⅞ x ⅝ in.
(10.2 x 2.2 x 1.6 cm)
Samuel Pike presented his wife, Ellen, with a pair of tiered diamond and emerald earrings as an enticement for her to head a promenade on the arm of the Prince of Wales at the Opera House in September 1860.

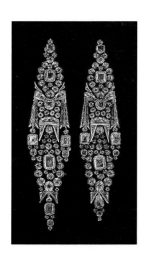

WAR AND DESTRUCTION

The excitement generated by the royal visit was soon eclipsed by Abraham Lincoln's election as the sixteenth President of the United States. All too clearly Cincinnatians saw war as inevitable and were faced with the stark fact that only the Ohio River separated them from the South and a Confederate invasion, even though Kentucky declared itself neutral.

Even more problematic was the fact that much of Cincinnati commerce was based on southern trade. Pike's best-selling whiskey bore the label, "Magnolia," chosen specifically for its appeal to his primary market in New Orleans. Pike, a strong Union supporter and pragmatic businessman, immediately shifted his territory and opened a second distillery in New York City to produce his new label, "Pike's Best." He exhibited his confidence in eventual Union victory by increasing his local investments through the purchase of one of Cincinnati's finest hotels, Burnet House, and the acquisition of land in New York City and northern New Jersey.

In 1864, moved by the ever lengthening list of Union dead and missing, Pike wrote an impassioned poem in nine stanzas and sent it to the *Enquirer*. "Why desolate our beauteous lands," he asked. "Why should friend and kindred smite/With bloody hands and savage steel?/Why should widows and orphans moan/When the lost dear ones fall in battle,/With mangled limbs and awful groan,/That rend deep curses with death's rattle?"[7]

On April 9, 1865, Lee surrendered at Appomattox. After a tumultuous celebration at the Opera House, Pike ordered it to be readied for a series of Shakespearian performances starring the great tragedian Junius Brutus Booth. On April 14, 1865, as Booth began the final act of that night's play, news spread that his younger brother John Wilkes Booth had shot President Lincoln. With frightening speed angry crowds gathered before the theater and Booth, fearing for his life, fled the theater leaving Pike with the prospect of a dark house until the next booking arrived. In Washington, actress Laura Keene's company, which was presenting the play Lincoln attended at Ford's Theater the night he was shot, was also out of work. The next morning Pike wired Keene to come to Cincinnati where she played to curious, sold out houses as Kate in Oliver Goldsmith's *She Stoops to Conquer* for the remainder of Booth's unfilled contract.

With the war over, civilian travel was once more easily available and Pike began making extended visits to New York to oversee his eastern interests. Even before the end of the war, he began to assess the future of his southern markets and determined that those in New York held the greater prospect for success. With each passing month, Pike was surer that his advantage lay in moving to New York. In preparation for the move, he sold his home and installed his family in the largest suite at Burnet House.

Even as Pike prepared to leave Cincinnati, the local press refused to give

ALICE AT FOUR, 1861
*Alice was the apple of
her father's eye, and she
looked forward to his return
home from work each day
so that she could dance
and sing for him.*

his decision credence. Cincinnati without Pike was unthinkable. They considered him as much a city landmark as his opera house. When, however, word finally reached Cincinnati from New York that Pike had purchased property from the heirs of the Episcopal Bishop Clement Clarke Moore (the author of *A Visit to Saint Nicholas*) for the purpose of building an opera house, his intention to leave Cincinnati was taken seriously.

Then, without warning, Pike's carefully organized plans were thrown into disarray. On the evening of March 22, 1866, Pike was at the Burnet House with his family. Earlier he had attended a performance of Shakespeare's *A Midsummer Night's Dream* at the Opera House. By 11 P.M. the Opera House was cleared and a few minutes before 11:30 P.M., the house manager began his inspection. He crossed over the stage behind the green baize grand curtain, but saw nothing out of order. The assistant house manager checked the auditorium and then left for dinner at a restaurant down the block. Finally, the night watchman completed his rounds and turned off the building's gas. Suddenly there was an earsplitting explosion so great that it blew out the entire rear of the opera house. When the house manager rushed back into the theater, it was already too late to stop the spread of the fire. Flames were already reaching around the grand curtain and climbing the velvet-covered walls of the auditorium toward the elaborately decorated boxes and frescoed dome. The roaring fire was fueled by masses of oil-painted canvas that earlier had been Titania's sylvan glen and Theseus's royal palace.

Within five minutes the blaze was visible not only in Cincinnati, but to people living fifty miles away. By 11:45 P.M., only fifteen minutes after the initial explosion, the fire spread beyond the Opera House to engulf the entire half square upon which it was situated, including the offices and printing plant of the *Cincinnati Enquirer* and neighboring stores. With each passing hour the flames grew higher and the entire downtown business section was threatened. The fire stopped only when it reached a large iron and brick building on the corner of Fourth and Vine. As dawn approached, the efforts of the exhausted fire brigade were completed by a soaking downpour.

The final loss to Pike was estimated at close to one million dollars, of which only $38,000 was covered by insurance. While the *Enquirer* suffered total loss as well, it was the destruction of the Opera House the populace most cared about. Cincinnati had lost the focus for its civic pride. And Pike? Sanguine as ever, he walked calmly from his suite to the front steps of Burnet House. He watched from there for a few minutes before he realized the better view of the destruction of his beloved Opera House was from the roof of the hotel.

Those who were with him that night remarked how quiet he was as he

THE BURNING OF PIKE'S
OPERA HOUSE, 1866
*On March 22, following a
performance of* A Midsum-
mer Night's Dream, *the
Opera House was destroyed
by a gas explosion caused
by a careless stagehand.*

stood watching, his ever-present cigar clenched between his teeth. A
reporter commented: "He viewed the tremendous scene, in which a million
of his property was vanishing, ...with more calmness than the majority of
the multitude of spectators. Whatever a dauntless spirit and an unwearied

energy on his part can do to repair his great loss, will certainly be done."[8]

The following day a letter from Pike was published in the paper express-ing his gratitude for the "generous sympathy" extended by his friends and members of the public. He also thanked the fire department for preventing the spread of the fire. The letter, however, did not conclude as many hoped it might with a promise to rebuild. Instead Pike wrote, "I can not now state what my plans for the future improvement of this property may be, but whatever I may do, I trust an energetic determination to overcome a loss of this nature...."[9]

Alice was among those who truly mourned the loss of the Opera House. In company with hundreds of fellow Cincinnatians, Alice, her sisters, and her brother went to see the ruins. It was a Dantesque scene that she re-membered for years after. Amidst the muck caused by the rain were still-glowing embers, and columns of smoke rising toward the sky. One wall remained standing and broken pillars, twisted iron, and piles of bricks lay everywhere blocking the major thoroughfares, necessitating a rerouting of the trolley line and the presence of the police to maintain order.

In spite of the destruction of his Opera House, Pike refused to allow his home life to be gloomy. As time passed, Alice could see her father's spirits lift. He was, however, as closemouthed with his family about his plans as with the public. Alice decided that her father must have a dream in mind. Since her home was not that far from the Opera House site, she would go frequently to inspect it, holding onto an older sister's hand. She saw the debris being carted away by a chain gang and noted that the ornamental stone fronting of the Opera House was not merely being dumped into a cart, but was being carefully marked before removal. She observed that special care was being taken to save the carved busts, musical medallions, cornices, window caps, frontals, pillars, and columns that had ornamented the front of the building. And like everyone else, Alice waited for some word from her father.

The major question for Cincinnatians became: would Pike rebuild or not? One newspaper ran a short article called "Dreaming Upon it," and a public campaign started to convince Pike to create another temple of music; for what was Cincinnati without its opera house? Even this pro-voked no response from Pike. He seemed preoccupied with his affairs in New York; his plans to move East were well along, including the erection of another opera house on New York's West Side.

The land at Fourth and Vine remained vacant and it was not until May 16, 1866, that Pike articulated his requirements for rebuilding the Opera House to a group of prominent citizens that had already organized them-selves as Pike's Opera House Committee. He outlined his plan publicly in a letter published in the *Commercial*:

My dear Sir.

In our conversation this morning, I mentioned that I had been solicited by many of my friends and citizens to build an opera house, and they had kindly offered to aid me pecuniarily if I so desired, and wished me to suggest some plan on which I would undertake it again. It is a compliment I highly appreciate, and I can not but express my thanks for the interest and sympathy our citizens have manifested in my misfortune. I know of no plan that could induce me to resume the arduous management of another opera house, but I fully feel the loss as a citizen, and would sacrifice a great deal to see the Opera House reestablished in Cincinnati, knowing as I do its importance to our merchants, and others interested in the welfare of our city's prosperity....There is one plan...which was for our citizens in committee to solicit subscriptions to the amount of $150,000, in payment of which they should receive tickets, for the amount of their subscription, for the first dramatic season after the Opera House is completed, which can be done 22nd March next. This suggestion seemed the only one that would induce me to rebuild and manage the Opera House, and if you, your friends, and the citizens desire, I will cheerfully undertake the task again, although for the past seven years it has not remunerated me pecuniarily, but has given me a great deal of pleasure to know that I had, in my humble endeavors, given satisfaction, to our community.[10]

The committee's response was to dissolve, and Pike's proposal for a cooperative venture was doomed. Within months Samuel Pike, his family, and all their household belongings were headed toward New York City. Behind them in Cincinnati was a gaping hole where once the Opera House had stood.

II
New York Ventures

The Pikes settled easily into their new home at 347 West Twenty-third Street. The house was fashioned after a French villa and was surrounded by a large lawn and colorful flower beds. Although the West Side was not the most fashionable section of town, Chelsea was quiet and gentrified.

Sixteen-year-old Jeannette and fourteen-year-old Hester were immediately enrolled in a local finishing school. They had been well-prepared by the classical education they received at the Cooper Seminary for Young Women in Dayton. Alice's high spirits and overactive imagination had been the despair of her governess, of the nuns at the convent school, and of her teachers during the one year she spent at Cooper Seminary. In New York she was once again turned over to the rigorous discipline of a convent school.

Of the four children, nineteen-year-old Lawrence was most captivated by the opportunities provided by the country's largest city. In Cincinnati he had walked in his father's shadow. Here he could become his own man, albeit financed by his father's money. Handsome and rich, he was soon a member of New York's young smart set. Although Pike still hoped Lawrence would become interested in the distillery, his obsession with the new opera house kept him from paying much attention to Lawrence's comings and goings. Lawrence, who much preferred socializing to dirtying his hands in commerce, carefully stayed out of his father's way. Pike found time only to enjoy the latest antics of his favorite child. When he arrived home, Alice sang to him the latest French ditty she had learned at her voice lesson or climbed onto his lap to read her lessons.

During the summer, Pike allowed Alice to have her own vegetable patch in the kitchen garden next to the rear door. Impatiently, she pulled up the plants to see how well they were growing and then carefully stuck them back into the ground if they looked too small. As father and daughter surveyed her efforts, it was clear to both her harvest would be small.

Of equal importance to Alice that first summer was the care and feeding of the goldfish swimming in the basin of the fountain in the front yard. She took her responsibility very seriously and watched anxiously as winter approached. On a particularly cold November day, not only did the goldfish pond freeze, but the goldfish as well. With the best of intentions she carefully carried each frozen fish into the house to thaw. Unfortunately, the last one slipped from her hand, fell to the ground, and broke in half. Her father arrived home to find her inconsolable. The next day her father's

ALICE, 1872

At fifteen Alice's carefree life was shattered by the death of her father. The effervescent child became the somber young woman captured by this tintype photograph.

partner, George Kidd, appeared at the door with a gift. Within moments
the tears were replaced by laughter at the antics of the little monkey she
named Jaco.

Day by day Alice's memories of Cincinnati dimmed as she settled into a
routine of school during the day, performing for her father at night, and
going to church on Sunday. It was not so easy for Pike. He not only had his
New York business to attend to, but the building of an opera house as well.
Moreover, Pike also had to deal with pressure from the Cincinnati merchants whose businesses were being seriously hurt by the loss of the opera
house clientele. Once again Pike reiterated his demand for $150,000 in
guaranteed ticket sales to ensure the success of the first season. When Pike
finally understood no support would be forthcoming, he issued orders for
construction of an office building on the site. When completed it contained
an auditorium suitable for concerts and exhibitions. Pike was noticeably
absent from the inaugural ceremony on February 12, 1867.

That spring was marked by an event that lodged in Alice's memory
because it was so unusual. The Pikes did not fight, primarily because Ellen
would do anything to keep peace. Thus, the entire household was thrown
into turmoil when Ellen put her foot down the day Pike told her he wanted
to buy a home in the far northern regions of Fifth Avenue. "Folly, total
folly," she yelled at Pike. "I did not move to New York City to live in the
country!" To the surprise of everyone, particularly Ellen, Pike gave in
because it was so genuinely unusual for her to express any opinion. The
battle over, Ellen retreated to her bedroom, her French novels, and her
blessed quiet. Pike, bewildered by the unexpected rebellion, began to
spend even greater time down at the corner overseeing the construction of
his new opera house.

Although the New York press knew Pike was building an opera house,
it was not until October 1867 when the main building was enclosed that its
scale was recognized. If New Yorkers had known Pike better, they would
have recognized he was not a man of small dreams. With an income of over
three million dollars a year, he was able to hire the very best architects,
engineers, and contractors available in New York.

The architectural firm of Thomas and Son was an early proponent of the
Second Empire style and the most advanced techniques of cast iron fram-
ing. Although this was its first theater, the firm had extensive experience in
designing grand buildings such as banks, stores, and office buildings,
which were as much commercial palaces as places of business. Construction oversight was awarded to Calvert Vaux, the premier builder of mansions for the rich along upper Fifth Avenue and was yet another indication
that the new opera house was going to be something special.

The stress laid on Pike from the spring of 1866 to the end of 1867 must have been tremendous. Yet, there is no record that Pike reacted in any way other than to go on quietly about his business. In spite of the optimism of New York reporters, the two enormous building projects a thousand miles apart stretched Pike's purse to the limit. A further irritant was the arrival at his home in New York of a contingent of Cincinnati Democrats who pressured him to return to the Queen City to run for mayor. Although privately chafing at the time wasted in meeting with the delegation, Pike refused politely. He was well aware of the dubiousness of the honor because he knew it was merely a ploy by a corrupt party to find an honest front man. A New York reporter summed up Pike's position:

> The good people of Cincinnati were not remarkably generous to Mr. S. N. Pike, when he proposed to rebuild an Opera House in place of the one destroyed by fire. Then Mr. Pike decided to build an Opera House in this city, and finally to remove his business hither. The distillery of 'Samuel N. Pike & Co.' is already in complete operation on the west side of town, and a new Opera House is quietly going up. At this point, the Cincinnatians threw out a bait to Mr. Pike in the shape of a Mayoralty nomination. The temptation comes too late. Mr. Pike is a New Yorker, and he 'respectfully declines' the proffered honor.[1]

THE SECOND OPERA HOUSE

As 1867 drew to a close, work at the opera house reached fever pitch. It was scheduled to open on Thursday, January 9, 1868, with Verdi's *Il Trovatore* sung by Max Strakosch's Operatic Company with Anna de la Grange as Leonora. Her debut performance in the role of Leonora at the National Academy of Music in 1855 had almost single-handedly raised the level of operatic performance in America, and music critics and aficionados all agreed that Pike had managed an operatic coup in engaging her for the opening. There was, however, a serious problem with Pike's new Opera House—its location. It was outside the boundaries of the established entertainment district. Although the city's center was rapidly moving north and west, it was not yet there. The primary question for New York's "Pike watchers" was: Would the sophisticated operagoer regularly travel over half a mile to hear music they could find more easily on Broadway?

Pike's million-dollar bet was that the Chelsea neighborhood would soon be at the heart of the city rather than on its outskirts. Reporters, impressed with his courage, cheered him on.

> Pike—Magnolia Pike—the Great Western Pike—the voracious Pike, who swallowed up all the little theatrical fishes out West, and has now come to New York to gulp down Wheatley, Wallack, Maretzek, Grau, Bateman, and Billy Birch [theatrical producers] at one swal-

low, will open his magnificent and costly establishment . . . with a grand opera troupe. Curiosity to see the result of Western taste and wealth will make the short opera season successful. After that the deluge. Cause, location. And that cause will hold good for at least five years to come.[2]

Whatever its chances for future success, there was unanimity of opinion among all the architectural and theater critics that Pike's Opera House was the finest New York had ever seen and its opening engendered columns of hyperbolic prose. One such lengthy report ended breathlessly: "We shall not attempt to give any detailed description of the house; but let it suffice when we say that art has been exhausted and skill has done its utmost to make this building worthy of the refining purpose to which it has been consecrated and also worthy of the great city which it preeminently adorns."

INTERIOR OF THE NEW YORK OPERA HOUSE, CA. 1875
The original interior of Pike's Opera House boasted a French decor of blues, whites, and golds, and could seat 2,600. It was considered the finest Opera House in New York, but it was doomed to failure due to its distance from the city's entertainment center on lower Broadway.

THE NEW YORK OPERA
HOUSE, CA. 1876
*Pike's second Opera House
at Twenty-third Street and
Eighth Avenue in New York
opened January 1868.*

Even allowing for hyperbole, Pike's Opera House was a significant addition to New York's architecture. John M. Moffit, an English sculptor, was given the challenge to engender awe for the arts through the exterior ornamentation. Pike wanted to follow the European model of using real sculpture as an integral part of the exterior design. The interior also received Pike's imprimatur. The predominant color scheme of the house was not the usual red plush so favored by theaters of the day. To Alice's delight and Ellen's dismay, it was decorated in French fashion with the prevailing colors of gold and white highlighted by rich blues and soft dove grays and accented by crimson and gold. The extraordinary architectural feature of the house was its dome. Twenty-five feet in diameter, it rose ten feet above the level of the deep blue ceiling and was encircled by warmly tinted frescos depicting the muses. At intervals along the base of the dome, papier-mâché figures held clusters of gaslights designed by Tiffany & Company.

The weather for the January 9 opening was fiercely cold and windy. The icy streets made it difficult for the carriages to make the trek from lower Fifth Avenue north and west to Eighth Avenue. Nevertheless, the opening night was sold out.

The hitherto unfrequented quarter of Eighth Avenue was blocked with carriages and crowded with fashionables, and the finest theatrical establishment in America was thrown open to the public for the first time. Through its spacious entrance poured in a crowd of elegantly dressed ladies, with their white-kidded cavaliers, and the vestibule was filled with opera-goers, uncloaking, unshawling, and otherwise reducing themselves to the requisite proportions of full dress before entering the brilliant auditorium. Box, parquet, and balcony were resplendent with rich toilets, and bright eyes flashed recognition of acquaintances in every part of the house.[3]

With spring came light opera and legitimate theater, but as the months sped by the audiences became noticeably smaller. The novelty wore off and it began to look as if the earlier forecasts of failure were coming true. In January 1869, *The New York Times* recorded that the box office receipts for Pike's Opera House in 1868 appeared excellent, second only to Niblo's Garden, the popular vaudeville house. By the time they were printed, however, the figures were meaningless for in December 1868, Pike was forced to sell his lovingly crafted theater to James Fiske, Jr., for $850,000 to become the headquarters of the New York & Erie Railroad.

Pike watched helplessly as Fiske destroyed the interior of his elegant building as thoroughly as fire gutted the one in Cincinnati. Fiske's florid remodeling included, in addition to a special suite of rooms for assignations with show girls, an overabundance of gilt, stained glass, and garish murals. Several years later, Alice took a friend to the site of her father's opera house and described the opera and theater she had seen there as a child. She told him "it was filled with such delightful memories for her. What momentous occasions had transpired there."

When the news of the sale reached Cincinnati, Pike was once more approached by a delegation of Cincinnati merchants to build an opera house for the Queen City. Pike appeared interested, but as in 1867, he wanted it to be a joint venture and requested a good faith investment of two-and-a-half million dollars. True to form, with the mention of money, the committee disbanded. This time, however, Pike was willing, and in 1871 he returned to Cincinnati for a short seven-week stay to oversee the transformation of the auditorium of his office building into an opera theater. The new opera house was enthusiastically received by sold-out crowds, and it quickly filled the place left vacant by the first opera house.

FINAL PROJECTS

After the successful opening night, Pike returned to New York to attend to the delayed matter of a proper house for his family. Now that there no

NEW YORK OPERA HOUSE ANNOUNCEMENT IN *THE SEASON*, 1868. Rigoletto *was one of the first operas performed in 1868 at Pike's New York Opera House. The Opera House was successful for only the first few months, and was sold by Pike within the year.*

ELLEN PIKE, C. 1868
Alice later wrote of Ellen, "Her Heaven [sic] was a place where one wore comfortable clothes, never had social obligations, read a new novel every day, ate quantities of black bridal-fruit cake, and consumed pitchers of ice water."

longer was any reason to live on Twenty-third Street, he purchased a new one uptown at 613 Fifth Avenue. Contrary to Ellen's fears, they were not faced with country living. The elegant neighborhood now included Gould and Vanderbilt mansions, the New York Yacht Club, and Saint Patrick's Cathedral.

Their new home was a five-story brownstone, simple and unpretentious. Pike undertook its decoration with the same attention to detail that he lavished formerly on his opera houses. Ellen had no interest in decorating the new house and happily turned the project over to her husband. Pike was often seen entering various stores with his youngest daughter on his arm, the only one of his children who seemed to share his delight in acquiring beautiful objects. Hours were spent at the fashionable Marcott shop selecting First Empire and Directoire furniture. Eschewing Victorian bric-a-brac, Pike invested in rare books, among them a portfolio of operatic costume designs that he displayed prominently along with the silver and Dutch paintings he had inherited from his parents and a new painting by the Spanish artist Alonzo Cano for which he paid ten thousand dollars.

Because she had helped with the decoration, the results were particularly pleasing to Alice. Moreover, it was a surprise for her mother, who was not allowed in the newly decorated downstairs rooms until the last of the workmen had left. On the day of completion Pike ceremoniously escorted Ellen downstairs to see the results. She inspected the grays, ivories, and deep blues of the draperies, upholstery, and carpets. Serenely, she rendered her opinion, "I much prefer red plush—like those draperies in the new Fifth Avenue Hotel." At this Pike threw up his hands in horror and retorted, "Ellen, you have no more taste than a cow," which was followed by the second and last argument Alice ever recalled between her parents.

The difference in age between Alice and her next oldest sister, Hessie, was much greater now that Hessie was a proper young lady rather than a schoolgirl. Jeannette lived another life altogether, one of balls and parties at Delmonico's. Lawrence's social life was so hectic that he was seldom seen at home by Alice since he rose long after she'd set out for school or singing lessons and by the time she returned he was off to a rousing dinner with his smart set. Ellen only came down for dinner and then retired immediately. Therefore, Pike and Alice spent many an early evening together enjoying her performance of arias she had heard at his New York City opera house.

Pike was now at that age in life when people speak of someone being in their prime. Having attained so much materially, he could with impunity spend the remainder of his life at leisure. Pike, however, was not a man to sit and survey life; he had to be an active part of it. With the distillery providing ready, ever-flowing capital, Pike created a new company called the Iron Dike and Land Reclamation Company for the purpose of acquiring and draining over six thousand acres of the Newark marshes. At a cost of nearly thirty million dollars, portions of the reclaimed land were to be diked and sold as rights of way to railroads coming from the south. When his expenses were recouped along with a hefty profit, he planned to sell the remaining acreage at just above cost to the immigrants who lived in the squalor of overcrowded slums on New York's Lower East Side. He envisioned what one hundred years later would become the American dream: every family in its own home on its own plot of land. Far ahead of his time, he foresaw the advantages of suburban living where children could grow up strong and healthy, free of rats, roaches, and dirt.[4]

It was an exciting project, and with his usual single-mindedness Pike devoted himself to it. Although it kept him away from his family, he made sure that Alice knew there was nothing he looked forward to more than spending time with her once his work was well in hand—a promise that this seemingly indefatigable man proved unable to keep.

On December 7, 1872, Pike went to work early at his office on Bridge Street followed by his usual lunch of a dozen oysters at Delmonico's with his partners. Suddenly he became sick and was carried back to his office. At 6:30 p.m., Samuel Pike died of a heart attack at the age of fifty.

For five days Pike's body lay on view in the front parlor of 613 Fifth Avenue. Not until December 12 did numerous business associates and musical and theatrical friends gather at the Pike home for the funeral. Following the ceremony, Pike's body was transported to Cyprus Hill Cemetery for burial.

With amazing swiftness Samuel Pike's name was forgotten in New York. Fiske had already renamed Pike's theater the Grand Opera House, and all that remained of its builder was the initial "P" on the back of the velvet seats. The distillery was sold and the diking company went out of business. When his will was presented for probate in January 1873, his estate was valued at three million dollars, approximately what he brought with him to New York.

Cincinnati, however, had a longer memory. Fifty years after his death,

Edwin Henderson, writing under the pseudonym of Conteur, was still evoking Samuel Napthali Pike.

> You rarely, in business life, come across a man who is not, in many of his characteristics, like the replica to the original, a mere one in many among men you have known. Seldom do you find one who seems absolutely a generis. But such a man was Mr. Pike. He was alert in business, with the eye of speculation directed toward the main chance; originator of, for his time, great ventures. At the same time he was debonair, chum of poet, painter, actor, singer, soldier. In the same day or week it seemed, his mind would be devoted to wholesaling whiskey, redeeming the marshes of New Jersey, erecting magnificent opera houses in Cincinnati and New York and in playing the flute at a benefit or dreaming over his poem, 'Dreaming.' He was a man of sentiment; soulful, magnetic. Intellectuality and an inclination to poetry marked his face in the delicate features, the slight retreat of dome and chin, the brilliant, thoughtful, kind eyes, the very droop of the mustache. He walked in a leisurely, careless way, like one who meditates upon the esthetics more than upon the grosser realities of daily life. He was a dreamer of the beautiful. And one of his dreams, nearly fifty years ago, was to so beautify the city of his adoption that it should be known the world over through his act. And this dream he fulfilled.[5]

With Samuel Pike's death, life in the Pike household changed dramatically. No longer did Alice have the encouragement and understanding that her father had given her. Her mother retreated further into French novels and removed herself from active participation in the life around her. The lives of her brother and sisters became even more remote and conventional to Alice now that she no longer had her father to share her dreams. In her memories, he was the central figure of her life; she would always be fifteen and he fifty. Never knowing him as an adult, or knowing his foibles, he became the ideal, a model to be emulated all her life.

III
Henry Morton Stanley

Memories of her father flooded Alice's mind at the end of every school day. Singing and dancing lessons, impromptu performances for her father, high spirits, and the laughter of young people gathered on the front stoop were all swallowed by the enveloping silence of the Pike home.

Part of the quiet came from unspoken grief, but the greater portion derived from the personality of the woman who now set its tone. As if overnight, the five-story house had become as sedate and conventional as Ellen. Her natural passivity, combined with her strict adherence to the rules of mourning, cast a pall over everyone who lived there. It was so unnaturally silent that if the servants hadn't vouched for their presence, callers would have thought Pike's children had been sent away to visit relatives.

Nonetheless, they were all there, from twenty-five-year-old Lawrence to sixteen-year-old Alice. It was long past the time for Lawrence to move out, but he had no desire to do so. At his father's insistence he had taken one abortive stab at business, but his attempt to manufacture shellac had ended in failure when he showed more interest in attending parties than appearing at his office. At twenty-three, he retired from the tedium of earning a living to concentrate on his social life.

Jeannette at twenty-two was also a social butterfly, her mind focused on the next party and the latest fashions. Of the three older children, only twenty-year-old Hessie seemed the inheritor of her mother's retiring nature. Moreover, Hessie was engaged, and it was easy for her to spend every day dreaming about her wedding to Tom Negus, which would occur once the year of deep mourning was concluded.

Of Pike's four children, Alice grieved most openly. Only with the greatest effort did she accept the new order imposed by her mother. Alice was by nature cheerful and curious. Her father had encouraged these attributes, but they were now looked upon as inappropriate. Once she had run down the hallway to greet her father when he returned from work. Now she tiptoed so that she would not disturb anyone.

There was something unnatural about the way in which Ellen took to mourning, and the family soon realized that her withdrawal from society was probably permanent. In later years Alice likened it to "a benign calm, of an almost oriental nature" where, "since everything meant nothing to her, nothing meant anything and in this vacuum she hibernated." Her only appearance outside the house was for a long daily drive. When visitors arrived they were immediately shown to Ellen's upstairs room, bypassing

HENRY MORTON
STANLEY, C. 1872
*This was Alice's favorite
picture of her first love,
one which she placed at her
bedside in later years. It
portrays him in his early
thirties, close to the time he
discovered Dr. Livingston
in deepest Africa.*

the elegant lower floors Alice and her father had decorated so enthusiastically.

No matter how much Ellen enjoyed her quiet life, her children found it confining. Even Hessie began to chaff at the constraining somberness of their days. The first anniversary of Pike's death came and went with no observable change in the fabric of Ellen's life. By Christmas 1873, Pike's daughters were committed to escaping the oppressive silence through taking the grand tour of Europe. They dreamed of seeing Zurich, Geneva, Milan, Florence, and Naples in addition to the obligatory extended stays in London, Rome, and Paris. All that remained was to convince Ellen of the reasonableness of their plan.

Any appeal to Ellen's sense of adventure was doomed to fail. Her children knew that all she really wanted from life was her comfortable lounging clothes, a stack of popular French novels, a ready supply of dark, rich bridal fruitcake, and gallons of ice water. Therefore, the way to gain her acquiescence was to convince her how readily these creature comforts could be found in Europe. She would have no responsibilities, her routine would remain the same, and above all, they would do nothing to worry her. Their faultless presentation reassured Ellen and she retired to her rooms and her novels during the hectic preparation.

Once the news was out that the Pikes were going to Europe for an extended visit, a steady procession of women came to say good-bye to Ellen. Alice was surprised at how many friends her mother had despite the fact that Ellen made no effort to make or keep them. But come they did, climbing the stairs to her cluttered second-floor sitting room that exuded the odor of freshly cut flowers. Perhaps, Alice mused many years later, they came because it was the only truly serene place in all of New York City where they could escape the constant pressure of pursuing or retaining a position in society. With Ellen they were free to pour out their troubles, confident she would never betray them. Ellen sat quietly and occasionally nodded or murmured encouragingly. What they never knew was that she had mastered the technique of appearing attentive while registering nothing. There were no confidences to break because she immediately forgot what was said. Her smile and a certain amused gleam in her eye provided them with the assurance that she understood them. Not one of them, however, understood her; she did not want it otherwise.

Ellen's preparations for the trip were marked by simplicity. She took the diamonds she never wore and the old and comfortable clothing she did. Finally the house was closed, and in early March 1874 the Pike family sailed to France. Hester, having given in to the urging of her sisters that she have a Parisian wedding, eagerly awaited Tom's arrival.

THE GRAND TOUR

Their first stop was the Hôtel Splendide in Paris. Alice felt as if she were in heaven. The hotel's decor reminded her of her father's taste. Its wood-paneled walls were painted ivory. Mirrors abounded, fancifully framed by delicate gold metalwork. Painted cherubs beamed down from the ceilings and delicate laces and blue pastel satin drapes hung on the floor-to-ceiling windows. When opened, the smells and sounds of Paris suffused the apartment.

Paris cast a spell on Alice. Her reaction was immediate and extreme; it was a magic city.

> It was amazing to Alice how everything was intensified in Paris. There was a stimulating animation and a heightening of color that exalted her. Color. It became a sudden world to her. The magic of the Louvre and the many galleries succeeded in increasing her desire for self-expression. Sometimes she drove over to the Left Bank and saw the artists in their native haunts... men with their black velvet jackets, their large black hats, black flowing ties, black eyes and black beards...

She was filled with the romance of it as only a seventeen-year-old could be.

Alice's first awareness that she possessed artistic talent occurred in Paris through an encounter with a fortune-hunting Count. The Count de Portelaise made it a point to pursue American heiresses in the hope of capturing one who would solve his financial problems. Having introduced himself to the Pikes when they were dining at the hotel, he selected Alice as the beneficiary of his charms.

Unlike many of her peers, Alice was not in Europe to acquire a husband, titled or otherwise. It was the furthest thing from her mind and there was nothing of Undine Spragg (the quintessential American social climber portrayed by Edith Wharton in her cynical comedy of manners *The Custom of the Country*) in Alice's character. The Count, however, was not deterred by Alice's lack of interest in his suit. Rather, it challenged him to new heights of creativity.

Part of his strategy was to pass himself off as a painter, although in truth his artistic pretensions were based more on the figure he cut in his painting attire than on any ability with a brush. As an excuse to spend time with Alice, the Count suggested he give Alice art lessons. What more fitting way for her to learn than by copying one of his own renderings of his château, which depicted in the foreground a groom leading two horses. As they worked, the Count extolled the virtues of his family home, suggesting how much better it would look if it were enlarged. Alice, in turn, ignored the hint and admired the horses.

To her surprise, Alice's copy far surpassed the original. Fearing to insult the Count, she reworked it to make it as clumsy as his. When the exercise was finished, the Count made his move. As they stood before the two paintings, he offered her his château, his title, and himself. To his utter surprise, Alice refused. After gathering up her paints, she graciously presented him with her copy in remembrance of their pleasant time together.

She also showed him a sketchbook she had begun, which was filled with drawings of the people she had observed during strolls around Paris. Portelaise adjusted his monocle and inspected them. The girl clearly had talent and it was with relief he acknowledged her refusal of his proposal. How terrible to be married to someone who was better than oneself; his ego would not have sustained it. There were, after all, a constant supply of rich young girls from America. He would just have to check next week's passenger manifests.

COUNT JEAN DE PORTE-
LAISE, C. 1874
*Alice may have been only
seventeen when she met the
Count Jean de Portelaise,
but she knew him for the
fortune hunter he was.*

When Tom Negus arrived in Paris, he and Hessie went off to face the intricacies of French bureaucracy. Although forewarned, they found it even more complicated and time-consuming than expected. Rather than wait for them to acquire all the necessary papers, Alice and Nettie decided to start the grand tour without them. Before leaving they reserved a suite "aux deuxieme etage" for late May and specified rooms sufficiently large to hold Hessie's wedding garments and an extensive trousseau, as well as all the necessities for the sisters and their mother.

Though they were "everlastingly rushing to catch trains," and constantly finding themselves "a trifle taxed" at each stop, the whirlwind tour offered endless opportunities for Alice to practice drawing. She sketched whatever struck her fancy: a dark, curly-haired peasant boy in Naples that she later turned into a painting, a bereaved father in Rome, a cavorting carnival celebrator in Milan. Her initial attempts were crude and untutored, but it satisfied her need to capture on paper the images that most excited her imagination. She could hardly wait for the London she had read of in Charles Dickens. She hoped by the time they got there, she would have improved enough to capture some of its colorful inhabitants.

As she worked at her drawing skills, she became more aware of other art forms and devel-

ALICE, 1874
Louis-August Malempré
Marble bust,
21 x 14 x 9.6 in.
(53.3 x 35.6 x 24.4 cm)
While in Rome, Alice's life-long love of the arts was cemented. One of her first exposures to the arts was through Malempré, who she later commissioned to sculpt her portrait in marble.

oped an appreciation for their interrelationships. They were all part of art with a capital "A," as Alice put it. Milan was especially important to Alice, not only for the sketches she made there, but because her father had based his Cincinnati Opera House upon La Scala. In Milan she awakened to the nuances of architecture and also purchased her first examples of the decorative arts—a table and ebony chairs inlaid with ivory and some Majolica plaques. Her eclectic approach to the arts was natural to her as she unconsciously laid the foundation for her lifelong aesthetic that held no one art form above another. In her emerging artistic lexicon, to know one artistic discipline was to understand and appreciate others.

In Rome she met a professional artist for the first time. Louis-Auguste Malempré was a French sculptor who was considered part of the English school. He was in Rome for the preparation of a large number of marble portrait busts for a forthcoming exhibition. Alice attended the opening of the exhibition and afterwards Malempré invited her to join a small party at his studio. Carried away with enthusiasm for Malempré's work and his skill at "successfully modelling all the 'best people,'" Alice commissioned a sculpture of herself. When she returned to the hotel and told Jeannette she had ordered a portrait bust from such a clever and handsome artist, Jeannette retorted that she had heard he did not even do his own work, but actually hired others to do it for him. This gave Alice the opportunity to show off her newly acquired knowledge: "My dear Nettie, of course he doesn't cut the stone! He leaves that to his men; he merely models in clay and then puts the finishing touches on the marble, naturally."

STANLEY AND LONDON

After leaving Rome they planned to spend at least a month in England. Alice's high expectations of the great British empire's capital city were quickly dashed to pieces upon entering the rooms reserved for them at the Langham Hotel on Regent's Park. The Langham catered almost exclusively to Americans and, therefore, its decor bore a great similarity to New York's Fifth Avenue Hotel. This was Victorian England with a style suited much more to Ellen's taste than to Alice's. Alice described her initial impression of London:

> It was the maiden-lady period of English society and all that was lavender was not left to scent the wardrobe chests but spread its stultifying sweetness over all the vigorous plush, frozen damask, frigid laces, becarved furniture, cabbage-patterned carpets, palms, and whatnot stands dizzily draped and paraletically weighted with this, that, and the other culled from home, abroad, and Aunt Ida's attic.

Among the guests when the Pikes arrived were Charles Armour of the

Chicago meat-packing family, who was a friend of Lawrence's from New York, and Henry Morton Stanley, reporter, explorer, and author of three books. Stanley was England's man-of-the-hour because he had searched for and found the great Dr. Livingston in deepest Africa. By 1874 the phrase, "Dr. Livingston, I presume," was already part of the English national consciousness. Alice later described his reception in London:

> All—yes—all London was at his feet. He had been commanded by the Queen...feted by royalty, interviewed, dined and even his sleep intruded upon in unforeseen ways as a result of his achievement. ...Having been in India before he went to Africa to find Livingston it was expected he might give the affair a native touch, but he had never consumed lentils in the shadow of a plaster-flaking arch with the natives, and so his contribution was, alas, not very edifying.

When Armour found that the Pikes were intrigued by Stanley's fame and wanted an introduction, he volunteered to act as intermediary.

The first member of the family to meet Stanley was Lawrence. The entry in Stanley's diary after the meeting was not flattering. Lawrence, he wrote, was "one of those useless young men fashionable New York produces every year, who become nothing, whom nobody ever hears of." Despite this poor impression, Stanley did agree to meet the Pike women. Jeannette did not fare much better than her brother. She was, according to Stanley, "rather fast" with a "disagreeably loud" voice. Equally distasteful to Stanley was her hairdo—a fashionable creation with fluffy, teased curls for bangs that looked to Stanley like "a lot of untidy hair hanging over the forehead." Mrs. Pike, on the other hand, was "good-looking, stout, and exceedingly good-tempered."

When Stanley began to write about Alice, there was an abrupt change in tone. Her profile was girlishly soft, her pale skin and large gray-blue eyes attractive, and her manner agreeably self-contained. Seemingly searching for something critical to say about her, Stanley wrote that "although her mouth was large but well-formed, her nose had a certain Jewish fullness at the point with the slightest possible rise halfway down." In the end he could find only one real criticism; she wore too many diamonds. Even this was subsumed when Alice arose from the table and the elegance of her figure was revealed as she stood before him in a black silk dress. Several days later Stanley confided to his diary, "I fear that if Miss Alice gives me as much encouragement as she has been giving me lately, I shall fall in love with her." The truth was that Stanley was already in love with Alice.[1]

Alice, on the other hand, was soon swept away as much by London as Stanley. In her autobiography she writes of both with the same breathless excitement:

'London-town! London-town! Lights come up as night comes down.'
...The fog, that brought curses from most people but repaid them with
red cheeks, made every bit of it a dream to her. The whole town, with
its rigid glamour floated around her in a misty bewilderment.... The
fog—the night—was full of it. Fantasy. It was London's aura. And,
she had met Stanley...she had met the lion of London...It meant the
lilt of life to her.

At seventeen Alice was both child and woman. She had all the aplomb
and poise to be expected of Samuel Pike's daughter. Her conversational
skills were based on remembered repartee from her childhood when she
had attended her father's after-theater dinner parties. Stanley could not
know that Alice's seeming sophistication—her proper manners and conversational ease—hid a young girl whose knowledge of affairs of the heart was
nonexistent. She had young male friends, but she had never thought of
them as anything more than compatriots in a good time. Certainly she had
never considered them potential husbands. She was quite unprepared to
face the emotions Stanley awakened in her. While infatuated by Stanley,
Alice had no idea if she were ready, or even willing, to love him.

Of Stanley's love for her there is no doubt. He was deeply and completely head-over-heels in love with an American heiress half his age. He could
not stay away from her. She enchanted him, beguiled him, challenged him.
They had pet names for each other—she was Lady Alice and he became
Morton when she professed her dislike of Henry. Only one thing disturbed
Stanley about Alice and that was her distinct lack of education. She was
totally ignorant about Africa, which was his passion. She was, however, a
quick study, and Stanley became teacher as well as suitor. As he talked
vividly of Africa, he hoped to draw her intimately into his life.

There was little in Alice's background to prepare her for an aggressive
man like Stanley. In personality he was far removed from the quiet and un-
assuming Samuel Pike or the laconic Lawrence. Stanley was often grandiose and abrasive. As an aggressive reporter for the *New York Herald*, he had
traveled and experienced more than most men. His assignments took him
to Paris, London, and Madrid and by thirty-three years of age he had conquered Africa. Queen Victoria called him "a determined, ugly, little man,"
but Alice saw him as a rugged individualist whose handsomeness derived
from strength and determination. As for his small stature of only five feet
five inches, Alice thought it nicely matched her own petite five feet.[2]

Alice was not the only one perturbed by her relationship with Stanley. It
was rapidly becoming apparent to the entire Pike household that this was a
serious romance, and Ellen was particularly troubled. Much as she hated
this interruption of her routine, she knew she had to speak to Stanley. Her

opportunity arrived one sunny day in mid-May when Stanley and Alice had planned an outing to Windsor Castle followed by lunch with the Queen's librarian. Stanley, who had discovered that Alice had little sense of time, came to the Pike's hotel rooms well before the appointed hour in order to ensure that they arrived at Windsor on time.

To his surprise the door was opened not by Alice or her maid, but by Ellen. Although he had not seen Mrs. Pike since their first meeting, Alice had told Stanley enough about her mother to know that her presence was highly unusual. He felt like a teenager caught out of school and searched his mind for some possible explanation, some indiscretion, but he could find none. True, he had been out with Alice every night since they had met, but he had always brought her home at a reasonable hour. Perhaps Mrs. Pike wanted to go with them. Maybe she thought it improper for Alice to visit Windsor unchaperoned. Perhaps Alice was sick.

He waited nervously for Ellen to come to the point, and after a brief exchange of pleasantries, she did. Alice, she asserted, might seem to be twenty, but she was really only a child of seventeen. She was obviously being swept away by the attentions of a famous man and enjoying it thoroughly. As her mother, Ellen was concerned that such a fairy tale romance so early in her life might ruin Alice's chances for real happiness when she finally reached a marriageable age.

Stanley was nonplussed. After a long pause, he declared that it was his desire to marry Alice, but only with Ellen's consent. Of course he had not actually asked Alice yet, but he was sure she would accept his proposal. Ellen's reply was quick and firm, "No, Mr. Stanley." Stanley began to plead his case. He promised to give up all further exploration. He would settle down with Alice in England or America, whichever Ellen preferred. He loved Alice. She made him young; she made him laugh and play—something he had never done before.

Ellen remained unmoved, but her regard for Stanley improved. He was obviously more than the lowborn adventurer she had thought. Unbending slightly, she told him that if he and Alice still loved each other in a few years, she might change her mind. For the moment, however, there must be no announcement of an engage-

ALICE AT SEVENTEEN, 1874
When Alice and Stanley parted in July 1874, Alice presented him with a copy of this portrait taken in Paris. She asked him to keep it next to his heart to help him endure the trials of his African journey.

ment, nor was he to attempt to bind Alice to a private one. As she turned to leave the room she said, "I do hope you're in time for your train...which reminds me, we're leaving for Paris soon."

Within moments Alice entered the room, and he could not help noticing how lovely she looked. Her dress was made of white cotton gauze, ruffled to the waist. She wore a black taffeta over-bodice that met the ruffled skirt in a point. Perched on her curls was a large white leghorn hat covered with white and black roses and long streamers of narrow black velvet. Her elbow-length gloves were black and her parasol was made of alternating black and white taffeta ruffles. Around her neck she wore a tiny locket with a ruby center. Inside was a picture of Stanley—the only gift that Ellen had allowed Alice to accept from him.

At eleven they arrived at the great brick Windsor train station, which had been the site of so many ceremonial arrivals by Queen Victoria and her family. Although the castle was only a short walk from the station, Stanley engaged a carriage to drive them through the massive Henry VIII gate, past the Horseshoe Cloister and St. George's Chapel to the State Apartments. There they were met by the Queen's librarian. Alice was very disappointed to learn the Queen was in Scotland.

The tour began, as all tours to Windsor do, at the grand staircase Queen Victoria built in 1866, which led majestically up to the second floor grand vestibule with its Gothic vaulting. As they strolled through the empty rooms, Alice's enthusiasm for English royal palaces waned. Alice later described it: "It looked as bad as the Fifth Avenue Hotel in New York, or was it that the Fifth Avenue Hotel was as bad as Windsor Castle....Here, everything was hung in plush: red, yellow, brown, green plush. The carpets were thick and had patterns writing all over them." Not until they reached the library did she find a room to honestly admire. Its mullioned windows were open and from there she saw the immaculately clipped lawns bordered by roses, mignonette, Canterbury bells, and phlox, whose fragrance was carried on a gentle breeze into the book-lined room.

The Queen's private chambers disappointed Alice the most. To Alice, they seemed dowdy and unattractive. How sad, she thought, "to be Queen and lose the opportunity of shining!" Lunch, however, redeemed the day. It was served in the library on gold-crested service and plate with crystal decorated with a gold coat of arms.

After lunch Stanley and Alice strolled around the upper town and then down the steep hill to the Thames. At one point Stanley weighed himself at a chemist's shop. To his dismay, he weighed 178 pounds, but he knew that whatever weight he had gained from being wined and dined in England would melt away in the heat of Africa. At the bottom of the street they walked toward the docks that jutted out into the placid Thames. Behind and above them the battlements of Windsor's round tower stood out against the blue of the sky. Impetuously Alice suggested a boat ride.[3]

As they floated quietly downstream overhanging trees shaded them from the sun and the pond lilies extending out from the bank divided as they slid by. The silence between them lengthened. Alice broke it to confess that not only had she eavesdropped on his talk with her mother, but that she agreed with Ellen. Another long silence ensued. Once again Alice was the one to break it.

Alice later repeated her faltering explanation: "I love you. You know I do, but Stanley, you have been everywhere, done everything and now you want me. I'm just starting out...I want to do, to know...just be myself...Then I, too, would be worthwhile." Stanley replied quietly, not really understanding anything other than that he had been refused, "Keep a spot for me, Alice." Alice could only respond, "We'll see, Stanley."

The Pikes began to pack. The date for Hessie's wedding was set for May 25. During their last week together, Stanley and Alice whirled off to one social engagement or another. Stanley extracted only one promise from Alice: they would spend their last evening alone together. In return, he promised her a thoroughly English dinner at the Cheshire Cheese Inn. A century earlier Samuel Johnson and his cronies had argued politics at the Cheshire, and it remained the place where writers and actors mingled with reporters, lawyers, and politicians. The pipes of the Johnson Club members were still lined up in the old pipe rack beside the chimney. Alice took all this in as Stanley escorted her past the bar and small tables filled with men drinking ale from jugs. They were seated at high-backed oak benches darkened with age, which were set before tables of the same wood.

The English evening was everything Stanley promised. Although Stanley had wanted something more private—a place where he could make his plea, declare his love, and, against Ellen's wishes, attempt to extract a promise from Alice that she would wait for him—her obvious enjoyment of the surroundings made up for that. On the ride back to her hotel she nestled against him, declaring herself totally satisfied with this last night together.

They were back at the Langham by eleven; for them an early evening. Stanley escorted her to the Pike suite, and it was time for their good-byes. Stanley found himself unable to say the words, and once again it was Alice who led the way. This time, however, glib words failed her, and she was not as sure her mother was right. As she reached out to assure him, she found herself being passionately kissed by him. Then, with equal abruptness, he dropped his arms to his side and stepped back to observe her in total silence. The unspoken gulf between them broadened. Finally Stanley spoke his piece: "To see you go, 'Lady Alice,' is like seeing a part of me being torn away....You're necessary to me. I can't help it. All I can say is, I love you. Maybe some day you'll understand that."

Alice was afraid to answer. She was feeling emotions that were unknown to her, and she feared their consequences. She held out her hand and smiled: "Let us just say 'au revoir.'" He remained still and then, as he turned to leave, he took one more long look at her. "I want you to remember. I'm hoping. I'm still hoping. I shall never give you up. Au revoir." Then he was gone. Alice began to cry, but she was still too young to know why.

Paris would be her tonic. It would help her forget Stanley. After all, she had come to Europe to have fun, and although she didn't fully understand why, her romantic interlude with Stanley had ceased being that. "In London," she wrote, "everything took on a serious aspect. In Paris...well, in Paris one laughed, one shrugged one's shoulders and met life anew with a bright eye, a smile and a joyous heart." In Paris she could be seventeen again.

The Pikes needed the large suite at the Hôtel Splendide. Every day they were inundated with goods from jewelers, dressmakers, and milliners. Since they were no longer in full mourning, grays and violet shades were permissible, and Alice selected a dress of amethyst colored velvet trimmed with embroidery for the wedding.

Although the Pikes were Episcopalians, the marriage ceremony was Roman Catholic, and its theatrical liturgy appealed to Alice. Afterwards the family and guests returned to the hotel for the wedding breakfast. Out of those invited, only Stanley was absent, and Alice wondered why she felt both hurt and relieved.

While Alice was in Paris, Stanley used the time to formulate plans for his next trip to Africa. He surrounded himself with books on Africa and took copious notes, carefully sketching proposed routes across the continent and making extensive lists of the supplies and equipment he would need. He accepted social engagements, but only for the purpose of interesting potential backers in his plan to find the source of the Nile and the headwaters of the Congo River. He wrote Alice every day, hoping that through sharing anecdotes about people they both knew she would write back to him. The days passed, but no letters came from Alice.[4]

The Pikes were booked to sail from Liverpool on Friday, June 12. Upon their arrival in England, Alice sent Stanley a note informing him that the Pikes were back at the Langham. Alice remained ambiguous toward Stanley, and she purposefully made herself unavailable by spending her days shopping and her nights attending the opera. She still feared his power over her and avoiding him was her way of making it clear they were not engaged; she believed "her heart was free." She knew she was hurting him, but she did not know how else to cool the strong attraction they felt for each other when they were together.

They met for dinner on June 11 at the Langham. The setting was carefully chosen by Alice to be as neutral as possible. She planned to say good-bye forever. Over dinner she regaled him with stories of the wedding, stated that she had been so busy that she had read very few of his letters, and attempted to shift her own failure to answer his letters by faulting him for not coming to Paris for the ceremony. Stanley sat there as she chattered on, but the expression on his face clearly mirrored his love for her and his determination to marry her. On Saturday he accompanied the Pikes to Liverpool. Alice waved good-bye from the upper deck as Stanley shouted "au revoir" from the dock.

THE MARRIAGE PACT

Alice could hardly contain herself as their ship sailed into New York harbor. She felt safe in her home port. Stanley could be relegated to the status of a summer romance—remembered fondly, but vaguely. Although they were gone for less than five months, exciting changes in the city's skyline loomed before them as they sailed to the dock. The city was growing up and the action on the docks seemed even more frenetic than when they had left. Waiting on the shore were various friends including her father's ex-partner, George Kidd, who would see that their twenty-eight pieces of luggage arrived safely at their home.

Of the four Pikes, Ellen was the most relieved that the trip was over. She could hardly wait to get out of her traveling clothes and into her comfortable lounging robe. At first Ellen's serenity was interrupted by numerous visitors who wanted to hear all about her trip and the wedding. In the mid-1870s, a European tour was still an event. Once they realized Ellen had little to tell them, they left her alone and within a few weeks, she was comfortably settled back into her familiar routine.

Jeannette, Alice, and Lawrence, on the other hand, were caught up in a whirl of welcome-home parties. The most lavish one was held at the Hotel Brevoort—a Palladian-style mansion at 24 Fifth Avenue built in 1834 by Henry Brevoort, one of New York's old family names. Alice, unrestrained by strictures of mourning, plunged into as many activities as possible: singing lessons, parties at Delmonico's, and participation in a charity concert organized by Nettie. She sang a duet from *Les Africanes* and in the quartet from *Rigoletto* and paid the price for doing too much by straining her singing voice so severely she never performed again in public. Nonetheless, she thought it a small price to pay because the Pike house was alive again, and Henry Morton Stanley no longer dominated her thoughts.

In England, Stanley worked to put Alice from his mind. His African trip

*HENRY MORTON
STANLEY*, C. 1927
Pastel on paper, 20⅛ x
16⅛ in. (51.1 x 41 cm)
*"He was," Alice was heard to
say in later life, "the only
man I ever really loved."*

needed all of his attention if it were to succeed. Although he had announced his intention to leave for Africa in September, he was still short of money. Lacking were funds necessary to purchase equipment, hire assistants, design and build a collapsible boat, or even buy passage to Zanzibar. Once in Africa, he would need additional money to hire porters, guides and mercenary soldiers, and supplies. His ambitious plan was to travel from Zanzibar on the Indian Ocean, cross several thousand miles of uncharted territory in the heart of Africa to reach his final destination—the mouth of the Congo River on the Atlantic Ocean. During his travels he hoped to find the source of the Nile, travel through lands that no white man had ever seen, and, if he survived, to discover the headwaters of the Congo. Finally, his enduring fame assured, he would travel to America and marry Alice.[5]

When Alice received Stanley's letter announcing his imminent arrival in New York to fulfill his American backer's contract, she was filled with mixed emotions. Stanley might be the hero of London, but most of her friends had never heard of him. Having rejoined the crowd made up of people her own age and social status, she wondered if Stanley wouldn't seem a bit uncouth and a trifle old and sedate in comparison. Obviously he would not fit in with the group who gathered in the evenings on her front stoop for informal parties—a group of seventeen to twenty-year-olds with scarcely a serious thought in their heads beyond where the next evening's party would be held. On the other hand, Stanley was famous, and she realized she should be flattered to be selected as the only girl he wanted to see in New York. The more she considered it, the more eager she became to see him.

Stanley arrived in New York filled with hope for his trip and visions of his life with Alice after it was over. He expected the meeting with his backer, James Gordon Bennett, owner of the *New York Herald* to be pro forma, and then he would be free to spend his remaining time with Alice. Bennett, unexpectedly, made himself unavailable, and Stanley was forced to cool his heels at the *Herald* office. As he waited, Stanley renewed old friendships on the staff, sharing his dream of life with Alice. He would build a magnificent home on the Hudson and retire for the remainder of his life. "I can see the house now—broad halls, a great gallery of rare pictures, rooms of Oriental grandeur, grounds with lakes, and wooded paths, an African *tembe* built especially for 'the boys,' like that in which I lived so long with Livingston, where my newspaper friends can come when they want to work or play; and all the surroundings of luxury and taste that the experience of a traveller can suggest."[6]

Buoyed by his dreams, Stanley was unprepared for Bennett's outright refusal to match the London *Telegraph*'s six thousand pound investment. Instead, Bennett told Stanley he would set up a fund for Stanley to draw upon when needed. To Stanley, it seemed a graceless offer, and he jotted down in his diary, "This is rather an unkind way to receive one he is about to send to complete the discoveries of so many great travellers in Central Africa."[7]

His first visit with Alice was equally disappointing. Almost despairing, he wrote in his diary, "No man had ever to work harder than I have for a wife."[8] He spent hours painting verbal pictures of Africa to touch her imagination. She could sail up the Nile to meet him and could while away the hours by filling up who knew how many sketchbooks. As he talked, Alice began to waver. He had touched her where she was most vulnerable—her imagination—and she felt herself yielding to him. Although for every argument of Stanley's, Alice made a counter argument, in the end, Stanley won. On Sunday, July 12, 1874, only five days before he was to leave, Alice and Stanley signed a marriage pact:

> We solemnly pledge ourselves to be faithful to each other and to be married to one another on the return of Henry Morton Stanley from Africa. We call God to witness this our pledge in writing.[9]

On their last evening, after dining and walking along Fifth Avenue, they returned to the Pike house where, as Stanley wrote in his diary, "she raised her lips in tempting proximity to mine and I kissed her on the lips, on her eyes, on her cheeks, and her neck, and she kissed me in return."[10] Alice remembered their last evening quite differently: "When they reached home they seated themselves by the fire silently....Now, he merely sat in the elegant gilt chair with its pale gray satin covering, dreading the moment he must leave. He looked up at Alice sitting quietly opposite him. As he looked at her, the flickering of the fire heightening the delicate color of her skin, she seemed the most desirable object in the world. Africa seemed a mere nothing to lay at her feet."

The following morning Alice went to see Stanley off accompanied by Nettie and her newly acquired fiancé, David Goin. The two lovers exchanged photographs, and Alice promised to write faithfully. Then, according to Stanley: "She repeated her vows to me as we stood together, and as I clasped her hands to bid her goodbye, she gave me such a look—a long, earnest, wide-eyed look—during which I thought she was striving to pierce the dark, gloomy picture, but I turned away—and the spell broke....I could not bear that the scene should be protracted, or that she should be pained with standing, and I motioned with my arm for them to be gone....Alice kissed her hand to me, and resolutely turned away."[11]

Perhaps it was her youth, but within weeks of Stanley's departure, Alice was once again caught up in a whirl of activities focused on the prenuptial festivities for Nettie's fall wedding. She scarcely thought of Stanley. Although Stanley wrote her daily, she was too busy to read most of the letters. One that she did read told her he had named his portable sailboat "The Lady Alice" in her honor. She also thought it was nice of him to send her presents from Zanzibar, but like the letters they remained for the most part unopened. She had them sent to the basement storage area for perusal some quiet, rainy day.

The letters she did write him were breezy in style and full of news of people they both knew and of her myriad activities. She sent him a clipping from the *Cincinnati Enquirer* about Nettie's wedding and wrote about attending the opera and dances, about strolls along Fifth Avenue, and about drives through Central Park. If there were indications in Alice's letters that she might prove anything other than steadfast, Stanley chose to ignore them. One letter that should have alarmed him read: "I should hate to be poor, how envious I would be of rich people. Just think if I had to give up my beautiful laces, silks and diamonds, my home and piano, horses and carriage."[12]

His letters to her contained detailed descriptions of his journey along with lengthy declarations of his love for her. One letter written March 4, 1875, told her that he had named an island [now called Bukerbe] in Lake Victoria for her. In closing he wrote:

In one of your very last letters which I received before starting from the sea, you asked me if you could not get married at once on my return, to which I answer that it shall be as you desire. The very hour I land in England I should like to marry you, but such a long time must elapse before I see you, that even to see your dear face again appears to me as a most improbable thing....I have often wondered how you pass your time. I suppose it is in one constant round of gaieties? What a contrast to yours are my surroundings....My present abode is a dark hut; through the chinks of the mud I can but faintly see these lines as I write. Outside naked men and women create a furious jangle and noise, bartering with my people for beads.[13]

This was another letter that Alice never read.

IV
Marrying Albert

In the spring of 1875, Alice traveled to Dayton, Ohio, for an extended visit with her mother's sister, Jeannette Schenck. Unknown to Alice, the invitation was not merely the desire of an aunt to see a favorite niece. Upon Stanley's reappearance, Ellen had become so alarmed that Alice might do something rash that she immediately wrote her sister for help. Even though Ellen knew nothing of Alice and Stanley's marriage contract, she was afraid something was in the wind. Moreover, she was concerned about the young city sports who flocked around Alice. They were too much like Lawrence—wealthy and spoiled. As she mulled the problem over, it became clear that the solution lay in putting Alice in her sister's competent hands. Jeannette was not only her sister, but a leader in Dayton society, and she would be able to find the right sort of man for Alice to marry, if anyone could.

When Alice stepped off the train in Dayton, she was met not only by her aunt and uncle, assorted cousins and childhood friends such as Carrie Dudley and Julia and John Patterson, but also by an unknown young man. In her autobiography Alice recalled: "There was also a very smart and handsome stranger in their midst, a rather short man in his late twenties, who was dressed with much taste and had about him a decided suave air of distinction. His name was Albert Clifford Barney and it did not take long for Alice to realize that he was 'it', namely the reason Aunt Nett had insisted that Alice come immediately to Dayton."

Albert Barney, like Alice, was the youngest child in a family of two girls and three boys. His father, E. E. Barney, moved from New York to Dayton, Ohio, in 1831 to accept the position of principal of the Dayton Academy. In 1844 he became headmaster of Cooper Seminary—the school for girls the Pike sisters attended before moving to New York. Barney's position was prestigious, but poorly paid, and students were boarded to make ends meet. E. E. Barney was a superb, progressive teacher who relied on more than rote and lectures to educate his students. He often took his botany and geology classes into the woods and fields surrounding Dayton to observe nature firsthand. One student later said of him: "We could not help learning. His teaching was as interesting as a story."[1]

With Albert's birth in 1849, Barney was forced to resign from the seminary to enter a more profitable business in order to provide a better living for his family. As Alice's father had five years earlier, Barney foresaw the possibilities awaiting a man willing to take a chance on the rapidly develop-

ALBERT CLIFFORD
BARNEY, C. 1876
In 1875 Albert Clifford Barney was considered Dayton's most eligible bachelor. Alice's aunt, Jeannette Schenck of Dayton, thought him the perfect match for Alice and made sure that they met.

ing Ohio valley. Although Dayton was Ohio's sixth largest city, it was only one-eighth the size of Cincinnati. Located at the fork of the Great Miami River, Dayton became the county seat for a lush, river-bottom farming region. Industry was not an important part of its economic growth until a railroad line was built in the late 1840s connecting Dayton to the port cities of Lake Erie to the north and a canal was dug to Cincinnati fifty miles to the south. E. E. Barney may have been a schoolteacher, but he had natural business sense and immediately perceived the potential of railroads in Dayton's future. Thus, when he founded the Dayton Car Works, it rapidly became a leading manufacturer of railroad cars for the Midwest. Just as he made Cooper Seminary one of the finest educational institutions in Ohio, he set about to make his factory a model of innovative mass production, assembly-line methods. In 1864 Barney took Preserved Smith as his partner and created the Barney-Smith Car

JULIA BARNEY, C. 1884
Following his mother's death, Albert used her estate to become a gentleman of leisure.

Works—a venture that lifted Barney's life-style from one of middle-class wealth to immense riches.

E. E. Barney expected all of his sons to enter the company after the completion of their education. Albert's scholastic achievements in early years led his father to send him to Phillips Academy, Exeter. He was accepted at Brown University at the age of sixteen and graduated with the class of 1868. Following a year abroad, he returned home in 1870 to enter the family business. Albert was expected to learn the business from the ground up by attaining proficiency in every job in every division.

For five years he moved slowly up through the plant's hierarchy, beginning in the molding department, until he reached the management level. Unlike his brothers who preceded him, Albert hated the Car Works. His only interest in the family business was that it provided him with social status and money for his pocket. He felt that his superior Ivy League education and continental polish exempted him from the exigencies of earning a living. Moreover, he resented being tied to his father's purse strings. If he had to work, he wanted it to be in an occupation more suited to his elevated tastes. As he watched Alice descend from her railroad coach, it may have crossed his mind that the young heiress could be the solution to his profound discontent.

It was obvious to everyone that Albert was taken with Alice from their

E. E. BARNEY, C. 1873
Albert's father, E. E. Barney, was both a scholar and a perspicacious businessman. His enlightened assembly-line practices became a model for other companies such as the National Cash Register Company.

first meeting at the Dayton depot. To the dismay of the Dayton belles, the town's most eligible bachelor immediately began to devote himself exclusively to the young lady from New York. No matter what the occasion, one was sure to see Albert with Alice on his arm. By early summer of 1875, everyone but Alice knew that a marriage proposal was in the offing. So unaware was she of Albert's intentions and so convoluted was the actual proposal that when it occurred Alice not only did not realize that he had asked her to marry him, but also that he had taken her smile for acceptance. Not until he called her aunt and uncle into the drawing room to announce, "Congratulate me! Alice and I are to be married," did she realize what had happened. As the family excitedly gathered around to congratulate them, she realized that all protestations to the contrary would only fall on deaf ears.

No matter how free in spirit Alice had believed herself, she now knew she was neither strong enough, nor courageous enough, to disentangle herself from this misunderstanding. Moreover, she was in shock. Only later, when she was finally alone in her room, did the doubts come. One by one she brushed them aside. He was a bit of a snob and seemed overly concerned with social position, but not so much so that it made him unlikable. She did not love him, but decided it did not matter. She was fond of him and she enjoyed his company. Marrying without love did not alarm her. As she wrote in her autobiography

> Desire for intimate relationship was not a part of her makeup. Not feeling the need for it, she did not go out seeking, so that when, unsolicited on her part, it was offered to her, and, just because it was offered expected the same thing in return, she could not compensate in kind; it filled her with no great sense of loss. Albert Clifford Barney, however, was wise enough to know that he pleased her in many ways, and so he did not play on her sentimentalities as other men had done….She thought it might as well be he as another, for she felt sure that she would never love anyone else.

If love meant experiencing the strange feelings that Stanley caused her, then she preferred to marry without love. Besides, her relatives expected it of her, and Ellen would be relieved to know she was marrying a suitable man. In the end, "she was almost glad it was decided for her—in a way...It would be so troublesome to change." Thoughts of Stanley intruded one last time on her reveries, but they were fleeting.

MARRIAGE TO ALBERT

What was true of Alice, however, was not true of Stanley. At times only the knowledge that Alice waited for him at the end of his journey gave him the courage to continue. He knew he had underestimated badly the time needed to cross the continent, but if he kept driving himself and his men to the limit, he might be home in time for the date chosen for his wedding to Alice. Stanley continued to write serial letters to Alice—a sentence here, a paragraph there—as time and circumstances permitted. He included them in his dispatches with only the faint hope they would be received.

In fall 1875, Alice returned to New York to prepare for her wedding. All the letters from Stanley that arrived during her absence had been carefully tied up in ribbons and put in a trunk in the basement. She refused to read them because she did not want her mind changed. In this way she acknowledged her weakness of character—choosing to do what was easiest and what pleased others. Constant activity, she decided, would alleviate guilt and so she immersed herself in shopping for her trousseau and planning the details of her wedding day. "Since she was going to be married, she was going to do it to the Queen's taste—not Queen Victoria's, but the airiest, blithest, most exquisite of fairy tale rulers."

On Tuesday, January 11, 1876, three days before her nineteenth birthday, Albert and Alice were married at the Pike home on Fifth Avenue by the Reverend Stephen H. Tyng in an Episcopal ceremony. Several hundred guests witnessed the ceremony. A reporter from the *New York Herald* who knew Stanley wrote: "The bride and groom stood under a bell composed of rare flowers. There was a reception lasting about two hours, during which a sumptuous repast was served. The bride was attired in an imported satin robe, literally covered with point lace, and decorated with silver oaks and lilies of the valley, ornaments—a rich diamond aigrette, bracelets and a cross—a gift from her mother." Stanley's name was not mentioned, even though the writer knew she had jilted him. A dozen years later the same reporter wrote in an article about Stanley that Alice's wedding reception was one of the most lavish and expensive he had ever attended. He pointedly remembered that "the bride, in point lace and diamonds, looked radiantly happy, and although I was one of the few who knew of her promise to Stanley when she accepted my congratulations, if there was a quiver of the hand or a glance in the eye that was not all joy, it was doubtless a mere fancy of mine—at best a flash of regret perhaps for the absent explorer. There was a shower of rice and old slippers as the carriage drove off, and to all appearances a happier pair never started along the journey of life."

ALICE PIKE BARNEY, IN
WEDDING GOWN, 1876
Jared Bradley Flagg
Oil on canvas, 42 x 29 in.
(106.7 x 73.7 cm)
A reporter attending Alice and
Albert's lavish wedding won-
dered if thoughts of Stanley
ever crossed Alice's mind.

The newlyweds left for a six-month honeymoon in New Orleans and Saint Augustine.[2]

Stanley reached Ujiji in May 1876. As it was a center of Arab slave trading, Stanley eagerly expected to find a bundle of mail awaiting him from Alice, but there was nothing. On June 2, 1876, he wrote Alice:

As I thought of Ujiji I flattered myself daily that I should receive letters and newspapers. I daily fed and lived on that hope....You may imagine how I felt when after enquiry about letters, I was met with 'There are none'...what would you have done, oh my Alice? Tear your hair, clothes, and shriek distractedly, run about and curse the Fates? I did not do anything so undignified, but I soberly grieved and felt discouraged....[3]

At the end of June, the newlyweds returned to Dayton and set up housekeeping on West Fifth Street not far from Albert's parents' home. Alice's trunks from New York were among the last things to be unpacked. Because Alice was five months pregnant, Albert stayed at home to help her sort through them. They worked quickly and quietly, savoring their new-found companionship. Without warning, domestic tranquility shattered as Albert thrust a packet of letters tied with ribbon at Alice. The travel-stained envelopes with exotic stamps on them were unopened, but many of the dates were recent and the name of the sender was clear.

Albert demanded an explanation in a tone of voice Alice had never before heard him use. As she tried to explain that the letters were unread, Albert watched her with a hard, cold look that filled her with fear. Even though each could easily reach out and touch the other, a barrier arose between them; on the other side of it was a stranger. Before Alice stood an unknown person looking at her with such bitterness that she felt faint.

Albert broke the silence and commanded her to take all of Stanley's letters and burn them in the fire. His authority was implacable. She moved to the fireplace in a daze and mechanically began to burn the letters. When she was finished, Albert told her she was a good wife and left the room. Alice remained motionless by the fire until the last piece of paper curled, blackened, and disintegrated into ash. Still she did not move. She stood mesmerized by the flames as the realization washed over her that she had made a terrible mistake in marrying Albert. Many years later she wrote:

It was as overwhelming as if she had been blind all her life and had one day arose and opened her eyes to the light of day....The pain of it was that she could do nothing about it...that is, so far as changing the external manifestations of her life. She would go right on. She was a 'good wife,' she would remain so. Obedient, subservient, thoroughly companionable, quite complete but now she knew that her heart would never be in it. She would be living out a pretense, just as she had heretofore, for now she realized that she had not been complete, never been a whole individual until that moment of realization when her husband had commanded her to destroy Stanley's letters.

APOLOGIES AND GOOD-BYES

Alice and Albert's first daughter, Natalie Clifford, was born on October 31, 1876. It was an event that should have brought Alice and Albert closer together, but there was no going back. Albert had revealed his true character to Alice, and no matter how witty, intelligent, and charming he could be, she knew that behind it was a narrow-minded bigot capable of violent jealousy against a much better man. Albert began to take pleasure in taunting her about Stanley's bastardy and his common life. No matter how much she protested that she had married him, not Stanley, Albert refused to listen.

While Albert denigrated Stanley in his home, the rest of the world applauded him. By August 1877 newspapers worldwide acclaimed his traverse of central Africa and the imminent completion of his successful trek. He wrote a long, final letter to Alice from the field and entrusted it to a Portuguese adventurer, Major Serpa Pinto, to send on to New York. Pinto wrote to a friend in Lisbon that Stanley seemed very worried that his *"pequeña* (girlfriend) might have forgotten him." Dutifully, Ellen sent Stanley's final letter on to Alice. Once she read it, Alice knew she must answer.[4]

Stanley reached Zanzibar on November 26, 1877. He eagerly sorted through the mail that had been waiting him for almost two years. There were several letters from Alice written before she went to Dayton. There was also a packet of clippings from the *Herald*. Among them was the column describing Alice's marriage and an announcement of the birth of her daughter. Stanley's dreams of his "Lady Alice" abruptly shattered. Devastated, he went into such deep depression that his aberrant behavior became news. A *New York Times* article described him as "sullen, morose, discontented and savage."[5]

He did not receive Alice's letter until he was back in England. In her letter dated November 26, 1877, she wrote:

> Dear Morton,
> Among the many congratulations and praises showered on you, receive my humble rejoicings also, of all you have accomplished. I am proud to know how bravely you have borne your many hard trials.
>
> Poor Stanley! How much you have lost, but your gain has been great indeed. I shed tears when I read of the fate of Kalulu and the 'Lady Alice.' I had hoped she would have proven a truer friend than the Alice she was named after, for you must know, by this time, I have done what millions of women have done before me, not been true to my promise. But you are so great, so honored and sought after, that you will scarcely miss your once true friend and always devoted admirer of your heroism. For indeed you are the hero of the day. That alone should console you for my loss. No doubt before long you will

think it a gain, for Stanley can easily find a wife all his heart could desire to grace high position and deservedly great name....

If you can forgive me, tell me so; if not, do please remain silent. Destroy my letters, as I have burnt all of yours. Adieu, Morton, I will not say farewell, for I hope in some future time we may meet—shall it be as friends?[6]

Two years went by. In 1879 Stanley sent Alice a copy of his two-volume book, *Through the Dark Continent*, carefully inscribed to "Lady Alice." Enclosed was a note: "You have helped me with my work, spurred me on to achievement which I could never have accomplished without you. Your image was always before me, Lady Alice. It beckoned me, it commanded, sustained, and now it rewards me. Africa has been conquered and you, not I, have conquered it. With love in my heart, I lay it at your feet, Lady Alice."

In 1877 Albert accepted the position of agent for the Pike estate in Cincinnati. Leaving Alice and Natalie in Dayton, Albert took rooms at a Cincinnati boarding house and turned his not inconsiderable intelligence toward running the estate. It was work much more to his liking than the Car Works and he excelled in his new position. In June 1878, the Pike family asked him to continue for another year. His position assured, he engaged a suite for his family at the Burnet House, still Cincinnati's most prestigious hotel. On November 30, 1879, their second daughter, Laura Alice, was born.[7]

Albert's father died on December 14, 1880, and his five children inherited equally. The primary stipulation of the will was that the major portion of E. E. Barney's estate would go to his wife, Julia Barney, until her death. Although Albert had hoped to be rich immediately, the money he received from his father's estate combined with his commission from the Pike family, allowed Albert to live as was described in one of his father's obituaries: "A wealthy citizen of Cincinnati, and a young gentleman of superior culture."

His first act on receiving part of his inheritance was to purchase a comparatively modest frame house on Auburn Avenue, a street known as "Cincinnati's Fifth Avenue." The exterior of the new house was unimposing, but it soon acquired a reputation for its elegant interior decoration. As one Cincinnati reporter noted, once the threshold was crossed "upon every side the wealth and refinement of its owner are made manifest."

A French governess was hired to assist with the children, and Albert began to indulge himself in what was to be a lifelong passion for fine horses and equally ostentatious carriages. There was a pony named Tricksie for Natalie and a dogcart for Laura. As chatelaine for this fashionable household, Alice dressed in the latest styles and established the Barneys as lavish entertainers.[8]

The mode of living that Albert insisted upon was expensive. Even with a steady income from the factory revenues, the Barneys lived only just within their means. Any thoughts Albert had of retiring from work would have to wait until his mother died. Until then, his income from managing the Pike estate continued to be essential.

By 1881, in spite of Albert's administrative skill, the opera house began to lose money. To Albert's relief, the Cincinnati Chamber of Commerce asked to lease the Opera House as a merchant's exchange while their own permanent headquarters was being built. It was a project that required extensive remodeling, and Albert sought permission from Pike's heirs. Only Ellen demurred because of her strong sentimental attachment to the Opera House as it was. Under strong pressure from her children, however, she reluctantly cabled her approval.[9]

INTIMATIONS OF FREEDOM

The summer of 1882 found the Barneys at the newly fashionable Long Beach Hotel on Long Island. It was their first visit East since their wedding six years before. To all outward appearances they were the perfect couple. They had two beautiful children, twenty-three-year-old Alice dressed in the latest fashions, they lived in the most elite section of Cincinnati, and they gave elegant parties, mingling comfortably with the city's wealthiest and most important citizens. With the exception of her children, Alice was happy with none of it. She felt unfulfilled. Her exuberance for life was held under tight reign by Albert, and she desperately missed the joy of artistic exploration she had shared with her father. Although she had sworn she would never become like her mother, she was following her mother's example—withdrawing into herself in order to avoid any confrontation with Albert. For appearances sake, she hid all signs of her unhappiness, especially from her mother, who held the highest opinion of Albert. For her own survival, Alice learned to laugh and toss her head gaily as she declared that her motto for happiness was "live and let live." Whatever inner sorrow she felt was well-masked. Years later Natalie assessed her mother's success in dealing with whatever life might bring:

> Live and let live was her motto....She had great patience with difficult characters, ungenial though they proved to be, and I never saw her cross. She was too aware of human shortcomings and simply tried to amend or to leave them alone. When anyone failed her, she was more sorry for them than for herself.[10]

That summer also saw the arrival of Oscar Wilde in America. He came to deliver a series of lectures on aesthetics, which met with varying success due in part to his poor declamatory skills in an era that thrived on oratory.

Following a short vacation trip through the Catskills in New York, Wilde was scheduled to appear at the Long Beach Hotel as a special attraction for its elite clientele at the same time that the Barneys were in residence. The lectures he gave there were successful because of the informality of the setting, which was replete with the sounds of children playing in the background and the laughter of guests on the way to the beach. Alice was among the audience, and like many others, she attended as much to see the outrageous playwright in person as to be enlightened by the content of his talk.

American audiences were already familiar with Wilde through the character of Bunthorne in the popular Gilbert and Sullivan operetta *Patience*, which had opened in London the previous season. Even though she had been introduced as a child to some outrageously theatrical personalities, Alice was taken aback by Wilde's flamboyant affectations of dress, which included knickers, ruffles at his sleeves, buckles on his oxfords, and a flower in his buttonhole. Yet she listened closely when he spoke about the importance of developing children's artistic tastes and how essential it was to decorate one's home aesthetically.[11]

Six-year-old Natalie was the first member of the Barney family to actually meet the famous man, and with a steadfastness that so often happens with early childhood attachments, Wilde became her lifelong hero. Natalie's long blond hair was both her most beautiful feature and the bane of her existence. Little boys loved to pull it, and one day, chased by a gang of boys bent on grabbing a hank, Natalie ran headlong through the hotel's lobby screaming in terror. Suddenly she found herself scooped up by a very large man who sat her down on his lap and immediately quieted her fears by telling her a fairy tale about a happy prince. By the time he was finished, her tears were gone and the boys had disappeared. As he ended his story, Alice appeared. Appreciative as she was of Wilde's help, as she led Natalie away she was not quite sure she approved of her daughter sitting on the lap of a man considered by the best people to be quite mad.[12]

Albert spent weekdays in the city conferring with Ellen about Cincinnati business affairs. Alice's afternoons were spent on the beach playing with Natalie while Laura napped in her blue satin-lined and flower-bedecked baby carriage on

LAURA AND NATALIE, c. 1881
The Barney sisters, Laura and Natalie, around the ages of two and five, respectively. The beautiful, blonde-haired Natalie was the apple of Albert's eye.

the hotel porch. As Alice basked in the sun mulling over Wilde's lecture and Natalie's adventure with him, she was startled from her reveries by the realization that a man had sat down beside her on her beach blanket. She thought it was Wilde, but he looked so different from the dandy she had met the night before. In spite of his 220 pounds, he looked handsome in his tight-fitting, striped, knee-length knit bathing suit with a brightly colored robe hung casually around his shoulders. His strong features and firm muscular physique gave little indication of the bloated and dissipated man he would become at the end of his life.

Seeing her puzzled look, Wilde reintroduced himself and, settling more comfortably onto the blanket, he began to comment on the fashionable beach attire worn by that year's trendsetters. He was thoroughly puzzled, he said, as to why women even bothered to come to the seashore. They covered themselves from head to foot with corsets, baggy pleated bloomers below the knee, heavy pleated skirts, long sleeves, stockings, and shoes, all of which he thought insulting to the sea. All that was missing was gloves, and he supposed that would be next. "I should like to shock those people with a little display of common sense," he stated mischievously. "I believe in following my natural impulses....After all, what are impulses? Gestures toward life. One must live, mustn't one? Expression is living; suppressing is dying, or worse. Don't you think so, Madame Alice?" To which Alice could only reply, "Yes."

It took her a few moments to realize that he was not merely making witty comments about bathing-suit fashions. She was disturbed not only by the fact that her own discontent was so obvious to a stranger, but also by his challenge to her. She began to fear that she had allowed herself to enter into a conversation she could not manage by her usual tactic of polite obliqueness.

Wilde abruptly changed the subject and asked Alice a surprising question: did she know Henry Morton Stanley? Nonplussed, Alice shrugged in what she hoped was a successful attempt at indifference, meanwhile wondering what Wilde was driving at. When Wilde persisted, she answered as coldly as possible that she had known Mr. Stanley. Perhaps if she were distant enough, Wilde would give up and go away. He was upsetting her and she did not like it. His next question took her completely by surprise. "What is your husband interested in, Madame Alice?"

Somehow, she knew that if she didn't answer truthfully, Wilde would find yet another way to unsettle her, and she paused to think about it before answering. She glanced at Natalie playing in her lap and answered, "Natalie." Wilde was silent as he looked at her, holding her eyes with his. It seemed to her that he looked right through her. When he next spoke, it was a statement, not a question. "Then it is true," he said simply. "What is

true?" questioned Alice, completely at a loss. "You love him." "Mr. Barney?" "No. Stanley!"

Alice was shocked. How did Wilde know her secret? It was uncanny. "You may not know it, Madame Alice, but you do. You may not even have the will to admit it; you're rather sluggish of mind, aren't you? Then you are terribly evanescent...oh, yes, you are. You've been absolutely drained of volition. Really, quite incomplete. Am I right?"

Alice was overwhelmed and tears began to form in her eyes. Haltingly, she heard herself say, "Natalie...Mr. Barney is interested in Natalie!" At this, Wilde rose to go, but she called him back because she was afraid to be alone with the thoughts of what she had thrown away in her life. Wilde seated himself on the sand at Alice's feet and stretched out his hands to Natalie. "Natalie want to ride to Canterbury?" Wilde tossed Natalie high in the air and swung her about as she laughed merrily.

When the nurse came for Natalie, Wilde and Alice were left alone. Suddenly he turned to her with a proposal: would she like to go swimming the next morning? She was not to wear her bathing skirt, shoes, or stockings.

ALICE, ALBERT, AND FRIENDS, C. 1886
Alice (seated top right) with Albert (standing extreme lower right), and friends on an outing in Cincinnati. Alice and Albert were part of the Queen City's smartest social set.

Volition? She would show him and she agreed, knowing that Albert would not return from New York until much later in the day.

At six the next morning there was a knock at Alice's door. As they ran to the beach, Wilde took her hand and laughingly intoned, "He who knows not daring knows not joy!" She was not a strong swimmer, but she was willing to bet that he was stronger than the ocean—he certainly looked so. Together they plunged into the water, but suddenly Alice was terrified the waves would drown her. Wilde told her to hold on to him, and he turned her around so that her back was to them. A particularly large wave came rolling in and as it broke over their heads, she was slammed against him.

A surge of pain went through her. She had broken her toe on his shin. "Help me, please," she cried, and when Wilde looked at her face he saw she was not joking. He carried her back to the beach and up to her hotel room, laying her gently on her bed. After the doctor had seen her and splinted her foot, Wilde sheepishly entered her room bearing a bunch of roses in humble apology. He was leaving in a few minutes, but he wanted to say he was sorry before he said good-bye. After he left she looked bemusedly at her foot and smiled. She would think of something to tell Albert. She laughed ruefully: "She had known daring and had gotten joy, plus a broken toe. It was worth it."

Once back in Cincinnati, however, her sense of daring and joy disappeared as she painfully hobbled about her home. Nor did Albert make life any easier. Since their return, Albert had been unable to talk about anything other than how much more sophisticated Eastern society was when compared with Cincinnati. He now found their Cincinnati social set provincial. The only solution for Albert was to move back East, and each day he thought up a new complaint about Cincinnatians' lack of manners and social acumen.

As his desire to move East grew, Albert became increasingly difficult to live with. He lashed out at his wife and children for not being perfect. He cursed his shortsightedness in agreeing to the terms of his father's will, which kept the balance of his inheritance out of his hands until his mother's death. He blamed Alice for her poor money management, which forced him to work at a job that demeaned him. At every turn, he expected Alice to provide immediate gratification of his every whim. Overriding everything was his growing love for whiskey. When he could not have his way, only a tumbler filled with Cincinnati's best whiskey could console him. As the fiery liquid slid down his throat, he was convinced he was superior—to everyone.

II
Trans-
forma-
tions

V

Discoveries

When Albert proposed they go to Europe in 1883 in order to find a suitable boarding school for the girls, Alice wholeheartedly supported him in the hope that a change of scene might make him happier and drink less. Although she disagreed with Albert's assessment that a European education was necessary to enhance their daughters' future marital eligibility, she looked forward to the trip as a means of renewing her acquaintance with the art of Europe's great museums and again trying her hand at recording her impressions through sketches of the people and sights they would experience.

Predictably, Albert was no happier in Paris than in Cincinnati, but the girls were successfully enrolled in Les Ruches, an elite boarding school at Fountainebleau. His fantasy of shepherding his docile and loving family on a sedate tour of the major cities of Europe was replaced by the reality of being stuck in Paris with three females who balked at everything he suggested. All the girls seemed to care about was the zoo, and Alice only wanted to visit museums. This left Albert to his own devices most of the time.

Like most children, Natalie and Laura's excitement over being in a foreign country wore off quickly, and they kept asking when they could go home to see their pets—two dogs, a Shetland pony, Jumbo the parrot, and Orisaba the parakeet. Raised by a French governess, both girls were bilingual, but when Albert tried to show them off to other Americans at their hotel, Natalie refused to cooperate. She became particularly sulky when Albert patted her on the head and called her his good little girl. She hated being called good.[1]

Albert made certain allowances for his children's lack of cooperation, but not for Alice. He expected her by his side at all times, but when he awoke late in the morning following a night's drinking bout, he usually found a note saying she was off to explore yet another museum. Her fascination for the arts was totally beyond him and, in his opinion, thoughtless. Not only did she clearly understand he did not share her appreciation for art, but he had told her repeatedly that he was suspicious and disapproving of people who did.

The longer they stayed in Paris, the less he liked it; he much preferred England with its orderly attention to proper manners. Above all, he enjoyed British clubs where he could sit comfortably in large, overstuffed chairs and be served brandy by servants trained to know their place. For him, Paris was noisy, dirty, and smelly. Even its famed gardens, such as the

ALICE, C. 1888
Alice in Paris was very different from Alice in Cincinnati, and Albert was not sure he approved. Her visits to museums and increasing artistic pursuits outside their marriage did not fit his conception of how a wife should behave.

Preceding pages:
Alcove of east studio, Studio House, c. 1904

Luxembourg, were offensively undisciplined with flower beds filled with wildly clashing colors so unlike the manicured perfection of London's sedate parks.

What disturbed him most was that Alice seemed a different person in Paris. The malleable young girl he had married had become a decisive woman with a mind of her own. While he could not fault her with openly disagreeing with him, she nevertheless seemed to do whatever she pleased with a new and disturbing insouciant air.

The new Alice was not completely Albert's delusion. Alice felt it, too. She drew energy from the artistic atmosphere of Paris. For the first time she began to evaluate honestly her life. As the emotional lethargy she had felt since her marriage to Albert lifted, it was replaced by a desire for action and commitment in her life. Finally she understood what Oscar Wilde had meant when he said the only person who could change her was herself.

EMERGING ARTISTIC AMBITIONS

Alice's metamorphosis continued upon the family's return to Cincinnati. Looking at the city with new eyes, she saw it was alive with creative energy. The long-ago success of Pike's Opera House was not the only indication that Cincinnatians valued their cultural life. For a number of years, Cincinnati had been a center not only for the fine arts, but also for the decorative arts. In 1869 the McMicken School of Design was established under the leadership of three of its wealthiest citizens: Joseph Longworth, Lars Anderson, and George Ward Nichols. While the school emulated the fine arts academies of Philadelphia and Boston, its curriculum also emphasized the industrial application of art and design. Among its offerings were courses in woodcarving, china painting, and mural decoration, augmented by more traditional fine arts classes in drawing, watercolor, oil painting, engraving, and sculpture.[2]

The philosophy of the school and its emphasis upon craftsmanship were based upon John Ruskin's aesthetic: One must "have nothing in your houses that you do not know to be useful, or believe to be beautiful." The leading Cincinnati proponent was the English woodcarver and teacher Ben Pitman, who brought the tenets of the Arts and Crafts movement to the women of Cincinnati. His teaching was predicated upon his belief that as female students decorated the interiors of their homes with furniture and decorative objects in the Gothic mode (then touted as the highest example of beauty enhancing function), their example would influence general public taste.[3]

In addition to Pitman, two other expatriate Englishmen, Henry L. Fry and his son William Henry Fry, also began classes for women in the art of woodcarving in 1872. By the time the Barneys moved to Cincinnati, the

LAURA, CINCINNATI,
C. 1882
*The Barney home on
Mount Auburn was modest
by Cincinnati standards,
but Albert made sure that
his children's trap and the
horses that pulled it were the
finest money could buy.*

Cincinnati decorative arts movement was in full swing. In 1880 Maria
Longworth Nichols established Rookwood Pottery. As with woodcarving,
the artists were primarily women, and, most importantly for Alice, they
were predominately members of the same or a higher social class than the
Barneys.[4]

Whatever her hopes for radically changing her life once they were home,
the reality was that marriage to Albert meant she was trapped in a "Doll's
House." However, unlike Ibsen's Nora, Alice found herself unable to leave.
She did receive permission from Albert to learn china painting—an art
acceptable to him because of the social prominence of the women who regularly displayed their efforts at Cincinnati's annual art exposition. The china
painting classes brought her into contact with women such as Elizabeth and
Adelaide Nourse and Maria Longworth Nichols. These were women who
took their craft very seriously and looked to Fry and Pittman as their
authorities on matters of art and decoration. With Albert's approval, Alice
began to buy furniture executed in the Fry studio for their home.

In 1884 Alice commissioned two paintings from Elizabeth Nourse. In
1883 she had purchased a decorative panel by Nourse depicting a flock of
geese in flight to hang over her mantel. The second was to be an oil of her
daughters. Although Elizabeth was two years younger than Alice, she was

already a professional who earned her living by painting decorative wall panels and illuminating inserts on furniture designed by Pittman and elaborately carved by her sisters Adelaide and Louise. During the course of the several sittings the portraits required, the two women formed a lifelong friendship. When Elizabeth learned that Alice had once tried her hand at painting, she insisted Alice set up her own easel. Once Elizabeth saw the extent of Alice's natural talent, she urged Alice to go to Paris and study art at an atelier. Although far from wealthy, Elizabeth told Alice she was putting aside every spare penny in preparation for a move to Paris, which she finally did in 1887.[5]

For Alice, the opportunity to study painting in Paris was totally dependent upon Albert, and, at the moment, it appeared unlikely that she would ever be free to go. Albert was experiencing a series of business setbacks, and, although his mother had died, her estate remained in probate. For the first time in several years, money was dear in the Barney household. The Chamber of Commerce's contract on the Opera House was due to end in 1886 and the Burnet House was in need of refurbishment. Although he had received firm offers from two separate parties for lucrative lifetime leases on both properties, it meant undertaking some very expensive renovations to both buildings. Once again he wrote Ellen for permission to make the necessary expenditures, and once again he found her adamantly opposed to making any changes to her husband's property.

Acting on Alice's behalf as one of the heirs, Albert personally borrowed the money to finance the renovations, planning to repay the banks and himself out of the proceeds from the rentals. He billed Alice's brother and sisters for a portion of the debt, pointing out that they would benefit from the rents collected on the improved properties. Only Hessie agreed to help pay a share of the debt; Nettie and Lawrence took Ellen's side. When Albert asked permission to sell the vacant distillery to settle the debt, Lawrence

FLOCK OF GEESE, c. 1883
Elizabeth Nourse
Oil on wood, 25⅞ x
55⅛ in. (65.7 x 140 cm)
Alice was so taken by this decorative panel executed by Nourse for Alice's living room mantel that she commissioned Nourse to paint a double portrait of Natalie and Laura.

advised his mother not to sell. Nettie and her husband, James Goin, believing Albert was being self-serving, also told Ellen not to cooperate. Enraged, Albert wrote a scathing letter to Ellen, condemning her for favoritism toward some of the heirs to the detriment of the others—notably his wife.

> I can hardly blame you because of clearly how you dread trouble and worry and how you naturally incline to those who are about you—to work their own interests. This partiality might pass in your position as mother; but will not do in your position as trustee. In Mr. Pike's will—each of his children shared equally and his trustee has no other duty than to carry out the purpose of that will—My accounts as agent with vouchers are ready to be filed in court and you as trustee must go over them all—then I hand in my resignation."[6]

Behind Albert's well-justified frustration with Ellen was his overwhelming desire to get Pike interests settled so that the moment his own mother's will was settled, he could shed himself of all responsibility and move East. The combined income from the two estates would allow him to devote himself completely to being a gentleman of leisure. Ellen's recalcitrance was the only impediment to his retirement from the workaday world.

Meantime, Alice continued to mine Cincinnati's artistic opportunities. In October of 1886, she signed up for one year of beginning drawing classes at the newly organized Cincinnati Museum Association's School of Art, which had taken over the McMicken School of Design.

Like its predecessor, enrollment in the museum's classes came primarily from the upper social strata. Therefore, Albert, in spite of his avowed antipathy towards the arts, became a museum shareholder and remained one until 1893. His intention was not, however, to support the arts, but rather to add another star to his social crown. As mysterious as Alice's new behavior and interests were, he was willing to go along with her if, as appeared to be true, she behaved no differently from the other women in her social strata.

By 1886 Albert had reached the heights of Cincinnati society, although he saw it as reaching the top of a hillock rather than a mountain. He was a member of the executive committee of the Commercial Club and a director of the Queen City Club, Cincinnati's first business and professional men's club. The latter boasted its own building where overworked businessmen could while away a few hours in the middle of the day by gaming or by having a quick one without fear of reproach. Yet there was something in his attitude, his way of giving himself airs, which did not go unnoticed by those he sought to impress. Several years after the Barneys had moved East, one of the Cincinnati papers poked fun at his pretensions:

One cannot help watching with growing interest the evolution of the Barney name. Formerly it was Al Barney, then Albert C. Barney, then Albert Clifford Barney, and now, behold how small a matter a tiny hyphen is! Rumor says that bets are being offered as to when the Clifford-Barneys shall have reached their last and final stage of development. Both of them are charming people and clever entertainers; many a bon vivant recalls with a thrill of pleasure stretching his legs under their mahogany in the 'umble' home on Mt. Auburn. But the place that knew them knows them no longer, and what is one to do? Banish those memories with the old home and name and rehabilitate then the Clifford-Barneys?..."[7]

ON TO PARIS

Although still mired in the financial difficulties surrounding the Pike properties, Albert nonetheless decided Laura and Natalie should begin their studies at Les Ruches. It was the chance for which Alice was waiting. Elizabeth Nourse and her sister Louise had left for Paris earlier in the summer, and the moment Albert mentioned Les Ruches, Alice started her campaign to join Elizabeth in studying art. To her surprise, he not only agreed that it was important for her to be near their daughters during their first year in a foreign boarding school, but that it might profit her to study art. While she was occupied with her painting lessons, he would be free to go to London or even back to America on business trips without having to worry about her or the myriad trunks with which she always traveled.

After ten years of marriage, the stage was being set for the establishment of a pattern based upon keeping up appearances. With the two daughters finally out of the home, the private facade of marital harmony could be abandoned. As long as Alice behaved herself, Albert would allow her to do whatever she wanted provided that the same was true for him. As for affection, he long ago had discovered other women who did not care how much he drank or what airs he gave himself. All that was important to him was discretion. Once he obtained Alice's promise that she would behave herself in Paris, he saw no reason why he could not abandon their marital farce and go to London. Let Alice amuse herself with putting brush to canvas.

Paris of the late 1880s was the undisputed cultural capital of the world. Although Henry Adams wrote his tribute to Paris in the early part of the twentieth century, it was just as applicable to the *fin de siècle*:

Inevitable Paris beckoned and resistance became more and more futile as the store of years grew less; for the world contains no other spot than Paris where education can be pursued from every side. ...Scores of artists—sculptors and painters, poets and drama-

LAURA, ALICE, AND
NATALIE, C. 1889
*In 1887, Laura and Natalie
were enrolled in Les Ruches
in Fountainebleau while
Alice studied art with Carolus-Duran in Paris.*

tists...designers in stuffs and furniture...were at work, a thousand
times as actively as ever before, and the mass and originality of their
products would have swamped any previous age, as it nearly
swamped its own.[8]

In 1887 Paris teemed with artists and art students. Edgar Degas, Claude
Monet, Pierre-August Renoir, Paul Cézanne, Berthe Morisot, Camille Pis-
saro, Alfred Sisley, and the American woman Mary Cassatt had shocked
the critics with their 1874 exhibition of Impressionism; ten years later they
were an accepted part of the art scene. *Au courant* were painters introducing
Symbolism, Primitivism, and Pointillism. This diversity was exactly what
appealed to Alice and from the moment she arrived she wanted nothing
more than to totally immerse herself in Art with a capital "A." In 1882 she
was an observer; now she would be a participant.

Wanting to be an artist and being one were two entirely different matters. Alice had talent, but she was limited by her lack of training. With few
exceptions, the innovative French artists she so admired were well-
schooled in classical techniques of drawing and painting exemplified by the
instruction presented at L'École des Beaux-Arts. Alice needed to begin
with the rudiments if she were ever to develop as an artist. As she had no
desire to attend L'École des Beaux-Arts, she soon found that the teaching
in the ateliers in large part duplicated its course of study.

At L'École des Beaux-Arts students went through a strict curriculum of classes that led toward mastery of the human form in drawing and competition for the Prix de Rome. A beginner might start with line engravings, move to copying plaster casts, and finally to copying paintings. Only the more advanced student worked from the live model. Painting instruction began when, and if, the student was deemed to have mastered drawing.

As it was still too early in the year for Natalie and Laura to enter school, Alice could not immediately enroll in an academy. Instead she sampled classes taught by Benjamin Constant and Jean-Paul Laurens that catered specifically to women. She sometimes joined Elizabeth at the Academie Julian where Gustave Boulanger and Jules Lefebvre held forth. In the meantime, she engaged the distinguished and popular portrait painter and teacher Charles Émile Auguste Carolus-Duran to execute oils of Laura and Natalie. Laura was depicted as a Regency era lass with broad-brimmed hat. Natalie, who was now ten years old and had a mind of her own, insisted upon being portrayed in the costume of Oscar Wilde's Happy Prince.[9]

During one of the early sittings, Alice asked if she might set up an easel and try her hand. With Carolus-Duran's consent, Alice began her own portrait of Natalie. In it she mimicked Carolus-Duran's style, but, as she lacked his skill and knowledge, the result was an obvious attempt by a beginner. It did, however, show promise, and, encouraged by Carolus-Duran's constructive criticism, Alice chose his academy to attend once the girls entered school.

The choice was fortuitous; Carolus-Duran was a master teacher whose students had included John Singer Sargent, Thomas Alexander Harrison, Theodore Robinson, Gwen Jones, J. Carroll Beckworth, Kenyon Cox, and Washington, D.C., painter Robert Hinckley, among others. With his commanding presence, accentuated by a bristling mustache and piercing eyes, Carolus-Duran inspired awe and rapt attention from his students. Her admiration of him was obvious in a newspaper article Alice wrote several years later.

> When Carolus-Duran, the keen eyed master came in (whose entrance caused a hush in the atelier), discussions about art, masters, religions, were dropped the instant the master's step was heard. The feeling of despair, of shyness, eager hope, of having to

CHARLES ÉMILE AUGUSTE CAROLUS-DURAN, C. 1890
Carolus-Duran, master portrait painter and teacher, counted John Singer Sargent among his students. Alice paid tribute to him in an article that appeared in the Washington Times *on July 4, 1895.*

Top:
ALICE, C. 1888
Elizabeth Nourse
Charcoal and chalk on
paper, 9½ x 12½ in.
(24.1 x 31.8 cm)
Alice modeled for this sketch
by her friend Elizabeth
Nourse in Paris.

Bottom:
LAURA AND NATALIE,
C. 1884
Elizabeth Nourse
Pencil on paper, 6 x 12 in.
(15.2 x 30.5 cm)
One of three extant prelimi-
nary sketches by Nourse for
an oil painting of Laura
and Natalie.

face the worst—as there is no escape—and you have just time for a hasty glance from your work to the model....As a drowning man reviews his past, so at the last glance, before Mons. Carolus steps in front of your canvas, you see faults in drawing, muddiness in colors, cold shadows; all the stumbling blocks so high that you see nothing else. With a despairing 'Bonjour, Mons. Carolus,' and a nervous smile, you make ready for the bolt which is sure to be hurled, some-times the blocks have shut out something which the master, being so very much taller, catches sight of, and then the 'Pas mal' makes your heart beat with a different sensation, and the smile changes from pathetic to something more pathetic as you are on the verge of tears of joy, but you are brought back to a sense of earth by the master, and after the sweet he gives a little tonic to do you good and make you strong.[10]

Alice also modeled frequently for class and friends. She enjoyed doing it. "I am a happy model, for this silence entertains me, and I have fancies and dreams which I leave in the study and take them up for consideration the following day." Often when the word got out that Alice was modeling, Elizabeth Nourse would rush over to join the group. One of her drawings of Alice shows her in an elegant gown with her waist tightly corseted and her breasts lifted high. A chiffon fichu is modestly draped about the top of the bodice, which emphasizes her elegant bare shoulders. Her gaze is serene, but there is in the curve of her jaw and the straight line of her nose an indi-cation of underlying resolve. Alice was in her milieu and she would never be the same.

During the summer of l888, Alice took the children to Brittany when Albert was called back to Cincinnati on business. While there she complet-ed four oil portraits of local peasants. One of them, a portrait of an old woman in Brittany bonnet, was submitted by Carolus-Duran to the Salon of 1889. It was accepted, but it failed to garner the attention Elizabeth Nourse's *La Mer* generated at the 1888 Salon. Alice was still very much a student with a student's deficiencies. She drew arms and hands poorly, and she had not yet gotten the knack for accurate portraiture. Alice knew the remedy was more study, greater self-discipline, and hard work. She was not discouraged by her own shortcomings as she signed up for another round of classes with Carolus-Duran to begin in October.

MOVING TO WASHINGTON, D.C.

When Albert returned to Paris in late September he brought totally unex-pected news. He had decided to move his family to Washington, D.C. He had finally and successfully settled all problems related to the Pike property in Cincinnati and, in addition, his mother's will was probated and her estate distributed to the heirs. Any mention of Alice's plans to study in France was brushed aside. He wanted her to return to Cincinnati with him at once to organize the move.

Within the month Alice was back in Cincinnati, her painting the furthest thing from her mind as she tackled the enormous job of closing the home in which they had lived for almost twelve years. It was her sole responsibility because during any moving preparations Albert absented himself to the conviviality of male conversation and a snifter of brandy at the Cincinnati Club.

The reason Albert had selected Washington, D.C., to be their future home was his confidence that he and his family would be immediately accepted into its top social echelon. Unlike New York, which looked at bloodlines as closely as it looked at financial statements, Washington society was made up of a curious mixture of parvenus, politicians, and the military. While old families did exist in Washington, their numbers were small enough to make their social power negligible. Most of the so-called elite of Washington had bought their way into society by money, by appointment to a high government post, or by election. After all, by Eastern standards Washington was a baby, having been founded by the compromise between North and South in 1790. It was also a city that seemed to have special allure for Ohioans. Presidents Ulysses S. Grant, Rutherford B. Hayes, and James A. Garfield—the latter two lifelong Ohioans—had succeeded one another to the nation's highest office. Following an eight-year hiatus, yet another Ohio man, Benjamin Harrison, was elected in 1889 as the twenty-third president of the United States.[11]

In the spring of 1889 the Barneys took up temporary residence in a large house at 1439 K Street, N.W., while their own home was being built at 1626 Rhode Island Avenue, N.W., just off Scott Circle in Washington's fashionable West End. The architects were the firm of Barry, Simpson, and Andrews and their finished product was to be a mansion that reflected Albert's taste—a pretentious Italianate palace with Gothic ornamentation. Not content to be known only for a prestigious Washington address, Albert also began building a twenty-six room cottage in Bar Harbor, Maine.

By the 1880s Bar Harbor was a major resort for the very wealthy and a close rival to Newport in the luxuriousness of its summer cottages. Originally discovered by French explorers, its real popularity began in the mid-1870s when it was rediscovered by wealthy Philadelphians who sought simplicity in a summer resort, eschewing the pretensions of Cape May, Long Branch, or Naragansset Pier, which they considered overrun by New York City nouveau riche. However, by the 1880s, improvements in train and ferry lines were depositing hundreds of these same New Yorkers in

ALICE, C. 1890
Alice standing in the door-way of Ban-y-Bryn, the Barney's twenty-six room cottage at Bar Harbor, Maine, where the Barneys summered when not in Europe.

Maine and with it the natural wildlife of Bar Harbor's Mount Desert gave way to grandiose pleasure palaces. Such prominent society figures as Pulitzer, Grant, McCormick, Whitney, and sundry Vanderbilts spent summers in Bar Harbor. The final blow was struck when James G. Blaine, former vice-president and presidential candidate, built his summer cottage there in the late 1880s. When Blaine came, so did many political sycophants and the easygoing ambience of Bar Harbor became a thing of the past. W. K. Vanderbilt entertained lavishly on board his yacht *Valiant*, which was docked in the landlocked bay surrounding Mount Desert. Where Philadelphians once had an unwritten law of no formal dress

allowed, by the 1890s reports of the elaborate attire worn at teas and balls were the meat of summer society columns that appeared in every East Coast newspaper.[12]

Albert engaged New York architect S. V. Stratton and local builder Captain Wheeler to create the twenty-six room cottage. In recognition of its castellated rear facade, the cottage was named Ban-y-Bryn after the Welsh castle it was supposed to resemble. Both houses met Albert's final criteria: instant notoriety proclaiming to one and all that the Albert Clifford Barneys from Cincinnati were people with whom to be reckoned. Because of the size of both construction projects, society reporters wrote avidly about

JULIET THOMPSON
AND ALICE, C. 1906
*Juliet Thompson and Alice
on an outing to the 1400
block of K Street, N.W.,
Washington, D. C., where
the Barneys first lived when
they moved to Washington.*

them and in particular about Ban-y-Bryn. Of particular interest to the reporters was the fact that the cottage included a studio for Alice in the second floor tower room. The studio had floor to ceiling windows and a fireplace. Albert allowed inclusion of the seventeen-by-fourteen-foot room, not in recognition of Alice's dedication to painting, but solely because it had become quite fashionable for women of high society to paint during their summer sojourns at Bar Harbor.

The construction of the Barney's Washington home attracted almost equal notice, although it was only one of many fine houses being built at the time in the neighborhood of Scott Circle. It had an inner court in emulation of Pike's second opera house that provided light and air to the interior rooms of the forty-six wide by one-hundred-sixteen feet deep townhouse. The English basement and first story were faced with buff-colored Ohio stone. The upper portions were covered with a matching buff brick with stone trimming. Inside, the staircase hall was Venetian Gothic in design, with stone columns and oak beams. On the next floor was a library and a drawing room with an adjacent music room. The most significant space was taken up by the picture gallery, which was fifty-eight feet long and seventeen feet wide.

Alice thought the new house was an ostentatious display of pedestrian taste. To her it looked just like every other house being built by wealthy people whose sole purpose was to impress other wealthy people. Albert had allowed Alice to decorate only two rooms—the reception room and the petite salon—following a terrible row after she learned part of the picture gallery was to be lined with yellow oak.

Although Ban-y-Bryn contained a studio, the Washington house did not. Albert saw no reason for one because he expected all of Alice's time to be occupied with running the house and her many social duties. With mixed feelings he read references in the society columns to the artistic quality of the guest cards she painted for their dinner parties: "Perfect little gems, and as such will always be preserved by those for whom they were designed." He was unprepared, however, for the mention she received in the press when her painting of the Brittany peasant was accepted in the 1889 Salon. He feared society might think his wife odd, but when it seemed to make them an even more popular couple, he allowed her to carve out a small space for her studio on the top floor of the new house.

Given her myriad social duties requiring attendance at afternoon 'at homes,' the ritual of calling cards on assigned days, formal teas, dinners, and balls, Alice found time to paint only in the morning. No matter how late she had been up the night before, she was always at work in her makeshift studio by ten o'clock. With the exception of preliminary charcoal sketches, she worked entirely in oil, wearing either a light colored smock or a kimono. She began by putting gobs of color on her palette, and then sitting before her easel on a large four-legged stool, she worked rapidly, often wiping away large areas if she was not satisfied with the effect. She had a fastidious nature and insisted that her painting equipment be kept in perfect order. When she finished her servants were instructed how to clean her palette and brushes.

It was at Bar Harbor, however, that Alice made the greatest progress toward perfecting her painting skills and with her improvement came the type of publicity so disturbing to Albert. First there was an illustrated article appearing in an issue of the Sunday *Boston Globe* entitled: "Quiet Nooks of Art Where Mrs. Montgomery Sears, Mrs. J. Madison Taylor, Miss Maria A'Becket and Mrs. A. C. Barney Do Serious Work Apart from the Whirl of Gayety." The article featured etchings of the individual ladies at their work and a paragraph devoted to each painter. Of Alice it said:

> One of the most prominent leaders in the gayeties of Bar Harbor life
> is very skillful with her brush. One visit to her studio in her hand-
> some cottage or rather stone villa on one of the high hills commanding
> a sweeping view of the bay and Sorrento in the far distance, assures
> the visitor of the ability with her brush of Mrs. Albert Clifford Bar-
> ney. Among the works in her studio is a group of men, in Greek
> sports, which discloses a dramatic moment, and on the easel is a fair
> woman's head....Turn where you will in this fine large studio, portraits
> meet your eye, each face is so varied, so strong, so beautiful, with
> such rare flesh tints that one must question when this gay, handsome
> woman has found time to study serious art?...She paints because she
> loves to. Only in certain moods does she take her palette, and when
> certain people appeal to her.[13]

In 1891 her success became a matter of great interest to more than just the society columnists. Much to the dismay of a number of prominent Washington portrait painters, Alice won a Congressionally funded competition to paint the official State Department portrait of former Secretary of State John C. Calhoun. Her finished painting created an uproar in Washington's small art world when it was finally exhibited. It was not because Alice's oil, which was based upon a well-known photograph of Calhoun, was a poor painting. Rather, it was unthinkable that a woman, and a wealthy one at that, had painted such a good one.

Albert, of course, was furious. What would happen to their social standing now that everyone knew he had a wife who took money for her art? Never mind that some critics touted it as one of the best portraits in the State Department's collection, they had revealed she received money for her effort, which made the event a cause célèbre. "I should think," one

John C. Calhoun, 1882
Oil on canvas, 28¼ x
22¼ in. (71.8 x 56.5 cm)
*Alice's portrait of the former
Secretary of State was based
on a photograph. The fact
that a woman, and a
wealthy woman at that,
was awarded a commission
to paint Calhoun caused
great consternation among
Washington's professional
art community.*

wrote, "it would make the men who paint for a living a little unhappy to see a rich society woman taking the laurels and the cash which they must naturally think belongs to them."[14]

While Albert raved and ranted at her indiscretion, Alice was gratified to learn she had supporters who were willing to print the entire story.

> The gay world of Washington knows Mrs. Alfred [sic] Barney as a hostess for whose elegantly appointed entertainments invitations are eagerly sought. It knows also that her pictures have been accorded a place on the walls of the Salon. But in Paris there are not a few struggling artists who know her in a still better and more womanly fashion. They know her as an artist whose work commands a satisfactory monetary return, which goes to defray their expenses and makes possible the art education upon which they rely for future support. Not a few of Mrs. Barney's friends, knowing her private wealth, were inclined to cavil when it became known that upon her had been conferred the honor to paint the portrait of John C. Calhoun which now adorns the walls of the private secretary's room in the State Department. That adverse verdict concerning the acceptance of the order would have been very different had the truth of the matter been known. The sum received for this portrait, in common with all other money earned by Mrs. Barney's brush, has been forwarded to an artists' fund in Paris which provides impecunious persons of ability with the means necessary to complete their art education.[15]

The final word on the Barneys continuing status in society lay not in Albert's perceptions or the pronouncements of art critics. Rather it was in the hands of the city's society reporters who held the power to make or break reputations. One of these, after expending many words describing one of Alice's ball gowns and comparing her looks to a Thomas Gainsborough portrait, wrote: "And Mrs. Barney is as clever as she is good looking. She is an artist, not a dilettante, BUT A GENUINE WORKER, who loves her art and strives to do something worth while."[16] For the moment that was enough for Albert. It was more than enough for Alice.

VI

Society and Art

I n the 1890s, if you were as wealthy as the Albert Clifford Barneys yet not as rich as the Astors or Vanderbilts, Washington, D.C., was the place to live. By the last decade of the nineteenth century, the nation's capital bore little resemblance to the town described in 1873 by Mark Twain and Charles Dudley Warner in the *Gilded Age*. Gone were the dingy stores and hotels that once lined its grand processional avenue. Rows of cheap little houses in nearby residential areas were replaced by fancy department stores, ponderous office buildings, elegant hotels, and pretentious mansions.

Washington, which was once famous for streets that turned to canals at spring thaw, now had miles of paved roads thanks to the efforts of Alexander "Boss" Shepherd in the mid-1870s. Shepherd had used his position as head of the Board of Public Works and Governor of the District of Columbia to line his own pockets through land speculation and to bankrupt the town with civic improvements. As a result of Shepherd's largess with other people's tax money, Congress abolished local suffrage, replaced the elected mayoral system with an appointed three-man commission, and took upon itself direct control of local affairs through committees in both Houses. Memories were short, however, and within ten years these selfsame disenfranchised citizens paid to have Shepherd immortalized in bronze. The new statue was placed in front of city hall in homage to the man who had "plucked [Washington] from the mire and set [it] as a jewel in the sight of men."[1]

Landscape architect Frederick Law Olmsted, who had designed the grounds for the United States Capitol, was currently engaged in drawing up preliminary plans for the orderly development of Washington's northwestern suburbs and the creation of a large new park that would rise from the swamps of the Potomac flatland just east of the Washington Monument. During the 1890s, with sewers and water lines completed, the typhoid and cholera epidemics that once ran rampant through the Irish slums of Foggy Bottom (where the State Department now stands) and through "Murder Bay" (now the Federal Triangle) were terrors of the past. Speculators rushed to build ostentatious apartment houses and mansions for wealthy clients or modest brick row houses for civil servants on whatever vacant lots were still left within the city's original boundary markers.

Washington's cultural life, however, had not kept pace with either the city's physical growth or its increasing numbers of wealthy and well-educated inhabitants—those who should most be expected to support a thriving

1626 RHODE ISLAND AVENUE, N.W., 1895
Alice always considered 1626 Rhode Island Avenue, N.W., a man's house because of Albert's masculine interior design. Laura and Albert stand before its main entrance, which looked toward Scott Circle.

artistic community. In 1840 a National Institute was founded to establish a national art museum, but failed for lack of interest and money. Ten years later another organization, the Washington Art Association, led by an impressive group of art lovers and artists, which included W. W. Corcoran, Asher B. Durand, Emanuel G. Leutze, and Robert W. Weir, once again tried to organize a national gallery of art. Although the Smithsonian Institution owned works of art that were primarily assigned to the anthropology department, at the turn of the century the only truly functioning art museum in Washington was the privately endowed Corcoran Gallery of Art.

There were only a handful of commercial art galleries, notably the V. G. Fisher Gallery and the Waggaman Gallery in Georgetown. Two local artists organizations formed during the 1890s: the Society of Washington Artists in 1890 and the Washington Water Color Club in 1895. A number of nationally recognized artists were among their members, but local artists received little support either from the federal government or from the public at large.

The nation's capital had no local symphony, opera, or dance company primarily because there was no large concert hall. In addition, there did not appear to be much of an audience for the performing arts in Washington. Traveling theater companies frequently played to half-filled houses at the old National Theater and the Lafayette Opera House. Ford's Theater, once a major house, had closed following Lincoln's assassination. In fact, compared with the artistic opportunities that Alice had known while she lived in Cincinnati, the nation's capital seemed a veritable cultural desert.[2]

In 1893, however, Alice's attention was not on Washington. Like so many others across the country, her interest was focused on the opening of the Columbian Exposition in Chicago's Jackson Park. Even newly elected President Cleveland seemed to have set aside for a moment his preoccupation with the repeal of the Sherman Silver Purchase Act, which he blamed for the depression that had gripped the country since 1890. The "White City" that arose on the shores of Lake Michigan spoke to America's nineteenth-century optimism and blithely ignored the poverty beyond its entrance gates.

Alice's personal interest in the exposition was centered on the United States Government Pavilion and the State Department's presentation of her portrait of John C. Calhoun as part of its exhibition of portraits of former Secretaries of State. It was the first time one of her works had been exhibited in the United States. And yet, she also felt a certain amount of disappointment. Payment for a painting was presumably one of the criteria for being considered a professional artist, yet she was not among those selected for inclusion in the highly publicized exhibition of female artists at the Women's Pavilion. Her omission did not go unremarked in Washington

ALICE PIKE BARNEY IN
WHITE SATIN, 1894
Hubert Vos
Oil on canvas, 71¾ x
42 in. (182.2 x 106.7 cm)
Albert commissioned Vos to
paint a portrait of Alice
during the summer of 1894
at Bar Harbor.

newspapers, and several local art critics chided the organizers of the women's exhibition for not including her, particularly once the photographic reproduction of her Calhoun portrait began to appear for sale in local store windows.

Alice did not go to Chicago, but one of the fair's representatives eventually came to her. A highlight of the Columbian Exhibition was the Fine Arts Pavilion where a visitor could view examples of a country's artistic heritage. Many nations appointed an official art ambassador and prominent among them was portrait painter Hubert Vos, Acting Royal Commissioner of Fine Arts for Holland. Vos was personable and outgoing with a seemingly insatiable curiosity about America. He used his time in the Western Hemisphere to travel from coast to coast and from the Great Lakes to Central America. He concluded his trip by spending the summer of 1894 with the Barneys at Ban-y-Bryn.

Even before coming to America, Vos had earned a reputation for his flattering portraits of wealthy Americans. A list of his subjects read like a social who's who and included Courtland Palmer, Robert Todd Lincoln, Horatio Alger, Jr., and William McKinley (when he was Governor of Ohio). A portrait by Vos was a mark of social standing, and so it was not surprising that Albert commissioned Vos to paint his beautiful young wife. Vos described his stay with the Barneys in the summer of 1894 as "three happy months of riding, feasting, driving, dreaming, walking, visiting, picnicking, golfing and working hard as well."[3]

His portrait of Alice was shown in September 1894 in the Portraits of Women exhibition at the National Academy of Design in New York. The exhibition was a charity fundraiser and the drawing card devised by the academy's board to entice visitors to pay the five-dollar admission fee for the opening was to have the subject stand by her picture during the evening. Thus, beside some six hundred depictions of sylphlike beauties with swan necks, slender waists, and serene expressions stood the actual models who came in all manner of sizes, clothed by Worth, dripping with diamonds, and most weighing considerably more than their flattering images. Of all the pictures in the exhibition, Vos's portrait of Alice was the most popular, perhaps because its model was as attractive as her likeness. Its success, however, also lay in Vos's execution—a lively, bravura style that captured a high-spirited Alice as she entered a light-filled room, a bouquet of tiger lilies resting in the crook of her arm, a laugh bubbling up just behind her slightly parted lips.

In review after review, Vos's portrait of Alice, which hung in the place of honor opposite a Whistler, was singled out for praise. "Abbott Thayer is refined in his color and Mr. Zorn is strong. But there is nothing in the galleries more original and delightful than Hubert Vos' portrait of Mrs. Barney. The little woman breaks in upon one like an audible laugh. It is sweet and fine and merry and its presence is cheering."[4]

In late fall, Vos visited the Barneys in Washington. Returning the favor for the now famous likeness, Alice painted a portrait of Vos. The social coup in being the first member of Washington society to pose for Vos was not lost on those who liked to poke fun at the very rich. Typical of such gossip items was one which appeared in a Washington society column: "Lately, since her return to Washington, she has been driving a good deal during the bright afternoons on Connecticut Avenue, and whether or not as a compliment to her guest, the distinguished Dutch artist, she generally has her arms heaped up with bright hued flowers, as though just returning from some horticultural show."[5]

Trading upon his success in the portrait show, Vos arranged a solo exhibition at the Ortgies Gallery in New York for December. Alice's portrait was once again the main attraction. If any one event or incident was needed to assure Alice's place in Washington society, the highly regarded Vos painting provided it. Conversely, Vos posing for Alice became the imprimatur that convinced the few remaining doubters that Alice was an artist worth watching. Until then, Alice had occupied a very ambiguous place in Washington's artistic life. While she did not exhibit her work, she had begun to be acknowledged as a professional artist. In 1895 Alice did a number of illustrations for the women's supplement of the *Washington Tribune*, wrote several articles on the problems facing women artists, and edited a July Fourth arts supplement for the *Washington Times*. Social columnists began reporting on her latest efforts. One article recounted the story of how her kitchen maid refused to model because she felt she was not being paid by Mrs. Barney to stand still. This prompted Alice to fire her as a maid, hire her as a model, then fire her as a model once the painting was completed and rehire her again as a maid.

Given the no-holds-barred style of social columns of the time, the stories written about Alice's artistic endeavors could have ripped her to shreds. Instead, the writers seemed delighted that they finally had an original and charming personality to write about in a city filled with predatory social climbers. They seemed to find a refreshing ingenuousness in Alice, who once blithely wrote in the city's most widely read newspaper that she knew no secret for success as an artist other than, perhaps, "Karma."

During the early 1890s, Alice's closest friend in Washington was Juliet Thompson, who had come to Washington to study art at the Corcoran School. They first met in 1889 when they both lived on K Street. Although Thompson was fourteen years younger, the disparity in age made little difference. Throughout the years, whether in New York, Washington, or Paris, the two remained good friends. In the same way that Elizabeth Nourse had encouraged Alice, so Alice encouraged Juliet. They frequently painted together, often sharing models. Occasionally they both worked on a single painting, and, since their styles were so similar, it is difficult to know where one stopped and the other began. In 1895, they exhibited at the Philadelphia Art Club's annual exhibition and were both highly praised. Thompson's work was given the place of honor while Alice's was touted as the discovery of the exhibition.

Alice needed a close woman friend and, for the time being, Juliet was the one. Beginning with Elizabeth Nourse in 1884, Alice's few intimates were women artists rather than fellow society matrons. A special closeness developed during the hours they spent together in front of their easels. The other reason for Alice often choosing female artists as friends was that they were not usually participants in the rigorous social life engaged in by Alice. That alone allowed them to view Alice's life objectively and assist her in maintaining her perspective.

FAMILY SECRETS

Although Alice was a positive person who seldom complained, her friends were aware of an underlying tension in her life. Through gentle prodding they uncovered the cause in the contrast between her cheerful public facade versus her discordant private life. Her marriage was increasingly unhappy and every moment spent with Albert was filled with the consequences of his drinking—consequences that conventional wisdom of the period told her to ignore.

At a time when masculinity was often measured by how well a man held his liquor or how successful he was in extramarital affairs, Albert had almost unlimited opportunity to indulge in both. Because the Barneys were members of the smartest social set, he was constantly surrounded by beautiful women. Women were attracted to Albert because he was handsome, charming, and very witty—when he wanted to be. He made few mistakes where women were concerned, but as the years passed he became less discreet. One of Natalie's most unpleasant adolescent memories of her father occurred during a reception in their home at which she saw a woman take a cigar from her father's lips and give him a passionate kiss.[6] Most of Albert's free time, however, was spent at one of his Washington clubs: the Metropolitan, Washington Golf, Alibi, or Chevy Chase, the latter of which he was a founding member. The real benefit of being a clubman for Albert was that it provided him with a safe place to get drunk, where, as long as he behaved himself, no one cared how much alcohol he consumed.

In 1892 both girls returned to America; Natalie to finish her education at Miss Ely's New York boarding school and Laura to enter Visitation, a Catholic convent school in Georgetown. Albert's excessive drinking, particularly during that summer at Bar Harbor, was the final step toward destroying any illusions Natalie still held about her father. A letter written to her closest friend, Eva Palmer, clearly conveyed the anger she felt at the person her father had become:

> The Japanese have a theory that every ill-begotten thought returns to vex he who utters it, but badly hurts the one for whom it is intended. This is not so clear for the people of the regions in which we live. But what is certain is that sensitive and impressionable individuals are affected by the unhealthy influence of nasty words. As a result of a scene caused only by my father's bad mood, I feel horribly oppressed by a murky cloud and engulfed in the worst of evils: pettiness. His snobbish thinking shocks me and his hard, egotistical words, his power to heap injustice on a world that is already filled with it, disgusts me with everything and poisons me on this magnificent night.[7]

NATALIE, C. 1897
Natalie was a superb horsewoman who frequently rode at breakneck speed with a second horse on lead galloping beside her.

The family secret was well kept, however, and, throughout the summer society columns reported on the activities of what they praised as one of the most charming Washington families to summer at Bar Harbor that season.

The striking looking Barney sisters were as opposite in personality as they were in coloring. Natalie was fearless, learning to drive her father's two-seater carriage and racing at a gallop across the island with her wild blonde hair streaming behind her. Laura, dark-haired and serious, spent many afternoons quietly posing for her mother. While Laura looked upon her parents with adoring eyes, unable to recognize that they might be less than perfect, Natalie harbored no illusions. By 1894 she was in full rebellion, so much so that arrangements were made for her to return to Europe for a grand tour under the strict and watchful eye of Miss Ely.

When Natalie was informed that Albert was coming to Paris to escort her back to Washington for her debut into society, she was filled with apprehension. Albert's behavior was so unpredictable. He could be totally charming; he could also be an ogre. She was also well aware that Albert's arrival would end what little freedom she had managed to carve out for herself with Miss Ely. In answer to a letter from Alice, Natalie wrote:

> I wonder how Papa and I will get on? I don't know either what would be the best way to treat him. At all events I can't and won't submit to his whims as you do. It doesn't pay. I think I shall be very polite and never answer him back, but have my own way when it's reasonable just the same. I wonder if that won't work.[8]

In Albert's imagination, Natalie was still his golden child, and he still loved her with the single mindedness that Alice had revealed to Oscar Wilde during their talk on the beach. But as Natalie approached adulthood, she became a puzzle to him, and the more he tried to control her, the more she defied him. She preferred to wear her long blonde hair loose in a golden untamed mane. She refused to wear corsets that restricted her body or stiff petticoats that encumbered movement.

In fact, at eighteen, Natalie was a beautiful, headstrong young woman, a Lorelei who inadvertently attracted men, but wanted only to ensnare women in her net. She took her first lover at fourteen, the equally beautiful red-haired Eva Palmer, daughter of a millionaire biscuit manufacturer. Her latest infatuation was a Mrs. Leonora Howland whom she had met on a boat between Norway and the continent. Therefore, the irony of her debut was not lost on Natalie. Its sole purpose was to catch a husband, and the only reason she decided to go through with it was the deliciousness of deceiving her father.

Alice was completely unaware of Natalie's sexual preference, but she did know how intensely Natalie reacted toward her father's every intrusion into her life. Natalie's letters to her disturbed her greatly, but she had no idea how to close the widening gulf between father and daughter. As she had done so many times before, Alice elected to ignore the situation. She turned for solace to her art and to an overwhelming list of things to be done in preparation for Natalie's debut. Included in the preparations was the construction of a large addition to the house that included a ballroom with a musician's gallery and a spacious studio overlooking the rear courtyard.

Albert arrived in Europe on March 31, 1895, and immediately began to spend money wildly on clothes for Natalie. He paid little attention to her wishes, and Natalie dashed off yet another letter to Alice complaining about his erratic behavior. "I wish you were here to help me," she wrote. "Papa is exasperating to go shopping with.... Clothes will be the death of me, clothes and Papa and time together."[9]

To show off his beautiful daughter, Albert took Natalie to the Paris opera. He insisted they sit in a box surrounded by other wealthy Americans who were obviously there to be seen, not to listen to music. Natalie was furious.

> Dear Mama,
> It almost drives me to distraction and I have no more idea about *Othello* than when I went. It's because the people at the opera kept giggling...there was no possible way of hearing or seeing the singers. I made up by looking at the celebrated millionaires and coquettes... Mrs. W. K. Vanderbilt and Gertrude were there and also Miss Gould, that was, with her titled husband. They both looked bored to death. So did everyone else. This Miss Gould is the most unwashed and dirty looking creature I ever laid eyes on and he the most insipid. *Quel menage*.

Albert gave dinner parties for her that she found "stiff and not very reassuring," and he drank too much. "Papa was in one of his moods last night and as insulting as ever over by-gones....I could hardly stand him, drinking again, I suppose."[10] Two months later on June 1, 1895, Albert's foray into concerned fatherhood ended as he and Natalie boarded an ocean liner in England to sail home.

Natalie was to have two debuts: the first at Bar Harbor, the second in Washington. On August 5 the Barneys presented Natalie to Bar Harbor society at the first private ball of the season. Over five hundred guests drove up the long drive to the pseudoWelsh castle perched on the crown of Howard Hill. Their way was lit by hundreds of Japanese lanterns hung from the towering branches of pine and spruce trees lining the avenue. Inside, the great hall was decorated with potted plants and flowers and festooned with trailing ground pine, among which were strewn silk-shaded candles and poppy-shaped lamps. The drawing room was cleared for danc-

NATALIE AT EIGHTEEN,
1895
*Natalie wearing her debut
gown designed by Worth*

ing, and the large veranda overlooking the bay was draped in silk to protect the guests from the fog-laden night air. Natalie and Alice stood side-by-side looking more like sisters than mother and daughter; Alice in a blue silk gown and Natalie in a simple white satin dress made by Worth's of Paris.

In October the Barneys returned to Washington to ready themselves for the winter debutante season. Natalie found herself constantly in the company of the nineteen other belles of the season. They included the two daughters of Vice-President Stevenson; Jane Fuller, daughter of the Chief Justice; Ethel Blanchard, daughter of Senator Blanchard of Louisiana; and Margaret Gana, daughter of the Minister of Chile. Natalie officially entered Washington society on December 18, 1895, at a five o'clock tea. The Barney mansion was neither as large nor as grand as some of the other debutantes' homes, but what it lacked in size was more than made up for by Alice's decorative artistry with flowers and her natural flair for the dramatic.

The house was illuminated with hundreds of candles rather than the brighter glow of gas jets. A roaring fire was laid in the new reception room's immense fireplace. On either side of it stood six-foot-high wrought iron candelabras ablaze with fifty candles each. The flickering light was reflected in the sparkling diamonds worn by the guests and shone in the gleaming silver vases and trays placed about the rooms.

In the music room mother and daughter received the guests. Alice wore a satin brocade of pink roses on a creme-colored background with an over-skirt of spangled chiffon and lace. Natalie stood beside her dressed in sheer white silk over white satin striped mull, its simple lines relieved by a light green velvet collar and girdle. She carried a shower bouquet of lilies of the valley bound by light green ribbons. Once again everyone remarked how much like sisters the two women looked.

Albert congratulated himself on the success of Natalie's entrance into society, but Natalie knew it was her swan song. Smiling sweetly, she played the role of demure daughter to the hilt, content because she knew it earned her a return ticket to Paris. She attended dinners and dances, helped her mother organize fencing lessons for young ladies in their new ballroom, and joined her parents in the dress circle of the Lafayette Opera House for concerts. Finally, Natalie completely fooled both parents when she announced her engagement to William Morrow of Pittsburgh.

Will was Natalie's friend and confidant and was well aware of her preference for women. With the naiveté and cockiness of youth, he agreed to a marriage in name only with each partner being able to have mistresses. Natalie remembered Will saying, "I love women too; why can't we both adore them?"[11]

BACK TO PAINTING

Lent marked the end of social frivolity. Ballrooms were closed, and the young set took to exercise—first ice skating and, when the weather was warmer, cycling and the hunt at the Chevy Chase Club. Natalie was so successful at being the dutiful daughter that even Alice stopped holding her breath in anticipation of an explosion between Natalie and her father. Alice took advantage of the comparative lull of the Lenten season to close herself up in her new studio. Following daily eight a.m. services at Saint John's Episcopal Church on Lafayette Square across from the White House, Alice would hurry back to her studio to continue working on three oil portraits: one of Natalie in a fur cape, another of Laura in a Japanese robe, and a self-portrait. It was imperative she finish the self-portrait to make the deadline for an invitational exhibit that was opening May 3 at the Cincinnati Music Hall. Along with it would go, at their request, her portrait by Vos.

The Cincinnati exhibition was based upon the popular 1894 National Academy of Design portrait exhibition, but it would feature paintings by Ohio artists in addition to an extensive display of works lent from individual collections. According to Frank Duveneck, the dean of Ohio painters, the Cincinnati show would be of higher quality than its New York predecessor because its core was provided by the works of native Ohioans and Ohio-trained artists such as Joseph Eaton, Henry Mosler, Thomas Buchanan Read, James H. Beard, Kenyon Cox, John H. Twachtman, and, of course, Duveneck. As a native Cincinnatian, Alice's artistic accomplishments had been followed with interest by those who remembered her, and the reviewers could not help but compare her self-portrait to Vos's portrait of her.

The self-portrait was strongly painted with firm decisive brush strokes. While the Vos portrait portrayed a woman who was merry, confiding, affectionate, and content, Alice's depiction of herself presented a strongly contrasting perception. In it she stood dressed in a long purple robe with her palette in one hand and brushes in the other. She replaced the soft, almost ethereal beauty of the Vos portrait with her own vision of herself as a woman possessed of seriousness of purpose and strength of character. According to printed reports, Cincinnatians considered her self-portrait "splendidly painted."[12]

At the end of Lent a combination of events once more saw the Barney family heading to Europe. Laura, whose leg had been seriously injured in a pony cart accident as a child, began to experience increasing pain as she entered adolescence. An operation was ordered and arrangements were made to have it performed in Paris where medical practice was deemed more up-to-date than in the United States. Natalie announced she wanted to further her study of French literature and invited Will to accompany them on the voyage. Alice, who needed to help Laura with her convalescence, saw the trip as an opportunity to resume her studies. Albert, knowing the proclivity of his wife and daughters to spend money freely, went along to monitor their expenses.

As was the custom in Washington, the Barneys rented out their furnished house for the season to Senator George Peabody Wetmore, Republican Senator from Rhode Island. On July 11, 1896, they sailed to England for a month's stay at Brighton. From there they traveled to Paris for Laura's surgery. Alice resumed her lessons with Carolus-Duran and took additional classes from the Spanish-born painter Claudio Castelucho. Castelucho's style differed significantly from that of Carolus-Duran. His bravura use of impasto and thick, short brush strokes to give form to his subjects—a departure from the emphasis upon solid drawing technique that Carolus-Duran insisted his students use before imparting one dab of paint to the canvas—was a challenge for Alice. Her lack of success in adapting Castelucho's method to her own is reflected in an unfinished canvas of a studio model, notable primarily for the blob of pale flesh-toned paint that appears at the end of the sitter's nose. Meant as a highlight, it ended up looking more like a large wart.

Although Alice had hoped to submit a new work to the 1897 Salon, she was unable to complete one that satisfied her in time. Instead, she entered her recently completed portrait of Natalie in a fur cape. All of her hard work over the past ten years came to fruition when the painting was hung on the line and chosen for reproduction in the Salon's *Catalogue Illustre*.

It did not take long for Albert to be bored by Paris. In early March 1897 he returned to Washington to participate in the opening of the golf season on the newly built links located on Fort Meyer Heights. The three women hardly noticed his absence. They were completely absorbed in their own pursuits, none of which either involved or interested him. Confined to bed, Laura spent her time studying philosophy and religion. Alice painted, and Natalie seemed totally occupied by classical French poetry and her plans to man a booth at the major charity event of the Paris social season: the Saint Raphael Orphanage Bazaar. At the end of April, Alice returned to the United States, staying first at the Waldorf Astoria before moving on to Bar Harbor for the summer.

French poetry and charity events were, however, the furthest things from Natalie's mind. Once both parents were safely out of the way, she lost no time trying to gain entry into the Parisian demimonde. Without connections it was proving almost as difficult to enter as New York society's Four-Hundred as defined by Mrs. Vanderbilt's guest list, which determined who was in and who was out. In looking for someone who might be able to help, she decided upon the model Carmen Rossi. An affair soon began, and Carmen was more than happy to provide the introductions. She took Natalie to the Bois de Bologne on weekends, where the leading courtesans showed off their beauty as they paraded along the allées in open carriages. Carmen also took her to the Neuilly Fair revels, which were famous for their outrageousness—planned and otherwise.[13]

On the morning of May 5, 1897, the Barneys opened their copy of the *New York Times* to read: "Fire Horror in Paris: Over 200 Lives Lost in a Bazaar Where the Duchesse d'Uzes Presided." Although Natalie was not scheduled to work at the bazaar until the tenth, May 4 was the opening and the Barneys had no way of knowing if Natalie was among the fifteen hundred or so visitors at the bazaar when the fire broke out. They immediately cabled Natalie, but received no answer.

The accounts of the fire filled them with mounting apprehension. It had taken only five minutes for the fire to completely consume the insubstantial wooden structure overhung with gauzy oriental hangings. Graphic descriptions of the victims' remains made it clear that unless some easily recognizable jewelry remained on or near a charred body, there was little hope of positive identification. Finally, Natalie cabled and confessed she spent the afternoon with Carmen and was nowhere near the disaster. Years later she revealed that when leaving Carmen's house that day, "she saw the reflection of the fire in the sky and declared that it was glowing to celebrate their love."[14] Once more Albert sailed to Europe to bring his daughter home.

SUMMER AT BAR HARBOR

The summer of 1897 was not as uneventful as Natalie feared it might be. Among the Barneys' summer guests at Bar Harbor were Prince and Princess Troubetzkoi. Pierre Troubetzkoi was an Italian portrait painter with a Russian surname, whose family settled in Italy many generations before. His wife, Amelie Rives, was not only a wealthy southern Virginia belle from the Tidewater area, but a widely published poet, novelist, and short story writer. They were the sort of cosmopolitan artistic folk that Alice delighted in entertaining. The beautiful Amelie provided her own fascination for Natalie with her petite figure, soft-spoken Virginia accent, and large, unusual violet-colored eyes framed by extravagantly long lashes.[15]

That summer Alice undertook her first theatrical venture. In previous

BAN-Y-BRYN, BAR
HARBOR, MAINE,
C. 1890
*Designed to mimic a
Welsh castle, Ban-y-Bryn
was the site of extravagant
entertainments whenever
the Barneys were in
residence.*

years she had presented small dramatic recitations for an evening's entertainment, but encouraged by her guests and looking for a way to engage
Natalie, she put together a series of unrelated scenes and presented a
vaudeville at the exclusive Bar Harbor Kebo Valley Club. The result pro-
voked a thoroughly tongue-in-cheek review:

> The Vaudeville is and is not. But the recollection of it shall become a
> thing of permanency....Society was deeply stirred over the impending
> event, and for a long time previous, it was the all-pervading theme of
> conversation. Urged on by the many weird and artistically suggestive
> posters by Mrs. Barney—what there is of Bar Harbor attended en
> masse. The final presentation achieved a splendid success. It was
> clever, unique, original. The acting was as good as the lassitude of
> summer would permit; the staging of the performance was artistic and
> even brilliant; the interest manifested by the audience attested to the
> wisdom and cleverness of the idea...."[16]

As the Barneys perused the review, each received a different message: Alice
read the words "clever, unique, original," while Albert saw "weird" and
"suggestive." The distance between them grew larger.

The Barneys returned to Washington in the fall, and Natalie was presented with the caveat that if she ever wanted to return to Paris she must
behave. Once more Natalie played the part expected of her. She even
attracted the attention of numerous young men as she participated with
seeming whole-heartedness in the activities of Washington's youthful smart

set. She missed Eva and Will who would have made her charade fun. Nevertheless, she hid her yawns, crossed her fingers, and threw herself into the social whirl with marked success.

Alice also chafed at the demands of the social season. Buoyed by her success at the 1897 salon, she decided to become an active member of Washington's artistic community, although endless entertaining kept her from serious work in her studio and contact with local artists. Now forty, and a serious painter for over a decade, she had never shown locally out of obedience to Albert. What mention there was of her art work, while complimentary, appeared in society columns and not on the art page. In anticipation of the frenzy of entertaining associated with Christmas, Alice finally took steps necessary to become part of Washington's sedate Bohemia.

First she joined the Washington Water Color Club, a group of local artists led by Henry Moser who exhibited drawings, pastels, and watercolors. The first showing of her paintings in Washington was with the Washington Water Color Club. The reviews of her entries, while encouraging, were not the uncritical acclamations of her talent that appeared on the society pages. Blance King, critic for the *Washington Post* stated that while her pastel technique was professional, the subject matter of one her pastels—a young woman with red hair—was ill chosen. King continued: "Although executed with a fearlessness of criticism that compels a certain admiration...as a picture, the coarse voluptuous face being framed in hanging has alas 'crimped' hair which no courtesy or poetic license could call by any other name than 'red,' and the lower portion being in flesh tones, whose chalkiness is too apparent to be overlooked."[17]

Alice then took the big step and applied for membership in the Society of Washington Artists, the city's most prestigious artist organization. In order to belong, her work was scrutinized by a selection jury comprised of the officers of the organization and a committee of the board of directors. Only upon their recommendation was her membership approved.[18] Although entrance was juried, membership increased yearly, and by 1898, the Society's gallery space was stretched to its limits. Moreover, the Society planned eventually to expand from a local exhibition to a national annual competition. Boston,

NATALIE AT TWENTY, 1898
Natalie in costume as La Cigale for Alice's Tableaux for the sick and wounded in war with Spain, presented May 9, 1898, in what is now the grand salon of the National Museum of American Art's Renwick Gallery.

LAURA AT
SEVENTEEN, 1897
Laura in costume as
Cleopatra for Alice's
vaudeville at Bar Harbor.
Laura was as intrigued
with theater as her mother,
which was surprising given
her naturally quiet and
retiring personality.

Philadelphia, and New York already hosted shows of nationwide importance, sponsored in large part by organizations such as the Society. Not only would this help establish Washington as a major art center, but the reputations of Washington artists would be enhanced by showing with widely recognized painters. Its second objective was to establish a federally supported art museum in Washington in conjunction with an art school patterned after L'École des Beaux-Arts in Paris. The Society's membership was convinced that if these steps were taken, Washington could become not only the nation's political capital, but its art capital as well.

Alice wholeheartedly supported the Society's goals and with her immense wealth and entrée to influential persons, Washington artists now had a badly needed and formidable ally. The state of the visual arts in Washington at the turn of the century was less than rosy, yet the city continued to attract artists and there were a number of knowledgeable patrons.[19] The most influential and well-known of the artists were James Henry Moser, president of the Washington Water Color Club and art critic for the *Washington Times* and eventually the *Washington Post*; painter Max Weyl; Richard Norris Brooke, president of the Society of Washington Artists; William Henry Holmes, who in 1920 became the director of the Smithsonian Institution's National Gallery of Art (the original name for what is now known as the National Museum of American Art); and Leila Mechlin, critic for the *Evening Star* and an amateur painter. As the number of professional artists living in Washington was small, Alice eventually came to know them all.

Now a member, Alice entered three pictures in the Society of Washington Artists's eighth annual exhibition. This time reviews were good. One picture was selected for high praise by Blance King because it reminded the critic of a Tennyson heroine with a "slim girlish form in a medieval gown of green velvet, that between the masses of yellowish auburn hair which almost envelops her, shows gleams of emerald light, white above it, fair and stately, rises the sweet girlish face, clear-eyed and innocent of aught but what has been instilled with words of learning and prudence." Moreover, King wrote, "in much of these subjects the execution is quite as much a matter for admiration as the motif itself, the drawing clear, decisive lines, and the handling of color being masterful as they are charming in effect."[20]

WAR ACTIVITIES

The pursuit of things artistic, however, was rudely interrupted by a declaration of war against Spain on April 25, 1898. While present-day historians believe the Spanish-American War was provoked more by William Randolph Hearst's yellow journalism than by a real threat to American security, citizens such as Isabella McKenna Duffield, who was living in Washington with her father Senator Joseph McKenna at the time, felt quite differently.

> Looking back on the Spanish American War, people speak of it now as 'a mere skirmish', but for those who lived through it the 'mere skirmish' seemed decidedly important. The blowing up of the 'Maine' was for us a fact in history as momentous as that of the firing on Fort Sumter for our grandmothers.[21]

A war, no matter how small, inevitably brings casualties; this one was no different. Veteran's benefits were notoriously meager and so the ladies of Washington, filled with patriotism, decided to help the war effort by putting on a theatrical event to raise money for the sick and wounded. Increasingly, Alice found satisfaction in the theatrical arts, looking upon them as an extension of the visual arts. It was in some way a return to her childhood pin theater, although now she had actors to direct rather than colored pins. It was exciting to see how one art reinforced the other and how easily she could move from one discipline to the other.

Fortified by her successful vaudeville venture the previous summer at Bar Harbor, Alice offered to arrange the evening's program. Under the direction of a nucleus of prominent women who were members of the Corcoran Gallery art loan committee, a stage was erected before a red-draped background hung across the eastern end of the grand salon of the Old Corcoran Gallery (now the Smithsonian's Renwick Gallery).

On May 9, five hundred members of the cream of Washington society crowded into the large and elegantly decorated gallery whose walls above the gleaming wooden wainscotting were hung to the ceiling with paintings provided by the loan committee. So great was the demand for tickets that the event was repeated the following week. After the second presentation one of the newspapers reckoned that each wounded soldier was at least $1,000 the richer.

Obviously, the success of the program was due at least as much to who was on stage and who was in the audience (including President McKinley) as to the cause it was supporting. The wife of the Minister of Austria-Hungary, the Baroness Hengelmuller, posed as "The Falcon," wearing a gold gown and ropes of pearls twined in her blonde hair. Chevalier Gaetano Trentanove, an Italian sculptor recently arrived in Washington to complete three commissions, sang "Non amo piu" from *Cavelleria Rusticana* and Alice's friend Prince Troubetzskoi lifted weights.

The finale was titled "War, Victory and Peace." War was draped in scarlet, her long dark hair flowing behind her. Cries of "War! War!" came from the audience, quieting only when Victory appeared costumed in white, wings fluttering bravely from her shoulders, as she raised a trumpet to her lips with one hand and held out laurels with the other. Finally Peace entered. Dressed in purple and gold, she carried a papier-mâché snow-white dove perched upon her finger. The three young women then formed a group allegorical pose for the finale as the United States Marine Band played the "Star-Spangled Banner."

One reporter wrote: "Mrs. Barney's greatest artistic triumph was perhaps the tableau which concluded the evening's entertainment. Each one of these were oil paintings in themselves, with every detail of the background, coloring, and picture effect thought carefully out."[22] There was little doubt that Alice had dazzled Washington society with her theatrical talents.

Laura, again in Paris pursuing her studies in philosophy while she continued extensive physical therapy, also developed patriotic feelings. In a letter to her father, she asked him to allow her to go to Key West, Florida, and nurse the wounded. "I am sure," she wrote, "that you will come to my conclusion that it is good and best to do every good action that can possibly cross one's path on this short life."[23]

Albert wired back an emphatic "No." Her letter had shaken him for it was the first time his compliant younger daughter had ever proposed anything other than the most conventional of acts. The mere fact that she asked this favor of him intensified his worst fears that the Barney women were out of control. Struggling to regain his mastery over them, he insisted that Alice and Natalie join him at Bar Harbor and made it clear that there would be no repeat of the prior year's vaudeville production. In return for their acquiescence, he agreed to take them back to France in the fall.

It was a very quiet summer. Then a letter unexpectedly arrived at Ban-y-Bryn from Alice's friend, the painter John White Alexander, whom she had met briefly in Paris. He informed her that circulars were appearing throughout the Latin Quarter announcing the opening of an Academie Whistler for the fall. Alexander, a respected member of the American art colony in Paris and a close friend of Whistler, asked Alice why she should not "dodge the obligations of society and take a studio in the Latin Quarter, live where the artists do, and have a taste of real life there?"[24] Enclosed was a letter of introduction to Whistler. Alice put the letter down. Why not, indeed.

VII

Friendship With Whistler

T he Alice Pike Barney who sailed to Paris in the fall of 1898 was a very different person from the seventeen-year-old girl who had first seen the City of Lights nearly a quarter of a century earlier. Then she was a slight, dark-haired girl, barely five feet tall. Her tightly corseted waist, crinolined skirt, and whale-boned bodice emphasized her hourglass silhouette. Now at forty-one she was a trifle stout and the gray in her hair was colored a Titian hue. She still moved, however, with the energy and grace of the girl she had once been.

On her first trip everything was new and marvelous: from the beauty of Louis XVI furniture to the exultation she felt at her first attempt at painting; Henry Morton Stanley courted her and life seemed an endless celebration. If at middle age the party was tedious and Albert, not Henry, shared her stateroom, Alice was still able to take delight in life's possibilities. She was going to Paris to study with the great James McNeill Whistler.

She leaned against the railing and watched the port of Le Havre take on definition as the ship drew closer to its destination. Beside Alice were Natalie and her unofficial fiancé, Will. She glanced at Natalie out of the corner of her eye as she often did, at a loss to understand fully just what went on beneath her crown of golden hair. Natalie was twenty-one, but she was not yet ready for complete freedom; not that Alice had any plans to closely monitor her daughter's activities in Paris. Rather she planned to use a loose rein to hold Natalie to the social boundaries Albert deemed so important.

She wondered often about Will and Natalie. He seemed so innocent and ingratiating, no match for Natalie's opinionated, strong-willed personality. She speculated on their relationship and why the engagement continued to remain unofficial. It probably did not matter in the long run. If Will were not the one, certainly there would be another.

She looked forward to seeing Laura again. Laura never caused problems. Sometimes she would look at her somber dark-haired daughter in amazement. Laura was so different from the rest of them, nothing but serious thoughts in her head—certainly not a family characteristic. Perhaps it was the daily presence of physical pain from her leg injury that had made her both introspective and practical in equal doses. So far, Laura's only lapse from the expected had been her extraordinary request to go to Florida to nurse wounded soldiers; yet maybe that urge was not quite so surprising after all.

Even as a small child, Laura had an overdeveloped sense of duty. It was

Self-portrait Reflected in Mirror, 1896
Oil on canvas, 35½ x 30⅞ in. (90.1 x 78.2)
Alice based this painting upon photographs taken by Frances Benjamin Johnston at the time of Natalie's debut.

Laura, not Natalie, who willingly posed for Alice. She was a diligent student, always trying to do better and always apologizing if her grades were not up to the standards she set for herself. While languages came easily to Natalie, Laura struggled until she mastered them. With little study, Natalie sailed through examinations and received the highest marks. Laura, who truly cared about her grades, spent hours in preparation. Alice ruefully remembered the almost indecipherable letters Laura dutifully mailed from Les Ruches, belabored and smudged, every other word misspelled. They always seemed to end on the same note: "Natalie refuses to help me. If she only would, I could be so much better."[1] Now roles were reversed, and it was Natalie who sought out the practical younger sister to take care of mundane matters.[2]

At Le Havre, Will parted company with the Barneys as they continued on to Étretat to spend what was left of the summer in a villa Albert had rented. To Albert, no one who was anyone went to Paris before the first of October. Paris society fled the city for the summer to escape the hordes of uncultivated tourists and would not return until the beginning of October. It was of absolutely no matter to him that both women could hardly wait to

ALICE, 1898
In 1898, Alice received a letter from John White Alexander urging her to go to Paris and study with Whistler. At forty-one, Alice was more than ready to shed her high society persona for that of an artist.

get to Paris, and the uncomfortable month at Étretat merely followed their pattern of letting Albert have his way. Natalie thought Alice was weak for always giving in to Albert's whims; but what Natalie never understood was that Alice's avoidance of scenes enabled her to keep a corner of her soul strictly to herself.

Upon reflection, Alice knew she had reached the point of pitying Albert. How terrible it must be for him to have to live with his own miserable self, always worried about appearances, always afraid that he, or one of his family, might make some faux pas that would cause people to laugh when they heard the Barney name. She remembered how upset he was when *Town Topics*, the salacious New York scandal sheet, printed the story about Natalie riding horseback astride during one of their Bar Harbor vacations; his mortification at his daughter's behavior was totally out of proportion to the deed. If social propriety had called for him to dress himself in sackcloth and ashes, Alice believed Albert probably would have done so.

On the first of October 1898, the Barneys moved to Paris. As if by magic, sidewalk cafés were once more filled with the idle rich, museums and galleries opened new exhibitions, and the great boulevards were crowded with carriages occupied by elegantly dressed men and women. That year there was a special thrill in the autumn air as the city readied itself for the centenary of its revolution as well as for the Universal Exposition scheduled for 1900. Dominating the skyline were the gigantic girders of the Eiffel Tower.

Of the many hotels and pensions that catered to the burgeoning business of lodging women artists in Paris, the Villa des Dames was considered one of the best.[3] Albert inspected its rooms and approved. Overjoyed, Alice began to count the days until he left for England. In her mind's eye she rearranged the furnishings to fit her image of a grand studio. There would be paintings in process artfully placed about the room and, in the afternoons, the air would hum with talk of art and culture by artists and friends as yet unmet. Lively exchanges on the latest aesthetic trends would replace the social gossip that she found so boring. She would serve tea and elegant hors d'oeuvres. Most importantly, once Albert was gone, her salon would be free of the tension she always felt at Washington parties. There she was always wondering if the

NATALIE AND LAURA, c. 1900
Blonde Natalie and brunette Laura were as different in temperament as they were in coloring. Natalie wanted nothing more than to live life to the hilt, while Laura found satisfaction in her studies and good works.

LAURA AT SIXTEEN, 1896
Oil on canvas, 30⅞ x 26⅝
in. (78.4 x 67.6 cm)
*Laura was always willing to
pose for her mother, and her
quiet temperament made her
a perfect model.*

Opposite:
NATALIE IN FUR CAPE,
1896
Oil on canvas, 36¼ x 23¼
in. (92.1 x 59.1 cm)
*This portrait of Natalie not
only hung in the 1897
Salon, but it also appeared
in the* Catalogue Illustré.

drink Albert grabbed from the silver tray would be the one that would finally cause him to spoil the evening. His behavior was always just at the edge of impropriety; his flirtations with women openly seductive and generally embarrassing to her.

It took almost a month before Albert was satisfied it was safe to leave them alone in Paris. The longer he stayed the more confirmed he was in his opinion that it was a thoroughly disagreeable city. The Dreyfus affair only reaffirmed Albert's belief that the French were an uncouth people. It was a cause célèbre in which a Jewish army officer was summarily convicted of treason on fraudulent evidence—so obviously fraudulent that he became a national figure. Mobs roamed the street and the government was put in jeopardy.

The case permeated the very air of Paris. Daily banner headlines showed advocates for both sides locked into positions far beyond the simple question of Dreyfus's guilt or innocence in giving military secrets to Germany. Pressure mounted as hundreds of scholars and writers throughout Europe and America publicly declared their support for the Dreyfusards.[4] The American writer Henry Adams condemned all Frenchmen supporting Dreyfus, particularly the great French writer Émile Zola, who was convicted of libel following the publication of his pro-Dreyfus letter, "J'Accuse." In Adams's opinion, not only did Zola belong on Devil's Island with Dreyfus, but so, too, did "as much more French rot as the island would hold, including most of the press, the greater part of the theatre, all the stockbrokers and a Rothschild or two for example."[5] Alice supported the Dreyfusards in opposition to Albert. She became an avid reader of the published lists of names of persons who supported Dreyfus and was relieved to note that they included few artists. That meant, as she informed Albert, that she would not be surrounded by Dreyfusards as she pursued her studies. He could leave her in Paris without the fear that she might become involved.

STUDYING WITH WHISTLER

As the gray-blue light of rainy afternoons reflected in the waters of the Seine alternated with the brilliant sunlight shimmering on the yellow leaves of the great plane-trees lining the walks of the Tuillerie Gardens, Americans vied with one another to buy the most extravagant costumes at the most exclusive dress designer in Paris—the House of Worth. It was not, however, the fashionable Right Bank with its alluring displays of expensive goods that called to Alice, but rather the narrow, winding streets of the Latin Quarter with their plainly adorned, tan and gray apartments and hotels. Alice believed that behind the high cloistered buildings guarded by locked gates and heavily barred doors lay a world very different from the one of which she was part. It was a world of artists and there she would meet Whistler.

At first it seemed her dream was to die aborning. Shortly after their arrival, a letter from Whistler appeared in the Paris papers written, as he put it:

> To correct an erroneous statement, or rather to modify an exaggeration, that an otherwise bona fide prospectus is circulating in Paris. An atelier is to be opened in the Passage Stanislas, and, in company with my friend, the distinguished sculptor, Mr. MacMonnies, I have promised to attend its classes. The patronne has issued a document in which this new Arcadia is described as the Academie Whistler.... I would like it to be understood that, having hitherto abstained from all plot of instruction, this is no sudden assertion...of my own.... I propose

JAMES MCNEILL
WHISTLER, C. 1898
*After class Whistler would
walk around the corner to
Alice's rooms at the Villa
des Dames for talk and a
cup of what she called the
"Emperor's tea."*

only, then to visit, as harmlessly as may
be, in turn with Mr. MacMonnies, the
new academy which has my best wishes,
and, if no other good comes out of it, at
least rigorously carry out my promise of
never appearing anywhere else."[6]

In spite of Whistler's public protestations, it
was well-known among potential art students
that even though Whistler had cold feet and
changed the name on the studio lease to that of
the model Carmen Rossi, it was his two hundred pounds that paid the rent. For a short
time, the sign over the front door to No. 6, Passage Stanislas, read "Academie Whistler," but
after his disclaimer it was removed and the
school officially renamed Academie Carmen.[7]
Word quickly spread among potential students
that no matter what the academie was called,
Whistler was still its master, and Alice confi-
dently enrolled in its class for women.

Once Albert sailed for the masculine comforts of England's clubs, Alice began making
over the apartment at the Villa des Dames into
her vision of the epitome of an artist's salon.
The main room was her studio and salon, and she filled it with choice furniture in Louis XVI style. It was a sunlit room with French doors opening
out for a view of the rear garden. Pale blue taffeta hangings marked the
entrance to its other rooms. There was a wood burning fireplace and the
lace-covered tea table was set. Flower arrangements abounded as did her
paintings, which stood unframed against the walls. A small easel placed
near a tall brocade screen completed the picture.[8]

Each day Alice walked around the corner to the Academie Carmen and
each day she returned disappointed when Whistler failed to appear.
Although Alice could afford the tuition and the wait, many of the other students could not and soon their grumbling turned into demands for the
return of their money. Carmen could ill afford to do so, and she arranged
hastily for Whistler to send a letter to his students which bore the saluta-
tion "To the distinguished pupils whom it is my pleasure to meet," and nam-
ing the day he would appear. Finally, the students heard Carmen speak the
words they were waiting to hear as she threw off her apron and rushed
down the stairs: "I hear wheels. The wheels of M. Weeslaire." In a few minutes the door flew open and she made her announcement: "Mr. Whistler."[9]

Totally engrossed in her painting, Alice not only failed to hear Carmen's announcement but also the hush that followed Whistler as he moved about the room examining the students' efforts. Finally, he came to her easel and her first inkling that he was standing there came as he said, "Ts! Ts! Ts!! How clever we are!" She abruptly swung around, totally annoyed at the interruption, and for the first time saw Whistler. She recognized him at once by the monocle and stark white forelock that were his trademarks.

As he drew off his black kid gloves, she looked back at her painting that was still in the preliminary stage of charcoal and wash and then turned back to him and smiled. "Thank you, Mr. Whistler. I understand." He nodded. "Thank you, Madame, for understanding." Cleverness, as the other students soon came to learn, was the cardinal sin in Whistler's artistic lexicon. It was Whistler's ultimate condemnation of a student's efforts.[10]

Satisfied that at least one student understood him, Whistler turned to the class and, asking the maître, Inez Bates, for palette and brush, began to prepare small mounds of flesh- and shadow-colored paint. His attention moved back and forth from model to palette. When the oils were mixed to his satisfaction, a blank, prepared canvas was set before him on an easel. "You see," he stated, "I must see the model and background on my palette before I begin. I mix before painting exactly what I will need, then half close my eyes and look at the model and so lose all the unimportant detail." For the next hour he concentrated on the shoulder area. Alice likened it to seeing "creation come into being...the first colors appeared, then the delicate broader lights and gradually the full strength, the gentle glow and completion lay spread before them, all in the color of a model's shoulder."

When finished, he turned to the students: "You see?" There was no answer. He handed palette and brush to Bates and began to pull on his gloves in preparation for leaving. Halfway to the door he paused and walked back to Alice, who was busy scraping down her painting with a palette knife:

'I should like very much to see more of your work sometime, Madame.'

'I should be delighted to welcome you, Mr. Whistler. I live at the Villa des Dames and am often in about four or five.'

'In the morning?' he smiled with a naughty twinkle in his eye.

'In the afternoon, Master. I am a very proper married lady with two young girls of my own!' Alice replied smilingly.

'In Paris one never knows. I will be there. I wish you good morning, ladies and gentlemen,' and making a bow, he left.

Whistler was as good as his word, and thus began one of many friendships not recorded in any biography of the more famous person because, in

THE SPANISH SHAWL,
C. 1900
Pastel on canvas,
51¼ x 38⅛ in.
130.2 x 96.8 cm)
Alice frequently used Natalie's friend Carmen as a model, with no idea that Carmen was also Natalie's lover.

the larger scheme of his activities, it is unimportant. On the other hand, it becomes the preeminent relationship in the life of the lesser known person. One searches in vain the biographies of Whistler for some mention of Alice's name. What one does find is that in 1898 he was a very lonely man. His beloved wife Trixie (Beatrice Godwin) died of cancer two years earlier. Without her humanizing influence he returned to his former practice of categorizing people as either followers or enemies. At sixty-four, Whistler was well on his way to becoming a caricature of himself. Where he was once entertainingly controversial, he was now boringly pugnacious. He suffered from mood swings so unpredictable that close friends began to avoid him. "There were limits to the price one should pay for Whistler's friendship," his compatriot William Rothenstein stated after being the recipient of one of Whistler's tirades.[11]

What attracted Whistler to the Villa des Dames was peace and friendship freely given. Alice made no demands upon him, only occasionally admonishing him to curb his tongue when his wit turned to cruelty. Alice's even temperament combined with her talent for repartee honed at her father's knee, touched the man and not the monster caricatured by Sir Max Beerbohm and Jean Boldini in widely reproduced drawings. Within a short time Whistler was making it a habit to join Alice at her apartment after class. Just as she had dreamed, she and Whistler sat and talked, sipping what Alice called her "sixty-dollar" tea, which was said to come from the first cuttings of the Japanese emperor's favorite tea bush.

Whistler seemed to treasure these moments of serenity as much as Alice. He disliked the intrusion of others, particularly people whose conversation he thought plodding and unimaginative. With the impishness of a small boy, the great Whistler would place his ear against the keyhole of the door to Alice's apartment before entering in order to ascertain who was there. If he did not like the visitor, he would tiptoe away. If he recognized the voice of a good friend, such as John White Alexander, he would knock for entrance and afternoon would stretch into evening as the two traded stories from their lives, the words flying fast and furious.

Sometimes they left her apartment and walked up to the Quai St. Michel to stroll along the Seine. On other occasions they explored the twisting, narrow streets of the Latin Quarter. Always they talked of art. One afternoon Alice and Whistler decided to explore the gardens of the Louvre together. As always on their walks, Whistler was master and Alice his student. To illustrate a point, Whistler dashed off a sketch of a woman seated on a bench holding her child and gave it to Alice.[12]

Alice never tired of listening to Whistler talk. At times, however, even she wearied of his egotistical monologues. Then she would gently interrupt him and remind him that conversation was also an art. Almost ritualisti

CARMEN, LAURA, AND
ALICE, C. 1898
*Alice works on a portrait
of Carmen during a visit
from Laura at Alice's
Paris studio.*

cally, he bowed and apologized for "going on so." She smiled graciously
and accepted his apology. Then off he would go again.

A question, a comment, sometimes only a quizzical look on her part,
were enough to set him off. She felt free, however, to interrupt him when
she did not understand what he was talking about. She would chide him
that to be a good teacher, he had to be clear. She remembered how difficult
it was for her to grasp what he meant by the term "seeing." If he were
incomprehensible, how could he possibly expect someone like herself to see
things the way he did? Whistler was taken by surprise that his usually

adept student did not instantly grasp what he meant. He began again, explaining with a touch of impatience that her figures must be part of their surroundings, so much so that they appeared to breathe the atmosphere in which they were placed. When she still failed to understand, Whistler took her to look in the windows of an art store on the Rue du Bac. Pointing to the pictures in the window, he indicated how the figures in one of the paintings stood out from the background, which caused too great a definition. To enforce his point, he directed Alice to look at people coming down the street. "See how they melt into their environment? The atmosphere seems to cling to them; it is a part of them and they of it. That is the effect to get into your pictures."[13]

One evening as Whistler relaxed in front of the fire, Alice gathered up her nerve and asked if she could sketch his portrait. It was the first favor she asked of him. She was always careful never to impose on him because even when they were most close, there still existed an undercurrent of the master-to-pupil relationship. To her surprise the question seemed to make him as nervous as she. He began to pace around the room, moving from fireplace to window to table. As she watched, waiting anxiously for his answer, he asked for another cup of tea first.

It was an indirect acquiescence, but she recognized it as the one she wanted. Then the reason for his anxiety came to her. She hid her smile. The silly dear was afraid that she was going to treat him in the same infamous way he treated his own sitters—hours at a time with dozens of sittings and no guarantee that there would be a picture at the end. With mock seriousness she poured another cup of tea, a stern look in her eye. Then she let the smile play across her face. "Don't worry, Master, I shan't make you pose for long. Just relax in that chair and talk away while I draw you."

While Whistler talked of Ruskin and Wilde, of the marriage of the English actress Ellen Terry, and of fellow artists Fantin-Latour and Degas, Alice quickly sketched his head in pastel, adding only the suggestion of collar and tie. At the end of forty minutes, Whistler rose and joined Alice at her easel. Alice held her breath. Had she been too audacious? Whistler surveyed the drawing from all angles. The silence lengthened. Finally, near tears and fearing the worst from this master of the cutting remark, Alice managed to blurt out, "It isn't finished!" She took a deep breath. "When can you come to pose again?" Whistler continued to examine the drawing. "It is very amusingly done, dear lady. I'll come again but you must not paint at it again, you might spoil it."[14]

On that night neither of them knew that it was to be one of their last times together. Whistler was bored with his academie, and he came less and less to critique the students. They, on their part, were equally restive at his acerbic remarks. Few were willing to subscribe to the contents of a mes-

JAMES MCNEILL
WHISTLER, 1898
Pastel on paperboard,
19¼ x 19¼ in.
(48.9 x 48.9 cm)
During one of his visits,
Alice asked Whistler if
she could sketch him.
"It is very amusingly
done, dear lady," was his
comment on the drawing.

sage from Whistler baldly stating, "Mr. Whistler expects, as the only acknowledgement that can be made him, complete acquiescence in his wishes—and complete loyalty—any doubtful hesitation being quite out of place and impossible among the distinguished pupils it is his pleasure to meet."[15] One by one they drifted away to rival ateliers whose masters were less demanding.

Following Whistler's departure that evening, Alice returned to study her portrait of him. She looked at it carefully and critically. She had not romanticized him, but she had caught something in her sketch that others seemed unable to see: "the kindliness of his manner" that accompanied "the frank genuineness of his criticism." As she studied her sketch, Alice began to see it as Whistler must have. Her work had changed under his tutelage, and she had not even realized it. This was no copy of the master's work or even of his style. It was hers alone, and it was "animated with life brought from quickening perceptions, deeper understanding, and [it] assumed the warmth gained only through wider sympathies."

Away from Albert and free from the responsibilities he imposed upon her, she had used her time well and found the key to her own work as an artist—concentration. What a simple word it was; yet the opportunity to do so was what heretofore had been missing in her life. She wondered just how long this freedom would continue.

LAST DAYS IN PARIS

Several weeks later her answer came. A letter arrived from Albert announcing he would join them in the spring and that he expected her to engage a house. He would not stay long, but the house was to be of sufficient size and elegance for entertaining. If she so desired, after his departure, she and Natalie could return to an apartment on the Left Bank. She engaged 53 Avenue Victor Hugo, one of the twelve tree-lined avenues radiating from the Arc de Triomphe. Like its imposing neighbors it was a four-storied Empire-style house. The paneled rooms were large and well-proportioned with floor-to-ceiling windows opening onto individual small balconies overlooking the avenue. Lovely as it was, she had no desire to live there—even for a short time.

Much as she tried to hide her sadness from Whistler on his next visit, he knew. That evening he was particularly gentle in his criticism of her painting and encouraged her to have faith in her new work. When Whistler returned several weeks later every corner of the room was filled with boxes and trunks in preparation for the move. As his visit drew to a close, he walked slowly to the door and then paused a moment before opening it.

'Good-by,' he turned to her, 'I fear only one thing.'

'And what is that?' asked Alice.

'Well,' and he pointed at her painting of him, 'you got over your 'cleverness' so 'cleverly,' I fear you'll slip back again.'

Alice laughed as she reassured him.

'No. I never shall. That I can promise.'

He left her slowly. 'I shall be a bit lonely for you,' and he was gone.

Alice looked around the room with tears welling up in her eyes. True, she might be back, but it would not be the same. She knew she would never see Whistler again. Other artists might people these rooms, but no one would ever replace him.

If Alice was unhappy about the temporary move, Natalie was angry. Throughout the winter of 1898–99, while Alice pursued her artistic life, Natalie engaged in a vastly different kind of enrichment. While the irony of living in the House of Women was lost on Alice it was not on Natalie, who used it as a base of operations for reviving her affair with Carmen. During the afternoons when Whistler conducted class, Carmen was temporarily relieved of her duties and she slipped around the corner into Natalie's waiting arms. In fact, Natalie never met Whistler, even though several years later Alice sent to Natalie a letter of introduction to Whistler with a request that he paint her portrait.

It was not that Natalie was excluded from Whistler's visits. Rather she chose to remain in her room and gave as her excuse her absorption in the novel she was writing—one that would have shocked Alice with its frankly autobiographical lesbian story. In reality, Natalie used much of the free time to write passionate love notes to her newest infatuation, Liane de Pougy, Paris's most notorious courtesan. Moreover, even as she thrived on the excitement of her double life, she loved and respected her mother too much to want to intentionally hurt or embarrass her. Therefore, she set up a routine of writing and study that put everyone off the scent, even the clearheaded Laura, who was a frequent visitor to the Villa des Dames. Natalie was well aware that any misstep on her part meant a swift trip to America.

What most worried Natalie about Albert's upcoming visit was his uncanny knack for uncovering what she really was up to. She resented the time and effort it took her to fool him, effort she preferred to direct toward her seduction of Liane. Natalie was, however, practical enough to know that as long as Albert controlled the purse strings, she must appear to do as he wished.

When Albert did finally arrive on the scene, he had all the graciousness of an inspector general. He was still driven by the fear that one of his family might sully the Barney name. All his attempts to establish authority over Alice, Laura, and Natalie might have been laughable, if they were not so unpleasant. Even more alarming was how ill he looked. His face was mottled, his eyes bloodshot and puffy, and he was losing weight. He suffered from shortness of breath and repeated colds. Although he drank less than before, Alice noticed that his tolerance for alcohol was diminished and its effect was often unpredictable. For the first time, Albert made an attempt at maintenance drinking—just enough to forestall withdrawal—and he regained his ability to behave without incident at social functions.

To Albert's relief, there were no rumors or innuendos whispered in his ears about his wife or daughters. Natalie, who was a true cause for worry, had been successfully discreet. As for the Dreyfus affair, which had distressed him so much the previous fall, it was no longer of concern. Dreyfus would have his day in court in August, and the French government seemed to have regained the upper hand over the anarchists and socialists of whom he so disapproved. Reassured after only a few weeks stay, Albert once again left his family in Paris and returned to America.

VIII

A French Salon

A lice remained on the Right Bank following Albert's departure in 1899. There was no reason to return to the Villa des Dames now that Whistler was gone from her life. His polite notes of regret when she invited him to visit her at her new home only confirmed that their relationship was over. Alice knew that Whistler hated the social life and even though she extended him her company, she knew he would never come. The scrawling handwriting of his note cards reminded her of impressionistic landscapes and she framed them and hung them in her bedroom. They were the last thing she saw before she turned off the light to go to sleep.

Alice turned one of the bedrooms into a studio and surrounded herself with drawings and paintings in various states of completion. Her tall, plain wooden easel was the focal point of the room and she moved it around to catch the changing light. She began painting in early morning and continued until the long shadows of the afternoon stopped her. Then she would lay aside her pastels and brushes, wash the chalk smudges from her face, push any stray wisps of hair back into place, and don a sumptuous silk robe patterned after a Japanese kimono. With a touch of rouge to cheeks and lips she was ready to join her circle of friends already assembled in the first-floor drawing room.

Alice's salon centered on the arts. Carefully chosen guests had in common not only love of the arts, but the ability to discuss them creatively and intelligently. As Alice moved about the room greeting people, she was constantly sensitive to the ebb and flow of conversation and made sure that no one was left out. If a discussion threatened to become too heated, she quickly diffused it for she was well aware that the success of her salon depended upon her talent to draw out the best in this group of people who understood that the art of talking about art was an essential ingredient of the art of living.

SELF-PORTRAIT IN PAINTING ROBE, 1896 Oil on canvas, 42¼ x 29⅜ in. (107.3 x 74.6 cm) *By the mid-1890s, Alice saw herself as a serious painter. This self-portrait was exhibited at the 1896 Cincinnati Portrait show along with her portrait by Hubert Vos.*

Most of those present were artists, including Americans John White Alexander, William Merritt Chase, and Frederick MacMonnies and Frenchmen Carolus-Duran, Edmund Francois Aman-Jean, and Lucien Levy-Dhurmer. Toward the end of her stay, the Swedish painter and etcher, Anders Zorn, joined the group. Two women artists were also among the regulars: Olga Boznanska from Poland and Swiss artist Ottilie Roederstein.[1] A few patrons of the arts attended, such as her old friend Phoebe Hearst from Washington, wife of newspaper baron William Randolph Hearst, and Jules Cambon, the former French Ambassador to the United

States. Natalie and Laura often attended; Natalie's quick mind and sharp wit enlivened conversations while Laura's serious questions often led to insightful observations on the part of those present. Among the younger set were: Eva Palmer, who was modeling for Aman-Jean and studying acting; Violet and Mary Shillito, former Cincinnati childhood friends; and the delicate Anglo-American poet Pauline Tarn, who would gain recognition under the name of Renée Vivian. When Will Morrow was in town he would stop by to see Natalie, whom he still referred to humorously as his fiancée.

Now that Whistler was no longer present to critique her work, Alice turned to the artists who came to her salon, and frequently part of the evening was spent looking over her latest endeavor. She particularly relied on the opinion of Alexander, Aman-Jean, and Levy-Dhurmer, all of whom were successful practitioners of the Symbolist style of painting.

Alice was most familiar with Symbolism through the popularity of Art Nouveau, which had taken many of its forms and images from the Symbolist iconography. She was particularly taken with the peacock symbol, one of the most ubiquitous of the movement's images. She commissioned a jeweled peacock feather dog collar from Millerio dits Meller Fabricants, a firm noted for the beauty and quality of its Art Nouveau jewelry. She explored the same symbol in her painting *Woman with Peacock*, which she based in part on Aman-Jean's 1895 painting *Girl with a Peacock*. Her painting's sensual linearity, however, was more reminiscent of Alexander's 1897 painting *Isabel and the Pot of Basil*, although the conscious harmonic value of its greens and blues derived from Whistler's style.

As Alice began to incorporate it into her art, Symbolism's challenge to traditional French art was already on the wane.[2] By 1899, what had begun as a conscious attempt at artistic reform was now part of art vernacular as evidenced by the broad popularity of Art Nouveau arts and crafts. In reality, the energy of the Symbolist movement had already begun to fade by the death in 1898 of its best-known poet Stèphane Mallarmé and of two of its leading artists, Puvis de Chavannes and Gustav Moreau.

Symbolism first came to the fore in England in 1848 with the publication of John Ruskin's *Modern Painters* and John Keats's poetry, both of which influenced a small group of artists, writers, and critics to form the Pre-Raphaelite Brotherhood. The Symbolist movement in France and in England was as much a literary and philosophical movement as it was a rebellion against the accepted artistic norms promulgated by the academicians who ran the Salon and L'École des Beaux-Arts. The Symbolist ranks included not only visual artists such as Odilon Redon, Paul Gauguin, Maurice Denis, Pierre Bonnard, and Henri Fantin-Latour, but poets such as Charles Baudelaire, Arthur Rimbaud, Pierre Louys, Paul Verlaine, and André Gide. There were also Symbolist musicians such as Claude

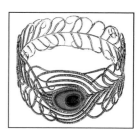

ALICE'S JEWELED COLLAR, 1900
Mellerio dits Meller
18 karat gold, enamel, diamonds, 4½ diam. x 2⅜ high in. (11.4 diam. x 6.0 high cm)
The jeweled, peacock-feather dog collar commissioned by Alice at the turn of the century is today considered one of the finest extant examples of Art Nouveau jewelry.

Debussy and Gabriel Fauré, as well as the playwright and poet Maurice Maeterlinck.

Their quest was for a multidisciplined aesthetic that would go beyond realism to reveal the hidden regions of the mind. In the 1880s, Charles Morice, the founder of the first Symbolist review, set forth the basic premise of the Symbolist movement: "Art...is essentially subjective. The appearance of things is only a symbol which it is the artist's task to interpret. Things have no truth except in that; they have only an inner truth."[3]

Although Alice grasped the basic philosophy, she never pretended to be an aesthetician. Symbolism's emphasis on the imagination and the interrelationship of the arts initially fascinated her and its inherent theatricality sustained her interest. Through Symbolism she came to understand that the essence of portraiture was not merely to capture a likeness, but to illuminate the inner spirit. As Carolus-Duran had strengthened her drawing and Whistler her painting, now the works of Alexander, Aman-Jean, and Levy-Dhurmer provided a foundation for her aesthetic.

LAURA, C. 1900
Laura often participated in the intellectual discussions among influential writers and artists at her mother's salon in Paris.

The appeal of Alexander's work was its overt theatricality as well as the linear stylistic cues taken from Japanese prints. Aman-Jean's work, on the other hand, was inspired more by Pre-Raphaelite images. In his paintings he sought to capture the psyche of his contemporary sitters as portrayed against a vortex of swirling arabesques. As she attempted to dissect Aman-Jean's style, she was most intrigued by the way in which he placed his subjects against lush backgrounds that suggested woodlands or garlanded bowers. These backgrounds seemed not only to enfold and caress the souls of the women who gazed out pensively from his canvases, but to also push the subject's psychic energy beyond the boundaries of the canvas.

Alice's painting *Woman with Peacock* was an unabashedly Symbolist painting in the Art Nouveau style and remarkably successful. Having painted in this overtly decorative style, however, she now chose to leave it, preferring the less meticulous, more obviously romantic swirling brushwork found in the oils of Aman-Jean.[4] Of the three Symbolist artists, however, it was Levy-Dhurmer whose work most influenced the direction Alice's art would take. He

Woman and Peacock,
c. 1900
Oil on canvas, 28¾ x
46½ in. (73 x 118.1 cm)
*This striking study in blues
and greens was strongly
influenced by the flowing line
of John White Alexander.*

Opposite:
Lucifer, 1902
Pastel on canvas, 30 x
25 in. (76.2 x 63.5 cm)
*Natalie modeled for this com-
panion piece to* Medusa.

worked primarily in pastel and used its soft, evasive edges to create dreamy images based on mythic literary themes.

Alice did not, however, spend all of her time during this prolific period copying other painter's styles. While copying was the quickest and easiest way for her to grasp another artist's style, she was well aware that it put her own individuality at risk. As a counterbalance to her predilection to absorb the work of other artists into her own paintings, she began to work closely with painters whose styles were far removed from her own. Ottilie Roederstein and Olga Boznanska were traditional portraitists and used oil as their primary medium. They both approached portraiture with an academic precision learned during their earlier studies in Germany. Of the two, Olga had most recently arrived in Paris, but at thirty-three she was not a novice. She had already won a gold medal for portraiture at the 1893 Viennese Exposition. At forty Ottilie was not only Alice's contemporary, but they shared a mutual friendship with Elizabeth Nourse. Like Alice, she pursued studies with Carolus-Duran and Jean-Jacques Henner. Ottilie's reputation as Switzerland's leading artist preceded her arrival in Paris and within a short period of time she was exhibited at the Salon and became an associate member of the Société Nationale des Beaux-Arts.

Alice offered her studio to Ottilie and Olga as a place where they could set up their easels and share a model (often the ubiquitous Carmen), or if one were unavailable, pose for each other. As the three women worked together they developed a close camaraderie. When Alice told them Natalie had asked her to provide illustrations for her first book of poetry, they shared her elation.

LOVE POEMS

Natalie's first book was to contain an introduction and at least thirty-five poems, all of which were to be written in French. It was scheduled for release in late spring of 1900 by Paul Ollendorff for his Société d'Éditions Littéraires et Artistiques. Alice's enthusiasm for the project came not only from the prospect of working closely with Natalie, but from the challenge of translating the symbols found in Natalie's poems into drawings. Taking her direction from Natalie's dedication of one poem to the late Symbolist poet Stèphane Mallarmé, Alice created four pastel portraits for the book. What seemed particularly serendipitous to Alice was that Mallarmé had not only been a friend of Whistler's, but an influence upon him as well.

NATALIE, C. 1900
From childhood Natalie was fascinated by Oscar Wilde's story of the Little Prince, and at the turn of the century she was photographed frequently in the costume

Both men had used their respective disciplines to explore the idea that art was best expressed through nuance and implication. While Mallarmé strove to create a music of language through symbolic images, Whistler's "Nocturnes" and "Symphonies" were symbolically conveyed by tonality and formal arrangements. What Mallarmé wrote of his poetic ideal was equally true for Whistler's art.

> To name an object is to destroy three-quarters of our pleasure in a poem—the joy of guessing, step by step. The ideal is to suggest the objects. We derive the most from the mystery that constitutes the symbol when we evoke the object step by step in order to portray a state of mind.[5]

Alice might not have been quite so enthusiastic about the project if she had understood the real nature of Natalie's book. It was not the project of a Victorian innocent. When Natalie asked Alice to illustrate her chapbook, she talked about style not substance. Natalie's nine-page preface, whimsi-

NATALIE AND EVA,
c. 1897
*Natalie (seated) and Eva
Palmer (kneeling) strike a
theatrical pose symbolizing
their love for one another.*

cally subtitled "for those who never read them,"
dealt almost entirely with her manipulation of
French poetic conventions of rhyme, syllabica-
tion, and versification. She explained her
audacity in offering "French verses to France"
by stating that, "In short, nothing about me
must surprise you. I am American." What
Natalie did not allude to in the preface, nor
mention to her mother, was that the majority of
the sonnets were thinly disguised love poems to
the women in her life. They were certainly
much more than the experiments in classical
French poetic form she claimed in her preface.

If Alice harbored any suspicions, Natalie
successfully put them to rest. When Alice wondered who to use to pose for the four poems she
was to illustrate, Natalie provided her with the
models. Three of them were Natalie's lovers,
but Alice remained none the wiser. When
Natalie was questioned about this years later,
she replied simply: "My mother loved to do portraits of my friends, who were so lovely."[6]

Alice looked first to the pastels of Levy-
Dhurmer for stylistic inspiration. Unlike the
popular drawings of the Pre-Raphaelite Brotherhood such as the work of Aubrey Beardsley,
or the concurrent Art Nouveau decorative
objects with their emphasis on linear
arabesques, the soft diffusion generated by Levy-Dhurmer's pastels
inspired Alice in her transposition of the substance of Natalie's poems into
a visual medium. Representative of her efforts was the drawing for "Rien
ne te peut toucher et rien ne t'emeut" [Nothing can move you and nothing
disturbs you], a poem Natalie dedicated to her cousin Ellen Goin.

The poetic image Natalie developed was of a malevolent water nymph
who floated beguilingly in the center of a watery vortex, and by her "joyless
laugh/Seeks what hovers and summons it for prey...." Her breasts were
"flowers in full bloom,/Cradling the poison of their longing for milk/Like
lotuses on a stagnant pond." The pastel facing it focuses on the head and
breasts. The head is turned slightly toward the viewer and the blond hair
mingles with the watery dark marine blues and grays of the background.
The white bodice of her dress is arranged in folds over her breasts to

WATERLILY, 1900
Pastel on paper, 16 x
21⅝ in. (40.6 x 54.9 cm)
*This pastel was one of the
illustrations Alice created
for Natalie's first book of
poetry. The model was
Ellen Goin.*

Opposite:
CERES, C. 1910
Pastel on canvas, 18⅛ x
14⅞ in. (46 x 37.8 cm)
*Alice frequently created
pastels as illustrations for
theatrical events. Ceres
appeared on the cover of a
program of classic dance
given at Studio House on
April 30, 1910.*

resemble lotus flowers floating on a pond. Underlying the tranquility of the watered image is a sense of menace—the slightly parted lips seductive and unsmiling.

In addition to the four pastels used in the chapbook, Alice later executed one other portrait, a sketch of Natalie inspired by the first line of Natalie's poem "De Moi-Meme." Drawn on mottled gray charcoal paper, it shows only Natalie's pensive face framed by her mane of flowing blonde hair. At the bottom Alice wrote "Sombre sans ennuis et triste sans distresse" [Somber without worry and sad without distress]. The sketch contains no artifice; it is a compelling portrait that echoes the central question of Natalie's verbal self-portrait: "What's wrong? I don't know, but I feel it deeply."[7]

Once the pastels were completed, Alice gave little thought to the slim chapbook other than her delight in its publication. She was far too engrossed in her own work and always residing in the back of her mind was the simple fact of the transitory nature of her sojourn in Paris. Eventually, Albert would summon her to return to a way of life she now knew was untenable—to a marriage that was a mistake from the first. Their differences were irreconcilable; their approach to life's exigencies so opposite. She reveled in life's adventures; he was wedded to the status quo. She welcomed change; even the threat of change was enough to send him into a rage and to the nearest liquor bottle.

Alice received weekly letters from Albert. They were short and dealt mainly with money. His usual complaint was that she and Natalie were trying to bankrupt him and in each he threatened to return to Paris to take charge. For the time being Alice knew this was unlikely; his dislike of Paris was too strong and only a crisis would precipitate his immediate arrival. Meanwhile, she began to plan the means by which she might gain control of her life following her inevitable return to Washington.

Although a free thinker in many areas, Alice did not believe in divorce. During what was now a two-year sojourn, she had grown stronger and wiser. Drawing upon the strength and wisdom acquired during her two-year separation from Albert, she began to contemplate her options. She realized the only way to keep her sanity upon her return was to make her mark as an artist in Washington. She was honest enough about her work to know that Alexander and Aman-Jean were not merely flattering her when they suggested she consider a one-woman show.

Other ideas also came to her as she recalled some of her conversations with Whistler about how badly Americans needed to be educated about art. Moreover, she was fascinated by the heated arguments she overheard on her visits to the Louvre. These were not high-flown aesthetic discussions among Parisian elite, rather they were intense critiques by workmen who chose to spend their lunchtime looking at art. In her wildest dreams, she could not imagine Americans of similar station discussing art with the intensity and perspicacity of those ordinary Parisians.

A whirlwind tour of several European capitals taken during the summer with her Washington friend Juliet Thompson provoked other ideas; it served to reaffirm the paucity of Washington's cultural life when compared with opportunities available in Europe. She realized how limited were the conversations held round her dinner table at Rhode Island Avenue when contrasted with the intellectual complexity of the subjects discussed at her weekly salon in Paris.

As Alice searched her mind for someone who might begin the process of bringing culture to her nation's capital, no name stood out. None, that is, except her own. It was time for her to be Samuel Pike's daughter. He had let nothing stand in the way of fulfilling his dream of enriching the cultural life of Cincinnati with an opera house. What stopped her from doing the same for Washington?

The more Alice thought about it, the more excited she became about being the person who would finally make culture flourish in America's capital. She realized, however, that the "why" was much easier to articulate than the "how." She would, of course, need Albert's permission to undertake any large project, but how could he refuse if she presented her case with a solemn promise to do nothing to embarrass him. For the present, however, the "how" could wait; she had no intention of returning to Washington until actually summoned. Paris was far too stimulating and she still had so much to learn.

DISCOVERED BY ALBERT

Alice probably blushed in amusement when she remembered the evening Natalie and Renée Vivien took her to one of Madame Saint-Marceau's Friday evenings on the Boulevard Malesherbes near the Alexanders. The featured performer was Isadora Duncan, accompanied on the piano by Maurice Ravel, in a program of interpretations of Chopin's waltzes and preludes. Few Americans were invited to Madame's salons. When Isadora heard American women were sitting in the front row, she whispered to Ravel to play the "Star-Spangled Banner" and improvised a dance for it on the spot. It was the ending of the dance that was memorable. As the song reached its peak, Isadora lifted her arms in salute, the hem of her Greek tunic clutched in her upraised hands and revealed, inadvertantly, that she was totally nude beneath her costume. Alice turned beet red. She whispered to Natalie, "Darling do you see what I see?" Natalie, choking with laughter, loudly repeated her question so that everyone could hear it.[8]

Shocked or not, Isadora's style of dance intrigued Alice. Her choreography was so different from the familiar movement of ballet. The dances were imaginative, and Alice recognized the possibilities of a dance form whose simple, understated gesticulation might make it possible for previously untrained dancers to perform. Alice began to envision a way to raise enormous amounts of money for charity, while at the same time painlessly introducing staid Washingtonians to a new art form. She could create a set suggesting a Greek ruin, dress a group of Washington belles in diaphanous robes, and show them a few simple steps. Dim lighting would cover a multitude of sins, and with the Marine Band playing exotic sounding music in the background, success was assured. Alice filed away these ideas for future consideration.

Alice paid little attention to Natalie's comings

RENÉE VIVIEN, 1900
In 1900 Natalie fell in love with Renée.

MRS. FLEMING NEWBOLD,
C. 1906
Pastel on paper, 40¾ x
22⅝ in. (103.5 x 57.5 cm)
Alice did many portraits of
prominent Washington
socialites who appeared in
her theatricals. As a young
woman, Mrs. Newbold played
Rosamond in Alice's Dream
of Queen Elizabeth.

Opposite:
SELF-PORTRAIT WITH HAT
AND VEIL, C. 1900
Pastel on paper, 25⅜ x
19¼ in. (64.5 x 48.9 cm)
By the turn of the century,
Alice was an accomplished
portraitist capturing not only
the visage, but the spirit of the
sitter. Here we see Alice as she
saw herself—confident and
self-assured of her talent.

and goings. She tried to ignore Natalie's acquaintance with Liane de Pougy, accepting as gospel Natalie's explanation that her only interest in Liane was to save the sophisticated courtesan from a life of sin. Instead, she encouraged Natalie to bring the well-brought up Renée to their home as frequently as possible because she was enchanted with Renée's delicate beauty, which contrasted so vividly with Natalie's robust physique. She sketched a portrait of Renée that emphasized her ethereal nature, not realizing that this quality came as much from opiates as it did from poetic sensitivity.

LIANE DE POUGY AND NATALIE, C. 1899
Natalie told Alice that she wanted to save the courtesan Liane de Pougy from a life of sin. In reality, Natalie was having an affair with Liane.

When Natalie traveled to England to meet Liane, purportedly to rescue her from sin, Alice wished her well. What neither of them knew was that a friend of Albert's saw Liane and Natalie together and wrote to Albert describing in detail what kind of relationship it really was. Albert immediately wrote to Natalie and demanded she return home at once. By return mail Natalie promised to behave herself. Although he should have known better, Albert chose to believe her and sent a conciliatory letter to her. Natalie's reply to him contained little to set his mind at rest.

> I have a heart, and am deeply touched—put me in the place I deserve though? Only God can do that, and the one 'in which I belong' you cannot judge what that is. Ever since I remember you, your one ambition for us was petty and worldly. Even religion was made a sort of social duty. One should go to church because it 'looked well, or because people would think it strange if we didn't.' You must understand how petty, how ugly our whole bringing up was. You showed me at the age of twelve all that marriage means—the jealousness, the scum, the tyrannies—nothing was hidden from me. I was even made a witness when still a mere child of the atrocious and lamentable consequences an uncontrolled temper has when visited on a then good and surely kindly woman. I hope you will not make me repeat twofold the harm you have done me, by being doubly insolent and cruel toward my mother—Seeing all this made me lose faith in you—respect for you. I no longer felt myself your daughter. Is any one fit to guide another who cannot even control his own passions? But Aunt Agnes and Lulu [Albert's sister and niece] tell me how thoughtful and lovely you were when a young man, how kind and even tender, and now

that your Xmas letter has come I can well believe it—For this shows me a glimpse of your better self—the self that has been put to sleep—hushed? stifled? killed? All why—all why? For these few soft words I love you, Father dear, and not to worry you I willingly give up seeing the woman.[9]

Much relieved, Albert chose to stay in Washington and pursue his bachelor existence rather than rush to Paris to confront Natalie. Part of the reason may have been that during Alice's absence, Albert worked out a particularly lucrative rental agreement for the Rhode Island Avenue house with Elihu Root, McKinley's Secretary of War and was comfortably settled at the Metropolitan Club. There he drank as much as he wanted, entertained lavishly, and knew that the night porter would make sure he was safely tucked in his bed.

Albert's feelings of bonhomie for his family ended abruptly when he picked up a review of Natalie's newly published chapbook, *Quelques Portraits—Sonnets de Femmes*, entitled "Sappho Sings in Washington." It did not matter to him that the reviewer, Henri Pene du Bois, praised her efforts highly and called her "a consummate artist" with a "miraculous power to write French verse."[10] It did not even matter that he did not have his own copy to read. He knew immediately what kind of poems they were and most embarrassing to him was the fact that Alice appeared to be equally culpable. How dare she provide the illustrations for such a scandalous book? This time they had both gone too far.

Albert stormed into Paris and purchased not only all the remaining copies of Natalie's book, but also its plates. With a decisiveness that had become increasingly unusual for him in the past few years, he swept up both women and moved them to Dinard, France, while he wrote ahead to have the Bar Harbor cottage readied for their imminent arrival. On July 7 Natalie, Alice, and Albert boarded the *Saint Louis* for America. Laura was exonerated by Albert and allowed to remain in Europe for the summer. Whether or not Alice and Natalie would ever be permitted to return to Paris was a question Albert refused to answer.

IX
New Independence

I t was two years since the Barneys last visit to Bar Harbor. In 1898 they led a social life, but in the summer of 1900 all was quiet at Ban-y-Bryn. For Albert, the uneventfulness of the summer was a relief after the emotional upheavals of the spring. Alice and Natalie were safely where he wanted them—under his thumb. For the first time in several years, he felt free to enjoy the Bar Harbor golf links and to spend the long summer evenings sipping brandy on the veranda overlooking the bay. Alice passed the days in her tower studio, while Natalie roamed Mount Desert on horseback. Natalie kept a small writing tablet in her pocket and jotted down her thoughts and new poems. As one day followed another, Albert continued to refuse to discuss returning to Paris in the fall.

In mid-July, the necessity for a decision by Albert was thrust upon him when he began to receive letters from Washington friends containing clippings from the *Washington Mirror*, a slick little gossip magazine. Its contents made clear that Alice's absence had not made some Washington society hearts grow fonder. No particular sins of omission or commission by Alice were cited; that was not the *Mirror*'s style. Instead, there were vague references to "some very grave mistakes in the early days of her residence...mistakes which were naturally to be looked for in a woman of her origin...."[1] Alice could not confront the real issues: she was Jewish and her father made his fortune in whiskey. Alice might have found the columns laughable if she were not so aware of their effect on their future in Washington society. When combined with the scandal caused by Natalie's book, retaining their status in Washington society seem doomed.

Although Alice never hid her background, she never went out of her way to publicize it, knowing full well the small-mindedness of many of her peers. She was aware of her Jewish heritage, but considered herself Christian. She was a communicant in good-standing at Saint John's Episcopal Church, one of the Diocese of Washington's wealthiest and most elite parishes. Both her daughters were baptized there and Albert was a member of the Washington Cathedral's initial building committee.

Her father's history as a distiller, however, was almost as problematic. The temperance movement was rapidly gaining strength and power. Moreover, Albert's drinking did not make it any easier for her to maintain her equanimity about the source of her wealth. She was savvy enough to know, however, that what really lay behind the articles in the *Mirror* was

SELF-PORTRAIT IN REPOSE,
c. 1906
Pastel on paper, 28½ x
22½ in. (72.4 x 57.2 cm)
Alice's friends thought of
her as a person in constant
motion. In this reflective
self-portrait, Alice reveals
a side of herself that others
seldom saw.

the jealousy of society matrons who envied Alice her success. Typically, Alice was more sorry for those unknown persons than for herself.[2]

In one sense, however, she did take the articles seriously. The comments about her Jewish heritage were clearly anti-Semitic, and she knew only too well the difficulties caused in France by the Dreyfus affair. Washington was known for its democratic acceptance of just about anyone into society. The publication of ethnic slurs marked a change in attitudes, paralleling the development of New York City's rigid social stratification. The reason for the change was simple enough: Washington was about to print its first social register, the only purpose of which was to define exclusivity. The compilers of Washington's Social Register looked to the long established New York Social Register for criteria; one of its leading unwritten rules was that Jews were excluded.[3]

That rule had not always been the case in New York. In earlier years, the majority of prestigious men's clubs claimed prominent Jews among their charter members. By the mid-1880s, however, their sons were being blackballed, and the long established and extremely wealthy German-Jewish families were excluded not only from the social register, but from the guest list devised by Ward McAllister for his patroness, Mrs. Astor. Because only four hundred persons could attend a party at Mrs. Astor's, the number four hundred became synonymous with exclusivity. When the names on the list were published in the *New York Times*, "Our Crowd," as the wealthiest Jews called themselves, discovered they were no longer part of society, even though the fortunes of such families as the Guggenheims, the Loebs, the Lehmans, or the Schiffs clearly rivaled the Vanderbilts and the Astors. Their ostracism was so complete that even their most outrageous scandals went unreported in New York's weekly society broadside *Town Topics*.[4] How soon Washington would follow suit depended upon how successful Washington's establishment (or "cave dwellers" as they were known) were in making its social register conform to New York's rules. The slurs against Alice seemed advance notice that the winnowing process had begun.

Alice was upset, but Albert was beside himself. He added one more resentment against Alice to his growing list of how she maligned his good name. He refused to either forget or forgive her part in the publication of Natalie's book. Not only was he sullied by marriage to a woman with a sordid past, all his hopes and dreams for social prominence were being destroyed.

As his anger mounted, so did his blood pressure and his drinking. It was a near fatal combination. In mid-July Albert suffered a heart attack while playing golf. He spent the next two months in bed nursed by the very per-

Page 150:
WOMAN CLOTHED WITH THE SUN, C. 1901
Pastel on canvas, 77¾ x 36 in. (197.5 x 91.4 cm)
The critics did not like this close to life-size pastel based on a verse from the Book of Revelation: "A great portent appeared in heaven; a woman clothed with the sun."

Page 151:
BABYLON, C. 1901
Pastel on canvas, 78 x 36 in. (198.1 x 91.4 cm)
This pastel was created as a companion piece to Woman Clothed with the Sun, *and was inspired by a verse in the Book of Revelation: "On her forehead was written a name of mystery: 'Babylon the great, mother of harlots and of earth's abominations."*

ALBERT CLIFFORD BARNEY,
1900
Ottilie Roederstein
Oil on canvas, 38¾ x
25¼ in. (98.4 X 64.1 cm)
*In a portrait commissioned
by Alice, Ottilie portrayed
Albert as an elegant, but
aging dandy.*

son he believed had ruined his life. When the doctors prescribed a change in scene, Albert quickly hustled Alice and Natalie back to Europe, bypassing Washington altogether.

They returned to the house on Avenue Victor Hugo, but did no entertaining. The only visitors were Alice's friends, her fellow artists, whom she invited up to her cluttered studio to help select the pastels and oils that would make the strongest presentation for the one-person show she planned to offer to the Corcoran Gallery of Art. To help Albert pass the time in the city he so disliked, Alice commissioned Ottilie Roederstein to paint his portrait. In the three-quarter-length oil, he is shown in full evening dress—an elegant, aging dandy wearing a brown fur opera coat draped over his shoulders. Working beside her, Alice also created a portrait depicting Albert in profile and revealing all of his fifty-one year. By the end of the sitting, Albert felt well enough to travel alone to Nauheim, Germany, and the healing properties of its saline thermal waters.

Alice immediately resumed lessons with Carolus-Duran and worked toward completion of an entry for the 1901 salon. There were no interruptions; Laura was in Egypt and Natalie was in England, carefully chaperoned by a Miss Colshoune, whom she heartily disliked but accepted for the moment.[5]

Albert returned to Paris at Christmas, and in January 1901 he and Alice sailed to the United States. They stayed at the Waldorf Astoria in New York because Albert still was unable to face Washington gossip. Albert remained weak, but he was strong enough to berate Alice constantly. The list of her sins was long, but always at the top was her failure to stop Natalie from publishing her book of sonnets.

Alice had never felt more alone than those first few months in New York. Daily, Albert reminded her of the evil in Natalie's character, which must have come from Alice. On her side, Alice felt betrayed and, for once, her equanimity left her. She now acknowledged what she previously denied—Natalie had been deceitful toward her—and it left her sick at heart. In late January 1901, she wrote Natalie, telling her that she had sinned against law and mankind. "Your poems," she wrote, "were the worst condemnation, for there is not the slightest loophole. You have closed every escape." By publishing them, Alice wrote, Natalie had "done the worst and that to a good honest name and a very sad and unhappy one. An unhappy woman, your mother is."[6]

Unexpectedly, Alice's tortuous condemnation of Natalie's conduct forged a bond between the two women that had not existed before. Instead of tearing them apart, Alice's letter was the beginning of a new relationship based upon open expression of feelings. Alice let Natalie see she was not always an even-tempered saint, and Natalie no longer pretended to be something she was not. As the year progressed, Natalie's letters to Alice became both more challenging and more open.

> And you, where are you little one? Putting up with the tyranny of A.C.B. so far as to vegetate in the Waldorf? Art with such impediments I should think impossible, and anything but the right sort of atmosphere for any works beyond the exertion of reading the newspapers or standing in the glary agitation of the corridors having sterile chats with adequate and effete individuals. I know and fear your theory that nothing is worth a row, but if thereby you were to gain unfretted peace?[7]

What Natalie did not understand was that Alice's art was already her path to "unfretted peace." It was her secret to the equanimity Natalie found so puzzling.

By the end of March, Alice found herself

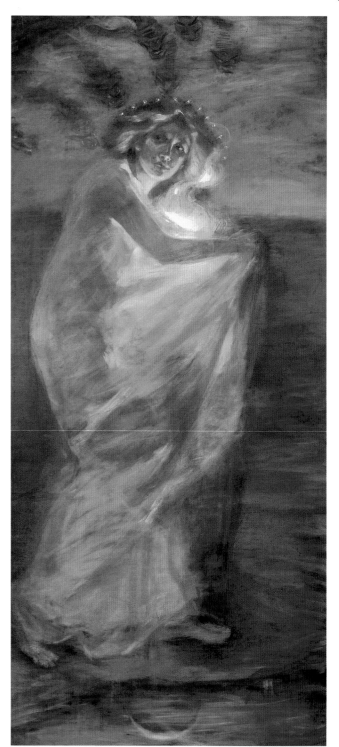

hounding the mail waiting for an answer to her letter to Frank McGuire, Director of the Corcoran Gallery of Art:

> Do you want an exhibition of my works? I have fifteen or twenty (most of them rather small) which have been liked by John Alexander, Zorn, Rex Harrison, and Carolus-Duran—and other of my painter friends. If you wish to show them I will have A. Zorn pick out the very best of them and send them to the gallery—where you may have them for as long or as short a time as you wish....If you will be good enough to let me know your wishes, I'll collect my paintings and take a count of them—should you want my things.[8]

McGuire's reply was in the affirmative, although he was unable to set an exact date. The Corcoran was closing June 15 for extensive remodeling and he was unsure when it would be ready to reopen.

With their house rented through the summer, Albert was able to further delay their return to Washington. Alice took a studio at the Carnegie Building on West Fifty-Seventh Street and began two of her most ambitious pastels. Inspired by verses from the Book of Revelations, both are almost life-size pastels rendered in a Symbolist style and using her niece Ellen Goin as the model. The first pastel depicts a woman in a diaphanous, golden gown, which modestly reveals her nude figure. The moon is at her feet and her flowing hair is crowned with twelve stars. The second picture portrays Ellen as the Whore of Babylon. Alice drew her seated on a throne with a slave at her feet, costumed in a yellow strapless wrap and a black Egyptian-style, shoulder-length wig.

As challenging and engrossing as the two pastels were, Alice's personal life kept intruding into the sanctity of her studio. For almost five years, she and Albert had managed to go their own way within certain well-defined limits, even when occupying the same home. In the close quarters of their hotel suite, however, there was no escaping each other. Even in her studio, the image of Albert's deteriorating visage arose before her mind's eye. Studio photographs taken of him during their stay at the Waldorf show a man grown old before his years. Whatever gains were made at Nauheim disappeared with his unabated drinking. Alice's concern was so great that she wrote both daughters to come to Bar Harbor for the summer. As an added inducement to Natalie, Alice invited Eva Palmer and Renée Vivian to come with her.

Albert continued to believe himself a man beset with troubles. Most were in his own head, but some were not. Shortly after arriving in New York, Albert was informed by the Elihu Roots that they were pulling out of their two-year lease on the Rhode Island Avenue house. From the *Washington Mirror* the Barneys learned that the Roots had found the Barney home so uncomfortably furnished that they had thrown out much of its "ecclesiastical" furniture and other "medieval truck" and replaced it with modern chairs and scores of pillows.

Soon thereafter, Albert was contacted by Alice's brother and sister, Lawrence and Hessie, who voiced fears about the security of the Pike estate. They were afraid that Nettie, with whom Ellen lived, was using undue influence to get their mother to change her will in the Goin's favor. They demanded that he, as the estate's trustee, fight for Alice's and their interests. Albert, however, no longer had any fight left in him and he resigned as trustee. His action was yet another indication to Alice that he was failing. Whatever his other flaws, Albert always had been a tenacious guardian of her inheritance. This unexpected abdication of power by Albert was followed by others. When Albert proved incapable of ordering Ban-y-Bryn opened for the summer or cabling money for steamer tickets to Laura and Natalie, Alice found herself taking charge.

Her preparations for her fall exhibition were harried as she added Albert's duties to her own. Before leaving New York she invited Anders Zorn, the popular Swedish painter and etcher she met briefly in Paris the preceding fall, to her studio to help her make the final selections. By late April the crated paintings were on their way, including the recently completed *Woman Clothed with the Sun* and the partially finished *Babylon*.

Now that Alice was in charge, the summer of 1901 was far different than the prior year's. In many ways this summer was more reminiscent of the Barneys' social whirl of 1897, although on a less grand scale. Alice gave private theatricals and invited select summer inhabitants to *fête champêtres*,

THE BARNEY'S PICTURE
GALLERY, C. 1895
*Alice always hated the pic-
ture gallery at 1626 Rhode
Island Avenue, N.W., as
it reflected Albert's taste,
not hers.*

or old-fashioned picnics. She now had an opportunity to practice educating her American peers in the arts as she had been inspired to do while in Paris. While Natalie spent her time frolicking with her friends Eva and Renée, Alice was in her element. East Coast newspapers followed her every move, with occasional swipes such as the *Mirror*'s declaration that Alice "ended up by all odds the favorite" in the competition to decide which woman at Bar Harbor revealed the most decolletage.[9]

An abrupt tearing of the social fabric came early on the afternoon of Friday, September 6, during a public reception in the Temple of Music at the Buffalo Pan-American Exposition. At approximately 1 p.m., Leon Czolgosz stepped up onto the platform ostensibly to shake hands with President McKinley. Instead, as the president extended his hand to him, Czolgosz fired two shots into McKinley's chest and stomach. Eight days later McKinley died of gangrene, and Theodore Roosevelt was sworn in as president. At Bar Harbor, where many summer residents were from the nation's capital, cottages were hastily closed so their inhabitants could return to Washington in time for the official ceremonies on September 17 when McKinley's body would lie in state in the Capitol rotunda.

Natalie, who had an aversion to anything even remotely connected to death or funerals begged to go with Eva to Bryn Mawr, taking Renée with her. Natalie told them she planned to audit classes and come to Washington at Christmas. This was acceptable to Alice who had more than enough to attend to in Washington without worrying about Natalie. Moreover, Laura was expected to arrive shortly from Paris, and, with her organizational

MARSHLANDS AT SUNDOWN, c. 1911
Pastel on fiberboard, 14 x 19⅜ in. (35.6 x 49.2 cm)
Of the few landscapes Alice executed, this pleine-aire rendering is one of her most striking. It shows the influence of Frank Edwin Scott in its muted tones.

Opposite:
THE FUR COAT, 1900
Oil on canvas, 22⅛ x 18¼ in. (56.2 x 46.4 cm)
At fifty-one Albert was still handsome man, but his drinking had begun to take its toll.

skills, she would be of much greater help to Alice than Natalie. That fall Natalie took a literature class, Eva pursued her Greek studies, and Renée, fortifying herself with a mixture of gin and chloral, wrote poems in the local cemetery.

When the Barneys arrived in Washington, they found the buildings on Pennsylvania Avenue flanking the route of the funeral procession from the White House to the Capitol draped in black. On that gray Tuesday, the city's church bells tolled as rain fell on the thousands of people who lined the street to view the funeral cortege of the amiable, popular McKinley and to catch a glimpse of his colorful replacement. Theodore Roosevelt was as unlike William McKinley as the twentieth century was from the nineteenth. With McKinley's death the presidency and the nation's capital would never be the same. At forty-two, Roosevelt was, and still remains, the youngest man to accede to the presidency.

FACING WASHINGTON

For that fall, however, Washington seemed more interested in the activities of Alice Pike Barney than in the new policies of the president. As Secretary of War and Mrs. Root had vacated 1626 Rhode Island Avenue in June, Alice moved back into the Barney home. The Roots had taken with them their modern chairs and multitudinous pillows and left behind a shambles for Alice to deal with. Amidst all the myriad housekeeping tasks, Alice found time to write to McGuire requesting a meeting to look through her work stored at the Corcoran: "I've just returned to find so many things to be done to my home that I dare not yet become interested in my exhibition."[10] She also dashed off a note to C. Powell Minnigerode, Clerk of the Corcoran, directing him to give the enclosed money to the laborers who uncrated her paintings because she had been so long in Europe that she no longer knew what was a proper tip in America.[11]

Alice's first one-person exhibition opened on November 2 and ran through the fourteenth. Her private four o'clock reception was described in great detail because it also marked the reopening of the Corcoran. Of the fifty-five works in the show, only two had been exhibited before in Washington. Although two small landscapes were included, the majority were portraits whose subjects ranged from children to studio models to her recently completed oil of Albert. In a departure from the standard exhibition practice of skying paintings, her pictures were hung in a row at eye level on the curved Hemicycle Gallery walls. In addition, at irregular intervals, the horizontal sweep of the exhibition was broken by four tall, vertical panels projecting from the wall on which were hung easily viewable groupings of smaller works.

The art critics' reviews from the major Washington dailies were unanimously laudatory and praised the marked improvement in her skill since her studies with Whistler, as well as the self-assured individuality of her style. Although they found "glints" of Elihu Vedder and Thomas Dewing, all recognized her work as "thoroughly individual." One critic even went so far as to say: "They are inspirations. They figure in the higher education of the soul."[12] In chorus, the local critics deemed that in spite of her wealth and social position, Alice Barney was an artist worthy of serious critical attention.

In his Sunday article for the *Washington Post,* Henry Moser, himself a painter, was particularly intrigued by Alice's choice of pastel as her primary medium. He noted that there were probably more pastel painters working in Washington than in any other major city in the country and that taken as a group, they could rightly claim the title, "the Washington Color School." His favorite work in the exhibition, however, was a small oil painting of a red-haired woman, veiled in black and holding a bouquet of poppies in her clasped hands. For him the profile portrait evoked echoes of Dante Gabriel Rossetti and Whistler. At the same time it illuminated Alice's ability to move beyond the influences of the European Symbolists to create her own vision.[13]

The *Star*'s critic Leila Mechlin, who was just beginning her forty-year career as one of Washington's most powerful arbiters of artistic taste, seconded Moser's perception. She felt Alice was not merely copying the work of modern Parisian masters, but had developed a unique style all her own through her poetic interpretations of people. For her the portraits revealed the "intense personalities" of the sitters, no matter how beautiful or handsome the person might be.[14]

Neither critic, however, was particularly taken with *Woman Clothed with the Sun* or the unfinished *Babylon.* Moser was candid about his lack of appreciation for art that attempted to illustrate "stories, lessons, problems, or sermons." Mechlin took a different tact and questioned why Alice even bothered to draw them in the first place. While Mechlin found them ambitious works by an artist equal to the task, she didn't think they measured up to Alice's more prosaic subjects, "which possess sufficient strength and much beauty."

It was Moser, however, who came closest to understanding that there was more to Alice's exhibition than met the eye. Writing after the show's closing, he said:

Mrs. Barney is being heartily congratulated upon her success, but to artists and those wiser ones who know there is a deeper and wider

Page 158:
FIRELIGHT, 1904
Pastel on paper, 27⅞ x 21¹⁵⁄₁₆ in. (50.5 x 41 cm)
Ellen Goin, Alice's favorite niece, posed in front of the west studio fireplace at Studio House.

Page 159:
DREAM BOOK, 1901
Oil on canvas, 19⅞ x 16⅛ in. (50.5 x 41 cm)
Alice liked to try her hand at incorporating the styles of other artists. Among the works in her collection by other artists was a portrait by Albert Herter, which Dream Book *strongly resembles.*

good to follow this charming display of the work of a local genius. It is the uplift that must follow the advent of a leader possessing academic skill, high poetic qualities, and the color faculty, and Mrs. Barney is an optimist....Our people are very conservative and Mrs. Barney can teach them what art is....Mrs. Barney's bold, free and original, although often experimental, work will encourage the guild to branch out not as imitators, but on individual lines, with more hope of support and approval."[15]

The accolades gave Alice a needed emotional boost that enabled her to replace the disarray of home with an orderly and satisfying involvement

ALBERT AT FIFTY-ONE, 1901
During the spring and summer of 1901, Albert and Alice lived in New York at the Waldorf Astoria. While Albert marked time until they could return to Washington, Alice rented a studio in the Carnegie Building and focused on her painting.

with Washington's art world. Within a week of the close of her exhibition, she was elected vice-president of the Society of Washington Artists. Moreover, in equally short time, Alice knew she had never lost her entrée into society when she joined with Harriet Lane Johnston (who, as niece of the bachelor president James Buchanan, was the White House's official hostess during his administration) and Mrs. Henry Satterlee, wife of Washington's Episcopal bishop, to arrange a concert in the ballroom of the New Willard to benefit the House of Mercy—a home for destitute and wayward girls. Alice was thrilled by the opportunity. She felt herself better equipped than in 1898 when she had presented her first Washington theatrical to benefit the wounded of the Spanish-American War. Furthermore, with this theatrical collaboration with two of Washington's most esteemed women, Alice knew that the Barney name had never really lost its status in society.

Alice's portion of the program consisted in part of a scene from Jean-Baptiste Molière's *The Misanthrope*, a recitation by Laura from a passage by Victor Hugo, and a vocal duet performed by Marguerite Cassini, the Russian ambassador's daughter, and Mrs. Stilson W. Hutchins, wife of the editor of the *Washington Times*. Within days tongues wagged over Laura's monologue, which, with its references to the Virgin Mary and Mary Magdalene, was considered blasphemous by Catholics in the audience. Although there were a few who chalked up one more black mark against Alice, the majority found her avant-garde proclivities *très chic*, particularly when bolstered by the imprimatur of two of Washington's most respected social leaders.

During this time, Albert retreated to the protective sanctity of the Alibi Club where he could do as he pleased with no eyebrows raised. Occasionally he walked through the large salon built for Natalie's debut and noted young women bearing prominent Washington names such as Sheridan, Lincoln, and Bell in various artistic poses. Although he acknowledged their presence, his thoughts were focused on the fine whiskey awaiting him at his club. Perhaps he should have paid more attention, for on February 2, 1902, when Albert opened the Sunday *Washington Times* to the front page of the society section, he was greeted by a picture of his wife and a large headline reading: "'What is Capital Life, After All?' Asks Mrs. Alice Barney. 'Small Talk and Lots to Eat, an Infinite Series of Teas and Dinners. Art? There is None!'"[16] As he continued to read the full page interview, he blanched. Whatever could Alice have been thinking of?

X

In the Public Eye

I n the velvet-gloved, cutthroat world of high society, very few refrained from using the press to establish their credentials. Dinner-guest lists, effusive reports of glittering parties, and salacious gossip were forwarded to reporters in an attempt to feed the seemingly endless appetite for self-aggrandizement and self-protection on the part of the rich and the correspondingly unappeasable interest of those who would never attain such heights. It was all part of a never-ending publicity game played out in detail in the daily press.

Alice decided that if her enemies could use the *Mirror* magazine to attack her, she could just as unabashedly manipulate a major newspaper for her own purposes. It was no accident that a *Washington Times* reporter was assigned to visit Alice. After all Alice and Mrs. Stilson W. Hutchins, the wife of its editor, had become friends during the staging of the House of Mercy benefit. The reporter, clutching pencil and notebook, thought she had come to discuss Alice's next charitable theatrical venture, an extravaganza starring well over fifty of Washington's most delectable young women and most eligible bachelors. Moreover, Alice had pulled a coup by enticing Constance Harrison, a native of Fairfax County, Virginia, to write the scenario for the pantomime *Reward of Amaryllis*. Harrison was the current literary darling of the social set and the author of such popular romantic novels as *A Daughter of the South*, *An Errant Wooing*, and *Sweet Bells Out of Tune*.

Alice greeted the reporter cordially, gave her a cup of tea, and then discharged her opening salvo: "Washington is an ideal city for art; but its people are not at all artistic." With that statement Alice made it immediately obvious to the innocent reporter that the interview had little to do with the forthcoming production. Instead, it was to be about Alice's opinion of Washington's cultural life.

For years, Alice noted, Washington had been considered a hardship post by foreign embassies more because of its cultural provinciality than its horrid summer weather. In her view there was no reason why it had to remain that way. With proper and knowledgeable leadership in the art community, Washington could take its place as the cultural capital of the world. Alice began to detail both her criticism of and solutions to the problem of changing Washington from cultural desert to arts oasis.

What was needed was someone who could grasp the complexities inherent in nurturing Washington's cultural life, someone who could understand

MODEL HOLDING DRAPERY, C. 1927
Pastel on fiberboard, 20 x 15 in. (50.8 x 38.1 cm)
In this memory portrait done two years before her own death, Alice draws herself as she was in the summer of 1903 at Onteora, New York, following Albert's death in 1902.

it from both the artist's and the patron's point of view. Alice thought little of those who laid claim to leading Washington's cultural life, but she pointed no fingers. That was not necessary, for society knew that at the top of the list was Mrs. John Henderson, wife of the retired senator from Missouri. Mrs. Henderson fancied herself an artistic leader because of her patronage of Lucien Powell, a prolific painter of Venetian scenes, who resided with her family in what was called Henderson's Castle. For Alice, merely supporting an artist, and not a particularly good one at that, did not a cultural leader make. By the end of the interview, no reader could doubt but that Alice, although she never said so, thought she was the most qualified to undertake the challenge.

Alice believed Washington's failure to develop as an art center lay in the attitude of the "ultra-fashionable folk of this city and the Congress of the United States for their seeming indifference to things artistic." Their indifference had all sorts of ramifications that she was more than ready to enumerate. First, for a city to be an art center it must attract artists. It is not unusual that "when an artist comes to Washington for the first time he is charmed by the beauty of the city. He probably decides to take a studio and is immediately disappointed...for the simple reason that Washington contains no studio building. ...The artist who wishes to make this city his home must either build a studio, which comparatively few of them can afford to do, or use an ordinary room as a makeshift."

Second, Alice stated, even if an artist decides to stay he finds not only that there are no suitable galleries to exhibit his work, but that the prices paid for pictures and sculptures in Washington are about one-fourth those paid in New York. Finally, she roundly chastised wealthy Washingtonians who refused to collect the work of Washington artists. "It is," she said, "indeed a great pity, for there is and has been much excellent artistic talent in Washington," and she ticked off the names of local artists in her own collection: Henry Moser, Max Weyl, Francis Hopkinson Smith, Juliet Thompson, and Hobart Nichols.

In her opinion, the absolute first step in the artistic education of Washington was to establish a national school of art, funded by Congress, modeled after the L'École des Beaux-Arts, and headed by "a strong, virile and typically American artist" such as her friend Frederick MacMonnies. Holding up her own studies with Carolus-Duran and Whistler as example, she declared that an artist developed only through lifelong study, which the Corcoran School of Art did not provide. She also advocated the removal of import duty from works of art imported into this country by Congress in order to enhance and broaden opportunities for the appreciation of art.

Above all, for Alice, was the need to change Washington's attitude about the place of art in its life. Art must be at the forefront, and only then would

Washington become the center for the nation's artistic life. She knew Washington had the wealth to make itself a second Paris, and she believed that "in this great country of ours, where so many other things have reached an approximate state of perfection, there certainly should be a place for art...and this is the ideal spot....Our national life is centered here."[1]

While Albert waited in horror for the fireworks, Alice chuckled over a poem she received from a local woman. Whatever the reaction from her peers, her faith that Washington could be the artistic center she envisioned was affirmed by A. Rosa Hausmann's tongue-in-cheek rhymed response to the *Times* interview:

I wish to ask you Mrs. Barney,
If it's true or only blarney,
That society's biggest feat,
Is small talk and lots to eat.
Are their souls from drinking tea,
So benumbed, they cannot see,
The beauty of the brush's creation?
If so, I envy not their station.
...How rich we are! the humble set
That knows not wealth or etiquette—
For whom no master lived in vain
That loves all art—the poet's rhymes
Also your page in the Sunday Times—
Appreciation of the arts
It dwells at least—in humble hearts.[2]

Alice knew Albert would be angry, but she was unprepared for the *Mirror*'s decision to deflate her pretensions with its review of the *Reward of Amaryllis*. It took two solid pages of the magazine to do it. The review, entitled, "Society Makes a Monkey of Itself in Amateur Theatricals," was a sentence-by-sentence put-down of every single person who took part in the production and of almost everyone who went to see it. It began with comments about the intelligence of an audience that would spend good money to see such a debacle and ended by forecasting that the career of its composer and conductor Reginald DeKoven ("this perspiring composer of other people's music") was over in Washington before it began. On stage debutante nymphs "galoomphed," the bachelor woodsmen were drunk, and Laura Barney as Medusa had a face only her mother could love. The article concluded that "as an amateur performance it was, without doubt, the worst that was ever attempted in this city—or elsewhere."[3] The *Mirror* followed up two weeks later by announcing that Alice was on "the verge of

social ostracism," and that her actions had caused "many of the more careful and reserved matrons to draw back from Mrs. Barney and her set."

A Baltimore paper finally came to Alice's defense:

It was the elder de Goncourt, was it not, who said that 'there are no women of genius; all women of genius are men?' Despite all epigrams to the contrary, there are women of genius and Mrs. Albert Clifford Barney is one of the cleverest women in America, but within her there burns that God-given *feu sacre*. And genius must be recognized, sooner or later; it is impossible that it pass unnoticed. Consequently all this talk about Mrs. Barney's social ostracism, because she and her two excessively clever daughters are, in their literary and artistic taste, what the narrow-minded individuals of this after all somewhat provincial town choose to call *tres-osée*, is as ridiculous as it is contemptible and will prove futile. Mrs. Barney stands nowhere near the verge of ostracism; she is most popular in the smartest set of the capital and has a greater vogue than any other woman in town. That is because she is the cleverest.[4]

Alice decided to let the press carry on the debate as she turned to more pressing matters. As vice-president of the Society of Washington Artists and a member of its executive committee, she was a juror for its annual exhibition. Previously, all entries were from local artists, but in 1902, at Alice's urging, the committee also invited important national artists to exhibit in a concerted effort to develop a national reputation for Washington. How well it succeeded depended both upon the caliber of the non-Washington artists who responded and the quality of the local talent whose canvases hung beside them.

Works by Thomas Eakins, Childe Hassam, Alfred Maurer, and Cecilia Beaux were placed alongside James Henry Moser, Bertha Childe, and Hobart Nichols. While overall the local entrants hung comfortably with better-known names, the most jarring entry was Alice's new pastel, *Medusa*. It was an eerie, compelling head study of the mythological monster. Using vivid tonalities of gray and blue emphasized by startling sweeps of red chalk, the pastel was disturbing because it was as much a realistic portrait as it was a treatment of an often seen Symbolist theme. Much of its power and immediacy came from her use of Laura as the costumed model. Whether it was art or not became a point of disagreement among the critics. One wrote of it, "I was cautioned to call it beautiful. It is so real that one stands before it and, hearing no sound, is horror-struck." A second called it "a weird creation, which is too horrible and too well done to be other than an outrage of the highest principles or aims of true art, as well as unworthy

Medusa, 1902
Pastel on canvas, 36½ x 28⅝ in. (92.7 x 72.7 cm)
Alice worked from an 1897 photograph of Laura in costume taken at Bar Harbor by fellow-artist, Mrs. Montgomery Sears. Laura recreated her Medusa tableau for Alice's Washington production of The Reward of Amaryllis *in 1902.*

of the genius of its skillful painter."[5] Whatever the picture's merits, and they were many, Alice had confounded Washington's little art world with her entry.

PLANNING STUDIO HOUSE

In the five short months since Alice's return to Washington, she had mounted a solo exhibition, directed two charity entertainments, been elected vice-president of the town's major artistic society, been interviewed by Washington's major newspaper, helped organize a national art exhibition, and managed to offend everyone in Washington society suffering from an overdeveloped sense of decorum. With the onset of Lent, that hectic pace abruptly ceased. Alice utilized the ensuing forty days to rest, retrench, and attend to private pursuits and projects.

In prior years Alice had devoted this time to painting and to morning prayer. This Lenten season, however, had a different focus. Although she still went into her studio each day, seldom did she work on a canvas. Rather, her days were taken up in pouring over architectural plans for what she called Studio House with the rising young Washington architect Waddy B. Wood. At thirty-three, Wood, who learned the principles of architecture in the reading room of the Library of Congress, was already an established member of the highly respected firm of Wood, Donn, and Deming. Of the three men, it was Wood's creativity that brought accolades to the firm and that caused Alice to seek him out. For Wood it was an opportunity to begin a new career, designing homes for the very rich.

Alice did not conceive the idea of Studio House full-blown upon her return to Washington. She had been considering it for almost four years since she discovered the importance of salons to the development of Paris's cultural life. She had observed that salons constituted the artistic and intellectual vitality of Paris. For Alice, therefore, of paramount importance to Washington's cultural maturity was the establishment of at least one salon conducted by someone already experienced in doing so. This idea became the linchpin of what was rapidly becoming her one-woman cultural crusade.

The fact that Albert was willing to let Alice purchase land and make contractual obligations in her own name was not a sign that he was suddenly a

FRONT ELEVATION OF STUDIO HOUSE BY WADDY WOOD, 1902 *Studio House was designed by Waddy B. Wood with a Spanish Mission exterior and decorated by Alice in her own eclectic style.*

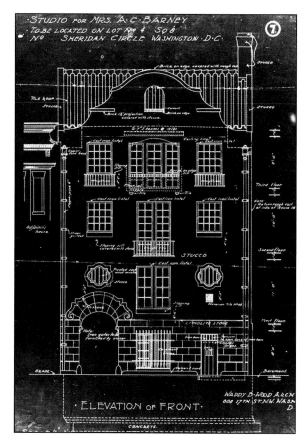

feminist or that he had begun to agree with Alice's ideas about art and society. Rather, it was further indication of his own deterioration. He no longer had the energy to say no to what was a decidedly unusual arrangement in an era when wives were seldom given either the responsibility for or the unrestricted use of family money. His capitulation was yet another sign of the ever-widening gulf between them.

Throughout Lent, Alice and Wood met and transferred to architectural plans her dream house. It had to provide a place to escape from the duties of a proper Washington hostess, have a quiet area for work, and, most importantly, have the atmosphere of a salon in which she could entertain and encourage patrons and practitioners of the visual, performing, and literary arts.

In contrast to her other two homes, Studio House was a reflection of Alice's own taste. Her ideas of architecture and design had been formed in Cincinnati during the height of its Arts and Crafts movement and influenced by her father's opera houses and Fifth Avenue house in New York. Therefore, she took more than an ordinary client's interest in construction and decorative details, regularly supplying Wood with her own architectural sketches that gave special attention to interior craftsmanship.[6] Finally, she could impose her artistic style on one of her dwellings. Like her father, she would brook no compromises to meet either the expectations of proper Washington society or Albert's penchant for yellowed oak paneling.

LAURA'S CONVERSION

For someone who had made sure she was constantly in the public eye since her return to Washington, the lack of reportage on Alice's new project reflected her concerted effort to keep it quiet. She would let the completed, fully decorated Studio House make her statement for her. On the Saturday before Easter, however, the *Mirror* mentioned in passing that Alice was building a "modest little structure...on the outskirts of Washington, overlooking Rock Creek." Unaware of the potential significance of Studio House to the nation's capital, the *Mirror* focused its article on Laura's conversion to the Bahai faith:

> Dear knows, our American girls have done worse things in the past than to have embraced the teachings of Behah Ullah....Preachings of Mirza Abul Fazel Gulpaygan may do good in its own peculiar way, certainly it is much more to be encouraged than the erotic languishings of Lord Alfred Douglass....let us encourage this latest fad of hers, it really is better after all to spend the time in prayer and fasting than inhaling the perfume of green carnations in an incense laden room.[7]

Laura was not amused by the article, and she was contemptuous of the ignorance it belied. An early feminist, Laura believed wholeheartedly in the teachings of its founder, Bahaullah: the unity of religions, the equality of men and women, and the elimination of racial prejudice. With characteristic single-mindedness, she only worked harder to further the cause of her faith in Washington.

In the spring of 1902, Laura was aided by the arrival of Mirza Abul Fazl, the leading Persian teacher of the faith, whom she had met during a visit to Egypt. Fazl, a convert to Bahaism in 1876, had dedicated the rest of his life to spreading Bahaullah's teachings. His Eastern garb of flowing white robes and turban around his long white hair were an exotic sight for Washingtonians at the turn of the century. Eyebrows were raised by his teachings that there is one God, or first cause, for all mankind and that God's divine teachings are revealed through many prophets. These beliefs were a far cry from traditional religion of the time, and, to the dismay of many prominent clergy, Fazl was attracting some of Washington's most prominent and wealthy churchgoers.

RUTH ST. DENIS, 1910
Pastel on canvas, 36⅞ x 23⅞ in. (93.7 x 60.6 cm)
In 1906 Alice brought St. Denis to Washington for a benefit performance of Radah.

Alice personally saw nothing paradoxical in being both an Episcopalian and a Bahai. Of the two, the Bahai faith with its emphasis upon women's equality was appealing to her. Moreover, the faith's Persian roots appealed to her sense of the exotic. When Laura asked her to help find housing for Abul Fazl and his coterie, Alice immediately guaranteed the rent at 1830 I Street, N.W.

Meanwhile, work on Studio House was progressing much too slowly for Alice's taste. She was used to quick resolutions of problems and felt frustrated. Unlike the design for a stage set, on which space is easily altered by rearranging the flats, architectural plans had to take into account building codes and engineering specifications. She found it difficult to accept that every time she changed her mind there were further delays.

During this period her artwork was not entirely forgotten. After going to the theater to see the great English actress, Mrs. Patrick Campbell, Alice sent a note inviting her to visit her studio in order to sketch a portrait of her. The resulting pastel of the well-known tragedi-

Left:
EN CRINOLINE, 1915
Pastel on fiberboard, 17¹⁄₁₆
x 14 in. (43.3 x 35.6 cm)
Throughout her life Alice was intrigued by the dance. Her 1915 collaboration with Pavlova was one of the highlights of her career in the arts.

Right:
MOON MADNESS, 1929
Pastel on fiberboard,
17⅞ x 13¹³⁄₁₆ in. (45.4 x
35.1 cm)
Alice often did pastel impressions of characters for her theatrical ventures. Illustrated is the character of Luna from the 1929 version of The Man in the Moon.

enne not only captured her likeness, but was infused with the dramatic intensity the actress brought to her most famous roles as Ophelia, Lady Macbeth, Hedda Gabler, and the second Mrs. Tanqueray. Upon completion it hung at the Corcoran along with Alice's study of Daisy Leiter, the youngest sister of Lady Curzon and the daughter of Levi Leiter, co-founder of Chicago's Marshall Field's Department Store. Through all this artistic activity, Alice continued to use the press's interest to enable her to express her opinions; found in the midst of comments about her own artwork would be yet another plea for the founding of a first-rate national art school in Washington.

In late May, Alice was treated to a rude shock as she leafed through the latest issue of the *Washington Mirror*. The object of its ridicule was once more Laura and the Bahais. The article was not only patronizing, it confused the Bahai faith with occult practices by painting a lurid scene of Laura as a medium leading incense-filled seances to contact Bahaullah. She was pictured as "etherealized in the receptive trance, while the exclusive few...listen in awe-stricken suspense, while Bab 'babbled.'" At the end it printed the address of the Bahai meeting place, which caused crowds to gather to gawk and laugh at those who came to hear the teachings of the venerable Fazl.[8]

When Albert realized what Laura was up to, he bought out the lease, closed the house where the meetings were held, and found himself stuck with a fistful of unpaid bills. His outrage at Alice and Laura knew no bounds, and the blow to his pride was more than his precarious health could stand; he suffered a second heart attack. On advice from his doctors, Albert sailed for Europe with Natalie to partake once again of Nauheim's healing waters.

Natalie was met in England by Eva Palmer, and, after a few weeks in London, the pair set off for Paris to search for an apartment to share while Albert continued on to Nauheim. Alice and Laura remained in Washington and soon found the Rhode Island Avenue mansion uncomfortably large. They closed the house, took an apartment at the fashionable Gordon Apartments, and settled in for the first time to survive Washington's summer heat and humidity so that Alice could concentrate on getting Studio House built.

On July 26, 1902, the contractor Charles A. Langley obtained a building permit for the erection of a dwelling and studio on Lot 4, Square 8 on Sheridan Circle with a street address of 2306 Massachusetts Avenue. The two adjoining lots Alice purchased for her Studio House were in the Kalorama Heights area of Washington, D.C. "Kalorama" was the Greek word for beautiful view, and from the rear of her land, it was possible to see across the Potomac palisades to Virginia if one ignored the more immediate scene of the dump which blighted the bank of Rock Creek directly across from her new property. The lots fronted on Massachusetts Avenue, facing the circle dedicated to Civil War hero General Philip Sheridan. At the time she bought the property, there was little to commend it—only her own conviction that it was an up-and-coming area. Only one other townhouse, a mundane affair of red brick, had been built on the newly plotted circle. In 1902, few foresaw that Sheridan Circle would eventually become one of Washington's most sought after addresses.

Langley estimated the cost of construction of the combined brick, limestone, and stucco building with red tile roof at $18,000. Because it was roughly one-quarter the size of the Barneys's residence on Rhode Island Avenue, Albert expected the construction bills to be proportionately less, but when they began to arrive for payment at Nauheim, they were almost

Mirza Abul Fazl, 1903
Pastel on paper, 29⁵⁄₁₆ x 20⅜ in. (74.5 x 51.8 cm)
In 1901, Fazl came to Washington, D.C. His Eastern garb, flowing white robes, and long white hair covered by a turban, were an exotic sight for turn-of-the-century Washingtonians. Fazl was called by a Bahai historian "the most erudite and accomplished scholar that the cause of Bahau'llah has ever won to its side."

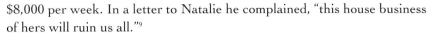

$8,000 per week. In a letter to Natalie he complained, "this house business of hers will ruin us all."[9]

ELLEN GOIN AND LAURA, c. 1902
Ellen (left) and Laura (right) were inveterate travelers and close friends as shown in this shipboard photograph.

While Studio House began to take shape on Sheridan Circle, Alice received urgent reports on Albert's health from Natalie. The news was not good. On his return from Nauheim to Paris, Albert became bedridden with pleurisy. He coughed all night and his lungs had to be cupped twice. Natalie urged her mother to insist he go to the south of France instead of attempting to return in November. She also wrote in astonishment of her own reactions to his illness: "When he is sick he is very pathetic and I, as I have been told, have turned into becoming quite a dutiful daughter. This pleases me to find that I am not such a bad lot and capable enough when I really see that it is required of me."[10]

A letter written in October displayed an even more acute understanding of her father as Natalie began to recognize what Alice had known long before, that he was a man sick not only in body, but in spirit.

> He seems to be getting better. He sails November 8 and speaks rather wildly about living his own life, cutting Mother out of his will and getting a divorce, but I don't believe that he means a word of it and that it would simply break his heart if he hadn't his awful family to nag and worry about and care for.[11]

Alice never saw Albert again. He was, in fact, too ill to make the ocean voyage and went instead to Monte Carlo. In the first week of December, Natalie was notified by Albert's concierge to come immediately to Monte Carlo because her father was dying. She arrived too late. She later wrote: "The only death I ever looked upon was that of my father, and his peace at last attained, seemed to warn me: Do not come too near, this is the only untroubled moment, the only quiet ever known. Keep the memory of it and do not mourn."[12] She had Albert's body photographed in his shroud and shipped his remains to Paris for cremation.

Accompanied by Eva and the Viscount of Canterbury, Natalie sailed for America with her father's ashes.

On December 5, 1902, slightly more than a month before her forty-sixth birthday and their twenty-seventh wedding anniversary, Alice received word that Albert was dead. She felt genuine sadness at his death even though she acknowledged that she had never loved him; the other emotion she felt was relief that it was finally over. For the first time in twenty-six years, Alice, Natalie, and Laura were completely free of the man who had tried to rule their lives.

Dressed in fashionable new black mourning outfits, Alice and Laura traveled to New York to meet Natalie. Natalie, the daughter who most fought everything her father stood for, was hysterical, alternately crying and laughing as she embraced her mother, and, as she later wrote, "felt how wildly our hearts beat alike."[13] Once she placed Albert's ashes in her mother's hands, Natalie felt her responsibility ended, and she refused further involvement. Alice and Laura returned to Washington to make preparations to bury Albert's ashes in Dayton. Local obituaries listed his clubs and his heirs, speculated on the size of his estate, and noted how much he would be missed in society. As he had lived, Albert died: the epitome of a clubman.

On December 26 Albert's will was filed for probate. The estate was to be held in trust with its income divided equally between his wife and two daughters. Alice could draw out her portion of the principal after a year; Laura and Natalie would receive theirs when they reached thirty. As the will was read and the extent of her inheritance was revealed, Alice realized that Albert's ravings that she would bankrupt the family by building Studio House were patently absurd. The combination of property and money in the bank easily exceeded three million dollars.

One final act remained. On January 26, 1903, a funeral service was held at the home of Albert's brother E. J. Barney, presided over by the Baptist minister of the church the Dayton Barneys attended. Only Alice, Laura, Ellen Goin, and Albert's brothers attended. Immediately following the funeral, the box containing Albert's ashes was placed into an full-size, dark wood casket and lowered into a grave in the Barney family plot at Woodland Cemetery. Before she left Alice commissioned a pseudo-Roman wellhead to mark the gravesite. She made no arrangement to be buried next to him when her own time came. [14]

LA ROSITA, 1909
Pastel on fiberboard,
26⅝ x 21½ in. (67.6 x 54.6 cm)
In December 1909, Alice Barney cast herself as La Rosita in her mime ballet The Man in the Moon. *She appeared in a torrid Spanish dance of jealousy, bartering her life for a bullfighter's cloak. Looking younger than her fifty-two years, she received not only loud applause from the audience, but rapt attention from one of the gentlemen in the cafe scene — Christian Dominique Hemmick. Two years later he became her second husband.*

XI
Tackling Washington

For Alice Pike Barney the first months of 1903 were more like the end of a year than the beginning. During this time several major chapters of her life closed. In January she buried her husband. In February a short story on the front page of the Washington Post told her that her father's second Cincinnati opera house had burned to the ground and with it her last link with Cincinnati. She realized that soon there would be few alive who would remember Pike's gift to his adopted city. Perhaps, she mused, there might be some way she could perpetuate his legacy. It was something to think about. Now, however, was not the time; she could not even continue with the projects she had already begun. The requirements of a year of deep mourning would not allow it.

As Alice secluded herself at the Gordon, the rest of society geared up for the "gayeties of the winter season" without her. "Le Toute Monde," as the *Washington Mirror* called society, eagerly awaited the imminent arrival of Monsieur Jesseurand, the new French Ambassador, who was reputed to be a lavish host. The Russian Ambassador Count Cassini and his vivacious daughter Marguerite moved the Russian Embassy to a large mansion on Rhode Island Avenue and planned to entertain on a grand scale. Extravagant dinners at the Barney home were given by the Lars Andersons who rented the house as they awaited the completion of their beaux arts palace a few blocks south of Studio House on Massachusetts Avenue near Dupont Circle.

Even President Theodore Roosevelt was infected by the preparations for the social season. At his direction the White House was being completely refurbished. Roosevelt hired American Neoclassical architect Charles McKim to bring it up to date for a cost of $668,000 in public funds. The controversial result was described as a "conglomeration of old English, both manorial and baronial, Gothic, monastic and colonial, with the last named style of interior decoration decidedly overshadowed by the others." In spite of the criticism, or perhaps because of it, invitations to the White House were more eagerly sought than ever.[1]

On the cultural front, the Washington Symphony Orchestra, under the baton of Reginald de Koven, began its inaugural season. The annual benefit performance for the House of Mercy, which Alice was scheduled to produce, went on without her. Thus, January seemed cold and dreary to Alice and February loomed even bleaker. For one so full of life as Alice, spending an entire year devoted to observing proprieties was tantamount to incarcer-

ALICE AT FORTY-SEVEN, 1904
Alice was the acknowledged queen of Washington culture when she was photographed in the first floor reception room of Studio House for a feature article in the prestigious Town & Country *magazine.*

ation. It was, however, important that she follow the rules. This was not the time to offend anyone who might help her enrich Washington's cultural life. Nevertheless, she could not help but chafe at the wasted time. Ironically, in death, Albert seemed more successful in curbing her artistic endeavors than he had when alive.

Feeling stifled, Alice turned, as she had so often in the past, to her painting for solace. In doing so, she wondered if her art might not provide a roundabout way of maintaining her momentum. She would let her art keep her name before the public. Thus, Alice's artistic accomplishments continued to be mentioned—not in the society listings, but in the Sunday art columns.

In mid-February Alice entered a pastel portrait of Laura in the annual juried exhibition of the Society of Washington Artists. The 1903 exhibition was a turning point in the society's history. Under the leadership of the executive committee, of which Alice was still vice-president, the Society mounted its first competitive national exhibition at the Corcoran. Of the seventy-three works shown, Alice's among them, over half were executed by non-Washington artists. To the Corcoran's delight, attendance increased dramatically.

Following the successful show, the Society believed it had proved without a doubt that Washington was ready for and would support a major annual national exhibition. The executive committee, therefore, proposed that the Corcoran take over the organization of the annual exhibition from the Society. Although the Corcoran did not immediately agree, Alice was gratified to see one of her major goals headed toward fruition. Equally important to Alice was her one-person exhibition scheduled for the end of February in New York.

Alice had come to the attention of the Durand-Ruel Gallery in New York with her 1901 Corcoran show. The gallery was famous for showing avant-garde art—particularly the work of American and French Impressionists. A New York show meant her work would be critiqued by unknown reviewers and not just good friends in Washington such as Moser and Mechlin. When Henri Pene du Bois's review appeared in the *American Magazine*, Moser reprinted it in his *Washington Post* art column. "Mental analysis and charm of reticence are united," du Bois wrote. "How? The heart in her work is naïve and her art is not....Mrs. Barney paints in pastels as if she were painting in oils....Her works are captivating."[2]

One last major juried exhibit remained for her to enter for the purpose of enhancing her artistic career. The Philadelphia Art Club Annual Exhibition of watercolors and pastels was a massive show of over two-hundred works with entries from all over the East Coast. The show was held in late March, and Alice once more received high praise from unknown critics.

The *Philadelphia Press* said that "the discovery of the exhibition is undoubtedly the three portrait heads by Mrs. Alice Barney....She has succeeded in giving a very remarkable quality to her pastel subjects, all feminine, and all having a certain sense of the possibility of conveying character by color, which is an entirely fresh and new note."[3]

STUDIO HOUSE COMPLETED

Satisfied that her artistic credentials were now impeccable, Alice turned to the completion of Studio House as her top priority. For this project, the free time imposed upon her by the year of deep mourning was a definite advantage. Little escaped her notice during daily on-site inspections to observe the building's progress. She was particularly struck by the skill with which the laborers performed their jobs and the pride they took in the performance of their various trades. Her respect grew daily as she watched their work translate her aesthetic ideas into practical form. Unskilled laborers and highly trained artisans, such as those provided by J.H. Corning's ornamental ironworks company, worked in concert to create the special ambience of Studio House. While the Spanish Mission exterior inspired by the Pan-American exposition in Buffalo provided Wood with the opportunity to explore the possibilities of a style still uncommon to Washington, the interior decor was Alice's design. The specific decorative details that marked it as a house devoted to art were based upon the precepts of John Ruskin and William Morris, which Alice had learned in Cincinnati some twenty years before. Moreover, her sojourns in Paris led her to integrate the swirling arabesques of Art Nouveau with elements of the Arts and Crafts Movement. The result was eclectic and to her taste. Side-by-side were irregular handcrafted Mercer tiles used to maximum effect in the foyer and the west studio, austere tongue-and-groove hard-pine wainscotting, stenciled arabesques on walls and wood, simple handcrafted wrought iron sconces, quatrefoil stained-glass windows, and tulip-shaped hand-blown glass shades.

Alice chose two mottoes for the house. The first was in Latin and, translated, it read: "To Overcome Calamity by Hard Work, 1903." Two tile plaques bearing the motto were installed: one on the exterior facade and the other on the wall facing the entryway stairs. A third rendition was fashioned from red-glazed tiles with black lettering and applied to the brick wall of the entrance stairwell. On the two plaques, Latin lettering formed the border around a square center tile of Alice's design: a heraldic pattern taken from a more illustrious branch of the Barneys showing a coat of arms with a large "M" over a stalking lion. When the time came to install the plaques, however, Alice's design did not work because she had not allowed for the grout between the tiles. Alice was thoroughly disappointed until she

THE MANTELPIECE IN THE RECEPTION-ROOM OF MRS. BARNEY'S HOME

AN ARTISTIC HOME IN WASHINGTON

Mrs. Alice Barney's Studio and Residence on Sheridan Circle

By ANNA P. THOMAS

A recognized patron of art and a liberal contributor to the Poor Artists' Fund of Paris, as well as an artist herself, Mrs. Alice Barney's cherished scheme is to be instrumental in establishing a National Museum of Art in her own Capital City of Washington. Her plan is to organize a select and permanent committee, made up of recognized authorities of both the United States and foreign countries, who shall have the controlling power to accept or reject every canvas submitted by private patrons who desire to loan their art treasures for a specified period for public exhibition, all accepted paintings to be regarded as government property for the time being, and as such, or under the public exhibition and museums law, to be admitted free of duty. She hopes thus to encourage private importation of pictures which hitherto have been neglected because of the heavy import tax, it being her intention thus to advance the higher education of persons who are unable to travel abroad. She would recommend the appropriation by Congress of a sum of money for the erection of a building, either separate or in connection with a suitable department of the government, where free admission would be granted to the public throughout the year. The idea is prompted by Mrs. Barney having been the victim of heavy loss on her return from Europe a year ago by the complete destruction of several of her most valued paintings t h r o u g h the careless handling of her importations by custom-house officials.

The suggestion brings ... nd an interesting ... which took place at ... e of the completion ... new residence on ... lan Circle. As a ... of appreciation on the part of the owner for their interest in her plans, which they had faithfully carried out, all of the artisans employed on its construction were entertained at a banquet in the house which had just been finished. The affair was unique in local annals and created widespread comment.

This residence, which is Mrs. Barney's studio home, is conspicuous among the handsome houses which have sprung up within the last few years on the shores of Rock Creek, in Washington's "New West End." One may approach the house by way of Massachusetts Avenue, one of the most fashionable driveways in the city, which embraces many of the palatial residences owned by multi-millionaires, who have been attracted to Washington as a place of yearly growing importance for a

MRS. BARNEY'S WASHINGTON RESIDENCE

winter residence. Last in line among its neighbors and unique in its Mexican style of architecture, her house, built of gray stone, with green parking before the entrance, faces the south side of Sheridan Circle, just a little back from the street. It looks out over the five avenues that converge upon the Circle, and in the rear it commands an uninterrupted view of the windings of Rock Creek and the Virginia hills beyond.

Imposing and attractive as the exterior is, the chief artistic interest is within doors, for here its artist owner, with money and leisure to travel, has arranged the objects of art which, with fancy or caprice and true American love of variety she has collected from all quarters of the globe. The visitor is conducted t h r o u g h a broad, low archway into a dark court, and thence up a short flight of steps to the iron-bound oak doorway that leads directly into the re-noticed one of the Italian tile setters struggling with the design. From where she stood she could see that he had removed one of the letters, yet the Latin seemed to make sense. More importantly, the integrity of the design remained. Faced with the choice between correct Latin and a pleasing design, Alice opted for the latter. When the plaques and the red and black wall tiles were installed, they read "Vici Calamitaem Labore MCMXIII" instead of "Vici Calamitatem Labore MCMXIII." However, it seemed fitting to Alice that in the end art had triumphed.

No compromises were made for the second motto stenciled in gold lettering across the base of the musicians' balcony in the great studio room. Taken from an 1872 English translation of Johann Goethe's *Truth and Poetry: From My Own Life*, it read: "The highest problem of art is to produce by appearance the illusion of higher reality." For Alice it was a constant reminder of Whistler and his warning to her against her own cleverness. The quotation's second line was implied: "But it is a false endeavor to realize the appearance until at last only something commonly real remains."

Alice had no worry about her studio house being "commonly real." Wood met her specifications and created an interior space that reeked of "higher reality." The unique ambience of the interior was Alice's design, but it was Wood's architectural acumen that made her imaginative variations on a typical Washington center-hall row house reality. The rooms to each side of the center core were of differing levels and geometric shapes. Floor to ceiling mirrors and shaped interior windows enhanced and augmented a sense of light and space. Large rooms were divided by raised levels or unexpected alcoves. The soaring two-story space of the west studio room with its musicians' balcony further emphasized the imaginative spatial design of Studio House.

There are no records of how far the costs of the house exceeded the $18,000 estimate, but in the end it did not matter. With her inheritance of some one million dollars, it was possible for Alice to indulge herself by decorating the house exactly as she wished. The furnishings were as eccentric and eclectic as the architecture, combining Art Nouveau, Arts and Crafts, Neo-Gothic, and other exotic styles to create her own highly intentional aesthetic. The most notable examples of furniture were the dining suite, which had been handcarved with renaissance motifs and ebonized at the Cincinnati firm of Henry L. Fry in the early 1880s especially for the Barneys. Displayed on every available surface were objects she had collected over the years: Venetian glass, French fans, a suit of armor, plaster busts, tapestries, and antique fabrics.

Large oriental rugs were woven in England especially for the house. Outstanding among them was a gold, Indian-design rug created to fit the octagonal shape of the dining room. From Washington's Woodward and

TOWN & COUNTRY ARTICLE, 1904 *Anna P. Thomas,* Town & Country *reporter, interviewed Alice in 1903 at Studio House.*

Lothrop department store she purchased ruby red damask to cover the walls of the first-floor salon and gold damask for the second-floor petite salon, which was outfitted in her father's favorite Louis XVI style. What brought these divergent and often clashing styles together was the single-mindedness with which she followed John Ruskin's dictum to "have nothing in your houses that you do not know to be useful, or believe to be beautiful."

At the end of March Alice and Laura moved from the Gordon Apartments into Studio House. Although it had been started for a different purpose, Studio House was home. On May 28, 1903, the house passed its final inspection and on July 5, although officially still in deep mourning, Alice gave the first party at her new home. The headline for the story in the *Washington Post* read: "Mrs. Barney Entertains Builders of Her Studio House. Quaint Old Custom Revived."[4]

The large Sunday afternoon party's guest list included everyone who was involved in building Studio House, ranging from architect Waddy B. Wood to masons, tilesetters, carpenters, plumbers, hod-carriers, and day laborers. The hot, humid July afternoon led many people to seek a breath of air by climbing the narrow stairway located in the west studio that rose from the musicians' balcony to the roof garden above. Through an opening set at an angle at the northwest corner of the building, guests admired the bucolic view up Rock Creek Park and the verdant green of the Virginia palisades. The high walls surrounding the roof garden effectively hid both the studio skylight well and the offending trash on the opposite bank of Rock Creek. In the kitchen located in the English basement three stories below, servants worked feverishly to prepare trays heaped with food to send up in the dumb waiter to butlers stationed on each floor.

Most of the guests had never before attended an affair of this sort; but then neither had most members of Washington society. Everything was arranged with an eye to making the arts an integral part of the celebration. It was partially an art exhibition with Alice's pastels and portraits hanging in profusion on the walls, partially a concert with chamber music and singing provided, and partially a dramatic presentation with Laura reciting selections in French from the writings of Victor Hugo. The artistic ambience was as different from the usual cultural evening given by elite Washington leaders as Alice could make it.

There was no question that Alice gave the party to honor the workmen who had made her dream become reality, but, as with so many of her activities during her year of deep mourning, there was also an underlying point she wished to make about Washington culture. The motivation for this event was to prove once and for all that an American cultural capital could not afford to be elitist. The success of her creative housewarming party

STUDIO HOUSE ROOF GARDEN, C. 1904
Alice entertained on her roof garden at Studio

House, where there was a view of the Virginia palisades and the upper valley of Rock Creek Park.

proved that not only the upper classes could appreciate the arts, but that there was an untapped audience among the laboring class. "How," Alice asked within the hearing of the reporter she invited to cover the event from the *Mirror*, "can we best discharge our responsibility to all the citizens of the nation's capital?" Since Alice provided no answer to her own question, the reporter left it to the readers' speculation.

The reception on Sunday is the beginning of a social crusade which will be energetically carried forward next winter....The exact nature of this campaign is not communicated even to Mrs. Barney's intimates, except that her work will all be along social lines — to provide entertainments for the poor and middle classes, similar to those given for the high born and the opulent. It opens a vista rich in promise and best of all, it gives Washington something to talk about.[5]

CREATIVE MOURNING

The seed planted, Alice and Laura left the city to continue what some members of society ironically referred to as their "picturesque mourning" at Onteora, an artists' resort in the Catskills.

Alice first learned about Onteora in Paris from John White Alexander, who often spent summers there. The resort would never have appealed to Albert because most of the summer colony were artists, not socialites. Alice looked forward to the relaxed atmosphere and to seeing John and Elizabeth Alexander again. She particularly anticipated the pleasure of renewing her friendship with Marietta Cotton (or Pansy as she was known to her friends), a Philadelphia portrait painter she met in Paris soon after Pansy received an honorable mention at the 1899 Salon. Pansy was eleven years younger than Alice and, like Alice, was a student of Carolus-Duran and Jean-Jacques Henner. Alice had followed Pansy's career since Paris and knew of her commissions for portraits of well-known personages such as the Duke and Duchess La Rochefoucauld, the Infanta Eulalie, and the Comtesse Eula R. Zichy, the former Mabel Wright of New York. At the end of the summer, Alice planned to bring Pansy back to Washington for an extended visit during which she hoped to use her influence to help Pansy obtain a solo exhibition at the Corcoran.

The summer season passed quietly and productively. Letters from Natalie arrived with regularity full of news of her new friends Lucy and Jesus Mardrus, and of Eva's acting success. The only jarring note of the summer was a hastily penciled postscript to one of Natalie's letters, which said: "Too bad Whistler dead!"[6] How typical of Natalie, Alice thought. Natalie never considered other people's feelings. It was yet another event in this year of endings. The master might be dead, but her memories of him were not. Someday she would have to capture his personality on paper, perhaps even on stage. Right now, however, she needed to paint. Painting made her feel alive. Why had Albert never understood that?

Whistler's death was the only exception to an otherwise idyllic summer. One highlight was putting down her own brush and posing provocatively for Pansy. The newly made widow leaned forward onto a black marble pedestal capped by a satyr's head. Her shoulders were bared and her ample

LAURA AT TWENTY-
THREE, 1902
*By 1902 Laura Barney
was active in Paris's
Bahai community and
was instrumental in estab-
lishing a Bahai presence in
Washington, D. C.*

bosom was barely covered by the red drape she managed to hold in place by crossing her arms across her torso. Her smiling lips, tousled hair, and gleaming sultry eyes held no hint of grief.

When the painting was exhibited the following January in New York at Knoedler's Art Gallery, it caused a sensation. *The Club-Fellow*, New York's society magazine, said: "It was a likeness which an artist only (as a subject) would permit. Mrs. Barney prophesied correctly when she maintained that it was not for the public, that only friends who knew her well would understand it."[7]

Alice was publicly circumspect about Pansy's painting, but she kept hidden a small pastel that she executed at the same time. Titled *Morning Mood*, Alice portrayed herself with lips parted provocatively, her head turned wistfully toward the viewer. Her breasts are barely concealed by loosely wrapped drapery. If Pansy's portrait was for selected friends, Alice's portrait was for herself, and patently revealed her new sense of freedom and playfulness.

In November 1903, Alice was reelected vice-president of the Society of Washington Artists. Its first meeting set the goals for the coming year. Following Alice's lead, the members unanimously agreed to devote themselves to developing Washington as a national arts center. The well-attended December meeting marked the end of Alice's year of mourning and was held at Studio House. For the first time, the house was filled with the conversation of those for whom it was built—Washington's artists. The evening's agenda focused upon creating a workable strategy to achieve their goals. They decided their primary thrust would be to lobby the Corcoran Board of Directors to decide whether or not they would take over sponsorship of what was to be the Society's fourteenth annual exhibition.

Alice's force in Washington art circles was confirmed in February when she was invited to show three works from her collection at an exhibition of American and European painters organized by the prestigious Cosmos Club. The Cosmos Club was Washington's male intellectual preserve, demanding proven success in the fields of science, writing, or the arts as a prerequisite for membership unlike other men's clubs that stressed social standing over accomplishments. Alice was thrilled; she knew that for a woman collector and artist to be invited to exhibit was a coup. Only three other Washington artists, all men, were similarly honored. They were the

ALICE, C. 1903
After Albert's death, Alice obeyed the dictates of her year-long official mourning by always appearing in society elegantly attired in black.

backbone of the city's art community—Henry Moser, Max Weyl, and Hobart Nichols.

Other painters whose work was exhibited ranged from Benjamin Constant, Sir Joshua Reynolds, Thomas Moran, and Henry Ward Ranger to Alice's teacher Carolus-Duran. They were culled from the personal collections of prominent Washingtonians with the largest group lent by Ralph Cross Johnson. Alice lent two Carolus-Duran oils of her daughters and her own pastel of Gwendolyn Ffoulke, eldest daughter of the highly respected art connoisseur and Cosmos Club member, Charles M. Ffoulke. The Ffoulke portrait was the largest of the exhibition and depicted Gwendolyn seated before a mirror in which her image was reflected. Its simple, unadorned oak frame was designed by Alice to echo the mirror's frame.

Alice's Studio House, however, received the most attention—and not just as a local phenomenon. In early December Anna Thomas, a writer for *Town & Country*, came from New York to see it for herself. The resulting article, which also garnered Alice a story in the *New York Times*, not only presented its readers with a vivid description of Studio House accompanied by photographs, but a taste for some of Alice's plans for Washington.[8] Alice was now well-versed in manipulating interviewers, so it was no accident that almost any report of her activities included yet another suggestion of how to make Washington the cultural capital of the Western Hemisphere.

The project Alice espoused in *Town & Country* was the establishment of a national museum of art in Washington. She had talked about it to reporters before, but never in such detail. For her, the obvious first step was the empowerment of an international committee of art experts to select what should be in it. The second step was for Congress to allocate funds to erect and administer the new art museum. Third, because she saw the primary objective of the new museum as the advancement of "the higher education of persons who are unable to travel abroad," admission must be free. Finally, to encourage collectors to buy the finest European art for the purpose of loaning it to the new museum, the import tax upon fine arts would be waived if it were accepted for exhibition at the new museum by the selection committee. Curiously, she did not see the government as art collector because she believed that ownership of artworks should remain in private hands.

OUT OF MOURNING

Alice breathed a sigh of relief when it was finally 1904, for it meant she no longer was restricted by the ritual of deep mourning. Even though the black outfits she wore during 1903 were ultra-fashionable, she welcomed the touch of color that now could be added to her toilette. While parties were still out of the question, the series of intimate, informal teas she initiated during the holidays for members of the artistic and diplomatic communities brought little criticism.

When Natalie arrived from Paris for a visit, Alice's spirits lifted further. As Natalie's trunks were being carried up the steep stairs to her fourth-floor bedroom suite, Laura's were being packed for a trip to meet with leaders of the Bahai faith in Egypt and Syria. It was not only Natalie's first visit to her mother's new home, but the first time they had been together since Albert's death. As Natalie explored Studio House, she noted how the fanciful, eclectic clutter that overlay the simple architectural lines of the house aptly reflected Alice's multifaceted, exuberant delight in the arts. Studio House was, in fact, altogether different from Natalie's remembered childhood residence, which evoked more the ambience of a men's club than a home.

For Natalie, there was nothing drearier than a Washington December, and so a fire burned continuously in the fireplace of the great studio room to dispel the damp and gloom. Most mornings were spent in the studio: Alice painting while Natalie read or wrote. Occasionally, when Natalie looked up from her work, she saw Alice staring at the fire, chalks held unnoticed in her hand. Not until Ellen Goin arrived for a visit, did Natalie discover the reason for Alice's concentration on the darting flames.

ELLEN GOIN, 1902
Ellen Goin married Manuel E. Rionda, a Cuban sugar magnate. They lived on a 150-acre estate, Glen Goin, near Alpine, New Jersey. Ellen was strongly influenced by Alice, and Glen Goin's decor was very similar to Studio House.

Unlike Natalie, who tended to fidget, Ellen was an excellent model and one of Alice's favorites. Once Ellen assumed a pose in a chair in front of the fireplace, Alice started to work immediately, the finished portrait already conceived in her mind. She rapidly sketched an outline of Ellen's head and torso at the foreground. Then she filled in the background with long, firm strokes of bright yellows, reds, and blues. Once the background shimmered with the brilliance of the primary colors, Alice returned to fleshing out Ellen's likeness. The finished portrait of Ellen portrayed her hair and skin bathed in the glow of the reflected firelight. To complement and extend the imagery, Alice designed a special frame for it, which utilized roughly hammered negative spaces to emphasize an overall flame pattern.

Alice worked at top speed in order to complete the picture in time to enter it in the Fourteenth Annual Society of Washington Artists Exhibition. Entitled *A Portrait by Firelight*, it was extravagantly praised, particularly by Moser in the *Post*. He found the work "a harmonious low-keyed fireside reverie that is Besnard-like, but better because it has the good qualities of color, strong, crisp drawing, and style of that noted Impressionist without being a discordant freak."[9]

With her mother and Ellen engrossed in the portrait, Natalie found herself at loose ends. Of the few Washington friends made on her infrequent visits to the city over the years, most were either married or had moved. On February 7, however, Natalie found a project that excited her. After reading the banner headlines of the burning of Baltimore's business district, she decided to organize a benefit for victims of the fire. Although the conflagration that destroyed Baltimore's business district did not rival the burning of Chicago, its effect on Washington's nearest neighbor was, nevertheless, devastating. Firefighters from all over the eastern seaboard joined to fight the blaze, but in the end only a few walls remained.

Huge sums were needed to rebuild, but unfortunately for Baltimore, Natalie did not have her mother's fundraising knack. Her choice of a lecture on Wagner's *Parsifal* by Walter Damrosh as the vehicle to which people would flock and pay benefit ticket prices was doomed from the start. The intellectual community of Washington, which might be attracted to such an esoteric event, was neither large nor wealthy, and Natalie badly underestimated the resistance of those who expected that they be entertained in exchange for their charitable dollars. Even though Mrs. Roosevelt attended, when the receipts were toted up against expenses, Natalie's personal contribution of $475 was the only reason the fundraiser ended in the black.

Alice was taken aback by her daughter's failure, for she was savvy enough to know that the successful organization of charitable events partially determined social standing. Thus, following close upon the heels of Natalie's fiasco were announcements that Alice was putting together a theatrical extravaganza for charity at the end of Lent. Rehearsals for *The Dream of Queen Elizabeth* began in March and from newspaper reports it was clear that Alice succeeded in making participation the most sought after activity in town. The president's daughter Alice Roosevelt wanted to be in it, only to be told by her father that no daughter of a president could appear on stage. With over one-hundred prominent patronesses listed in the program, advance ticket sales were enormous, even though the beneficiary was not yet announced. The reason no specific charity was named was that Alice was in a quandary. On one hand she felt obliged to raise money for victims of the Baltimore fire to make up for Natalie's failure. On the other, she wanted to use this entertainment as the vehicle to bring a new charity to public attention.

In 1901 Alice had served briefly as the vice-president of the Associated Charities, a precursor of the United Way. In the course of her short tenure, she came to know and respect its energetic, young executive director, Charles Weller. Weller was also director of Neighborhood House, a settlement house in the southwest area of Washington modeled after the successful English social movement begun in 1844.

In Washington it was the custom of wealthy women to choose a single charity with which to associate their name. The charity Alice selected was Neighborhood House, which she believed could provide a model for the development of cultural awareness among blue-collar workers.[10] She remembered the perceptiveness of Parisian working men enjoying the Louvre and saw no reason why the same could not be true of Washington's populace. After due consideration, however, Alice decided to put her public support of Neighborhood House in abeyance. A week before the show opened, she announced that all money raised would benefit the families of men killed in an explosion on the battleship "Missouri."

If constant ballyhoo could guarantee success, *The Dream of Queen Elizabeth* was a smash hit long before the doors of the theater opened. Daily reports on the progress of rehearsals, ticket sales, and patron solicitation were published in papers up and down the East Coast. Whenever interest appeared to lag, Alice added a new twist such as inviting Emma Calvé, the great diva, to watch a rehearsal. Reporters stood outside Studio House waiting for Calvé to emerge, eagerly seeking her opinion of the singing ability of leading actors and actresses. Calvé, who was no stranger to handling the press, fielded the questions with finesse and assumed an air of humble appreciation for what she had just heard. Alice even provided an item for Moser's art column in the *Post* by dashing off a sketch of Queen Elizabeth and placing it in the window of the Veerhoff Gallery on Connecticut Avenue where it would be seen by the elite on their Sunday promenades.

Since everyone knew Alice was a consummate portraitist and that the queen was played by the beautiful Sally Anderson Fremont, widow of Admiral John Fremont, Moser's comments about the portrait aroused great curiosity. "The virgin

PROGRAM COVER, 1904
The Washington Mirror, *a weekly gossip magazine, called Alice's 1904 production of* The Dream of Queen Elizabeth, *"The Queen's Nightmare."*

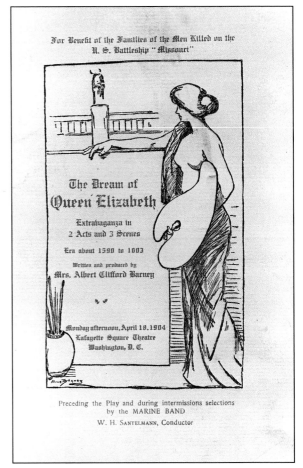

For Benefit of the Families of the Men Killed on the U. S. Battleship "Missouri"

The Dream of
Queen Elizabeth

Extravaganza in
2 Acts and 3 Scenes

Era about 1590 to 1603

Written and produced by
Mrs. Albert Clifford Barney

Monday afternoon, April 18, 1904
Lafayette Square Theatre
Washington, D. C.

Preceding the Play and during intermissions selections by the MARINE BAND
W. H. Santelmann, Conductor

COUNTESS MARGUERITE
CASSINI, 1904
*The Russian Countess
Marguerite Cassini
appeared as Judith in*
The Dream of Queen
Elizabeth. *The Countess
later remembered she
appeared in a costume wearing a "pair of lace curtains
and some Chinese brocades."*

queen! This decrepit old woman, full of indomitable will power, was pictured in a merciless fashion, which one would look for only in a Lenbach, or Gude. One shuddered at it, but it was a page from history as a painter alone, and one of skill and genius, could make."[11] It would be worth the price of a ticket to see Sally in makeup.

In many ways the actual event was an anticlimax. The *Washington Mirror* had a field day tearing the production apart in an article titled "The Queen's Nightmare," and probably gave a more accurate account of the amateur event than the major dailies, which skirted the merits of the play and gushed in praise of the beautiful actresses, the glittering prominence of the audience that included Alice Roosevelt in a pale yellow gown, and the enormous net at the box office.

Alice Barney's success at the charity fundraising game was clear. She knew how to do it better than anyone else. In the future others would call upon her services, and she intended to assist them, knowing full well that it meant she would tote up important IOUs, which she had every intention of using to further her own plans for Washington's cultural life.

At Natalie's urging and Alice's own need for the artistic refreshment of the continent, the two women boarded the *Deutschland* on June 9 for Europe and at least a year's absence. Alice's personal attention to her various projects were put on hold, but movement in all areas was not halted. In fact, behind the scenes, several of Alice's schemes were already in process. While to outward appearances she appeared to be abrogating her leadership of Washington's cultural life, in reality she was leaving it on simmer to have some badly needed carefree fun. When she returned she was fully prepared to stir the pot once more.

III
Later
Years

XII
Setting an Example

When Alice returned to the United States in November 1905, following a tour of southern Europe and a visit to Cairo to meet the leader of the Bahais, Abdul Baha, she launched into a round of activities that was to form the pattern for the rest of her life. Like her father, she was a woman of action rather than contemplation, and she had been inactive far too long.

She began quietly enough by sending carefully selected diplomats, judges, senators, and society leaders a small, tastefully printed invitation to attend an "Evening at Studio House" on December 18. In addition to dinner, an imaginative entertainment was promised. It would showcase the acting talent of her holiday guest Eva Palmer. The chosen vehicle was the balcony scene from *Romeo and Juliet* with Eva as Romeo and Edith Harlan Child, granddaughter of Supreme Court Justice John Marshall Harlan, as Juliet. Dressed in hose and buskin, Eva spoke Romeo's words of love to Edith who stood hovering above her on the musicians' balcony of the great studio room. Although there were a few whispers in the audience about Eva's overly realistic amorous pursuit, it was attributed to the fact that Eva had studied in Paris where Sarah Bernhardt's emotional acting was the model. Moreover, Alice made sure that everyone knew Eva had been selected personally by the divine Sarah to join her company in the spring. Whatever the artistic quality of the event, there was no question that Alice's evening was a welcome respite from the standard fare of musical recitals routinely presented by Washington hostesses.

In the following month Alice took a different tack by inviting some well-known theatrical personages to dine with her at Studio House. The first was her girlhood friend Caroline Louise Dudley, who had awaited Alice at the Dayton railway station and witnessed Alice's introduction to Albert. At forty-four, Carrie (better known by her stage name of Mrs. Leslie Carter) was the acknowledged queen of America's emotional actresses and called the American Sarah Bernhardt as the result of her portrayals of Madame du Barry and Zaza under the tutelage of the great impresario David Belasco. At Carrrie's request, Alice sketched a portrait of her that, when exhibited in March 1906 at the Corcoran, caused *Washington Post* critic Henry Moser to write that while on first glance the picture exhibited the "coarsest, most breezy, high-keyed technique imaginable," on further study a viewer "will discover that through its broken color and 'unfinish' there appears a living, breathing personality, a sense of red-blooded, wholesome life and happiness."[1]

ALICE IN STUDIO HOUSE, C. 1915
Alice poses with her portrait of Whistler. In her hand she holds a peacock feather, representing the preeminent Symbolist image.

Preceding pages:
First floor reception room with stage at South End, Studio House, c. 1911

Her second guest was Ben Greet, an English Shakespearean actor and producer (and later a cofounder of the Royal Shakespeare Academy) who was in America to promote the idea of performing Shakespearean plays on the green and to find a place suitable for such a production in Washington. His purpose in presenting Shakespeare out-of-doors was to disencumber Shakespearean plays from almost three hundred years of accumulated theatrical baggage and bowdlerization. In alfresco productions Shakespeare's genius could shine through, uncluttered by creaking stage effects, cumbersome scenery, or happy endings. In Alice he found a willing convert as she readily visualized the dramatic power of a performance relying equally upon the strength of the audience's imagination and Shakespeare's words. So taken was Alice by Greet and his ideas that she immediately began writing a synopsis for a spring theatrical to be presented out-of-doors.

UNDERLYING MOTIVE

The hospitality Alice extended to artists and friends alike was not totally disingenuous. Behind each extension of hospitality was an iron-willed purpose: someone must show Washingtonians how to live a cultured life. While support of the visual arts was expected, her forays into theater were not. What Alice attempted to illustrate by example was that to be truly cultured a person needed to understand that the arts were interrelated. Indeed, for Alice, to limit her enjoyment of the arts to only one discipline was tantamount to a living death. Even worse was to abjure the arts as Albert had done. Thus, her own highly publicized forays into varied artistic experiences ranged from theatricals to concerts to poetry readings to art exhibitions—all aimed at providing an example to Washington of how to live artistically. She was particularly solicitous of young performers, and they most benefited from the regular assemblage of Washington's elite for her "evenings."

Much of her understanding of art and artists derived from being an artist herself. While Alice took great pride in her patronage of the arts, she was well aware that much of her credibility as a spokesperson for the arts came from being a practicing artist. Her nearest rival for the title of Wash-

MRS. LESLIE CARTER,
C. 1904
Alice's childhood friend from Dayton, Ohio, Caroline Louise Dudley was better known as Mrs. Leslie Carter, the queen of America's emotional actresses and the American Sarah Bernhardt.

ington's Queen of Culture remained Mrs. Johan Henderson who tried to call the city's cultural shots from her castle at Sixteenth and Florida Avenue, N.W. But no matter how much Mrs. Henderson tried to be the leading light of Washington's arts arena, Alice retained the upper hand because she not only talked art, she produced it.

As an artist, Alice was acutely aware that the problem of a lack of suitable exhibition spaces remained unsolved during her time in Europe. To get people thinking, she decided to give Washington's art patrons a model solution at Studio House. On January 12, 1906, the cream of society gathered in her studio to see an exhibition of pastel portraits by Juliet Thompson and miniatures by Andrea Lenrique. It was a grand gesture, but no one seemed willing to follow suit. On January 21, after a long delay, the Corcoran's Board of Directors finally voted to accept the Society of Washington Artists' proposal to sponsor a juried annual national exhibition. When the Corcoran limited entries to oils, the significance of Alice's attempt to open up large private homes for exhibition space took on a greater importance.

When the idea found no takers, Alice returned to her painting until she was ready to fire another salvo. Her next prominent sitter was the Cuban Minister, Gonzalo de Quesada. Not since painting Albert's portrait in 1898 had she attempted to capture a man's likeness in oil. She asked Quesada to pose for the same reason she chose all her models—his looks fascinated her. A singularly handsome man with flowing black hair and full handlebar mustache, Quesada observed Washington through heavy-lidded, piercing dark eyes.

As Alice learned while sketching Whistler, her success in depicting men depended as much on her ability to get them to talk about themselves as her talent to create a likeness. When the sittings began, she and Quesada were merely social acquaintances, and when the painting was complete, they were close friends. Alice was a sympathetic listener, and the ardent Cuban patriot had much on his mind. He held one of the most difficult posts in Washington representing a free Cuba at a time when America's paternalistic foreign policy toward Cuba was predicated on the constant threat of U.S. invasion. In the end, Alice was so fascinated by Quesada that she attempted two portraits of him, only one of which was finished.

The completed oil was a three-quarter frontal portrait similar in composition to Ottilie Roederstein's painting of Albert. The contrast between the two portraits, however, was not in execution, but in what it revealed of the sitter. Ottilie's portrait of Albert showed a man reaching the end of his life, while Alice's portrait of Quesada was that of a man in his prime. Quesada was depicted as the consummate diplomat, relaxed in stance but poised for action. It was a portrait of tension and captured the pressure of the diplomatic tightrope upon which Quesada walked. When she showed it for the

first time at the Corcoran, Moser pronounced it "a Spanish nocturne which would have delighted Whistler."[2]

On March 19 Alice was informed of the death of her brother, Lawrence, from a heart attack in his hotel room at the San Remo Hotel on Central Park West. The obituary in the *New York Times* was short. There was not much to say about him, Alice thought, because since his one attempt at business in the mid-1870s, Lawrence had spent the remainder of his life bent on pleasure. There were only his clubs (Lotus, Manhattan, and New York Yacht Club) and his siblings to list. Over the years, Lawrence had developed into such a self-centered person that neither Alice nor her sisters

WEST STUDIO, STUDIO HOUSE, 1904
The west studio of Studio House was the epitome of a turn-of-the-century studio, eclectic and artfully arranged to be both studio and salon.

had made any pretext of keeping up close ties with their older brother. Nevertheless, Alice pulled a few black dresses to the front of her closet for attending his small private funeral. She would not, however, observe a lengthy mourning period for a brother with whom she had so little contact for so many years. Thus, less than a month later on April 1, the *Post* announced that Alice would produce a benefit performance the first week in May.

For the next sixteen days, the *Post* bombarded the public with daily progress reports because the site for the event was the grounds of Friendship, the summer home of John R. McLean, founder of the *Washington Post*. Alice's production was to be an original pageant in the style of an eighteenth century pastorale inspired by those given at Versailles. Alice looked forward to the event with as much eagerness as her performers; it was her first opportunity to test Greet's theories of outdoor theater. On April 18, 1906, however, all ballyhoo for the pageant ceased as news reached the East Coast of the devastating San Francisco earthquake.

CHARITABLE BENEFITS

For some twenty years the wealthy of Washington had demonstrated their charitable largesse by vigorously and wholeheartedly supporting a plethora of local and national causes. Benefits were so important to Washington society that social acceptance was judged as much by the ability to raise money as personal wealth or lineage. It was not surprising, therefore, that from the moment Alice learned about the earthquake, she put her play on hold and began to look for a particularly exciting and creative drawing card to fill the coffers of a newly created fund to aid earthquake victims.

As time was of the essence, Alice asked Martha Wadsworth to help her. Martha, like Alice, was a midwesterner and owned a proven track record as a fundraiser. Common interests made the two women close friends, rather than competitors, in Washington's social life. Like Alice, Martha had a flair for architecture; when Martha built her home at 1801 Massachusetts Avenue, it was designed and decorated almost entirely by her. Her husband, Herbert, was often heard to declare: "There is only one thing that house lacks. The arch over the carriage entrance should have written on it, in Gothic letters, 'Marfy done it!'"[3] Where Alice looked at all the arts as her purview, Martha concentrated mainly on music while retaining an avid interest in other arts. In 1902 Martha availed herself of her husband's seemingly bottomless pockets and backed the founding of the short-lived Washington Philharmonic Orchestra. She also held formal recitals in her ballroom, which featured not only international greats but members of her private singing class.

The two women began to look for a very special program, one that must be absolutely new to Washington and that would titillate as well as capti-vate. Word had recently reached the capital that New York had a new star that was all the rage. Moreover, the prestigious Isabelle Gardner of Boston had summoned her to perform at a private party at Fenway Court. It was the Boston event that convinced Alice and Martha that Washington society would pay good money to see the daring avant-garde dancer, Ruth St. Denis. She was just the artistically unique performer they were looking for.

St. Denis's act was like nothing ever seen before on the American stage. Although some remarked on its resemblance to Little Egypt's hootchie-kootchie act at the 1893 Columbian Exposition, others recognized that her choreography went far beyond the conventions of the midway. St. Denis's dances were created from all the sources available to a person who never went to India: books on Hindu myth, East Indian photographs, Delsartian movement, and readings from popular literature on the mysteries of India, as well as several visits to carnival sideshows. At St. Denis's debut of her new creation in a vaudeville turn at the New York Theatre on January 28, 1906, she left her audience puzzled, intrigued, and clamoring for more.[4]

St. Denis called her program *Radha*, although only the last piece actually went by that title. The music was ersatz oriental, chosen because it met the popular romantic notion of what exotic music should sound like. Two of the dances were choreographed to music from Léo Delibes's opera *Lakme*. The third was inspired by a composition by Harvey Worthington Loomis, an American composer of operettas.

"The Incense" was the first dance. St. Denis, draped in white gauze, slowly and sinuously moved forward through a series of oriental hangings to the front of the stage. Behind her, fragrant smoke wafted upward from the incense brazier she held majestically before her. She placed the brazier on the stage apron and began weaving in and out of the rising smoke. As the music neared its finale, she slowly undulated backward and disap-peared behind the arras leaving a stage filled with smoke as the curtains slowly closed.

"The Cobras" followed. Like the first piece, it was based upon simple Delsartian movement but with quickened tempo. This dance was St. Denis's conception of a dervish at a bazaar. On the index and little finger of each hand she wore large gold rings embedded with a prominent green stone to simulate the eye of a cobra. With a combination of arm and hand movements she pantomimed the twisting and turning of two cobras. When the music reached its peak, she rushed to the front of the stage and pointed the snake's eye rings directly at the audience causing, it was said, several women in the audience to faint.

The final dance, "Radha," was a fully-staged temple dance with a set, a cast of extras, and a story line. More fully realized than the other dances, she shocked audiences by appearing with bare feet, bare midriff, and thighs and legs teasingly glimpsed through her skirt of glittering gold-colored gauze. Of the three dances, "Radha" was the one Alice and Martha wanted presented.[5]

Wearing black chiffon over white satin, Alice sat transfixed in her theater box as St. Denis transported her and other audience members "across the seas to the land of neophra flowers and mysticism."[6] There was much discussion about who was the most daring—Ruth St. Denis for dancing almost nude on the stage or Alice for bringing her to Washington.

Just as St. Denis left an impression upon staid Washingtonians, Alice left one upon St. Denis. In her autobiography St. Denis wrote:

> I went to Washington at the invitation of that remarkable and delightful individual, Mrs. Alice Barney, to appear for another charity. The diplomatic group and the president's daughter, Mrs. Nicholas Longworth, were there. Mrs. Barney was an eccentric, talented individual with butterscotch-colored hair which flew in all directions, and an extraordinary taste in clothes. She had a flair for assisting artists and giving original parties. Her organizing capacities were amazing; at parties she managed to be in four rooms at once, seeing to everything, reaching over four or five heads to say hello to someone she had not seen for twenty years and yet recognized immediately.[7]

Bringing St. Denis to Washington was a passing triumph for Alice, as she frantically readied her pastorale for performance at the McLean's estate. At times like this she felt most like her father's daughter. She felt his passion for theater in her genes and wished he were there to see her theatrical achievements. At this point they could not begin to measure up to what he had accomplished, but perhaps one day, she, too, would be able to found a theater.

The grounds of the McLean estate were perfect for theater on the green. Its Italianate formal gardens were lined with box hedges that delineated the boundaries of the out-of-door auditorium and the grassy stage area was demarcated by the spreading limbs of two giant oaks silhouetted against the McLean's magnificent yellow palazzo. While the production did not have the polish of Ben Greet's Shakespearean plays running concurrently at Woodley in the Cleveland Park area of Washington, much of what Alice learned in the process she used later for other out-of-door theater ventures.

SUMMER TRAVELS

By June, Washington was in the midst of a heat wave. The elegant alfresco meals Alice gave for her cast during May were no longer possible, and the summer resorts prepared for an early influx of Washington residents. In the western sector of the city front doors were boarded up and shades drawn. With the exception of congressmen, everyone who could afford to do so headed for the seashore or the mountains. Ban-y-Bryn remained closed as Alice left to summer at Stony Man Mountain in the Blue Ridge Mountains of Page County, Virginia. Toward the end of the summer, she traveled to Canada where, like her peers in resorts up and down the East Coast, she remained until October and cooler weather. In Europe, Natalie left Paris for Orange in southern France to attend a play written by her friend and now lover Lucy Delarue-Mardrus, then on to Bayrueth and finally to the isle of Lesbos. Laura, ever in search of spiritual enlightenment, spent the summer visiting Bahais in Egypt, Turkey, and Persia.

Alice returned to Washington in late fall to the good news that a collection of paintings bequeathed to the United States by President Buchanan's niece, Harriet Lane Johnson, would form the nucleus of a federal art collection under the aegis of the Smithsonian Institution. The collection was to be housed in a hall at the National Museum (now the National Museum of Natural History) on Constitution Avenue. Although the new art bureau did not have its own edifice, nor was it organized in the manner Alice thought most efficacious for growth, she fully supported the federal government's action because it signaled a major step toward the creation of a full-fledged national gallery of art.

As 1907 began, Alice appeared to her friends, when she had the time to stop for a minute and talk with them, to be engaged in a whirlwind of artistic endeavors. If by the end of the winter season, they said among themselves, society did not know how to live artistically, they had not been paying attention to Alice Barney. There were tableaux at the Willard, programs at Studio House, and a visit from the portrait painter Pansy Cotton. On top of this was Alice's growing involvement with Neighborhood House. In 1905 she had purchased one of Washington's oldest residences, the former Judge Crane home in the southwestern sector of the city, and provided it rent-free to Neighborhood House. The primary stipulation was that the Crane house be called Barney Neighborhood Club Building and be used to develop an industrial arts program modeled after the former McMicken School of Design. The curriculum was to stress practical

LUCY DELARUE-MARDRUS WITH HER HUSBAND, DR. JESUS CHRIST MARDRUS, C. 1909.
Dr. Mardrus gained fame for his translation of A Thousand and One Nights. *Lucy, who was one of Natalie's loves, wrote a poem to Circe in accompaniment to Alice's Symbolist pastel of the same name.*

LAURA, HAIFA, 1906
*Laura frequently traveled
to the Middle East to meet
with Bahais. Sitting just
below her and to her left is
Hippolyte Dreyfus, whom
she would marry in 1911.*

training in decorative arts skills that could be transfered by youths to non-arts employment as adults.

Alice's largesse was not without headaches for the new director of Neighborhood House, John P. S. Neligh. She not only had very definite opinions about the program to be carried on in her house, but about its decor as well. She also felt her generosity entitled her to an exchange, and Neligh found himself caretaker of Studio House when Alice left that summer for Europe. Moreover, he discovered that his patroness could be quite tight with her money and that where repairs to Studio House were involved, he needed to be very careful. He received a particularly irate letter from Alice castigating him for his failure to find an inexpensive roofer to repair leaks at Studio House.

Having left detailed instructions for Neligh, Alice headed once again for Paris and the anticipation of focusing on her painting. It was a period of prolific creation, spent partly with Natalie at her home in the Bois de Bologne and partly in London in what had once been Whistler's White

House on Tite Street. In March 1908 she invited friends and critics into her Parisian studio to view her latest work. In July she exhibited fifty-eight pastel portraits and sketches at London's Modern Gallery. Among them were portrait sketches of essayist and novelist G. K. Chesterton and playwright George Bernard Shaw, whom she had invited to pose in her studio in exchange for tea and conversation.

Parisian critics admired her work, particularly *Circe*, which had inspired the poetess Lucy Delarue-Mardrus to write:

> The eternal clamor of this open mouth
> Warns humans of their ultimate ruin
> Those who deliver themselves to Circe's
>   love
> Will see their brains cracked against her
>   breasts.
> Because for her always unsatisfied depths,
> She demands not men, but beasts![8]

On the other hand, London reviewers intensely disliked the very same work, writing that her seeming originality of style only created confusion.

One would have thought by this time Alice would have been inured to criticism, but even she was surprised by how deeply hurt she was by London's appraisal of her work. She had such a long string of successes that she was unprepared for negative criticism. Leaving instructions at the Bond Gallery on where to send her pictures after the close of the show, she immediately left for Paris and the comfort of friends who understood her.

MANIFESTOS

Still smarting, she was not ready for the telegram informing her of her mother's death. More troubling was a letter from her favorite sister Hester. Enclosed with it was a copy of a letter Hessie had written to Nettie's daughter, Ellen Goin. Shortly before her death, their mother had changed her will and left the entire Pike estate to Jeannette. In her letter Hester charged that Jeannette had coerced Ellen into ignoring her other two daughters.

Alice had never been quite so angry. She was driven to sit down at her desk and pen her own will. In it she made absolutely clear that Jeannette's greed had severed whatever tenuous relationship still existed between them. Thus, to her, Alice left "all that which she has already taken."

ALICE'S LONDON HOME, 1908
In 1908 Alice lived and painted in a home that had been Whistler's White House on Tite Street in London. While Whistler's house has been demolished, the former residences of Oscar Wilde and James Singer Sargent still stand on this residential street in Chelsea.

Opposite top:
GEORGE BERNARD SHAW, 1908
Pastel on fiberboard, 27⅞ x 19⅛ in. (70.8 x 48.6 cm)
Shaw and G. K. Chesterton were among the well-known London figures Alice met during her year in London.

Ellen Goin, Jeannette's only daughter was still Alice's favorite niece, and while she could not bring herself to leave money, she did leave her a piece of jewelry. It also seemed a good time to settle grievances with both sides of the family, and so a niece on Albert's side of the family, Lulu Platt Hunt, who had gossiped viciously about Natalie's lifestyle, was left only "the forgiveness of all her petty unkindness to me and mine." While she was at it, she decided to add two other bequests, both of which she thought would have pleased her father. The first directed Laura to allot one-third of Alice's estate for educational purposes including the printing of books and the staging of plays. The second donated Studio House to the City of Washington "to be kept as a museum and for a meeting place for the Rock Creek Valley Commission, for charity concerts and lectures, and any purpose of this kind." Moreover, with the exception of objects her daughters might want, all of her paintings, tapestries, and furniture were to remain with the house. With the writing of her will, Alice's anger at her sister and the hurt from her reviews evaporated. Her vigor and outlook renewed, in October, Alice left Paris for Washington, eager to continue the challenge of developing Washington's cultural life.

Her opening shot was a manifesto issued on November 28, 1908. The subject was "free art." She still was not satisfied that the federal government was totally dedicated to creating a national art museum, nor did she think it understood the dilatory effect of the tariff act on the entrance of artwork into the country for the benefit of the public. She sent her manifesto to the House Ways and Means Committee then holding hearings on the question of import duty on works of art.

Her statement was an expansion of her earlier position on the tariff as reported in the press. At the forefront was her insistence that a committee of experts must be established to pass judgment on all art entering the country. The committee she envisioned would be composed of "gentlemen of leisure and high artistic qualifications...who would be willing to serve without a salary, and just for the honor and pleasure which a participation in the artistic development of their country would afford them." Artwork judged mediocre would continue to be taxed at thirty percent of value. For

CATALOG, 1908
*Alice's one-woman
exhibition at the Modern
Gallery included her
sketch of G. B. Shaw.*

works considered of high quality, the owners would lend them for a period of two years to the federal government for exhibition at the national museum in Washington in lieu of paying the tax. The result of the adoption of her proposal would be that:

> the government, too, will not be without a material profit: (1) It will receive duties on second-class works of art; (2) it will receive half duties for works of art whose owners would not be willing to loan them for a period extending beyond one year; (3) it could charge a small admission from all those who wish to enter the museum, allowing certain days in the month during which all would be admitted free; (4) that now that limited 'free art' is not allowed, many yearly spend large sums of money abroad in order to visit and study works of art while by having limited 'free art' in America the bulk of that money would be spent in America itself.

In addition to being part of the House Ways and Means Committee's hearing records, her manifesto was printed in *American Art News*, a nationally distributed arts journal. An accompanying editorial pointed out its basic flaw: the committee of experts would have to examine every piece of art entering the country wherever customs examinations were made. "It would be, we think, impossible to secure the services of men sufficiently accomplished to pass upon importations at New York, Boston, Philadelphia, Baltimore, Savannah, etc." The editorial failed, however, to address the underlying concerns she sought to address in her proposal. "More harm," she wrote, "can be done in the long run to the public in showing them non-genuine works of art and corrupting their sense of art appreciation than by not showing them any works of art at all....A National Building erected by the Government for the exhibition of works of Art would prove of invaluable importance to the nation at large."[9]

PRESS COVERAGE

Her opinion presented, Alice decided that if she were going to talk about educating the general populace to the value of the arts, it was time to do something about it on the practical level. Thus she volunteered at Neighborhood House because it offered an opportunity for hands-on involvement. She had never been one to stand idly by doling out money to this or that cause.

Every so often she arrived unannounced to inspect the industrial arts building and to assure herself that it was being properly utilized. During the winter of 1907–1908, she decided to try her hand at teaching. She called her class, "The Rainbow School," and in it students learned the art of tie-dying silk. To illustrate how crafts could earn the maker money, Alice took it upon herself to sell the unique gossamer, multihued, silk chiffon scarves to her friends.

There were very few weeks when there was not some mention of Alice Barney in the press. Although it was good to keep her name in the forefront, she was annoyed that most mentions were in the society columns where it seemed more important to report what she wore than what she did. Typical was *Washington Post* coverage of an opening at the Corcoran, in which more lines of type were used to describe her dress than the exhibition's paintings. Alice Barney, the *Post* reported, sailed through galleries examining paintings through a diamond-studded lorgnette and wearing a black tulle dress with green and gold palettes sewn on it to form an overall pattern of peacock eyes. In her hair she wore a peacock green ornament from which hung a long, uncurled ostrich plume.

This was not the type of publicity Alice needed to assert her leadership of Washington culture. It was time to once again use the press for her own purposes. On January 5, 1909, Alice held a news conference to announce her bequest of Studio House to Washington as a museum and intimate cultural center. As Washington papers were quick to point out, the only other example of such a gift in America was Isabelle Stewart Gardner's gift of her home in Fenway Park as a museum for Boston.

The other coverage she sought out was for the special events held at Studio House, at least those that provided an example of what should occur in a cultured setting. Among them was a lecture series on Persian life by Mme. Ali Kuli Khan (the former Florence Breed of Boston), wife of the chargé d'affaires at the Persian embassy. On another afternoon she entertained fifty guests at a musicale featuring the English baritone Cecil Fanning.

The most ambitious event of the winter of 1909 was an evening of ten tableaux held in the studio accompanied by a diverse group of musical selections sung by Fanning. Among them were the "Prologue" from *I Pagliacci*; "Herr Oluf" by Johann Loewe; "Dante's Traum" by Martin Pluddemann; and "Menuet d'Exaudet." The exotic "Vision Fugitive" from *Herodiade* by Jules-Émile-Frédéric Massenet provided the finale. In attendance were senators, leaders of Washington society, and a sizeable contingent of ministers and ambassadors from Hungary, Italy, Russia, Switzerland, Portugal, Spain, Sweden, and England.

As Washington prepared for the inauguration of President William Howard Taft on March 4, 1909, Alice readied her annual spring theatrical event. That year it was to be an operetta written in collaboration with composer Harvey Wheaton Howard called *About Thebes*. Although it contained the obligatory crowd scenes and dancing girls to ensure ticket sales, the script marked her first attempt at conventional dramatic form with plot and dialogue.

The play was set in Egypt and told of a greedy American scientist who used the Khedive of Egypt's lust for a young American woman to obtain the secret of awakening the dead, its key hidden in scrolls buried with the mummies of Egyptian kings. Once deciphered, Ramses and Cleopatra came to life and became a threat to the Khedive. In turn, the Khedive threatened the life of the young woman if the scientist did not reveal how to send Cleopatra and Ramses back to their sarcophogi. All was put to right, however, when the scientist fell in love with the young woman halfway through the second act. By the fall of the curtain, the ancient Egyptian rulers were returned to the dead, and the loving couple were seen leaving the stage to sail for America to be married and live happily ever after.

When finally performed before an audience that included President and Mrs. Taft, few people noticed the absurd plot or stilted dialogue. Their attention was riveted on the dance that opened the second act. For several weeks prior to the premiere, notices appeared announcing that Mme. Geraldine Clifford of Paris had consented to dance a part, the first and last time she would perform in America. Although no one knew who Mme. Clifford was, no one had forgotten Alice's importation of Ruth St. Denis to Washington in 1906.

The curtain rose on the interior of the Tomb of Kings. The stage was filled with vapors from a smoke machine. Halfway down a long stairway at the rear of the stage, a lone figure stood bathed in green light. Slowly the apparition descended the stairs. The glittering batlike wings attached to the back of her gown quivered in sympathy with the oriental harmonies of the flute section. Disembodied rhythmic chanting sounded from various parts of the stage. When the mysterious figure reached the bottom of the stairs she began a sensuous twirling dance. It was the famous Mme. Geraldine. Lorgnettes and monocles were raised as the audience leaned forward to get a better look at Alice's latest coup. The figure danced closer to the apron of the stage. Suddenly gasps were heard from the house as the members of the audience with the best eyesight realized that Mme. Geraldine Clifford was none other than Alice Barney. The amazing sight of a fiftyish widow moving her barely concealed body provocatively about the stage raised a question repeated in drawing rooms throughout Washington, "what would Alice Barney do next?"

WHIRLWIND OF ACTIVITY

Next for Alice was to prove with finality that she was a professional artist. In response to an invitation from the Knoedler Gallery in New York, she shipped fifty-four pastels for exhibition in May. Most were seen previously in London and Paris, but included were new works such as a sketch of Sarah Bernhardt and portraits of Washington luminaries Alice Roosevelt

Longworth, the Baroness von Heugelmuller (wife of the Austrian Ambassador), and Ali Kuli Kahn of the Persian Embassy.

After her experience with the London critics, Alice was undeniably nervous about New York. In a letter to Leila Mechlin, she admitted her fear of her work "being a little too imaginative and personal for America's taste."[10] In the end, her fears proved groundless, although no review was without criticism. There was unanimity on the high level of her skill with pastel and the quality of her head and half-length sketches. Opinions on her larger portraits and studies varied. What one critic praised, another would denigrate, but, on the whole, the majority of her pastels were favorably received.

One criticism, however, appeared consistently in all the reviews she received. Not one critic liked her pastels executed in a Symbolist style. The *New York Times* critic thought them bizarre and the *New York Post* writer stated bluntly that he did not care for them. The two most salutary reviews merely hedged when it came to the Symbolist pastels. One said that although they tended toward bizarre sensationalism, they were well done "and good in color. The artist would seem to be a follower of no particular school, and her work appears to be the expression of an unusual individuality."[11] The other critic formulated his own philosophy about their import:

> It is only right that the suffragists of the future shall have their own bards and painters. In Mrs. Barney they will have an artist of singular merit, who shows very plainly her preference for women as sitters and as the subjects of ideal creations....To Mrs. Barney even the devil is a woman, as we see at once from her "Lucifer."
>
> Hell fire may play across these features as it will, rendering as red as roast sinner one part of the face, but ghastly green another; dull glowing points of ruby may shine in Lucifer's eyes—he is a she all the same.[12]

That spring, as viewers formed their opinion of her work at Knoedler's, Alice was busy at Neighborhood House. She purchased a second house for the organization's use as an infant day-care center, or baby dispensary, as it was called. As in 1907, she had set yet another record for artistic activity. What was clear to all was that she thrived on it. She was fit, lithe, and full of energy, looking and acting years younger than her peers. Still, she did take a long break each year, and by May she was on her way to the cool weather of Bar Harbor.

She had not been to Maine since Albert's death and was happy Laura joined her in her first summer as the widow Barney. Because Ban-y-Bryn was rented, they stayed at the Malvern Hotel. Unable to paint without a studio, Alice sat at the desk in her room and dashed off *The Bridal Veil*, a

Greek-style pastoral that was presented on the green before an enthusiastic audience of fifteen hundred of the East Coast's top society with music provided by the Boston Symphony, which she imported to Bar Harbor especially for the occasion. Even though it had been her purpose in going to Maine, to sit totally still was not part of her personality.

In October Alice stopped in Boston on her way to Washington to attend the opening of her exhibition at the Walter Kimball and Company Gallery on Arlington Street and to speak before the Boston Professional Women's Club. In the introductory paragraph of an interview run in Boston's *Reveille*, Alice was described as a member of a new breed of wealthy women, "the busy rich," who raise funds for charity through their own talent and invest time as well as money in their chosen philanthropies. Alice's talk before the women's club stressed a similar theme. Although she admitted for the first time that her involvement in such a multitude of activities (charities, social duties, painting, and trips) often tired her, her conscience did not allow her to rest for long. Moreover, she told her receptive audience, "work well done was the highest form of worship and that no one had the right to be idle."[13] Like her father, Alice had only disdain for the idle rich. Projects made life worth living.

Following the successful showing in Boston, Alice's pictures were shipped to Paris for a November exhibition at the Bernheim Jeune Gallery. The crated pastels were to return to Washington at the end of that month to be ready for Alice's second one-person show at the Corcoran Gallery of Art in late December. If that were not enough, Alice then embarked upon producing her most ambitious charity production to date. Thinking big, she booked the Shubert Theater chain's Belasco Theater on Twelfth Street, N.W., and immediately began rehearsing her new play, *The Man in the Moon*, at Studio House.

The benefit's designated charity was Neighborhood House and, in particular, the industrial arts program of the Barney Club. Under Alice's direction, the sets, costumes, and properties were executed for the performance

SOCIETY WOMAN WRITES PLAYS AND THEN ACTS THEM HERSELF

MRS. A. C. BARNEY.

The versatile Mrs. Albert Clifford Barney of Washington is rehearsing another play. Mrs. Barney not only writes plays, but acts in them and even dances. Her latest play, which is to be given for a charity at the Belasco theater in Washington Dec. 20, is called "The Man in the Moon," and in it Mrs. Barney will do a dance of jealousy called "Etude d'Espagne." She is pictured here in the costume she will wear during this dance—a costume of gold and silver Spanish church lace." The photograph is by Virginia M. Prall, one of the most artistic of the women photographers in the United States.

ALICE AT FIFTY-TWO, 1909
Alice in costume for her Spanish dance in her charitable extravaganza, The Man in the Moon. *She realized that this photograph would be a valuable publicity tool.*

by students enrolled in the club. Alice spent every waking moment getting her play into top shape. Every year brought a new crop of amateurs to grace the stage and this year was no exception. There were the season's debutantes to train in rudimentary stage craft, as well as the ever changing rank of bachelors who must be cajoled to step on the stage. Each day the incipient thespians gathered at the house on Sheridan Circle to practice songs and dances. Once it leaked out that Mme. Geraldine would make another appearance, ticket sales soared. Mrs. Taft reserved the President's box, and, by the date of the performance, only a few seats remained to be filled. A sold-out house was assured when Washington papers began to carry a picture of Alice dressed as a Spanish dancer: her head was thrown back, her brightly painted lips parted in a come-hither smile, a tightly corseted hip canted rakishly toward the camera. Everyone knew that *The Man in the Moon* was going to be very special.

XIII
Love Behind the Scenes

Nothing is so guaranteed to provoke instant intimacy among total strangers as putting on a play. Relationships often continue long after the final curtain; a stage romance can become reality. For Alice romance arose during performances of her production of *Man in the Moon*. Her torrid Spanish dance of jealousy (in which she bartered her life for a bullfighter's cloak) was not only received with enthusiasm by the audience, but with adoring looks by Christian Hemmick. Hemmick was one of the myriad supernumeraries in the cast who had been chosen for their ability to decorate the stage, proving the point that good looks, not talent, were Alice's primary criteria.

Alice was fifty-two in 1909, but she looked and acted much younger. She hid the gray in her hair with a Titian red henna rinse and the lines around her eyes with black mascara and eyeliner. It was, however, her boundless energy and enthusiasm for life that subtracted at least ten years from her chronological age. For Christian, who saw her through a scrim backlit by love, she was ageless.

Christian Dominique Hemmick was twenty-two years old when he agreed to take a small part in *Man in the Moon*. He had spent a number of years abroad while his father served as the consul to Geneva. Although he was cultivated, urbane, and well-educated, he had yet to find a woman he fancied. Upon returning to Washington in 1909, Christian became one of society's most popular bachelors and was much in demand as an escort during the debutante season. When he learned that being in one of Mrs. Barney's plays was the thing to do, he followed his crowd to rehearsals at Studio House. He was also curious about the eccentric Mrs. Barney and her fabled home.

According to both Christian and Alice, it was love at first sight. Christian was her Greek god; she was his queen. Night after night he stood in the crowd and watched her move to the seductive rhythms of flamenco, knowing that she danced just for him. Amazingly, as engrossed as they were in each other, no one in the large cast guessed their secret. Perhaps, it was because the very idea of an affair of the heart between Alice and Christian was preposterous—a woman past her prime and a callow youth. No one questioned the frequency with which they met beyond the appointed rehearsal time as Alice often worked individually with the more inexperienced members of her cast. Even the fact that Christian escorted her to numerous social functions aroused no suspicion as Alice always surrounded

ALICE IN COSTUME, C. 1909
Alice in costume for her role in The Man in the Moon, *created to benefit Alice's favorite charity, Neighborhood House.*

herself with attractive young people. It was the secret of her perpetual youth. When Christian posed for a portrait sketch, no one remarked on it. Alice was always sketching beautiful people.

If someone had been paying attention, they might have noticed how circumspect Alice was in 1910; she became the soul of discretion. There were no two-inch headlines trumpeting her latest opinion on Washington's cultural life and when her name appeared in social columns, it was as a patroness of the arts rather than a prophet. Articles still were written about her, but they had a different tone. They were affectionate and filled with hometown pride. Admittedly, Alice was slightly different from her peers, but it was her eccentricities that made her so delightful. Alice's Studio House was lauded as Washington's "meeting place for wit and wisdom, genius and talent, which fine material is leavened by fashionable folk, who would like to be a bit Bohemian if they only knew how, with the result that Mrs. Barney's entertainments, her dinners, luncheons, teas, receptions have a piquant and unusual flavor different from any other attempted here and not unlike, though on a smaller and more modest scale, those given by Mrs. Jack Gardner in her famous Venetian palace in the Boston Fens."[1] When she was elected to the board of the National Society of Fine Arts, people took it as a sign that she had finally decided to join Washington's cultural mainstream rather than continually approaching it as a harbinger of change. Alice-watchers began to talk about how nicely she was mellowing with age.

As the winter season of 1909–10 continued, Alice's guests ranged from Justice and Mrs. Oliver Wendell Holmes to Ruth St. Denis, who came to town in a return engagement as Radha. There was also the usual assortment of ambassadors, senators, cabinet officials, military officers, and members of high society. Her neighbor Isabel Anderson described one of Alice's evenings in her book, *Presidents and Pies*:

Some theatricals were given in an artist's house—a queer, low-ceilinged structure of a style called Spanish, with only a few dim lights hung here and there. Incense curled about us and blurred the weird sketches of wild-eyed people who peered down from the walls as we groped our way about, running into mirrors and each other.

I am sure the house had never been dusted, and it smelled as if it had never been aired—even the tapestries on the walls were musty and the air reeked with perfume. In the center of a room in which we eventually found ourselves, several more or less undraped ladies with bare feet were posing and whirling rhythmically. It was all quite unusual, but highly diverting. At that time barefoot dancing,

Mrs. Barney assisted by Mrs. Barber of Boston
presents

The DAPHNEPHORIA
An Ancient Greek Festival
For the
Benefit of Neighborhood House

Monday, May 23ᵈ
at four-thirty P. M.
At
The Oaks; 31st and R Sts. N. W.

Music by the MARINE BAND

Admission Tickets, ONE DOLLAR

Reserved seats $2 each, Boxes $25 and $40, and Special
admission tickets for Children 50 cents, may be secured at
T. ARTHUR SMITH'S, 1411 F STREET

G A L A T E A

POSTER, 1910

*The poster for Alice's Greek-
style tribute to Apollo,
The Daphnephoria,
featured a photograph of a
dancer who danced profes-
sionally as Galatea, but was
better known to Washing-
tonians as the widowed
Mrs. Frances Noyes.*

now so common, was in its early stages, and
this party caused considerable talk.[2]

With Lent came events of more serious note.
Professor Christian of Sweden was invited to
speak at Studio House on Esperanto. He was a
man dedicated, as was George Bernard Shaw, to
furthering this artificial language as a replacement for French or English as the lingua franca
of international communication. The other major
event held at Studio House that season was a
reception for the officers of the Suffrage Associa-
tion, who were in town to present petitions to Congress and to hold their
annual convention. To avoid controversy, Alice publicly asserted her neutrality toward issues of suffrage. She had offered her house for the occasion, she
said, because she believed in the exchange of ideas. Those who knew Alice
wondered how long it would take her to embrace the cause. When she did,
they had no doubt she would do it in style.

With the blossoming of the cherry blossoms, daffodils, and azaleas that
make Washington in spring one of the most beautiful cities in the country
came Alice's annual spring theatrical to raise money for Neighborhood
House. Entitled *The Daphnephoria*, it was presented out-of-doors at the Oaks
in Georgetown. She based her script on an ancient Greek festival in honor of
Apollo and the return of spring in order to give the debutantes and bachelors
an opportunity to don Greek garb and wear garlands in their hair. Alice
danced the role of Narcissus à la Isadora Duncan and raised thousands of
dollars for her favorite charity. Christian was cast as Narcissus's lover and
Alice kissed him gently on the lips before an unsuspecting audience. The
deepening relationship remained secret. The special sparkle in Alice's eye
was attributed to the overwhelming success of her fundraiser.

WEDDING PLANS

Once the production was over, she rented Studio House to the Peruvian
Minister and quietly left Washington for an eighteen-month stay in Paris.
She took with her the newly completed pastel of Christian as a Greek god to
hang in her bedroom. Everyone assumed Alice was merely making one of
her biannual pilgrimages to Paris to refresh her artistic soul, but they could
not have been more mistaken. Christian and Alice intended to marry in
Paris, and Alice sailed to Paris in late spring to allow plenty of time to
extract a blessing on the marriage from Laura and Natalie before he arrived
the following February. As she lay in her cabin, the seasickness from which
she suffered only added to her foreboding of what her daughters would say.

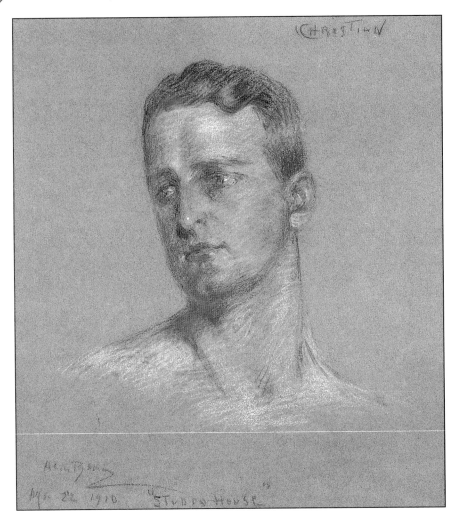

When Alice told her daughters of her wedding plans, they were even more vehemently opposed than she had imagined. Laura led the attack by denouncing Christian as a gigolo who wanted to marry Alice for her money. She said it was ludicrous for Alice to marry someone who was eight years younger than her youngest daughter. Furthermore, Laura was sure that they had nothing in common and that all Alice would get out of this marriage was ridicule followed by ostracism. Although Natalie had the more acerbic tongue, she took a gentler tack. She praised Alice for all her accomplishments as an artist, a philanthropist, and a cultural leader and reminded her she was able to accomplish these things only after she had become a totally free person. Was she really sure that she wanted to tie herself to another man? How could she remain true to herself? In the end,

CHRISTIAN, 1910
Pastel on paper, 20⅝ x 19 in. (52.4 x 48.3 cm)
With eyes blinded by love, Alice drew Christian as a Greek god.

however, Laura and Natalie realized that their arguments fell on deaf ears. Grudgingly, they backed down because, more than anything else, they were moved by Alice's obvious happiness. Whatever the future held, it had been many years since either of them had seen her look so radiant.

With the confrontation behind her, Alice began to work on several projects to fill time until Christian joined her. Always seeking to hone her artistic skills, she began to study privately with the American artist Frank Edwin Scott. Although Scott was almost unknown in the United States, American artists in Paris were familiar with his work. He was dubbed the modern Whistler and the dean of American Impressionists currently living in Paris.

The differences between Scott's style and her own intrigued Alice. Scott was an Impressionist and a master of the plein-aire landscape. He specialized in oils of familiar views of monumental Paris, which he executed in the early morning hours of gray, cold, damp days. His palette was composed of low-keyed browns, grays, and blues. The minute touches of subdued white, ocher, ultramarine, and burnt sienna he used were liberally mixed with turpentine to diminish highlights. Scott's technique contradicted everything Alice had learned from Carolus-Duran, although not what she had learned from Whistler. Moreover, Scott was openly passionate about his distaste for Sargentesque colors, bravura brush strokes, and heightened contrast, all frequently employed by Alice in her portraits.

Scott's influence on Alice's work was subtle. She did not attempt to copy either his style or subject matter; pastel portraits continued to be her métier. The result of his teaching was revealed in a softening of the colors — dusty rose instead of alizarin crimson, or background and foreground integrated by gradual shading rather than contrasted by black lines and pulsating color.

Scott also differed significantly in personality from either Carolus-Duran or Whistler, who were both witty, sociable men. He was taciturn and unrelentingly serious about work. He insisted on absolute quiet in his studio. Alice found herself awed by Scott in a way she had not been by the two more famous painters. His military bearing, augmented by a ramrod carriage, snow-white hair and mustache, and deliberate manner of speaking reinforced his single-minded devotion to his art, as well as his expectation that his students be of like mind.[3]

The more Alice tried to engage him in conversation, the more he insisted that she develop self-discipline. Alice was not to be totally denied, however, and with the help of Scott's second wife Josephine Sanford, she cajoled him to show with her at her already scheduled exhibition at the Parisian Gallery Devambez in May of 1911.

NATALIE'S SALON

Although Alice tried to be the devoted art student Scott expected, it just was not in her nature to limit herself solely to one activity. The first time she set foot in Natalie's villa at 20 Rue Jacob, she realized she must do something about its decor. She knew Natalie would never do it for herself. Natalie had occupied the premises for almost a year, but to Alice it still appeared unfurnished. It was not that Natalie did not like having nice things around her; it was just too much bother to shop.

Until Alice arrived and began to search for suitable furniture from auctions at Hôtel Drouot, Natalie had made do with Laura's castoffs. Among them were two brass lamps with Art Nouveau shades that Natalie hated, but kept until she died. Unlike Alice, Natalie was not a conscious collector of things, but, once owned, nothing was given away. What was important to Natalie were the intangibles—being true to oneself in intellect, heart, and spirit. She was, therefore, quite content to let her mother decorate her apartment and to be bemused by Alice's ability to communicate with the tradesmen in what to her was the mysterious language of upholsters, drapers, and rug merchants.[4]

Like Alice's Studio House in Washington, 20 Rue Jacob was to become much more than the place where Natalie lived. Her move there, however, was not preconceived as was Alice's move to Studio House. Yet when Natalie found 20 Rue Jacob with its small replica of a Doric temple tucked away in a corner of its overgrown garden, she knew she must have it.

Natalie might have remained permanently in fashionable Neuilly-sur-Seine on the Right Bank where she had lived for almost ten years except for the impetus of an eviction notice from her landlord. It was the result of one of the entertainments she liked to present in its garden. The offending presentation was *Équivoque* (first presented in 1906), an original one-act play she wrote about the Sappho myth. Although scholarly in approach (when published in 1910 her classic French verse was footnoted in Greek), it offended her landlord's masculine French sensibilities. Adding fuel to the fire was an article in *Comoedia* on May 23, 1909, which described Natalie's residence in Neuilly as the place where "chaste nudes gathered in the shade of her garden."[5]

EVA PALMER, 1906
In 1906, Natalie's presentation of Équivoque *about Sappho's life offended her landlord's sensibilities. Prominent among the players was Eva Palmer. In 1907 Eva married Angelos Sicillianos and the couple devoted their lives to reviving the customs of antiquity and restoring the ancient culture of Greece.*

NATALIE'S HOMAGE TO
SAPPHO, 1906
*With Penelope Sikelianos,
Isadora Duncan's sister-in-
law on the lyre, Natalie's
friends danced their tribute
to Lesbos in Natalie's
garden in Neuilly.*

In reality, that afternoon in 1909 was much tamer than some of Natalie's earlier entertainments, including the one described by Colette in which Mata Hari came riding out of the bushes toward the audience wearing only a crown of tinsel. The performance that so raised the ire of her landlord, occurred on a sunny May day amidst a circular colonnade of Greek columns that surrounded a five-foot high wrought iron incense brazier at the center of the circle. Dressed in Greek robes, the players included Eva Palmer, her long red hair enhanced by a diaphanous veil; Colette in a thigh-length tunic; and actress Marguerite Moreno and actor Sacha Guitry. Penelope Sikelianos accompanied the Greek line dances, which were choreographed by her husband Raymond Duncan, on a Greek harp.

By 1910, 20 Rue Jacob was well on its way to becoming the site of one of Paris's most famous salons. Natalie modeled it after those she had seen her mother give in Paris at the turn of the century and at Studio House. From her mother, Natalie inherited the talent of bringing interesting and diverse people together, as well as the art of stirring the conversational pot to create a sumptuous stew. Natalie was able to gather some of the most important and provocative artists and writers of the early twentieth century, all of whom thronged to Paris because it was the artistic capital of the western world. They were personages who would never dream of going to Washington, D.C.

Over the years, T. S. Eliot, Ezra Pound, and Wanda Landowska downed champagne and fruit tarts on a Friday, as did Paul Valéry, George Antheil, Gertrude Stein, and Alice B. Toklas. The Indian poet Rabindranath Tagore attended, as did Isadora Duncan, Ida Rubenstein, Colette, James Joyce, Virgil Thomson, and André Gide. In fact, the world's intellectual and artistic elite continued to make the pilgrimage to Natalie's for some sixty years, spanning the decades from Marcel Proust to Truman Capote.

There was, however, another difference. Instead of the debutantes and bejewelled socialites invited by Alice to add the beauty of youth to her soirees, Natalie's salon was graced by the crème de la crème of Paris's lesbian community. The women were witty and brilliant—writers, painters, composers, scholars, musicians—and they more than held their own with their more conventionally famous male counterparts.[6]

Alice long ago had applied her live and let live philosophy to Natalie, although she remained incapable of giving her blessing to Natalie's lifestyle. No matter how understanding she tried to be, Natalie's lesbianism was one of the few areas in which Alice remained a product of her generation and upbringing. Nevertheless, she was proud of Natalie's accomplishments, and, even though she could not understand it, she was open enough to appreciate that Natalie's relationships brought happiness to her. Alice did not, however, feel comfortable staying for any length of time at Natalie's. Within a few weeks, she moved to Laura's apartment, even though, as she ruefully admitted to herself, it was not half so interesting or fun as being at Natalie's. In some ways, Laura was as puzzling as Natalie. Alice often wondered how she could have produced a daughter who took every minute of life so seriously.

THE STATUE INCIDENT

By early fall 1910, Alice was as happy as it was possible to be without Christian. Her output of pastels was prolific. She induced several members of Natalie's circle to pose for her, among them the 1908 Goncourt Prize-winner Francis de Miomandre, poetess Lucy Delarue-Mardrus, harpsichordist Wanda Landowska, writer Elizabeth de Gramont, the Duchess de Clermont-Tonnerre, archeologist Samuel Reinach, and Lady Anglesey who had introduced Natalie to Romaine Brooks. Unlike her 1900 pastels of Natalie's lovers in *Quelques Portraits-Sonnets de Femmes*, Alice harbored no illusion about the women. Also unlike 1900, there was no one to whom it mattered.

This quiet period of Alice's life was short-lived. On October 10, 1910, Washingtonians opened their *Washington Times* to find the banner headline for the lead story on page one was "BARNEY STATUE SHOCKS ARTISTIC POLICE CHIEF." The subhead stated: "Dew Covered Work of Art Exposed In Sheridan Circle to Be Draped by Policeman Under Orders of Major Sylvestre."[7] The accompanying article revealed shocking news that Alice had shipped to Washington a reclining nude statue sculpted by Laura. Anyone passing by Studio House could see what looked like a life-size version of Natalie in the all-together on the front lawn.

At a time when laws were being proposed in the Massachusetts legislature to provide clothing for all nude statues on display in public museums and parks, the notoriety was immediate and not unexpected. Up the street, mothers told their children they could no longer roller-skate around the circle in front of Mrs. Barney's house. The street ringing Sheridan Circle became blocked by hundreds of automobiles and tour buses filled with curiosity seekers.

At the forefront of the viewers were the members of the Watch and Ward Society, an organization of women devoted to upholding the morals of the nation's capital. After a long look, the ladies announced their opin-

RECLINING NUDE, 1910
Laura Barney
Cast concrete,
18¼ x 82 x 27½ in.
(46.4 x 208.3 x 69 cm)
When shipped to Washington and placed on the front lawn of Studio House, everyone saw in the nude statue a likeness to Natalie, which caused a sensation in society circles.

ion—the sculpture was immodest and immoral and must be removed at once. Chief of Police Sylvestre, who was more concerned with crowd control than aesthetics, ordered the statue covered with a pup tent.[8]

If Sylvestre thought he had ended the problem, he was mistaken. The following morning brought even larger crowds to Sheridan Circle and by day's end an estimated 25,000 persons had passed in review. The reason for the crowd's return was that during the night a group of drunken men moved from Finucan's Saloon near Dupont Circle, snuck up Massachusetts Avenue, lifted the statue from the front lawn of Studio House, and placed it directly under the nose of General Sheridan's horse.

Unfortunately for the Barneys, it was a slow week in the news, and the statue incident became page one material not only in Washington, but across America and finally over the Atlantic Ocean to the English language newspapers of all the European capitals. Alice was beside herself when the story broke in the Paris edition of the *New York Herald*. She could not contain her anger and wrote a scathing letter to the *Herald* requesting an immediate interview. It was a disastrous mistake in judgment. Instead of killing the story, it ensured its continuance as page one news and guaranteed that whenever Alice's activities were written about in the future, the statue story would be rehashed in the lead paragraph.

From the day the story first appeared, Natalie was identified as the model. No matter how much Alice insisted that the model was a well-known Parisian model, no one believed her. Moreover, none of Alice's Washington friends believed her either. They knew Natalie when they saw her, even without any clothes on. Natalie in her own interview with the *Herald* only muddied the waters when she claimed Laura had put her head on the model's body. Washington artists familiar with the model immediately pooh-poohed that assertion. The model who Alice had said posed for the sculpture was well-known for her large, abundant figure. Natalie, on the other hand was petite and, at this time in her life, slender. The sculpture was in perfect proportion to her figure. The jury was in. The sculpture was Natalie; the Barney women did protest too much.[9]

Alice's anger at the closed minds of Washington became well-known when excerpts from her letter and interview published originally in the *Herald* were reprinted in the *Washington Times*.

> It is deplorable enough for our country that from a lack of artistic education people should be censured for a work of art, which everywhere else has been considered perfectly decent, without giving spread to a slanderous report.
>
> I do not know what I shall do with the statue. I regard it as a

perfectly simple work of art and I anticipated no trouble with it. I do not know what the laws in Washington are. They seem to be rather strange.[10]

Upon reading Alice's statements, the Watch and Ward society were galvanized into action. Armed with petitions, they marched to the office of the Chief of Police and demanded removal of the offending sculpture. Sylvestre, ducking moral and artistic issues, issued an edict. Stating it was his sworn duty to protect the sanctity of Alice's front yard, he ordered the statue placed inside Studio House and mounted a twenty-four hour guard at the front door.[11]

A DOUBLE WEDDING

As the affair of the statue came to a head in Washington, something equally unexpected made it seem terribly unimportant to the Barney women in Paris. Serious Laura had fallen in love with Hippolyte Dreyfus, a widely published oriental scholar and a leader of the Bahai community in Paris. He was an intellectual who tempered his intense brilliance with humor. He was also a gentle and compassionate man possessed with infinite patience when it came to Laura. Above all, he made her laugh.

Although Laura continued to devote herself to just causes, particularly the plight of oppressed women in Persia and the growth of the Bahai faith, for the first time in her life she seemed almost carefree. When Alice tentatively suggested a double wedding ceremony, Laura, in a gesture of harmony with her mother, agreed to a joint civil ceremony. For once Laura's heart overruled her critical personality. She found herself wanting to share her happiness with her Little One, as she called Alice, and if that meant a double wedding, then that was what she would do.

In February 1911, headlines raged with the news of Alice and Christian's engagement: "SWEARS TO LOVE FOR RICH WIDOW IS STORY TOLD: MRS. A. C. BARNEY, NOW IN EUROPE, WOMAN IN CASE," "RICH WIDOW, 61, TO MARRY MAN OF 26," or "MRS. BARNEY WEDS YOUNG HEMMICK: ROMANCE OF THEATRICALS." Almost every paper or magazine in Washington had something to say about the surprising May/December marriage. When Christian finally arrived in Paris in April 1911, he brought his own surprise, a sworn deposition stating he loved her for herself alone and that nothing could induce him to touch a penny of her money. He offered also to legally sign away his right to any portion of Alice's income. The resulting headlines were even larger and bolder than the announcement of their engagement.

Christian came from a wealthy family, but he was no millionaire. He was, however, very much in love with Alice, and it was important to him

that she know he loved her for herself, not her money. Too many of the stories being printed implied otherwise.

> Chris is evidently very much in love, and it is safe to hazard that his prospective wife will lavish all that a wealth of affection can supply to his comfort and pleasure, for her affection is said to be almost as unstinted as her wealth, and Alice Barney is lavish in all things.[12]

After consultation with her lawyers, Alice placed the principal from Albert's estate into a trust controlled by Laura. She and Christian could live on the interest, which was still a princely sum. With the flourish of a pen, Alice and Christian blithely entered into a marriage contract that denied them direct access to three million dollars. "WIDOW, 61, GIVES AWAY $3,000,000 TO WED BOY" was but one of the headlines in this new chapter in the Barney/Hemmick romance.

The marriage took place on April 15 in a Catholic ceremony at the Church of Saint Joseph, Avenue Hoche, following a joint civil ceremony for Laura and Hippolyte. Afterward, the new Mr. and Mrs. Hemmick took a short honeymoon trip to Venice because Alice needed to return to Paris by the end of May in time for the opening of her exhibition at the Gallery

HIPPOLYTE DREYFUS AND LAURA, 1911
Hippolyte Dreyfus had the rare ability to make Laura laugh and be playful. They are shown here on their honeymoon at Montreux.

Devambez. A more leisurely trip was planned for July and August to Marienbad and the Dolomites before returning to Washington.

It was fortunate that the reviews for her exhibition with Edwin Scott in late May were so favorable, because the publicity surrounding her marriage to Christian had left a sour taste in her mouth. Family members on both sides seemed unable to find words for congratulations. A letter to Alice from Christian's brother, William, who was studying for the priesthood at The Catholic University of America in Washington, D.C., was typical.

> Chris and I you know have gone through life hand and hand, and have never been separated for long; and naturally when there was the question of his taking such a serious step as marriage I could not but feel deeply concerned....With your knowledge of the world and men and things I feel that you will understand Chris perhaps better than any one else, and understanding brings contentment and happiness....In my prayers I will often think of you both, and always I will ask that your hearts may be filled with happiness and that God's blessing may be with you always."[13]

Alice's sisters did not write until mid-August. Jeannette penned only three sentences: "I have never had any misgivings as to the happy outcome of your marriage. You are too clever a woman to botch a matter of such vital importance as that and I congratulate Mr. Hemmick from the bottom of my heart. I shall hope we may all know him some of these days." Hester, on the other hand, completely ignored the whole affair and chose to wax eloquent about the success of Alice's exhibition. In closing, however, she wished Alice and Christian (whom she called Mr. Hemmick), "a safe and pleasant journey home."[14]

The reviews for Alice's show were excellent and the inclusion of Scott's paintings helped the critics to find it one of the most interesting shows seen in Paris that spring. Although she did not know it at the time, it was the last exhibition of her work for almost twenty years. She was praised for having "masculine intelligence combined with feminine comprehension," and Scott must have been pleased with his pupil when he read that "with her extremely sensitive eye, she works with a firm touch and a sound understanding of light and shade. Her broad style eliminates all unnecessary detail."[15]

Alice and Christian's honeymoon to the Dolomites was more leisurely than Christian could stand. From the start the difference in their age intruded. Christian had the energy of a man in his twenties; Alice needed her beauty sleep. In a letter to Laura, Christian unwittingly revealed his misgivings, although he tried to jokingly pass it off.

CATALOG COVER, 1911
In 1911, Alice decided to share her already-scheduled one-woman exhibition at the Galerie Devambez in Paris with Edwin Scott. The taciturn Scott accepted only after much prodding from his wife and Alice.

Souls alone! This place is deader than a graveyard. Your dear Mother and I sit like Darby and Joan at night—and she goes to bed at 9:30 and I sit and read. Read! why I read my eyes out—sat up until 12 P.M. reading Balzac's *Memoires*. Tell Hyppo—I am becoming so serious I hardly can believe it—if this keeps up he had better start in himself and 'study up' if he expects to keep up with me....Alice and I have not had but one little misunderstanding. I walk with her—and enjoy her so much. I never argue. I am "dumb"—and you know Laura it *is* working beautifully."[16]

EXHIBITION AT GALERIE DEVAMBEZ, 1911
The French government purchased a portrait of Natalie for its Museé du Luxembourg from the exhibition at Galerie Devambez in Paris. At far left is Alice's portrait of Wanda Landowska, the renowned harpsichordist.

Christian's next letter, written as they sailed toward America on the T.S.S. *Lapland*, was considerably happier and sounded more like a love-dazed bridegroom.

> As I tell your darling Mother, I don't see how I had courage ever to ask her to marry me—but I did—and I have never regretted my step and there isn't a day I would live over again,...oh! Laura they [the honeymoon] were really days one imagines one would live through in heaven—we were so happy being there so alone to climb and wander through those wonderful mountains.[17]

In closing he promised to "write you all details and tell you of all that has happened there and what people say."

As the Hemmicks steamed toward America, they hoped that by the time they docked in New York, their marriage would no longer be news. In that they were disappointed. An item in *Washington Society* magazine was typical.

> With the return of Mrs. Barney and her husband or—a thousand pardons—Mr. Hemmick and his bride, to spend the winter in the unique studio-house of Mrs. Hemmick, they could not be in any community without adding to its festivities and its interest in every way.[18]

In her absence, Alice had hired J. P. S. Neligh, director of the industrial arts program at Neighborhood House, to redecorate Studio House as a wedding present for Christian. The changes Neligh made to Alice's specifications almost totally hid Waddy Wood's simple Arts and Crafts interior under layers of fringe and fabric and religious artifacts, which Alice now added to the decor out of tribute to Christian's Catholicism.

The walls of the foyers on the first and second floor were heavily stenciled and the furniture was reupholstered in high Spanish Renaissance style. Any nooks or crannies not filled by Alice prior to her marriage were now cluttered with ornate church silver purchased in Italy. In addition she contracted with the J. R. Moore Company to construct a two-story garage to the rear of the lot adjoining Studio House. Its design replicated the facade of Studio House with its red tile roof and tan stuccoed Mission style.

The Hemmicks were met in New York by Christian's brother Will, now an ordained priest. The following day Will blessed the couple at a private mass. From New York they traveled to Washington and their new life together at Studio House.

© G.V. Buck

XIV
The Course of True Love

Christian searched the papers for amusing gossip about himself and Alice to send to Laura and Hippolyte in Paris, but little attention was being paid to the newlyweds. So he wrote instead about all the changes that had occurred in Washington since Laura's visit in 1907. Sheridan Circle, for example, was no longer considered the hinterlands. Twenty-fourth Street had replaced Sixteenth Street as the imaginary western boundary for fashionable homes. Massachusetts Avenue, on which Studio House faced, was now a major thoroughfare lined with magnificent mansions. The bridge that would carry Massachusetts Avenue over Rock Creek was finally being built and enormous homes were in the process of being erected on the few lots remaining on Sheridan Circle.

On the artistic front, the Freer Gallery of Oriental Art had just opened on the Mall, and entrepreneurs proposed building a combined national school of music, dramatic art, and dancing, and a theater, concert hall, and roof garden grandiously named the American Palace of Art. Some aspects of Washington life, however, were immutable. The city remained:

> Essentially political with scrapings both of the cosmopolitan and the provincial. It was cosmopolitan in winter to a degree that exceeded any other American city, since it drew the brains and wit of every city—and through the diplomatic corps of all foreign countries—to its houses. It was provincial in the fact that no theatrical company, concert orchestra, opera or other type of creative art called Washington its home.
>
> So, having no other primary interest, it made SOCIETY in capital letters its primary interest.[1]

One social item sure to pique the interest of Laura and Hippolyte was generated by the visit of Abdul Baha, the frail, aging leader of the Bahais. "All yesterday afternoon," one reporter wrote, "women in automobiles and carriages arrived for private conversations with the aged leader. A few poorer people came, but most of the visitors were wealthy....Mrs. Nicholas Longworth [Alice Roosevelt] occupied a seat far back in the audience with two other women, and seemed greatly interested in the afternoon's entertainment."[2]

Abdul Baha spent the major portion of his eight-day stay speaking to the faithful and illuminating the teachings of Bahaullah through cogent elucidation of the sect's sacred literature. He also visited several prominent

ALICE AT FIFTY-EIGHT, 1915
Alice stands before the gold damask-covered walls of the East Studio alcove at Studio House.

Washington Bahais, including Alice, whom he had met in the Middle East in 1905. She honored him with a luncheon and two evening receptions. Since all three events were sedate affairs, *The Club-Fellow and Washington Mirror* was forced to put a different spin on its coverage of Studio House happenings in order to titillate its readers.

Without checking facts, something it seldom did, the *Mirror* announced that Christian had turned his back on Catholicism to become a Bahai because rumor had it that he now sat on the floor and ate oriental suppers while wearing loose flowing Eastern robes instead of a dinner coat. Although Christian may have joined Alice in breaking bread with the revered Bahai leader in the Eastern style, seated on cushions around a low table, his imputed conversion was patently false. On the other hand, Alice's adoption of Catholicism was tenuous at best—a choice made for true love rather than belief. The Bahai faith, which proclaimed full equality for women as a basic tenet, mirrored her own values more close-ly. Although Alice made no attempt to proselytize

Christian, she expected him to have an open mind, particularly where women were concerned.

As the months passed, Christian realized that his fears about how he and Alice would be received as a married couple were groundless. People weren't talking—at least not openly—and most of Alice's friends welcomed her back with open arms. It was almost as if she had merely returned from one of her regular European sojourns. The few stories that mentioned them tended to compliment Alice on the changes her marriage had made in her appearance such as letting her hair go gray and eschewing heavy makeup.

So little was written about Christian that it was almost as if his only *rai-son d'être* was to provide Alice with a new last name. Mrs. Hemmick's varied interests were regularly highlighted and differed very little from those of Mrs. Barney. She reinstituted her popular Friday afternoon teas. Her Sunday evening entertainments in her studio once more sparkled with bejeweled and bemedaled society figures who came to applaud the originality of her tableaux, musicales, and interpretive dances. On an evening one might see Chief Justice Edward Douglass White and his wife, a sprinkling of admirals and generals, Miss Mabel Boardman of Red Cross fame, and

LAURA AND NATALIE, c. 1910
The Barney sisters lived the majority of their lives in Paris. The Club-Fellow and Washington Mirror *told its readers in 1910 that the sisters "agreed to dis-agree and to live separate and apart." As they aged, they had little to do with one another for neither sister accepted the direction the other's life had taken.*

representatives of the diplomatic corps with none ranked lower than first secretary.

Although appearances were to the contrary, Alice's real focus was on her marriage, for which she was prepared to do whatever was necessary to make it succeed. The most important decision she made was to eschew the solitary art of painting that excluded Christian for the communal art of theater in which they could work together. Her life was finally forcing her to live up to her philosophy that all arts were interrelated and that the more one knew about one, the more one knew about another. At fifty-five she prepared to discard an activity that had given her life meaning for over a quarter of a century, all for the sake of love.

EMMA CALVÉ, C. 1898
By the time Emma Calvé visited Alice at Studio House in 1912, the vision of her as Carmen was but a distant memory, although her rich coloratura soprano voice continued to enchant all who heard it.

NEW TALENT

In June 1912, Hippolyte and Laura came to Washington to see for themselves how the newlyweds were faring. Later in the month, the foursome left for Bar Harbor. As the Hemmicks departed, *The Club-Fellow and Washington Mirror* sniped:

> After the seven days' wonderment Alice Barney kicked up and delighted in, by her marriage to the poor, handsome and willing Chris she slipped back onto her old mode of living, went on with her pursuit of art and artistic effects, mystic cults and curiosities, and found Chris a willing follower....They will wind up the season at Bar Harbor, but Mrs. Hemmick coyly infers that they have not had enough of wooing, and intend to spend long and happy days, weeks, yea perhaps even months, in the enjoyment of each other far from the madding crowd. Hence, except that eventually she will trail her draperies and handsome young husband at Bar Harbor, there is no way for the world to discover where Alice's fancy will lead her.[3]

Bar Harbor was full of its usual social demands, and the Hemmicks whirled from one party to the next. Writing to Natalie, Alice spoke of their gaieties: "The house is certainly most comfortable and the servants are good....You too would have enjoyed the party.

I lent to Mrs. Noyes one of the robes and there was a fancy dress ball and we are all going. Laura and Hippo as pirates and Christian as Spanish if he can manage the Spanish britches."[4] In late fall rumors circulated that Alice and Christian would rent Studio House for the winter season and go to Europe, but at October's end the Hemmicks returned to Washington.

Alice's inaugural social event of the 1912–13 season was a high tea followed by an intimate dinner for her old friend Emma Calvé. Calvé, one of opera's greatest coloratura sopranos, was in Washington for a concert appearance. By 1912, her visually sensual Carmen only existed in an opera buff's memory, the singer a victim of the vicissitudes of age and rich food. Only a good friend such as Alice could imagine the overweight woman seated at her dining room table as the vibrant Carmen she had sketched in 1900. Calvé's voice, however, remained magnificent and she could still move an audience to tears with her rendition of Carmen's final aria.

By the end of dinner, Calvé knew Alice had more in mind than wining and dining an old friend. It seemed that the shy, exceedingly handsome young man seated directly across from her was a tenor. No doubt Alice planned to have her discovery, Louis Thompson, sing for her. Calvé prayed his voice would be as satisfying as his looks, for in her experience middle-aged wealthy women often judged a young man's talent by his looks. Calvé respected Alice's musical sensibilities, but as she glanced toward the head of the table where Christian sat, she speculated on Alice's judgement in men.

Having made up her mind to devote herself to the performing arts, Alice had begun to investigate the talent available in Washington. Alice first heard Thompson's clear tenor voice during tryouts for a Neighborhood House benefit the previous spring and thought it exceptional for someone only nineteen years old. He was, however, her first discovery, and she was still unsure of herself. She needed someone of Calvé's stature to validate her instincts.

After dinner the guests adjourned to the east studio on the second floor, located at the front of the house opposite her great studio room. Thompson sang "Pale Hands" from Amy Woodford Frinden's *Indian Love Lyrics*, as well as several arias. As he performed, Alice watched Calvé's face closely. At the conclusion of his short recital, Mme. Calvé congratulated his teacher with bravos and praised Thompson for his good breath control and resonance of tone, adding that he was one of the freshest and most sympathetic tenors she had heard in years. Thompson was a find; Alice was on her way.

A NEW ADMINISTRATION

By late February 1913, Washington was gearing up not for one of Alice's theatricals, but for the inaugural of Woodrow Wilson as president of the United States. Like most of Washington's resident society, Alice hung back

CAST OF A BAR HARBOR THEATRICAL, 1912
Even after her marriage to Christian, summers in Bar Harbor meant costume parties and theatricals. This cast picture, taken at the

Kebo Club, shows Alice and Christian (center) with Hippolyte dressed as a sheik (center, first row) and Laura in a vaguely Middle Eastern costume seated behind him.

in voicing an opinion on what direction social life in the capital would take under its new Democratic administration. To all observers, it did not bode well. Unlike Roosevelt and Taft, Wilson was a rigid, serious man who seemed disinclined to waste time on frivolity.

Wilson set the tone for his administration in his inaugural address. "This is not a day of triumph, it is a day of dedication," he stated. "Men's hearts wait upon us; men's lives hang in the balance; men's hopes call upon us to say what we will do. Who shall live up to this great trust? Who dares fail to try? I summon all honest men, all patriotic, all forward looking men, to my side. God helping me, I will not fail them, if they but will counsel and sustain me!"[5]

Of forward-looking women, there was no mention. To those who supported the suffrage amendment giving women the right to vote, Wilson's omission of women in his inaugural address did not bode well. The suffragettes were the most vocal in their protest, but other highly placed women were equally disturbed. Here was the incontrovertible evidence that Wilson, for the sake of politics, was a traitor to the cause of suffrage. The irony was that until the 1912 convention, Wilson had actively courted the suffragettes. Once he received the nomination, however, he refused to see their delegations and worked actively to defeat the proposed suffrage plank in the party platform. Alice was one of the many women in Washington who was outraged at Wilson's violation of his support.

Wilson's intransigence led the suffragettes to public expression of their dissatisfaction—a counter inaugural parade that culminated in a tableau written and staged by Hazel MacKaye on the steps of the Treasury Building next door to the White House. Many prominent women sat in the stands before the columned Treasury Building to see the performance of their more militant sisters rather than using their invitations to see Wilson's swearing in at the Capitol. Among them were the wife and daughter of outgoing President Taft and Alice Barney Hemmick. Alice was inflamed by the tableau, a theatrical form she had used many a time, and vowed to join the ranks of the protesting suffragettes.

Within the month, Alice went public with her allegiance to the suffrage cause and began to actively support the movement with all the passion she had formerly felt for her art. She lent 1626 Rhode Island Avenue to the National American Women's Suffrage Association for its Washington headquarters and at white heat wrote two plays for the benefit of its Congressional Union, which was the Washington branch led by the militant feminist Alice Paul. On the afternoon of May 20, a standing-room only audience comprised primarily of women attended the performance. The main play, *The Woman*, was vintage Alice—a series of scenes in didactic, allegorical style. The curtain opened to show Woman (played by professional actress Izetta Jewell) bound to a bush by Man (portrayed by Christian Hemmick) and his cohorts, Sin and Ignorance. After a series of formal arguments were presented by the men, they were answered by the female character of Freedom. Then the goddess of Justice freed Woman. As part of her argument, Freedom called forth a succession of tableaux depicting the accomplishments of a series of famous women from history, including Sappho, Esther, Queen Zenobia, Elizabeth of Hungary, Saint Hilda, Joan

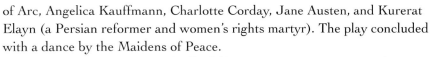

of Arc, Angelica Kauffmann, Charlotte Corday, Jane Austen, and Kurerat Elayn (a Persian reformer and women's rights martyr). The play concluded with a dance by the Maidens of Peace.

The curtain raiser was markedly different. *In Some Years Hence,* Alice was inspired by Oscar Wilde's witty dialogue and George Bernard Shaw's experiments with farce, which couched serious theses in comedic form. The play was a loosely constructed comedy in which she aimed sharp-tongued barbs at the sexist prejudices of her generation—men and women alike—reflecting more closely the views of the mainstream women's groups than the militant feminists.

She set the play in the year 2013 because she speculated that by then women would be equal to men because, by 2013, there would be no idleness, ignorance, war, illness, yellow journalism, old age, marriages for titles or money, alcoholism, loud street noises, or servant problems, and women

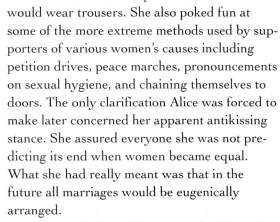

would wear trousers. She also poked fun at some of the more extreme methods used by supporters of various women's causes including petition drives, peace marches, pronouncements on sexual hygiene, and chaining themselves to doors. The only clarification Alice was forced to make later concerned her apparent antikissing stance. She assured everyone she was not predicting its end when women became equal. What she had really meant was that in the future all marriages would be eugenically arranged.

At its conclusion, Alice was pushed from the wings onto the stage for a standing ovation. She was, one reporter wrote, "a picture to marvel at—lithe, graceful and fascinating, scorning her real age of—we won't say what—and passing for a charming person in her twenties."[6] Christian appeared by her side, took her hand, and led her forward to the footlights to receive the crowd's applause.

Although Christian played the male lead in *Woman,* he felt unappreciated; Alice received the accolades, not he. He needed his own applause, but could not figure out how to obtain it. A long summer loomed ahead and he was bored. While Alice fantasized that she and Christian were drawing closer through their

ALICE AS MADAME GERALDINE, 1909
Alice often created roles for herself in her theatricals. Here she is Madame Geraldine dressed for her dance in the Tomb of Kings from About Thebes.

shared theatrical endeavors, the opposite was proving true. Even though Alice no longer painted, Christian continued to feel left out as he waited for Alice to finish writing her plays, return from auditions for a play in which he was already cast, complete her costume and set designs, or reappear after lengthy afternoon meetings with the women who ensured the publicity went out and the tickets were sold. While Alice worked zealously, Christian lounged around Studio House. He lacked the skill, talent, imagination, or temperament to help her in any way other than to strike a pose on stage. Thus, by default, the highlight of Christian's day was watching the servants clean house.

He followed them around, a sidewalk supervisor, since they already had their instructions from Alice. One thing that Christian noticed was that, unlike the scented oils hand rubbed into the ebonized furniture, ordinary cleaning pastes smelled noxious. He had always liked the scents that came from the jumbled assortment of jars, bowls, and sachets Alice kept on her dressing table. Like a small boy with his first chemistry set, Christian took one of the cleansers from the scullery and began to experiment by adding various combinations of Alice's herbs, spices, and perfumes.

After much trial and error, he proudly presented the spicy concoction and a crudely drawn label to Alice. She was overjoyed; not once had Albert shown the initiative or ingenuity evinced in Christian's modest effort. Alice's mind raced ahead envisioning possibilities for marketing, sales, and, of course, an office for Christian in his own soap factory. Like her father, Alice was there to take thought and make it actuality. Within weeks Christian found himself leaving Studio House to go to his office to oversee the production of his scented cleaning paste. By summer's end, however, he tired of the project, worn out in part by Alice's enthusiasm. Increasingly, he looked forward to the end of the day when he could return home to bask in Alice's fond declarations of affection for her "pink pet."

TRAVELS WITH LAURA AND HIPPOLYTE

In November 1913 Laura and Hippolyte arrived in Washington on the first leg of a planned round-the-world trip. They asked Alice to come with them as far as San Francisco. The leisurely, circuitous train trip would take them to New Orleans, El Paso, Mexico, San Diego, and Hollywood—all places the well-traveled trio had never been. Believing Christian totally occupied by his new-found work, Alice left him behind in Washington to tend to his business. Laura, never able to totally stifle her disapproval of Christian, hoped the trip might provide an opportunity to find out if her mother were still happy in her marriage.

On January 25, 1914, Hippolyte, Laura, and Alice left Union Station for points south and west. In the journal she kept, Laura wrote:

My lady mother wears a cherry-colored nightgown for sleeping in the cars. Why this signal of danger? I do not know. As she is the nimbler of limb and of temper, it is she who climbs into the upper berth of our compartment; I see her plump legs ascending the ladder which a brawny negro holds firmly! An Aubrey Beardsley picture in _rouge et noire_ interspersed with white.[7]

The itinerary for the first leg of the trip was one that would have daunted a woman younger than Alice. They rode south through Atlanta and Birmingham to New Orleans, the city where Samuel Pike's sales of Magnolia whiskey ensured his first millions. From New Orleans, they traveled to El Paso and switched trains for an excursion to Juarez, Mexico, the headquarters for Pancho Villa. They walked to Villa's headquarters to present their visiting cards. A burly, bandoliered guard informed them he was busy, but could see them at 3 P.M. The bullets and guns were enough to convince the trio they had nothing in common with Villa, and they spent the afternoon in the relative safety of the local racetrack waiting for the first train back to civilization. Alice mentally filed the event away and later drew on it when she wrote her only novel, _The Iron Tower_, an antidrug potboiler set in Mexico.

From El Paso they rode across the vast, vacant lands of New Mexico and Arizona until they reached San Diego. Here they disembarked to visit Katherine Augusta Tingley, leader of the Theosophical colony of the Universal Brotherhood on Point Loma. Hippolyte and Laura were interested in learning more about the American version of Theosophy, particularly in discovering if the Bahai faith and Theosophy had beliefs in common. Tingley conducted the tour personally. They found they held a belief in universal brotherhood in common, but as Tingley discoursed on the centrality of reincarnation and the occult to the Theosophical belief system, Laura and Hippolyte were disturbed by its irrationality and abruptly, but politely, bid their adieus. Alice's imagination, on the other hand, was fueled by the talk of spirits. Like the experience in Mexico, Tingley's talk of reincarnation was filed away as grist for future writing.

The final stop before reaching San Francisco was Hollywood. Alice was in her element in the capital of make-believe, while Laura and Hippolyte were anxious to move on. The more Laura saw of America, the more grateful she became that she lived in Paris. Once they reached San Francisco, however, much of her criticism of the United States was mitigated by the beauty of the Bay City. In mid-March, Laura and Hippolyte boarded their ship for Japan. Eventually, they hoped to see Korea, China, India, and Persia as they moved ever westward toward Paris.

XV
War Efforts

Not once on the trip across the United States did Alice speak a harsh word about Christian. If she were having second thoughts about her marriage, she chose not to confide in Laura. But as the train carried her back toward Washington from San Francisco, her thoughts turned to Christian and their marriage. Washington society also wondered about the Hemmicks. Although there were no outward signs of trouble, the marriage had always struck most of Alice's peers as ridiculous. The fact that it had lasted this long surprised everyone. While she was away, the editor of *The Club-Fellow and Washington Mirror* wrote that "rumors are flying about to the effect that all is not well with the couple. It will be interesting to watch and see what happens. For my own part, I have been watching ever since the two were married, and have been patiently waiting for the separation, which people are now saying is imminent."[1]

Out of Alice's musings came one decision: the National Women's Party would have to vacate the Rhode Island Avenue house. She would move into it with Christian and rent Studio House. Rhode Island Avenue was more of a man's house with its yellow oak interior trim than Studio House, and Christian could be its master. Once decided, workmen began its refurbishment.

By early May, Alice was sending out invitations to a combination housewarming and fundraiser for Neighborhood House complete with a new entertainment she had dashed off called *The Mystery of the East.* It was a hodgepodge that included readings from Tagore, exotic dances à la Ruth St. Denis, and songs by Louis Thompson. It was set in three Eastern locales—India, Egypt, and Persia—chosen to make extensive use of the hand-dyed liberty silk the industrial arts classes at Neighborhood House produced under her direction. The sophistication of the process of producing tie dye silk scarves at Neighborhood House was far beyond what it had been when Alice began the project in 1909. She had discovered that the use of a simple household chemical gave the dyes a metallic luster, and the unique result made them eagerly sought after by fashionable Washington. Alice's hands-on work at the settlement house was as unusual as the product. Women of Alice's station graced charities with their presence, they did not get their hands dirty.

When interviewers asked why she personally supervised the project, her reply remained the same as her response to a Boston magazine interviewer in 1909: "Work, good, honest toil is as much an obligation of the rich as it is

ALICE, C. 1913
With the outbreak of war in Europe, Alice became a strong advocate for peace and cochaired the Peace Party's artistic committee with poet Hazel MacKaye.

a necessity to the poor. It is part of my creed. The Bahai faith teaches it. I believe that every man and woman should earn his or her place in the world by honest application to whatever trade, profession or art he or she is best fitted for."[2] Meanwhile, Christian's "honest application to a trade" was drawing to a close. By the end of September, his scented cleaning paste business was a memory.

THE GREAT WAR

Although Alice worried about Christian, newspaper dispatches from the Far East made her more concerned about the safety of Laura and Hippolyte. Rumors of war had followed Laura and Hippolyte from Japan to Korea and into China, but they chose to ignore them. When they finally arrived at Tsingtao, China, in late July 1914, they found that the former Chinese fishing village, which was ceded by China to Germany at the turn of the century, had been turned into a modern heavily fortified international naval port. On August 1, the Germans declared martial law and within the week the English vice consul ordered all allied visitors to leave immediately. By the time Laura and Hippolyte reached Shanghai, even they realized that a major war was inevitable. On August 23, 1914, Japan declared war on Germany and landed troops in Shantung province for an attack on Tsingtao. In Europe, Germany invaded Belgium, France's army was mobilized, and England declared war. The great war had begun.

Natalie was as worried about Laura as Alice. From her vantage point in Paris, she had a more realistic view of the storm rising in Europe:

Agitated times my Laura bird....I telegraphed to you at Palace Hotel Shanghai telling you war is about declared and hoping things would not be too interrupted to get a telegram back telling me of your plans. I do so hope you won't come back, but remain safely in Egypt or somewhere like that....Of course you would love to nurse the wounded, but I have much hope that you won't be able to get to them, and so have your dear nerves spared at least this....Perhaps you'll go across the Pacific again instead of back this way? But I'm at any rate so glad that all my dear ones are far off....I logically stay where I am the most wanted and needed. You have Hippo, Mother, Christian — and—I all four of you—would that it might be more often.[3]

As Alice and Christian waited anxiously for word from Laura and Hippolyte that they were safe, Washington society reporters began to call attention to the worsening world situation in their columns.

The autumn season in its first month is not likely to present any extensive social programs here or elsewhere. It will be more particu-

ROMAINE BROOKS, c. 1908
The relationship between painter Romaine Brooks, right, and Natalie lasted almost forty years. Romaine created compelling drawings and paintings of their circle of friends. During World War I, she collaborated with poet Gabriele D'Annunzio to publish a limited edition of his poem based upon her painting Le Rouge Croix.

larly than usual a period of home-coming....So many Americans who have spent recent years in European capitals find that career at an end and the participation of hundreds of these traveled persons in the life of this city within the near future is expected to be an interesting phase to result from the war.[4]

Laura and Hippolyte were equally eager to leave the eastern war zone, but the only passage they could find forced them to retrace their steps to Paris through America. After arriving in the United States and waiting two months in New York for tickets, they boarded *La France* on its last voyage as a passenger ship. By December's end, Hippolyte was a member of the French Army and Laura a Red Cross nurse.

At first Natalie refused to become involved in the war efforts in Paris, preferring to concentrate on her latest love, the painter Romaine Brooks, and she continued to hold her salons almost as if the war did not exist. By the end of the year, however, Natalie, too, was distributing supplies and doing clerical work with a French-American women's war relief committee. Doubtless she was inspired less by Laura than by Romaine's collaboration with poet Gabriele D'Annunzio to publish a limited edition of his poems accompanied by a lithograph of Romaine's painting, *Le Rouge Croix*.

Although the United States followed a policy of strict neutrality, members of high society rapidly involved themselves in various fundraisers and charitable acts such as knitting hats and gloves for the relief of victims in the war. Some of the younger women left for assignments as nurses for the International Red Cross. Prominent socialites, who had never done anything more serious than make sure their clothes were made by the correct Parisian couture, took up sewing or gave balls of yarn to genteel ladies residing at local retirement homes who in turn made up sweaters, caps, gloves, and scarves for the brave allies in the trenches.

By the end of 1914, the Germans and French faced each other across trench lines that did not vary by more than ten miles during the remainder of the war. In Washington the issue of American intervention was discussed by Wilson. As president, he was prepared to do whatever was necessary to keep the United States out of the war. Although antiwar, Alice was moved by reports from Laura and Natalie about the plight of the families of French artists who were serving in the trenches. When she learned that the charity selected for the annual Beaux Arts ball was a relief fund for the next of kin of artists fighting the Huns, she volunteered to write and produce an entertainment for the event. Working at peak form, she dashed off a series of tableaux and dances, enlisting the New York painter and craftsman Albert Herter to design the program cover.

The Judgment of the Muses was presented on February 8 and 9, 1915, at the New Willard Hotel under the combined auspices of the Society of Beaux-Arts Architects, the Washington Chapter of the American Institute of Architects, the Washington Architectural Club, and the Society of Washington Artists. The hotel's ballroom was decorated to resemble a French country fair, and food, drink, and confetti were in plentiful supply as five hundred East Coast artists, art students, and elite danced through the night.

To be sure that everyone understood that she had raised funds specifically for artists, and not as an endorsement of a just cause, Alice assisted the local chapter of the Women's Peace Party to open its headquarters at 1338 F Street, N.W. On the same day, the United States government officially protested the German proclamation that it was establishing a submarine blockade of England on February 18.

The Women's Peace Party was founded by Jane Addams, an American social worker who opened Chicago's Hull-House in 1889 and who was both antiwar and prosuffrage. Alice embraced the joint cause wholeheartedly and was elected president of its Washington branch. The purpose of the new party was to "enlist all American women in arousing the nation to respect the sacredness of human life and to abolish war." Its constitution called for replacing the warring armies with an international police force, demanded that the warring nations meet to plan for peace by agreeing to arms limitations, and concluded that peace required "the further humanizing of the nation by giving votes to women."[5]

Alice also cochaired the Peace Party's artistic committee with Hazel MacKaye, who had produced the suffrage tableau during President Wilson's inauguration. The purpose of the committee was to encourage artists, musicians, and writers to create entertainments promoting peace. One project was the establishment of a nationwide touring company to perform Euripides's *Trojan Women*. The other was the creation of a tableau as the main attraction for a mass meeting on February 21 at the New Masonic Temple (the current site of the Women's Museum of Art). The thesis for

PROGRAM COVER, 1915
Alice helped to raise money for the families of French artists fighting the Huns with productions such as The Dispute of the Muses.

the production came from a chance remark by President Wilson that when peace is made as beautiful as war, peace will come. The sentiment appealed to Alice who, according to the *Sunday Star*, held to a "creed that beauty can be carried into every form of activity."[6] Titled *The Awakening*, the piece consisted of ten tableaux depicting how man's greed for commercial supremacy caused war.

The first six tableaux—"Sowing the Seed," "The Cause of War," "Call to Arms," "Youth's Illusion of War," "Reality," and "Reaping the Harvest"—depicted how wars began. The turning point was the seventh tableau, "Women's Demands." The next two, "Justice" and "Attainments," inexorably led to the evening's concluding tableau, "Peace."

As planned by Alice and the artistic committee, the extensive publicity generated by the tableaux gave exposure to the platform of the National Women's Peace Party. Reactions ranged from avid support to virulent opposition as epitomized in a letter written by former president Theodore Roosevelt to a member of the local chapter, which was published in its entirety in the *Evening Star*. The demands of the Women's Peace Party, declared Roosevelt, were "base and silly," and he compared their activities to that of Civil War copperheads. "I assume, of course," he wrote, "that you are for peace in reality and not merely for the name of peace, and that you are for peace based on justice and right and not for peace that consecrates successful wrong; for peace that consecrates wrong may be actually worse than any war." He concluded with a final broadside against the treacherous ideas being circulated by the women of the Peace Party.

> Let them do something to show that they mean what they say and that they are really striving for righteousness. Until they do this let every wise and upright man and woman refuse to have anything more to do with a movement which is certainly both foolish and noxious, which is accompanied by a peculiarly ignoble abandonment of national duty and which if successful would do only harm, and the mere attempt to accomplish which rightly exposes our people to measureless contempt.[7]

Alice declined to respond realizing that engaging in a war of letters with a former president was pointless. Instead, she and MacKaye planned a surprise for Roosevelt that would garner even greater publicity for the cause than their Masonic Temple tableaux. As for his contention that the women of the Peace Party were not righteous, neither Alice, nor the Washington women who made the Peace Party their cause, believed they needed any defense. The women who worked with Alice in the Washington branch of the Peace Party were the same women praised the month before by the *Sunday Star* for their charitable works. It was important work, according to

the *Star* because they carried "the burden of responsibility upon their shoulders to found and maintain countless philanthropies." For example, "Mrs. Christian Hemmick, is laboring hard to produce a play of the East dealing with the opium question for the benefit of Washington's poor. The list could be indefinitely extended."[8]

BATTLES ON THE HOME FRONT

The Opium Pipe was written by Laura in 1912 in reaction to Renée Vivien's death in 1909 from anorexia and substance abuse. During the years in which Renée was part of Natalie's life, Laura and Alice grew very fond of her. Alice's pastel portrait of Renée, superbly captured the vulnerability of the ethereal poet. Even though neither mother nor daughter saw Renée after she and Natalie went their separate ways in 1904, both women mourned her death. They were well aware, however, of Renée's last years, which were spent either wandering throughout the Middle East and the Orient or in her dimly lit, claustrophobic apartment. There, surrounded by oriental artifacts with the air heavy with incense, she penned her obsessive verses on death and dead loves.[9]

CHRISTIAN AND CAST MEMBER, 1915
Alice cast Christian (left) as the lead in her antidrug opus, The Opium Pipe. *He played the Oriental potentate who surrendered to the temptations of the opium pipe and caused the death of his one true love.*

CAST PHOTO,
THE OPIUM PIPE, 1915
*The lead actors and actresses
from* The Opium Pipe
*gathered in the gardens of the
Pan American Union to pose
for this cast photograph.*

In 1915, Alice substantially reworked much of Laura's play to enhance its production values and credited herself as co-author. To ensure authenticity, she enlisted the aid of Ali Kuli Khan, chargé d'affaires for the Persian embassy. The authentic hangings, furniture, and rugs offered for the production turned it into the most lavish set decoration ever seen in Washington. As soon as word got around about its exotic theme, patrons, actors, and backstage hands lined up to be part of what they were certain was going to be the most daring production Alice had ever presented.

The first newspaper stories about Alice's new play focused on the controversy it was causing in society's theatrical circles. Alice was at first not concerned, knowing full well that such articles would only attract larger audiences. The Washington chapter of the Drama League of America had the authority to sanction all amateur plays given in Washington. Even though rehearsals were scheduled to begin within the month, the League's officers pronounced *The Opium Pipe* devoid of literary merit and, therefore, unsanctionable. What this meant was that no member of the League, which included the majority of those who regularly worked on or appeared in the city's amateur dramas, would be allowed to participate in Alice's play.

Although Alice's even temper was well known, she refused to accept the League's literary slap on the hand with her usual magnanimity. For Alice this would necessitate a battle royal, for more was at stake than the actual play. The fight was really over control of Washington's amateur theater, which was the city's only alternative to the professional touring companies appearing at the Belasco and the National theaters. Just how high Alice felt the stakes to be was evident in her statements about the League printed in the *Washington Times*.

> The forces of post-impressionistic art contending against those of conservative dramatic art, caused the rift which has resulted in the formation of the Amateur Authors' and Players' Group. 'The Opium Pipe' is a modern play, evidently diametrically opposed from a technical standpoint, to the type of plays sanctioned by the Drama League.
>
> The ultra-modern play, though highly moral and beautiful, introduces touches of oriental weirdness, fantastic snake dances, and strange lights, with now and then a dash of tom-tom music. Here we have the rock upon which the local chapter of the Drama League broke.
>
> The conservative element in the parent organization holds to the view that 'Uncle Tom's Cabin' and 'She Stoops to Conquer' are the proper types of plays for production by amateurs. Little wonder that the board of the Drama League objected and declined to permit the production of 'The Opium Pipe' under its auspices. The Drama League board declared that my play was not a literary play, while my adherents claimed that it was literary and even something more.[10]

LOUIS B. THOMPSON, 1915
The singer Louis B. Thompson became Alice's protégé. She cast him as a court entertainer in The Opium Pipe, *which allowed him to display his superb tenor voice.*

The Washington chapter of the Drama League thoroughly misjudged Alice's charisma, and in short order its membership was decimated while former members flocked to join the newly formed Amateur Authors' and Players' Group of Washington. Alice was its first president and joining her were Mrs. Albert Burleson, wife of the Postmaster General, Mrs. Barnett, wife of the commandant of the Marine Corps, Maude Howell Smith and Izetta Jewel Brown, the most prominent local amateur and professional actresses, respectively, and George O. Totten, architect, as well as a host of high society who much preferred the fun of being in Alice's idiosyncratic plays to appearing in approved drama. Alice's fifteen years as leader of Washington's cultural life came to fruition in this theatrical palace coup. Even Albert might have been proud.

Perhaps, Alice fought so hard because she personally wanted more than to raise the consciousness of Washington's culture mavens. Her private intention was to use the production as a means of revitalizing her marriage. She intended to involve Christian as much as possible in the venture by casting him in the leading role of the young prince who falls prey to opium. In doing so, she blinded herself to the obvious—the enthusiastic, good-looking boy she married had in four years become a sullen, overweight man. Nevertheless, her plan seemed to work, and the minute rehearsals started, she thought she saw the Christian she had fallen in love with emerge from his lethargy.

Following four sold-out performances, Alice added a fifth one for Laura's favorite cause, the French Ambulance Motor Fund. In order to lure back some of the earlier audience, Alice engaged Paul Swan, a New York dancer and a protégé of the great actress Alla Nazimova, to come to Washington to play the role of the blind dancer of the opium den. Inordinately handsome, as well as a superb dancer, Swan's agent billed him as "the most beautiful man in the world." He was, however, much more than a well-built, graceful dancer and poseur. He held his own salons in New York, was a gifted raconteur and a highly acclaimed painter and sculptor. Christian had never met anyone like him. Swan combined all the artistic energy that Christian found fascinating in Alice, but more than that, he had a disarming charm that took Christian's breath away. Although Christian did not yet know it, he was in love.

In a lengthy interview with the *Evening Star*, Swan said that even though he had no illusions about how being called a "Greek god" or the "handsomest man" in the world affected people's perception of him, he wanted his art taken seriously.

> I am not merely a pretty doll and a poseur, I do not loll in bed in pink silk pajamas until noon, as many suppose....I work, for it is a tenet of my religion that I owe it to life to contribute something vital to the world, some creation of my brain and talents that will live. The men and women who have made the highest art, the real art of today, take me seriously as the one exponent of classic dancing. I am a pioneer. I am trying to show those whose opinion is of account that dancing is not really an effeminate accomplishment. Among the Greeks it was deemed just as necessary for boys and men to participate in their dances as for girls.[11]

Swan's interview echoed Alice's own feelings about art, and her delight in having gotten him to appear in her play blinded her to Christian's infatuation. When Christian announced he wanted to enter the diplomatic corps, she wholeheartedly supported him. When this required frequent trips to

ANTIWAR TABLEAUX,
1915
*"The Cause of War," one
of eleven antiwar tableaux
from Alice's* The Awaken-
ing *presented at the foot of
the Washington Monument
in 1915, bluntly made the
point that commercial greed
caused wars. Alice produced
the event while president of
the Washington branch of
the Peace Party.*

New York, she saw him off at Union Station. Because she was preoccupied with her own projects, she failed to notice any change in Christian.

On May 7, 1915, the *Lusitania* was sunk by the Germans, and the ensuing national furor challenged the entire peace movement. The Women's Peace Party looked for a way to counter prevailing public opinion, which swayed precipitously toward American military involvement in Europe. The Washington chapter decided a large public event was needed immediately.

Within the week, Washington was leafleted with the announcement of a tableau, *The Awakening*, which would be presented at the base of the Washington Monument on Memorial Day. Alice hurriedly arranged for bleachers to surround the monument and rented a portable spotlight to illuminate the performance. On May 31 wreaths were laid on graves at Arlington, Congressional, and other cemeteries in and around Washington. By mid-afternoon crowds had begun to assemble at the base of the monument, and by 8 P.M. over six thousand people were gathered to see Alice's tableaux on war and peace.

The program began with a speech by Janet Richards, one of the party's national vice-presidents. She read a statement which explained that the purpose of the tableaux was to educate and teach Americans about the "awfulness, the stupidity, insanity and uselessness of war." In rebuttal to Roosevelt and other hawks, Richard stated that "the party recognized that it was the duty of the United States to protect its people, to promote its commerce, and to see to it that, if war should come, the country is prepared to meet the enemy. Preparedness in time of peace is no threat that war is about to be waged."[12]

The tableaux were presented twice so that those whose view of the first show was blocked by the enormous crowd did not go home disappointed. Alice was thrilled by the unexpected size of the audience. It was her first real proof that if free artistic performances were offered, a large and enthusiastic audience would assemble to see them. Alice stored her insight away for future reference.

With summer came the usual announcements of where the rich would spend the season. Mr. Hemmick, it was noted, would remain in Washington to prepare for the diplomatic corps; Mrs. Hemmick would spend the summer in New Hampshire, the fall in New York City, and not return to Washington until early November. It meant that during 1915, the Hemmicks would be together less than five months. Rather than rattle around in the huge Rhode Island Avenue house for the next six months, Christian returned to Studio House. The roof garden overlooking Rock Creek park, with its view of the Virginia palisades, was equipped with awnings and bamboo summer furniture. Whatever breezes might be found in the humid Washington summer air could be felt in this secluded aerie.

While Alice thought Christian was hard at study, in reality he was spending every waking moment thinking of Paul Swan. Unfortunately, Christian never considered the possibility that his affections might not only be unreciprocated, but vigorously repulsed. Soon snide remarks circulated about Christian and how he seemed to be trying to look like Paul Swan. He bleached his hair blond to match Paul's curls. He doused himself with Alice's perfume, because Paul liked cologne. Unfortunately, when he tried to dress like Paul in high fashion clothes with an artistic flair, Christian only became a caricature of an overweight, overdressed dandy. One wag remarked that Christian looked as if he were trying out for the first row of a chorus instead of a diplomatic receiving line. Another wondered if Christian always made it a point to use perfumed notepaper in writing male friends, or had he accidentally spilled some of Alice's sachet powder on it by mistake? Innuendo after innuendo, Alice's husband was being tarred and feathered cruelly, albeit anonymously, as was the polite way of society when engaged in doing someone in.

XVI
A Ballet for Pavlova

I n August of her fifty-eighth year and her fourth year as Mrs. Hemmick, Alice was invited to New York by sculptress Malvina Hoffman to have lunch with Hoffman's good friend and frequent model, Anna Pavlova. Hoffman was aware of Alice's fascination with dance and her use of it in her theatricals. She was sure, therefore, that Pavlova and Alice would be kindred spirits, even though she knew Alice's preference for the experimental choreography of Isadora Duncan or Ruth St. Denis over classical ballet.

Unlike St. Denis, whom Alice sponsored at the start of her career, Pavlova was by 1915 considered by dance aficionados and the public at large as the world's premier interpreter of classical ballet. The secret of her success was her absolute mastery of balletic movement, which allowed her the freedom to overlay it with the naturalness and fluidity of a Duncan and enhance it with the exoticism and theatricality of a St. Denis. Descriptions of Pavlova's choreography in her most famous solo dance, the "Dying Swan" from *Swan Lake*, resonated with earlier reviews of St. Denis in the cobra dance from *Radha*. In both, the choreography focused on arm, head, and upper torso articulation with intricate footwork subsumed by the movements of the upper body.

Behind Pavlova the dancer was a visionary who believed that the arts must be accessible to all, not just to devotees. Although conservative in her dance aesthetic and a strict adherent to proper technique, Pavlova recognized that ballet needed to be able to incorporate elements of folk and oriental dance in its choreography. With the creation of her own company, she began to include new components into her repertoire, although they were always circumscribed by the traditional movement of ballet.

Alice also knew that the future of the arts lay in accessibility, although she approached it as a producer and educator who believed that high ticket prices and lack of exposure were what separated the arts from its potential public. Although their approaches were different, their goal was the same: to bring people to the arts. In spite of Pavlova's broken English, the two women easily understood one another. They agreed that the arts were interrelated, and they discovered each attempted the other's art for pleasure; Pavlova sculpted, Alice danced. Pavlova often described her own dancing in terms of other artistic disciplines. "I try to express by dancing," she said, "what the composer puts into his music, what the painter expresses with his colors and brushes, the actor with the spoken word. I try to express them with my body and my spirit, that most universal of all languages."[1]

COSTUME SKETCH,
L'ÉCOLE EN CRINOLINE,
1915
Anna Pavlova in her role as the mischievous student Emelie in L'École en Crinoline. *Pavlova enjoyed the opportunity to display her mimetic and comedic talents in Alice's one-act ballet.*

Alice's stated guiding principal for her artistic endeavors was to take from one to enhance the other. As Hoffman had predicted, the two women had much to discuss.

As lunch drew to a close, Alice asked if Pavlova might be interested in reading the outline of a short ballet she had brought with her. Quickly perusing the proffered script, Pavlova announced that if expanded it would be the perfect addition to her forthcoming season. The only proviso was that she would have to convince her personal manager, her common-law husband Victor D'andré, to include it. As Pavlova departed, Alice gave her an inducement—to ensure her ballet's production, she would underwrite the company's Washington appearance.

Alice's offer was an expensive proposition. At the time of the lunch, Pavlova's Imperial Ballet Russe was contractually obligated for a season's tour with the Boston Grand Opera Company under the managing director-ship of Max Rabinoff. In addition to the conductor, chorus master, stage manager, and set designer, the opera company included seventy singers and a sixty-member orchestra. The Ballet Russe carried approximately forty-five persons on its own payroll, including its conductor, Adolph Schmid, and its ballet master, Ivan Clustine. A further expense was the transport of the ballet company's 400 pieces of luggage of which 160 were crates for sets and costumes. Rabinoff was well aware that full houses were not enough to cover the total costs and much of his time was spent courting local patrons for each stop of the tour. Alice's guarantee immediately added Washington, which had been bypassed because professional ballet and opera companies considered it a box-office disaster.

In the long run, however, the decision to include Alice's ballet in Pavlo-va's repertoire was artistic rather than financial. It was Pavlova the dancer, not D'andré the manager, who would have the final word. D'andré argued that it was impossible for Pavlova to add a new piece so close to the begin-ning of the tour; she demanded its inclusion. For some time she had searched for a piece to display her comedic and mimetic abilities to their fullest advantage. Alice's ballet, *L'École en Crinoline*, filled the bill. In the end her word was law and for the first time in many years, Washingtonians would see fully staged opera and ballet. Much of Pavlova's repertoire con-sisted of showcase divertissments and one-act ballets, generally preceded by a full-length ballet. For the 1915 season, however, an opera would pre-cede the one-act ballet.

Alice wired Christian to join her at Bar Harbor while she worked on the ballet in the relative quiet of Ban-y-Bryn. At the end of October 1915, he returned to Washington to take classes for the foreign service test while Alice went to New York to put the final touches on the ballet's script. Once it was finished to her satisfaction, she returned to Washington only to find

COSTUME SKETCH,
L'ÉCOLE EN CRINOLINE,
1915
*Emelie (played by Anna
Pavlova) presents flowers to
the school's headmistress.*

that Christian had dropped his studies. He said he was unable to concentrate, but gave no reason since he could not admit to his wife his infatuation with Swan.

Alice thought that if she took his mind off the test, he might relax enough to pass it, and she enlisted his help in soliciting patrons for the upcoming arrival of the Ballet Russe and the Boston Opera Company. By November 30, with only twenty of the ninety patrons needed to meet the guarantee, Alice was called to Boston by Pavlova to direct the final rehearsals of *L'École en Crinoline*. As an inducement, Pavlova promised Alice as much time as she thought necessary. Alice took the first train to Boston leaving Christian in Washington to find the remaining sponsors. If he failed, her little ballet was going to be costly to the Hemmick pocketbook.

Alice took full advantage of Pavlova's promise of unlimited rehearsal time, and the company's Washington opening was delayed for three days. The result was that *L'École en Crinoline* was placed on the prestigious opening night bill rather than, as originally scheduled, on the Saturday matinee bill. On December 20, the curtain rose on the Washington premiere of Montemezzi's *L'Amore dei Tre Re* followed by the world premiere of Alice Barney Hemmick's *L'École en Crinoline*.

Alice set *L'École en Crinoline* in 1830 at a fashionable girls boarding school. She designed a black-and-white set and hoopskirted crinoline costumes to recall the popular early nineteenth-century black silhouette cutouts pasted on a white background. The plot summary, including a quarter-page drawing of the set, was inserted into the company's program:

> The Artistic Soul of Emelie (Mlle. Pavlova) loving to create scissor-pictures (so much in vogue) of Pierrot, Harlequin, and such lovely beings, rebels against the drudgery of lessons. This neglect brings punishment, for she is forbidden to attend the Garden Party—to which all have been invited by the Curate—instead she must study. The lessons are dull and she falls asleep and dreams that one of her beloved portraits is endowed with life and kneels at her feet—telling her she threw him a kiss, which gave him a heart and that heart loves her. He invites her to the Joy of the Dance.[2]

At the dance's end, Emelie once more falls asleep, to be awakened by the return of her classmates from the party.

The next day the city's three major papers, the *Evening Star*, the *Post*, and the *Times*, reported on the event. A lengthy article appeared in *Washington Society* magazine the following Friday. They primarily focused on it as a social event of the first rank with lengthy reports on attendance and the gowns worn for the affair. The reviews of the ballet itself were unanimous; it was a success. Typical was the *Washington Times*'s review.

> 'The School in Crinoline,' the ballet given by Pavlova, Volinine, and some dozen of their Ballet Russe, presented a most striking and quaint picture in a most charming conventionalized setting, worked

ADVERTISEMENT FOR *L'École en Crinoline*, 1915
Following its premiere in Washington, D.C., on December 20, 1915, L'École en Crinoline was regularly presented across the United States by Pavlova's Imperial Ballet Russe during its short-lived joint tour with the Boston Grand Opera Company.

ANNA PAVLOVA, C. 1915
*Although Alice wrote a
second ballet for Pavlova, the
two women never collaborated
again. The above photograph
of Pavlova was inscribed by
the ballerina to Alice as a
souvenir of their joint effort.*

out in black and white, in striped effect, with but a touch of turquoise. It attests highly the artistic skill and originality of Mrs. Christian Hemmick, whose pantomime play was a dainty comedy of hoopskirt days, which allowed Mme. Pavlova a delightful comedy role through which she pirouetted on her toes as fascinatingly as ever. In an interlude that was a dream, a Pierrot, in most effective black and white, enters to find a fair Columbine awaiting him and to the ingratiating music of Chaminade, to which the ballet is set, Pavlova and Volinine present a lovely 'pas de deux.'[3]

Alice's success lay in the two words used repeatedly by reviewers—simple and charming. These were unusual adjectives to apply to any production in which Alice had her hand. Her theatrical efforts were most noted for their large casts, lavish costumes and sets, and turgid plots. The secret of the stylistic success of *L'École en Crinoline* was that for the first and last time, Alice did not start from the visual to create a theatrical piece, but took as her inspiration the simple piano pieces of Cecile Chaminade. Chaminade's music spoke to her of "quaint, amusing situations" in which "the people are creatures of charm with here a touch of drollness, there elegance and grace, and again simplicity and beauty." It meant that "the composition of this dance-drama was by no means a hard task. In fact, it seemed to compose itself from the serious situations that the music suggests."[4] In gratitude for providing her with such a popular vehicle, Pavlova sent Alice an autographed photo inscribed in French "In memory of our collaboration in your charming ballet 'En Crinoline,' Anna Pavlova."[5]

Washingtonian's viewed Alice with new respect; she was no longer their leading dramatic amateur, she was a professional. It was rumored that Pavlova had requested another ballet and that Alice was at work on one based loosely on her 1909 play, *Man in the Moon*, the production that had brought Christian into her life. Although she sent Pavlova her synopsis for *Moon Man*, *L'École en Crinoline* was their only collaboration. By late spring, the Boston Opera's touring company was bankrupt, and Pavlova was left to fill the commitment of both companies. Her company's losses were stag-

gering and she had no money to mount a new
ballet. Only the tried and true could remain in
production and Alice's ballet was among the
casualties of the reduced repertoire.

As her fifty-ninth birthday approached in
1916, Alice moved from project to project at a
pace her friends found exhausting. She seemed
driven in a way no one understood, even Alice.
But by keeping constantly involved in myriad
projects, there was no time to examine her personal life.

In February she staged an Egyptian pageant
for the annual Beaux Arts Ball to raise more
money for the artist-soldiers of France and to
recognize the invaluable services offered to
American art students by the L'École des Beaux-
Arts. Her contribution was *An Echo of the Nile*,
which starred Christian as Marc Antony. In
March she joined a committee planning a sale
and exhibit of Neighborhood House crafts, and
within days the small project was expanded from
a crafts sale to a full-fledged carnival including
an original entertainment by Alice. The Hemmicks began entertaining again on Friday
evenings, regularly having as many as eighteen
guests for dinner.

While Alice followed what she now catego-
rized as her religion—constant work—Christian

CHRISTIAN, C. 1918
*With his pince-nez eyeglass-
es and added weight, by
1918, Christian looked less
and less like the Greek God
Alice had married in 1911.*

once again prepared for the foreign service exams. This time Alice was able
to observe the lackadaisical way he studied and the ease with which he was
distracted. She was increasingly uneasy, but held her tongue. She feared to
confide her dismay even to her closest friends for fear of what they might
say. *The Club-Fellow and Washington Mirror*, ever ready to lob a pot-shot at
Christian, noted:

> Chris Hemmick is another who is hearkening to the call of the diplo-
> matic corps, spurred on by some pride which he still possesses and
> likewise by his indomitable, motherly wife. He is now devoting much
> time to study for the examinations, and well he may, though of course
> the tremendous influence which they can bring to bear, might result
> in rating up his educational qualifications with more success than
> attended the last examinations for the consular service. But surely

Alice cannot expect a ministerial post for her husband, even though she herself would grace any barbaric court, and yet I cannot picture her as being willing to subside into a minor role as wife of a mere secretary or attache.[6]

Such well aimed barbs hit home in Christian's over-sensitive ego and merely added fuel to his fire for Swan. At least with Swan, he was in no danger of being considered a mama's boy.

At this point in their marriage, Alice would have accommodated herself to any success of Christian's for even she had to admit that her Greek God was less than enchanting. She began to notice Christian's growing fondness for wines and brandies, although she saw none of the belligerence displayed by Albert when he drank too much.[7] Rather, Christian became increasingly withdrawn, and since no one remarked upon his lassitude, she was not sure if their dinner guests noticed. In the long run, Alice decided to ignore Christian's constant tippling, but she refused to give up hope for their marriage. Instead, she continued on with her own obsessive activity. "Work," she would remind any friend who dared suggest she slow down, "was her religion," and, as always, it distracted her from the problems in her marriage.

XVII
A National Theater

To Alice-watchers, it must have seemed that she had done everything a person might want to do in the arts. She painted, produced plays, scripted ballets, and they had heard it rumored that at one time she had a superb musical voice. She even provided an example for artistic living from her bohemian Studio House. Surely, she had done it all, and yet, one never knew with Alice.

In early April, Alice, who was still president of the Amateur Authors' and Players' Group, noted that as no professional theater group seemed inclined to honor the three hundredth birthday of William Shakespeare, she and her group would do so. Drawing upon her newfound cachet as a professional, she enticed the widely regarded husband and wife Shakespearean acting team of R. D. Shepherd and Odette Tyler to appear as the stars. The tercentenary provided her a perfect opportunity to test her long-held belief that a large, untapped audience for theater existed in Washington. If six thousand people had flocked to her amateur tableaux at the Washington Monument, how many might she draw if she used professionals? Handed to her on a silver platter was the opportunity to provide an answer to a question she had raised some thirteen years before: "How can we best discharge our responsibility to all the citizens of the nation's capital?" The answer she believed was simple: free theater.

On May 26, 1916, the elite flocked to Henry F. Blount's estate, The Oaks, in Georgetown (now known as Dumbarton Oaks), to see *Shakespeare Triumphant*, an evening of scenes from Shakespeare selected by Alice. The earnings were earmarked to support a free presentation of the masque the following night at the base of the Washington Monument.

That evening, William Shakespeare sat at one corner of a temporary stage. A muse would approach him and then a scene from one of his plays was performed by the Shepherds supported by Alice's regular amateur actors. The boys' choir from the Washington Cathedral sang Elizabethan music in counterpoint to the dramatic presentations, which included selections from *The Merchant of Venice*, *Romeo and Juliet*, and *The Taming of the Shrew*.

When the production moved the next evening to the base of the Washington Monument, it faced the same logistical problems that had plagued *The Awakening* the preceding May. The audience was too large for the allotted space, and the thousands unable to see went home disappointed. The next day, Alice called an emergency meeting at Studio House

ALICE AT SIXTY, 1917
Alice had herself specially photographed in preparation for the opening of the National Sylvan Theatre in 1917.

to address the problem and within days the *Evening Star* reported that she and Odette Tyler would shoulder the task of providing Washington with a sylvan theater on the grounds of the Washington Monument for the free production of Shakespeare and other classical plays.

Even for Alice the project was daunting because it involved negotiations with the federal government. While others might have despaired, not so Alice and the equally unflappable Odette. According to Louis B. Thompson, the young tenor whose career Alice had launched at a Studio House evening, the key to their success lay with the redoubtable Colonel W. W. Harts, superintendent of public buildings and grounds for the nation's capital and aide to President Wilson. If Harts could be persuaded, he, in turn, would persuade Congress to appropriate money for the project.

Although Alice and Harts did not move in the same circles, she knew Thompson had met Harts at one of his singing engagements. Over dinner, she worked to enlist Thompson to her cause. Of their discussion, Thompson later wrote:

> Lady Alice, as it seemed to me, had abandoned her marvelous achievement, painting, and had gone berserk with the drama and dancing. She informed me one evening at dinner that it was a national disgrace that the nation's Capital did not have an outdoor theatre. She was going to see to that. 'You know, Louis, you will have to help me.' 'How can I do it?' It has been often said if you can sell a piano you can sell anything. I don't know why but with my youth and inexperience I fell for it and went to work on the act. Lady Alice thought the theatre should be a little clump of trees just southeast from the Washington Monument. Lady Alice knew what she wanted and she generally got it.[1]

Then, putting his doubts aside, Thompson told Alice what he knew about Harts.

> I met him on several occasions at the apartment of Mrs. George Pickett, the widow of Gen. Geo. Pickett of the Gettysburg charge fame. The colonel was quite the gorgeous thing—waxed moustache, marshal's stick, and all the trimmings. He was quite aware of the fact that promotion in the Army did not come by soldiery in a remote Army Post. He had found the spot he wanted, Washington, D.C. After all this was headquarters for everything.[2]

Alice and Odette met Harts on May 29 and rode with him to survey the site for the proposed theater. They pointed out that the topography of the site they had selected made expenses minimal. The natural stand of trees and bushes already in place formed the basic lines of the stage and wings.

The hill of the monument provided a natural amphitheater for thousands of seats. A national sylvan theater for Washington would, Alice said, "bring the greatest good to the greatest number." Furthermore, the two women argued, "they knew of mothers from all parts of the city who had arrived with their children more than three hours before the start of the Shakespearean tercentenary performance in order to ensure that their little ones were able to see the production."[3]

Colonel Harts, while polite, was not totally convinced. He estimated it would cost approximately six hundred dollars to provide what the two women wanted, and he was not sure Congress, which faced the possibility of America entering the war, would be willing to fund it. Once more Alice called on Thompson for advice; "Soften him up with a few dinners," he advised. Soon Colonel Harts was seen arriving at Studio House for alfresco dinners held on the Hemmicks' roof garden. By July, the *Washington Courier* reported that not only was the Colonel enthusiastic over the matter personally, but when an audience finally gathered to enjoy a performance at the new outdoor theater, "Col. Harts will be the hero of the event, laying the stage hero in the shade."[4]

As Thompson summed it up later, "The little chocolate soldier took the bait."[5]

From summer's end to late fall, grounds keepers worked to create the natural sylvan theater setting Alice envisioned. The sodded stage area was to be as large as the Metropolitan Opera's. High, dense shrubbery was needed on both sides of the stage to provide wings and a natural screen for dressing rooms. Six mature chestnut trees were planted at the rear of the stage as a sounding board.

Harts fully endorsed Alice's proposal that she be named chairman of the Production Committee. With the title came the power and responsibility to produce a series of Shakespearean plays for the summer and fall of 1917. The Shepherds would play the leads with supporting cast drawn from Alice's Players' Group. From time to time, Alice planned to allow other organizations to produce events, but for Alice and the Shepherds the immediate object of the entire project was to "aid the public of Washington in a better understanding of Shakespeare and his plays."[6]

The idea of open-air theater was not original to Alice. The years immediately preceding the United States's entry into World War I saw a spontaneous revival of outdoor performances throughout the country. The particular design of an outdoor theater generally determined the style of the dramas to be performed in it. The Sylvan Theatre was based upon the most versatile of them, a classic garden theater with the stage area delineated by trees and shrubs allowing performance of both traditional plays in which the words were important and masques and pageants that were primarily visual in import. Even as she espoused her allegiance to Shakespearean theater, Alice was seeing masques and pageants in her mind's eye. No matter what type of production would eventually be presented, it was Alice's belief that the arts were for everyone that was finally being tested. If she were correct, the National Sylvan Theatre would be the nation's first truly democratic playhouse where caste distinctions among inhabitants of box, dress circle, orchestra, balcony and gallery were obliterated.

COURTING BERNHARDT

As she had when Studio House was being built, Alice chose to remain in Washington for the summer so that she could check on the progress of the National Sylvan Theatre. She also thought Christian might need cheering because, for the second time, he failed his diplomatic tests. In that, Alice was mistaken, for he appeared both cheerful and unconcerned. The reason was that Christian had discovered a group that thought him a splendid fellow and gave him plenty to do, which kept him away from Alice and the possibility of her accidentally discovering who was present in his nightly dreams.

Christian had been taken under the wing of a group of artists and patrons (or "dilettantes," as *The Club-Fellow and Washington Mirror* preferred to call them) led by sculptor Paul Bartlett and painter Herbert Bush-Read, sculptor U. S. G. Dunbar, and cartoonist Felix Mahoney who were attempting to start up a new club in Washington. Christian became a member of the Board of Governors and was named membership chairman for the fledgling Arts Club of Washington.

The group leased the colonial home of Dr. Trueman Abbey on I Street as their headquarters and worked toward opening its doors in the fall. On October 8, over four hundred artists and arts followers walked through its blue-green doorway into the high ceilinged, purple-painted rooms intended to provide Washington with a place where politics were eschewed in favor of the arts. Christian, as chairman of the initial membership drive, was credited with much of the new club's success. He accepted the praise; but those in the know noticed that Alice was the chairman of its Dramatic Committee and one of its artist members, and they wondered how many of the memberships were the result of her influence.

On November 5, 1916, Jean Eliot, a *Washington Times* society columnist, broke the news that Alice had accomplished the cultural coup of the season. Sarah Bernhardt, who was in Washington for two weeks of performances at the National Theater, had accepted an invitation to Studio House on November 10 for tea and an original entertainment in her honor. Writing in the inimitable gushing style of gossip columnists, Eliot informed her readers:

It's a very delightful entertainment Mrs. Christian Hemmick is planning in honor of Mme. Sarah Bernhardt, but not a big reception. Dear me no! In the first place, Studio House is not very large; moreover, the 'artistic hour' is planned with a view to interesting and entertaining Mme. Bernhardt, and she certainly would not derive much pleasure from shaking hands with three or four hundred people.

Mrs. Hemmick has asked fifty or sixty people...members of the French embassy staff, friends of Mme. Bernhardt's and a very few of her own friends. There will be tea, of course; and a performance in miniature along the lines of the artistic masques, pageants, and spectacles Mrs. Hemmick has staged so frequently in Washington. Music, sans doute—I hear Louis Thompson is to sing, and that's a treat in itself—dancing, by some of the clever and talented young people Mrs. Hemmick so delights to bring before the public, gorgeous and colorful costuming, spectacular lighting effects—all this will contribute to the gay and original entertainment.[7]

The guests invited by Alice to her *L'Heure Artistique* were chosen as much for their ability to speak French as for their social status. They began arriving at Studio House shortly before the 4:30 P.M. time specified on the invitation. Among the early arrivals at the tea table in the dining room presided over by Mrs. John Biddle and Miss Sheridan was Marietta Minnigerode Andrews. Mrs. Andrews then climbed the stairs to the large west studio room to await the performance of her daughter Mary Lord Andrews, who was one of seven young women and men appearing in *Temple d'El Kaffa*, a dance drama written by Alice especially for Mme. Bernhardt. Marietta, an artist and longtime friend of Alice, later described the event:

The studio, which is the top floor of her strange house on Sheridan Circle, was filled with the elite of Washington. That day the lights were dim; Mrs. Barney knows how to make us all look our best; the lighting of her rooms lends a touch of mystery to the most prosaic— age looks young, while youth takes on just enough dignity to be interesting; unbecoming details melt away in the fragrant half tones of that salon. On the dark red tiled floor against a background of tapestries and old carvings she staged that afternoon an oriental tableau in honor of her distinguished friend and guest, Mme Bernhardt. My dear daughter, Mary Lord, immovable, in vivid green—kneeling on the terra cotta floor—took the part of an Egyptian idol—the beautiful Ruth Hitchcock, a queen, before whom the various snake charmers and dancers displayed their art.

Madame Bernhardt arrived promptly, borne in a chair by four men. She was badly crippled at that time, very faint and suffering.

The object of her visit to America was to collect funds for the French widows and orphans—the ovation given her I need not describe. It was not only to her, it was to France! My dear Mary Lord, spoke French well, and had the honor of a brief conversation with her, receiving a word of praise for her costume and the brave way in which throughout the performance she held a difficult pose.[8]

For those who watched both Hemmicks, of equal interest to the Sarah Bernhardt reception was a short announcement appearing in the *Washington Times*. It stated that Christian Hemmick would spend the greater part of the winter in Pittsburgh on an unspecified motion picture venture. Immediately, whispers began to circulate about the imminent dissolution of the Hemmick marriage, but no word was forthcoming from 2306 Sheridan Circle because, whatever his failings, Alice still needed Christian. She could not reconcile herself to the fact that she may have made as terrible a mistake with her second marriage as with her first, and so, in an attempt to maintain her equilibrium, she continued to pretend to herself, Christian, and everyone else that all was well.

WAR APPROACHING

Meantime, Alice plunged herself into work to keep herself from facing the reality of her relationship with Christian, as well as to keep her deep-seated fear for her daughters' safety at bay. Although she received letters from Laura and Natalie assuring her they were fine, newspaper accounts of the heavy losses at the Battle of Verdun in the spring and the Battle of the Somme in the fall, combined with constant zeppelin raids on Paris, did little to ease her mind. As disappointed as she might be in Christian, he allayed her fears with his presence. But now, with Christian in Pittsburgh, she was lost. Even though she was not sure he would understand, she sent him a letter full of loneliness and longing.

> I felt so lonely last night, it was really terrible. I pictured my dear ones in that awful plight. Natalie with her beautiful mind torn from the quiet of her work to a realization that the world is sinking—that it is full of

HIPPOLYTE AND LAURA, C. 1915
In France, Hippolyte and Laura met infrequently because of their respective war duties: Hippolyte as a soldier and Laura as a nurse. After the war, Laura was made a Chevalier of the French Legion of Honor for her work among the wounded.

misery and fear. And Alice [Laura]—with the brave look I've seen so often when something must be met without flinching.

You know that girl has been through Hell, and god knows I went with her. Christian—have you ever suffered through others? I have been so tortured that I thought I could not live. It all came back to me last night. I lived over the agonies of my life. I felt very alone— they will be quiet and calm. We never cry out, but I know every expression—the meaning of the indrawing of Alice's nostrils, the opening bewilderment of Natalie's eyes. I know each of them—every line, every signal of meaning.

Christian—the wind was terrible last night. This morning Charles brought me some coffee and my paper at seven, and I see that both our houses near the Seine, and our apartment, must be ruined— and all beautiful Paris. Dear beautiful smiling Paris, and the kindly warm-hearted people. It's very terrible. I think I can't stop here. I believe I'll have to go to Europe next Wednesday. I may be of some use to some one. Don't you think that I should?

At the French embassy yesterday they told me things were much exaggerated, and that I need not worry—but these reports, and my feeling, I'm not a panic sort of person, fills me with alarm. These two dear friends of mine are the only ones in the whole world who care for me and know me, and I am full of fears. Yes, you are right, I am the commonplace woman—and I feel very lonely. No one but you knows how I feel. I can't tell why I tell you—you a boy—everything. Yes, I'll prepare to leave Wednesday. I can't stay here so alone. I'll say nothing to anyone, only start off.[9]

No record exists of Christian's reply, but he must have reassured her enough to keep her from going to France.

While awaiting summer and the opening of the Sylvan Theatre, Alice began to discuss the possibility of allowing the Rhode Island Avenue property to become the national headquarters of the National American Women's Suffrage Association of which Carrie Chapman Catt was president. As early as 1914, Alice had begun to disassociate herself from the more militant Congressional Union. Under successive leadership, the Union, along with its parent organization, the Women's Peace Party had changed its tactics, moving beyond what Alice considered suitable protest tactics. Although Alice continued to support the right of women to vote, she no longer was willing to lend her name or talents to the organization. She believed the party had showed particularly bad manners when it unfurled a suffrage banner in the halls of Congress. In her mind a well-attended theater piece to protest women's inequality was one thing, but

invading the halls of Congress was a different matter altogether.

Instead she joined the National American Women's Suffrage Association, a middle-of-the-road group that used lobbying as a tactic instead of dramatic gestures such as chaining themselves to wrought iron gates. Like the Peace Party before it, the NAWSA was now large enough to warrant a permanent Washington presence. With its twenty-six furnished rooms, 1626 Rhode Island Avenue would serve admirably as its new headquarters. Both Ruth White, the organization's secretary, and Mrs. Thomas Jefferson Smith of Louisville, the national board member assigned to work with the local chapter, planned to live on the premises, and other bedrooms were to be at the ready for the arrival of out-of-town members coming to Washington to lobby their congressmen. The ballroom built for Natalie's debut was designated the Susan B. Anthony room. Important suffrage movement memorabilia, which included the table upon which Anthony drafted the original suffrage amendment, was to be on exhibition. Tongue in cheek, the Association let it be known that all other spaces would be known as "Root for Suffrage rooms," a joke at the expense of Alice's former tenant, the staunchly antisuffrage, Senator Elihu Root. Senator Root, Mrs. Catt announced, was welcome to visit at any time.

BALLROOM OF 1626 RHODE ISLAND AVE., N.W., 1895
Alice allowed the National American Woman's Suffrage Association to use 1626 Rhode Island Ave., N.W., as their headquarters. The women designated the ballroom originally built for Natalie's debut as the Susan B. Anthony room and filled it with suffrage memorabilia.

OPENING OF THE SYLVAN THEATRE

As 1916 drew to a close, Alice arranged to sublet Ben Ali Haggin's studio and apartment at the Hotel des Artistes on West Fifty-seventh Street in New York and began the process of cajoling numerous stars into appearing at the Sylvan Theatre's opening gala on June 1. By the end of March, her plans were complete, and, even though war was declared on April 4, 1917, the date for the dedication of the National Sylvan Theatre remained on the official government calendar as June 1. In April both Christian and Alice returned to Washington to take up residence at Studio House.

Publicity for the opening program promised something for everyone. It included an allegorical pageant in three parts produced, directed, choreographed, and costumed by Alice with roles for nearly a hundred of Washington's elite. The local amateurs were to be assisted by a host of professional singers, actors, and dancers invited by Alice to appear free of charge. Among the parade of stars were Andras Pavley, lead dancer for the Chicago Opera, Serge Oukrainsky of the Ballet Russe, Kathryn Lee of the Boston Grand Opera Company, and Sophie Braslau of the Metropolitan Opera. Tamki Miura of the Boston Grand Opera planned to sing an aria from *Madame Butterfly* and the R. D. Shepherds would perform several Shakespearean scenes. The finale was to be a medley of Lily Langtry singing "Brittania," Sophie Braslau performing "La Marseillaise," and Anna Case leading the crowd in "The Star-Spangled Banner."

A crowd estimated at thirteen thousand began to gather on the Washington Monument grounds early in the afternoon of June 1. Those who could not find seats set up their camp stools and opened picnic baskets on the sloped hill leading up to the monument. Excitement ran high, for Alice's extravagant opening program at the National Sylvan Theatre had been ballyhooed for weeks in the press. Directly in front of the stage was a roped-off section reserved for dignitaries such as the president, his cabinet, Supreme Court justices, and Congress. Pre-opening parties, which delayed the dignitaries, were held throughout the city. When they arrived they found their seats taken by a band of noisy boys who ignored all threats and settled in to enjoy the show. The amateur

SERGE OUKRAINSKY, c. 1914

Among the performers Alice gathered together for the opening performance of the National Sylvan Theatre was Serge Oukrainsky of the Ballet Russe who later became ballet master and premier dancer of the Chicago Opera.

actors arrived, worth among them an aggregate of at least some forty million dollars. The audience was orderly and hushed in anticipation. Members of the Marine Band, resplendent in their red uniforms, waited for Captain James K. Hackett to raise his baton. Then the one thing happened that Alice could not control. It poured rain. Everyone scurried for shelter and the show was called off. The entire opening performance was rescheduled for the following evening at 8 P.M.

Despite threatening weather the following day, an even larger crowd assembled for the second try at inaugurating the National Sylvan Theatre. Precisely at 8 P.M., Captain Hackett once more lifted his baton and this time the clouds overhead cooperated; Alice's National Sylvan Theatre was a reality. At the close of the festivities, a moment of tribute was paid to Alice as a letter written to her for the occasion by Sarah Bernhardt was read aloud to the assembled throng:

> I am very glad that it is a woman who has realized one of my dreams, and I am especially glad that woman is yourself. I have always dreamt for this wonderful country a national theater. That theater is now established. ...Brava, dear madame! Brava! And many thanks.[10]

As the notes of the national anthem faded away, the Marine Band struck up a rousing rendition of "Dixie" to mark the end of the program. Even then, according to contemporary reports, "the spectators seemed loathe to depart, until spattering raindrops warned them that the threatened storm would not be much longer delayed, so they hied themselves happily homeward to tell their families and future generations how they witnessed the opening of the first national theater in America—alfresco, at that."

The inauguration of the National Sylvan Theatre was the proudest moment of Alice's life. While her father had given a theater to a city, she had obtained one for the nation. He would have been proud of her. If she did nothing else, she would always have this moment to remember and savor.

The success or failure of Alice's idea for a National Sylvan Theatre did not, however, ultimately rest on its opening night. Rather, the true test was how funds were raised and audiences

PROGRAM COVER, SYLVAN THEATRE, 1917
Although the opening night of the Sylvan Theatre at the Washington Monument grounds was rained out, it remained one of the proudest days of Alice's life. This site is used to this day for many national and local celebrations.

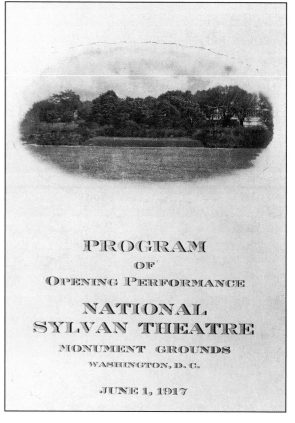

NATIONAL SYLVAN THEATRE

DEDICATION OF THE NATION'S FIRST

FOURTH OF JULY CELEBRATION

1917

AT EIGHT O'CLOCK

ON THE

WASHINGTON MONUMENT GROUNDS

EXECUTIVE COMMITTEE

Superintendent of the National Sylvan Theatre............Col. Wm. H. Harts
Chairman of Productions...........................Mrs. Christian Hemmick
Treasurer...Robert Elmore
Stage Managers.................John F. Luitich and Denis E. Connell
Manager of Properties.................................Mortimer Clarke
Mechanical Director.....................................John S. Neilegh
Director of Lighting..................................Morven Thompson

PART ONE

Musical programme and Community Singing conducted by Reginald de Kovan. the American composer. Mrs. Edna Thomas, contralto. Mrs. Annie Brett Sumey, soprano. Mr. Louis Thompson, tenor. Prof. Stansfield and Mrs. Wilder, leaders of chorus. Marine Band, Mr. Branson, conductor.

PART TWO

THE CALL OF THE ALLIES

A Propaganda Pageant

Written and Produced by Mrs. Christian Hemmick

ARGUMENT

Prologue

Spoken by Mr. Denis E. Connell

Joy and her spirits are joined by Peace, Liberty, and Freedom. They are chased off by the Fire Brands of War who wreak destruction and light this vast conflagration of the whole world. In the wan light of the break of day fleeing multitudes with their hastily gathered possessions and their little children are vaguely seen, their muffled moans being heard breaking the calm. (End of Prologue.)

Brutal man and his men of Power and Greed enter with Peace and Liberty in chains. Justice, drugged by gold, lies senseless upon her throne. Servia's cry is heard: "All I gave to proud Austria's demands, all but one, mine honor"; Belgium tells of their endeavor to save, but their frailness proved unequal to the task, but their mighty deeds of courage proved a Christlike service to the world.

England and France enter; Imperial Russia, gloomy and austere, watches the Siberian exiles. The sorrows inspire the spirit of New Russia. Armenia with cries of woe for the cruelties she suffers—Poland and all the other Allies beg of Freedom for aid. When their doom seems deepest Columbia comes, Peace and Liberty are released, Justice is awakened, Columbia's millions of millions of sons heed the cries of agonized Europe and will fight and die and prove their courage and their honor in this vast war, A WAR TO END WAR.

CHARACTERS

Freedom ....Mr. Milton Bryan
Peace ....Miss Virginia Hereford
Liberty ....Miss Vietta Droney
Man ....Mr. Arthur White
Justice ....Miss Lou White
Servia ....Mrs. Chase
Belgium ....Mr. Maurice Jarvis
England ....Mr. Henry Dolan
England's colonies ....Mrs. Wilcox and Mr. L. Kent Morrison
France ....Mr. Denis E. Connell
France's colonies—
    Tunis ....Miss Helen Griffith
    Algeria ....Mr. Reybeau
Imperial Russia ....Mr. Charles Shaw
New Russia ....Miss Katherine Drain
Armenia ....Mrs. Maud Howell Smith
Italy ....Miss Grecbella Rivero
Roumania ....Mr. Hatfield
Japan ....Mr. Antonia Rivero
Poland ....Mr. Finley Hayes
Men of Power and Greed,
    Messrs. Mortimer Clarke, Neilegh, McMullen, Underwood, Lewis, Thompson, and others.
Columbia ....Mrs. Anne Brett Sumey
Sibtrian Exiles, Belgian Refugees, and War Victims,—Fire Brands of War, led by Miss Katherine Drain, Mrs. O'Dede, and Mr. Mason Wright.
Dancers of Joy, led by Miss Charlotte Hogan.

PROGRAM,

THE CALL OF THE

ALLIES, 1917

Alice's propaganda pageant,

The Call of the Allies, *was*

presented at Washington's

first Fourth of July

celebration at the National

Sylvan Theatre in 1917.

built to ensure its existence over the long run. As chairman of the Sylvan Theatre's production committee, it was Alice's responsibility to see that both were found. With the entrance of the United States into the war, the potential audience increased exponentially as thousands of new civil servants working on the war effort arrived in Washington. Funds for the support of the proposed season of two Shakespearean works and two non-classic plays were, however, another matter altogether.

By mid-June the *Washington Times* and the *Washington Post* announced that the third production, a play called *Sundown*, scheduled for June 26 might be the last. Subscription sales for reserved seats directly in front of the stage had raised only half the amount needed to continue the season. Moreover, the low treasury threatened Alice's Fourth of July propaganda pageant, which was already in rehearsal. It was noted that the special guests would be soldiers in training at Fort Meyers and Washington barracks.

The news that the capital's first official Fourth of July celebration was aimed at providing entertainment for the nation's fighting men opened the coffers of no less a venerable and culturally conservative organization than the National Society of the Daughters of the American Revolution. In return for ensuring Alice's production, the DAR insisted on sharing Alice's allotted time with a presentation of its own.

Alice's part of the program was a series of tableaux called *The Call of the Allies*. The prologue spoken by Mr. Denis E. Connell, stated the thesis of the play:

Joy and her spirits are joined by Peace, Liberty, and Freedom. They are chased off by the Fire Brands of War who wreak destruction and light this vast conflagration of the whole world. In the wan light of the break of day fleeing multitudes with their hastily gathered possessions and their little children are vaguely seen, their muffled moans being heard breaking the calm.[11]

In order to ensure that there could be no doubt to what was happening on stage, Alice also printed a narrative of the action in the program. To make it even clearer, as each character appeared, the Marine Band played the national anthem of the nation represented.

She had every reason to do so. It took a great deal of imagination to follow the plot, even with the program. Enough of Alice's regular performers, augmented by some new faces from the Neighborhood House staff, were in town to provide the gigantic cast needed to field several armies and a multitude of refugees. Missing from the actual performance, however, was Louis B. Thompson, even though his name was listed on the program. Having been privy from the beginning to Alice's plans for the Fourth of July celebration, he bluntly refused to have anything to do with what he believed was an artistic disaster. Of the affair Thompson wrote:

> There was to be a formidable army of Turks; red fezes, cardboard scimitars painted silver and rubber boots. I was to be the general or head Turk. The Turkish Army was to chase the Armenian women from the trees and bushes. The poor Armenian women were all sizes, tall and thin and short and fat....Lady Alice was quite provoked when I refused to be the Head Turk and asked to be excluded from any part of this artistic debacle. I agreed to attend the dress rehearsal and help with suggestions.
>
> The Marine Band, eighty-five strong, all aglow in their summer dress uniforms, were there for the rehearsal. Colonel Harts had really gone to town. A Captain Stansfield [sic] was the leader of the band. He was the typical German type, fat, long black gay nineties moustache, and he wore glasses which seemed to be a half inch thick. The rehearsal progressed smoothly until the refugees came crawling out of the bushes. Lady Alice without warning grabbed the baton arm of a very much bewildered German and said, 'Captain, STOP—the music isn't terrible enough.' He replied, 'Mrs. Barney the Marine Band can't play terrible music.' The rehearsal came to an abrupt end with everyone in convulsion. This included the Turkish Army, the refugees, and most of the Marine band. I made a swift exit to 17th Street where I found a taxi and made off for the Studio House. Lady Alice came home most disconsolate.[12]

Although the pageant was repeated on Bastille Day in honor of "French Day and of the Visiting Allies," the plays planned for August and September were scrapped for lack of funds. The audience was there, but the money was not. Alice stepped down as chairperson of the production committee and turned the reins over to Colonel Harts. The remainder of the summer of 1917 saw the National Sylvan Theatre serve as the site for a series of military band concerts, weekday preachers, patriotic speeches, and children's choirs. Alice learned a hard and disappointing lesson from the experience—she had misjudged the readiness of Washington's elite to support cultural opportunities for the masses.

Alice retreated to the cool mountains of West Virginia in an attempt to recover her equanimity and consider other ways in which to bring about the changes in cultural attitudes so sorely needed in Washington. Christian, for his part, decided he wanted to be a soldier and applied to attend the August officers' training camp at Fort Meyer. *The Club-Fellow and Washington Mirror* caustically noted that "Alice's pink and pampered darling" would probably find army life exceedingly difficult "for the life in the training camp is vastly different from that of idle luxury to which Chris has become accustomed in the past eight years. No manicure parlors or perfumery shops occupy the sites of the army post." When, on the first of August the list for the second camp at Fort Meyer was released, Christian's name was missing. "Poor Chris," said the writer for *The Club-Fellow*, "he seems never to have succeeded at anything since catching the Widow Barney."[13]

The barb stuck and Alice could no longer ignore the fact that something was basically wrong with her marriage. It did not lie in the difference in their ages, although at times that rankled Christian. Rather, the problems were congenital to their distinctive personalities. Where Alice might be temporarily defeated, Christian failed. While Alice used personal setbacks as the impetus for exploring new avenues of endeavor, Christian seemed to tuck his tail between his legs and flee in the opposite direction. Where Albert had been able to maintain a public facade of success to the very end, Christian was constantly pilloried for failure. In the privacy of Studio House, the arguments began. Christian gave her paintings hung about the walls of the great Studio Room a disdainful glance and declared them punk. "But it is work," she retorted. "You won't do any work." Then Christian, the erstwhile Greek God with the highly publicized 4-F physique, drew his lips closed and uttered a sound like escaping steam or hissing snakes. Alice was terrified by the sound and unsure whether it was one of menace or imminent demise.

XVIII
The End of a Marriage

W as it finally over, the romantic Hemmick marriage? If the romance were gone, then all that was left for the two participants was to face each other over morning coffee. She had given up painting for him, what had he done for her? She had supported him with her money, what had he ever contributed toward running their household? Alice refused to honor these unbidden questions with answers because to do so would be to admit defeat and she was not yet prepared to do so. Thus, when Christian said he was interested in producing a play, she grabbed at his proposal, willing to provide whatever it cost to help him succeed in this new venture. Maybe this time the result would be different.

Alice acted swiftly and by the end of August 1917, Studio House was rented and the Hemmicks moved into an apartment at the Hotel des Artistes in New York. The Hotel des Artistes was filled with theatrical luminaries, including the exotic Alla Nazimova, who Alice hoped could guide Christian toward a profitable theatrical venture. She became an active member of New York's Actors and Authors' Theater and hosted their meetings. Among the participants was Walter Knight whose patriotic play was to open in Pittsburgh in mid-October. It looked a sure thing, and she purchased a share of it in Christian's name.

On October 16, Alice and her in-laws, Perry and Katherine Johnson, went to Pittsburgh for opening night. The play clearly needed more work before it reached New York, but they were assured by Knight that it would be improved before its Boston preview. Knight elicited additional money from Alice's seemingly bottomless purse, and the Hemmicks returned to Washington with the Johnsons. They spent the remainder of the week at the theater so that Alice could give Christian a crash course on drama. If he were really serious about the producing business, he had to know what made for successful theater. *The Club-Fellow* was quick to note their presence on the local scene.

The Christian Hemmicks have been attending all the first nights at Washington theaters, and they always attract a good deal of attention, to the obvious delight of Alice to whom the limelight is as the breath of life. She fusses out of her motor and into the lobby, down the aisle and into her seat, the faithful Christian fussing along beside her, helping her off and on with her wraps, holding her fan and her bag, and

ALICE IN STUDIO HOUSE, C. 1908
Alice attracted attention wherever she went. At the reopening of the Corcoran in 1908, her peacock green hair ornament, complete with an uncurled peacock feather, attracted as much press notice as the newly installed galleries.

assuring that her hair is all right and that everything is at it should be! If anybody else so much as shuffles a foot or rustles a programme during the performance, Mrs. Hemmick says "shush!"[1]

At week's end, Christian went straightaway to Boston to be on hand for his play's next round of previews while Alice returned to New York and her own dramatic project. *When a Woman Loves* opened at the Grand Opera House in Brooklyn on December 17. The play was largely autobiographical, although its happy ending was more wishful thinking on Alice's part than reality. According to press releases, it was a story of "all-consuming passions of perfect love—its happiness, sorrows, elysium, self-sacrifice and devotion. The central character was a woman of

fashion and wealth who dares to defy customs and condition to enjoy the god-given gift of perfect love."[2] The starring role was played by Cecil Spooner, for many years Otis Skinner's leading lady. The professional actors in Spooner's resident stock company played the remaining characters. To ensure that the critics crossed the Brooklyn Bridge to review the show, the press was informed that the author was using the pseudonym of Mrs. Christian so that the play could be critiqued on its own merits. The reviews were kind, and Alice was encouraged enough by them to begin the arduous task of attempting a traditional three-act play. In the long run, however, what Alice did next depended not upon the reviews of *When a Woman Loves*, but on Christian.

Boston reviews for Christian's first producing venture were scathing, and the play closed summarily. His producing career was over almost before it began. He returned to the Hotel des Artistes, Alice, and the unobtainable Paul Swan. Rumors circulated in Washington that Christian was turning his hand to playwriting and that the plot was very intense. *The Club-Fellow* wondered "will friend wife be the heroine—or merely the backer?"[3]

As winter turned into spring, Alice wondered too. By now Alice knew Christian well enough to realize that his talk of writing and producing his own play was mere fantasy. He was not only incapable of undertaking the hard work involved, but his grasp of drama remained limited. Moreover, her purse was not bottomless, and Christian's dramatic pursuits were draining. Perhaps, it was Christian's arrogant assumption that she would continue to fund whatever he did that finally helped Alice to decide. By spring she began to talk about divorce, but no matter how she tried to convince him that it was the best thing for both of them, Christian refused to consider it because he was Catholic.

In desperation, she investigated grounds for divorce in New York. There was only one, adultery, and she was aghast. Friends recalling that time remembered her saying: "How crude. Then of course, I can't get it here." They recommended that she establish a residence in New Jersey and sue for desertion. "I just can't live in New Jersey," she was reported as saying. The Hemmicks were at an impasse.

In late spring of 1918, Christian went to Pittsburgh on a second foray in producing. Alice moved from the Hotel des Artistes to a smaller apartment at Number 30 Central Park South. She worried about Studio House because it stood empty and the War Department was requisitioning vacant homes around Dupont Circle for office space. In spite of this, she was reluctant to move back to Washington until the matter with Christian was resolved. Moreover, the relative solitude of her new apartment allowed her to concentrate on her latest play, *The Color of Her Soul*, which she planned to submit to the New York Theatre Guild.

On November 11, 1918, the Great War ended, but in January 1919, Alice's personal war with Christian began in earnest. In that month Alice learned that her husband was pursuing not only a theatrical career as a play broker in Pittsburgh, but a young male actor as well. Armed with this information, Alice phoned Christian and announced that her purse was closed and the marriage over.

Alice never referred to Christian's new attachment among her friends, although she did finally reveal it to her daughters. Rather, she provided close acquaintances with an edited version. "'I didn't expect much attention from Christian,' she said plaintively. 'But toward the last I got none. He was angry because I wouldn't sign any more large checks for him and went away. He took up the society of actors. Of course Christian's family took his part. His sister [Katherine Johnson] said: 'It is positively absurd of Alice to object to Christian's friendships. She herself has stage friends.' 'But I did mind.'"[4] When Natalie learned the truth she wrote a scathing letter to Alice, castigating her mother for her "lavishness" toward her "worthless-boy pederast husband and the thousands of dollars wasted upon him." Laura was more sanguine. "Dear Little One," she wrote, "you have fortu-nately been able to prevent Christian's wastefulness getting away with much of your money; and since your marriage there have practically been no good years."[5]

Letters continued to fly back and forth across the Atlantic with advice from Laura and Natalie on just how Alice should divest herself of her unwanted husband. In the long run it was Laura who knew Christian's

WASHINGTON POST
HEADLINES, 1920
In January, the Washington Post *broke the story
of the unusual way in which
Alice announced the end of
her marriage to Christian.
The feature article was
picked up by newspapers
around the country.*

character the best. Let him sue for divorce. If need be pay him off, being sure the amount is large enough to end it, but small enough to make a point. In the meantime, Laura counseled, Alice must get on with her life and go back to Washington.

In October, Washington society began to receive invitations to small at-home entertainments at 1626 Rhode Island Avenue where Alice stayed while Studio House was being readied for her. Christian's absence was explained away by Alice and the dreaded word "divorce" was not mentioned. By November Alice sent out invitations from Studio House for a large reception at 1626 Rhode Island Avenue. It provided the press up and down the East Coast with one of the juiciest stories in years.

The front page headlines of the November 21, 1919, edition of the *Washington Times* were only the beginning:

> Society Leader Discards Husband's Name; Begins New Social Campaign: Mrs. Alice Barney today inaugurated a new social campaign in which society immediately became interested and is curious to know just what she has in mind. Society also is surprised to learn that she has discarded the name of her husband, Christian D. Hemmick; Has Not Been Divorced; How Mrs. Hemmick Astonished Washington Society.[6]

On January 18, 1920, the *Washington Post* published a full-page story of the event, which was reprinted in papers as far away as Oakland, California. "She Sent Out 'At Home' Cards For a Big Reception at Her Rhode Island Avenue Residence and Eliminated Her Husband's Name from the Invitation—Divorce? Oh! No. Just Her Way to Announce Her Estrangement," read the subheadline. Part of the article's impact was the accompanying illustrations, which showed a pair of women's hands using a scissors to cut off the name Hemmick from a calling card imprinted with the name "Mrs. Alice Barney Hemmick." A full-length profile, 1911 photograph of Alice blown-up large loomed over smaller pictures of her studio and of Christian in costume for his Roman general's role in *About Thebes*. The story was a gossip columnist's dream.

> Just a few days ago, fashionable Washington rubbed its eyes and raised its eyebrows in utter perplexity. To the charmed inner circle had come an invitation to a certain function— 'Mrs. Alice Barney requests,' etc.
>
> But who was Mrs. Alice Barney? There had only been one lady of that name and she was now Mrs. Christian Hemmick!
>
> Strange, too, the address was Mrs. Christian Hemmick's Sheridan Circle house!
>
> If this Mrs. Alice Barney was Mrs. Alice Barney Hemmick, what had become of the Hemmick? It had been acquired by due ceremony. Legally and in the eyes of the law as well as her friends she was Mrs. Christian Hemmick. There had been no reports of separation, none at all of any legal action whereby the fashionable lady was authorized to return to her pre matrimonial nomenclature. What could it all mean? Surely there must be some mistake.
>
> Those who had received the invitations and dutifully presented themselves found that there was no mistake. There was no longer a Mrs. Christian Hemmick. There was only the former Mrs. Alice Barney.
>
> Had she been divorced so secretly that not even her closest friends had heard of it?
>
> Oh, no, it was just her way of announcing that she had dropped her husband!
>
> It was so delightfully simple. It saved money, minimized gossip. The marriage had been a mistake and so she just decided to go right back and begin again where she had left off when she had placed her life in the hands of her young Greek God.
>
> 'Well,' gasped fashionable society again, 'Alice certainly does do things differently.'[7]

The press was merciless; the story was too good to be forgotten. With relief, Alice accepted Natalie's invitation to stay with her until some other scandal grabbed the attention of the public. She sailed to France in June and was, therefore, unavailable to attend the hearing held on August 28 in Chicago where Judge Frank Johnston, Jr., granted Christian's petition of divorce from Alice on grounds of desertion. Christian testified that Alice had refused to live with him since she did not wish a husband in the theater business and that "without so much as a good-bye left him...to live again in Paris."[8] What was not brought out in the hearing was the $10,000 check he had received from Alice before she sailed accompanied by a letter from her lawyer stating that she owed him nothing further.

ESCAPE TO PARIS

Few of her fellow travelers noticed the short, plump, well-dressed, gray-haired woman who leaned against the rail watching the French shore come into focus. From the dark circles under her eyes and the paleness of her skin, she appeared to be one of the unfortunates who suffered seasickness. Yet, she moved jauntily, even gaily, down the gangplank to greet the two middle-aged women who waited with to take her to Paris. Her bulging trunks packed with clothes, jewels, and scripts followed in a hired car.

Upon arrival at 20 Rue Jacob, Alice's belongings were carried to the bedroom assigned her and as soon as she refreshed herself, Alice joined Natalie and her lover, Romaine Brooks, in the dining room. Through its French doors Alice glimpsed the Temple a l'Amitie, that ghostly architectural remnant partially hidden in the deep shadows of Natalie's overgrown garden. Everywhere within Natalie's apartment hung the fustian smell of someone who paid little attention to housekeeping. Even the large square room, with its ceiling panels of succulent nudes painted by Albert Besnard, in which Natalie held her Friday salons, showed her disinterest in matters not of the mind or the heart.

Within weeks Alice realized she had erred in staying at Natalie's. Natalie neither forgave nor forgot easily, and her sharp-tongued commentary on the mess Alice had made of her life was unrelenting. The obvious choice was to move to Laura and Hippolyte's apartment, but they were on an extended visit with Bahais in the Middle East. Alice, therefore, remained at Rue Jacob and busied herself with shopping for things to brighten Natalie's apartment, writing ballet scenarios, and making contact with potential producers.

For her mother's amusement, Natalie tried her own hand at writing *The Lighthouse*, a contemporary, full-length play in English. Alice critiqued it for production value, and, in turn, Natalie suggested how Alice might improve her ballets to increase their appeal to European sensibilities. Later in the

NATALIE AND ALICE,
C. 1920
*One of Alice and Natalie's
many feuds was over Alice's
critique and eventual rewrite
of one of Natalie's dramatic
efforts,* The Lighthouse.
*However, whatever their
differences, Natalie and
Alice loved one another
dearly and enjoyed a close
relationship.*

summer Alice went to Monte Carlo in an attempt to interest a producer
who was the brother of actress Mary Gordon in *Atlantis*, a ballet about the
fall of the mythical continent.

In spite of Natalie's opinion that the ballet was old fashioned and trite, it
was well received. Alice also showed them Natalie's play, which was not. In
a letter from Monte Carlo, she attempted to explain to Natalie what was
wrong with her play, which was little different from what she had already
told her. "No one," she wrote, "wants to risk things for higher circles. They
are too few and they [producers] must have something to please the middle
circles."[9] In the same letter she asked Natalie to contact Igor Stravinsky or
Francis Poulenc and see if they might be interested in composing music for
two of the scenes of *Atlantis*. On the whole, however, she preferred to offer
a guaranteed two thousand francs to Arthur Honneger for a complete
score.

In October Alice moved to the Ritz Hotel in London. Not having heard
from Natalie about the results of her contact with the two composers, Alice

engaged two others: Eugene Goossens for *Danse en Crinoline* and Gustuv Holtz for *Atlantis*. She also began an all out rewrite of Natalie's play. Letters flew back and forth across the channel about how to make it more dramatically appealing. In a long letter to Natalie, she attempted once again to explain why it needed a complete revision. Alice cited as an example a successful play produced by Belasco in New York, which had failed miserably in London. "It's because," she wrote, "one must understand their public. What is a public? Intellectuals? No. They are too lazy, too occupied to go to the theatre. The public is the great mass of people needing amusement." As it stood, Alice thought Natalie's play too fine and subtle. Above all, the speeches were too long. The play, she wrote, was "right at the very first, but wrong all through." "Also," she continued, "the scenes must be less quiet and more passionate to carry well, especially the lead. And the audience, except a few intellectuals, would not 'get' the idea...what would be called the big scene at the end....The last is too genteel, too in the air." Alice offered to "work on the lines, spoil the play a little perhaps with a few, but it will grip the many, that's what a manager looks to." She would start with the name and change it from *The Lighthouse* to *The Beacon*.[10]

Natalie not only disagreed with Alice's suggestions, but sent her mother an acerbic opinion of the proposed changes. Ten days later Alice washed her hands of the entire project. The new ending Natalie proposed in her letter was to Alice, "not nearly enough, for my interest in the play is over and I really don't care to work on it." She continued, "You have killed all desire or possibility....I'll return it to you...I had no intention of making the play maudlin, only stronger and more explained in putting in what I felt needed...I could not now touch it. You always offer something and then regret...in this case, go ahead and do what you like. So I beg that you offer nothing else...as for me, well, I'd better not sign lovingly Mother."[11]

IDA RUBENSTEIN, C. 1918
Unlike her many successes in Washington, Alice had many difficulties producing her theatrical efforts in Paris. She hoped that the dancer Ida Rubenstein would star in the ballet she wrote especially for her, but Rubenstein never bothered to respond to Alice's overtures.

Alice received a few nibbles on her ballets. A former partner of Pavlova, Hubert Stowitts, approached her. He was in London to present Ida Rubenstein in a Javanese ballet and promised Alice he would arrange a meeting between them. Alice was philosophical, however, about interesting Rubenstein. When Pavlova had failed to show interest in *Moon Man*, she believed it was because, in the end, Russians were unreliable. Rubenstein was well-known for her inability to commit herself to a project. Nonetheless, Stowitts remained optimistic that a collaboration was possible.

When Alice received a copy of Natalie's new book, *Pensées d'une Amazone*, she knew their feud was over and dashed off a note of congratulations.

> How very beautiful. Why such a title? Between heartbreaks, what a wealth you have given. Can anything be left? It seemed to me wonderful....I am more than anxious for the book to be published in English and I'll do all and everything to further it. Too bad there's littleness mixed in, but that's us.
>
> I'm terribly proud of you. I want everyone to see these wonderful things you say and say so finely, Natalie. How can you, whence does it come? I can't express my admiration, my child.[12]

At the beginning of 1921, Natalie received another letter from Alice. She had finally read the book from cover to cover.

> You terrify me, you seem more buoyant than anyone in the world. You know much dear, much too much. That's terrible. How has it happened? In some ways you are like a searcher who knows all ills, but who knowing does not address but merely explains and walks away. Truth yes and much beauty you have, courage, yes, yet you frighten me. I feel there's too much of the mixture, but I suppose that's you and me though one has great value, offered by more I find hateful, like a flag on the face. All have keenness, but some are so very fine that I hate them to touch with the others. Truth is terrific, truth is terrible, its nakedness should be closed when ugly as my body.
>
> This book makes me realize how much of myself I've passed on to you. You're cultivated and I not, but we've got the same traits, grabbing here and there, dashing from this to that. So much of the monkey in us.[13]

What Alice perceived clearly for the first time through Natalie's book was that her daughter had attained a sophistication far beyond her's and that she was possessed of an intellectual capacity that Alice would never have. At the same time, Alice saw the cost to Natalie, one Alice would never pay. Natalie used truth both to illuminate and to hurt; Alice tried to make truth beautiful. Alice saw that Natalie was a woman of the head, while she was one of the heart. She was frightened for Natalie; she would not, Alice thought, ever know real happiness.

During 1921 Alice traveled back and forth between Paris and London pursuing producers for her ballets. She stayed at the Plaza through the summer because when warm weather came to Paris, Natalie and Romaine retreated to the south of France. In one letter to Natalie Alice recounted her amazing encounter with Igor Stravinsky.

> I saw again the young Russian who has played on the piano and the week before some of his own things. He was in a fury, an absolute fury, demanding me that he should write my ballet. I told him it was necessary for me to have known composers or my ballet wouldn't be accepted. He said the young should be given a chance. I told him when I had been accepted, he should then write me a ballet....His belief in himself was astonishing. I wish I had it.
>
> Doubt, delicacy, shyness have not found a place in his makeup. He compelled me to think of him. Of course, I was revolted by the sweat in his brow and around the upper lip, by the clammy damp warmth of his hand. Ugh. But his desire to do, also impressed me and I felt sorry and apologetic too. Patience is a hard thing and it dampens one's inspiration. He does not know the old also suffer.[14]

It was an odd thing for Alice to write, for belief in herself and her talent seemed to be her strongest trait. Yet she had lived long enough to know that she could not always be successful or right, and that even when she believed in herself, others might not. These beliefs Stravinsky had yet to learn; he was still young and impressed with his genius. She was more sanguine about herself—talented, yes; a genius, no. Only time would tell if Stravinsky's faith in himself was well-founded.

She was in fact impatient with genius, proven or not. She had heard nothing from Ida Rubenstein even though she had sent her a script written especially for her called *The Courtesan of Rome*. Much more troubling was the behavior of Eugene Goossens, the composer she had commissioned to write a new score for *Danse en Crinoline*, an expanded version of *L'École en Crinoline*.

With great difficulty, Alice had succeeded in getting the management of the Paris Opera House interested in the ballet. Adding it to their coming season hinged upon a successful audition of Goossens's music. Goossens forgot his score for the first audition and did not even show up for the second. Terribly discouraged, and for once feeling all of her sixty-four years, Alice wrote Natalie:

I have little persistence. I'll just give it all up and not bother. Only, hope has a hold upon me and I can't just subside into a Mrs. Black — an old lady. I may be forced to bury my talents, letting younger ones push to the fore.[15]

As 1921 drew to a close, hope won over discouragement and soon potential English producers were receiving Alice's theatrical resume. In it she talked of being Pike's daughter and her memories of his Cincinnati opera house, of the thousands of dollars she had raised through her theatrical endeavors in Washington, her ballet for Pavlova, and her most important achievement, the establishment of the National Sylvan Theatre. "Had the United States not have been forced into the war, by now, she believes, the plans and foundations of a United States National Theatre would have been." The fourth and final page announced:

Mrs. Barney is at London, in the quiet of the Ritz and she is writing other plays and ballets, (Mr. Eugene Goossens is composing the music of some of these latter. Miss Phyllis Neilson-Terry has taken one of the former). When Mrs. Barney held an exhibition, when last in London, fifteen years ago, (when she occupied 'The White House', Chelsea, Mr. Whistler's house and studio) the only thing which seemed to hold the critic's attention was her 'versatility.' They all said her exhibition looked like the work of a dozen different painters. So it is with her writings — she is working on Musical Comedy, Farce Comedy, Tragic Drama, Ballets. She is sending one Ballet to the Chicago Opera, the music is by Armande de Polignac (the Countess de Chabannes), a great friend of Mrs. Barney. Another Ballet "The Lure" has music composed by Gustave Holst, (the composer of 'The Planets'). It resembles his ballet (for his own opera) 'The Perfect Fool'.[16]

DISASTER IN WASHINGTON

The waiting began; there were no nibbles. Instead, she received a letter from Washington in which the realtor managing her various properties informed her that an extraordinary blizzard on February 22, 1922, had caused extensive damage to 2223 R Street, a house she built for rental in 1907. He had no news of Studio House or 1626 Rhode Island Avenue. For the time being, he asked that she not expect any rent money from any of the houses until all repairs were made. Alarmed, Alice decided to forego another summer in Europe and return to Washington in June.

No fanfare greeted Alice's arrival in Washington, although her friends were glad to see her back. She took rooms at the Wardman Park Hotel and inspected her homes. In addition to the extensive work at 2223 R Street,

she had to install new downspouts and repaint water-damaged walls at
1626 Rhode Island Avenue, as well as recover the flat roof over her studio
at Studio House. As for social activities, a tea was given in her honor at
Neighborhood House where she inspected the work of the students in the
industrial arts program.

It was a short respite. By December, at the urging of its president,
Mrs. Oliver Belmont, and its vice-president, Alice Paul, Alice enrolled as a
founding member of the National Woman's Party. Although the Nineteenth
Amendment was ratified in 1920, it had not brought women equal rights.
A benefit for the new organization was in order, and with Alice Barney's
return to Washington, what better way to raise money than to have her do
a play? Thus, by the performance date of February 4, 1923, it was as if
Alice had never left.

If Alice had been out of her depth in Europe where theater was concerned, she was not in Washington. Local newspapers touted the forthcoming performance of the city's most prolific playwright, which was to be held
at the Belasco Theatre. Washington had not seen a Barney play in almost
five years and all fourteen performances were quickly sold out. Society
partly bought tickets out of curiosity to see what the pen of their favorite
Bohemian would produce after her European sojourn. Tickets also sold,
however, because Alice had never disappointed her audience in providing a
good time while parting the rich from their money.

For the occasion, Alice composed a traditional one-act play, entitled

THE PETITE SALON AT
RHODE ISLAND AVENUE,
C. 1898
*What became known in
Washington, D. C., as the
great Knickerbocker snow-
storm of 1922 brought a
worried Alice back to the
city from Paris to assess
the damage to her various
houses. She was particularly
concerned about the petite
salon at Rhode Island
Avenue, one of the few
rooms Albert had let her
decorate to her own taste.*

Driven. The assignment provided Alice with the opportunity to test the dramatic theories she had espoused to Natalie of how to write a play that would appeal to an audience. She knew that something different was expected from her by the audiences, and that was what she planned to give them. It was time to show Washington that she knew more about writing plays than mere scenarios for pretty pictures on the stage.

As Alice was to discover, she not only underestimated the growth in sophistication of her audience while she had been away, but her own ability to write plausible dialogue. The cast for *Driven* was made up of four of Washington's most experienced actors. The lead role was played by Maude Howell Smith, queen of amateur theatricals, who appeared as a mother who suffers and endures an unbearable marriage because an unjust law ordained that a mother and children were the husband's chattel. The result was that if she were to leave her wastrel husband, he could deny her access to her daughter. The four actors tried, but they were hard put to breathe life into the script's stilted lines. There were many curtain calls, but the applause was for the actors' valiant effort. The general opinion from those who remembered Alice's earlier efforts was that she should stick to her spectaculars and forget the words.

An invitation to Alice from her sister Hester to come to Los Angeles in April for an extended visit arrived none too soon for Alice's bruised ego. Not until she stepped from the train in 1923 and smelled the orange blossoms, did sixty-six year-old Alice realize that she had found what she had been seeking in New York, Paris, and London since her divorce three years before—a place to start over.

XIX

Life in Hollywood

T he first item on Alice's agenda once she moved to southern California was to find a place to live. Only with difficulty did Alice convince the realtors that she did not want a palace in Beverly Hills. She may have looked elderly, but she led the agents on a merry chase, inspecting one property after another until she was finally shown a small farmhouse built in 1882 by one of California's pioneers, Jacob Miller. Located at 1635 Ogden Drive, its privacy was ensured by a dense grove of avocado and palm trees that screened the property from the street. On the northern side of the large lot was a small garage with enough space to provide sleeping quarters for a chauffeur. She barely listened as the realtor droned on about escrow and mortgage payments. From her purse Alice withdrew a check for the entire amount and handed it to the astonished agent. Terms like escrow, Alice remarked, were much too confusing.

Within weeks the two-story Miller homestead rang with sounds of hammers and saws as it was transformed into a residence for Alice. A large one-story wing was added at a right angle to the original two-story house, the primary space of which was designated for a large reception room where Alice planned to hang her art and hold salons. Behind it was a small dining room. When finished, the Miller farmhouse, now resurrected as Old Garden Cottage, bore a striking resemblance to Studio House with its simple dark wood trim, arched doorways and tiled floors. It seemed almost as if she had transferred the essential spaces of Studio House to the foot of the Hollywood hills.

While she waited for the renovation of Old Garden Cottage to be completed, Alice worked diligently on polishing a one-act play to enter in the first one-act play contest sponsored by the Arts Club of Washington. If she won, her reputation as a playwright would be redeemed in Washington. If she lost, no one would be the wiser, except the clerk who mailed it back to her, since the plays were judged anonymously.

False Value was a semiautobiographical portrayal of the dark side of her relationship with Christian. It told the story of a middle-aged woman who discovered the secret of eternal youth through her liaisons with young men. At the end of the play, she realizes that her pursuit of youth had destroyed whatever chance she had for real happiness with someone her own age. Removing all makeup and donning a dress suitable to her real age, the woman sends away the one innocent boy she actually loved.

As melodramatic as it was, there was a ring of truth to the central char-

ALICE AT FIFTY-NINE, 1916
Alice posed in costume before the French tapestry hanging in the west studio at Studio House.

acter that attracted the attention of the judges, which included her longtime friend, Maude Howell Smith. After reading all the entries, *False Value* received first prize. With her head held high, Alice returned to Washington to receive her award and attend the play's premiere performance on the Arts Club's stage.

Feeling magnanimous, she agreed to produce one last theatrical spectacle as a benefit for Barney Neighborhood House. Held at Twin Oaks, the home of Mrs. Charles J. Bell, *Fantasie Indienne in Three Episodes*, showed Washingtonians that Alice had not lost her ability to produce exciting, fun extravaganzas. Alice knew that when she finally left Washington, her unofficial title as Washington's most successful fundraiser remained intact.

Since her move to California was to be permanent, Alice took a suite of rooms at the Wardman Hotel and remained in Washington for the remainder of spring 1924. She needed the time to wind up a number of business matters including sale of the Bar Harbor cottage and several lots on upper Massachusetts Avenue. She asked her realtor to put out feelers for prospective buyers for Studio House (she had long since changed her mind about donating the house to the city of Washington), but there were no takers and the house was once more put on the rental market. Shipping only a few selected pieces of furniture to California, Alice, by late fall, returned to Hollywood to prepare her California debut as a cultural leader.

On Sunday, November 22, 1925, a selected group of writers, critics, musicians, and friends arrived at Old Garden Cottage for a five o'clock program in the drawing room followed by supper. The purpose of the event

OLD GARDEN COTTAGE, C. 1927
Built as a small farmhouse in 1882, Alice turned Old Garden Cottage in Hollywood into a California version of Studio House, but on a much smaller scale.

ALICE AT SEVENTY, 1927
*Alice seated by the lily pond
at Old Garden Cottage.*

was to hear selections from the book of Alice's comedy-opera, *Luna, The Man in the Moon*, a rewrite of her 1909 play. Her composer, Sol Cohen, played some of the score on his violin, followed by performances of other songs by up-and-coming Los Angeles singers. At dinner Alice courted potential backers for the production. As in Paris and London, interest was expressed, but wallets and purses remained closed. This time she was not discouraged. She realized she would have to prove herself first, but she believed wholeheartedly that success in the golden land was assured.

In America, unlike Europe, Alice knew how to work the system and, in particular, the press. Los Angeles papers were already aware of the theatrical whirlwind from the East and had begun to write of the genius of Mrs. Barney, founder of the National Sylvan Theatre. Within weeks the Los Angeles papers were publicizing a two-week engagement of *Passions*, booked by Alice at San Francisco's Columbia Theater in mid-February— far enough from Los Angeles to keep its critics away. It proved to be a very smart move. She chose to open the play in San Francisco because, while that city's critics might pan her play, little note would be taken of them in the southern part of the state. She already had learned that Los Angeles critics had little use for their snobbish northern counterparts.

In fact, the critics did pan the play, but they were remarkably kind to the playwright. Writing in the *Chronicle*, theater critic George Warren stated that although Alice was a woman of wide experience, unquestioned taste, artistic bent, and a writer of some note, these qualities were of no assistance to her in writing *Passions*. "It is cruel," he wrote, "to have to say such things when one wishes the producers, the actors, and the author every success, but the crudities of the play are too obvious to be overlooked."[1] Alice read the top of the review, ignored the end, and proudly pasted it into her scrapbook.

Spring passed into summer with no word from her realtor that Studio House was sold. Although she had not wanted to, Alice decided to return to Washington to try to sell it herself. She would stay the winter, and, if she met with no more success than the realtor, she would select some more furnishings for Old Garden Cottage and leave the rest for whoever rented the house. To make the time pass more quickly, she planned to write her autobiography. Her life had been full of incidents and meetings with people of interest that would fascinate many. So, with her usual zeal for undertaking sometimes shocking enterprises, she planned it to be a long and spicy account of her love affair with Stanley, her friendship with Whistler, and various other tidbits.

A further inducement to go to Washington for one last time was an announcement she had received concerning a playwriting contest being conducted by the D.C. chapter of the Drama League of America. After her lengthy fight with them over the artistic merit of *The Opium Pipe*, Alice thought it would be amusing to take first prize. The play she chose to enter was *The Lighthouse*—her rewrite of Natalie's play. Her justification to her conscience in using another person's play was that she had so reworked the play that it bore little resemblance to Natalie's original. The cover page could honestly show but one name, hers, and when she did win, she accepted the award graciously and not without a bit of glee.

Alice waited through the winter and into the spring of 1927 for someone to indicate interest in buying Studio House or the Rhode Island Avenue mansion. When no one emerged, she signed rental agreements for both and instructed her live-in secretary, William Huntington, to make sure the moving men placed every last picture, bibelot, and piece of furniture she had earmarked for California on a truck. Then, without looking back, Alice boarded the train for Los Angeles and her new life.

THEATRE MART

That new life was theater, theater, and more theater, all of which she was prepared to fund from her own purse. Having reached seventy, Alice planned to do exactly as she pleased. In January 1928, she opened two plays at the Hollywood Play House for four performances. The first was a comedy, *Legitimate Lovers*, an acknowledged collaboration between Alice and Natalie. The second, *The Lighthouse*, was billed as being from Alice's pen. Natalie accepted her invitation to come to the opening of the two plays, more

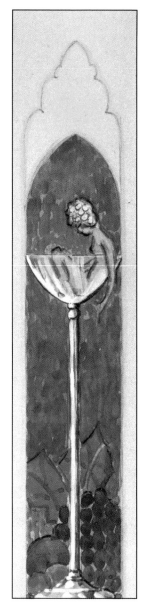

SKETCH, *MAN IN THE MOON*, 1928
Sketch by Alice of a pivot flat for the café scene in the 1928 ballet version of Man in the Moon.

CAST PHOTO,
MOON MADNESS, 1929
*Alice's musical version
of* Moon Madness *was
presented at the Theatre
Mart in 1929. As was
usual with her Theatre
Mart productions, the set
was decorated with Alice's
personal furnishings and
pictures.*

to assess how her mother was spending the family money, than to see the plays. She was even prepared to confront Alice about her monetary profligacy, but she was unable to do so—just as she was unable to attack her mother for stealing her play and claiming it as her own.

Natalie had never forgotten a conversation she had with Alice in Paris in the 1920s. Even with all her disappointments in failing to find a producer for her ballets, Alice had appeared cheerful. Natalie could not understand it:

> We were discreetly intimate, and once only I ventured to remark: 'Why, Mother, you have so happy a temperament that I cannot imagine that anything has ever been able to cause you more than a passing sorrow.' She looked doubtful about this overstatement, but kept an embarrassed silence, and as I laughingly pressed her as to what that sorrow may have been, she turned her head away, and as though speaking to herself, merely muttered: 'You.'[2]

Thus, when she saw that Alice was truly happy, bustling about like a fairy godmother spreading culture left and right, she held her tongue. She could not inflict further unhappiness upon the mother she loved so much.

Moreover, Natalie realized for the first time that the mother who she and Laura fondly called "Little One" was old. Years later, Natalie wrote an essay called "Meeting Death." In two sentences she was able to describe the essence of that moment feared by every mother and daughter. "That mothers should die filled me with a consternation that I never outgrew. And when my own mother, looking into my eyes when I last left her in her 'Old

Garden Cottage,' said: 'Isn't it dreadful?,' I trembled, for I guessed what was meant."[3]

Despite Natalie's concern, in 1928 Alice felt more alive than she had in years. She took dance lessons to stay limber, dressed in the latest fashions, and invited to her home the most interesting people she could find in the small town of Hollywood. Although her invitations seldom extended to movie stars, she made it a point to include up and coming actors and actresses such as Anna May Wong and Edward Leiter to mingle with her peers. The majority were people who had made their money elsewhere and were now seeking new life in the healing California sunshine. Some founded the Hollywood Bowl or amused themselves by building an authentic Japanese Garden on the slopes of the Hollywood Hills. Others formed literary or music clubs and built architecturally unusual structures in which to hold their meetings. They were, Alice hoped, the people most likely to support the theater she had decided to found.

ALICE PAINTING EDWARD LEITER, 1927
After many years of not painting, Alice began to try her hand again at Old Garden Cottage in Hollywood. Among her subjects were actors such as Edward Leiter.

As she looked for a suitable building for her theater, Alice ended a twenty year hiatus and set up her easel at the edge of the lily pond at Old Garden Cottage and began turning out pastel portraits of new friends made in California as well as old friends from her past such as the R. D. Shepherds. The free-flowing strokes of her earlier pastels eluded her and were replaced by solid, heavy shading. Her skill at capturing likenesses, however, did not desert her. Eventually, she hoped to exhibit them at the Stendahl Art Galleries located in the Ambassador Hotel.

In October 1928, *California Graphic* magazine announced:

> The latest activity to challenge attention...is called Theatre Mart.... According to the program announcement, Theatre Mart is not an 'art theatre,' not a 'community theatre,' not a 'repertoire theatre,' not a 'little theatre;' neither is it a 'haven for struggling artists,' nor is it for 'amateurs.' If it was not any of those ventures, then what was it. According to the program, the Theatre Mart 'is—or desires to be—*something new*'. Surely a modest claim! 'It is unique,'...It is a link between the artist and the commercial theatre....It appears that Theatre Mart is dedicated to trying out new plays, for the purpose of giving the unproduced playwright a chance to see his work in action and

MRS. ALICE P. BARNEY,
GENERAL DIRECTOR

THEATRE MART

PHONES: OLYMPIA 2951
OLYMPIA 2952

605 N. JUANITA AVENUE

WHICH IS ONE BLOCK SOUTH OF MELROSE AND ONE BLOCK EAST OF VERMONT

EVENINGS 8:15

THRILLING
COMEDY DRAMA

"MATA HARI"

PRODUCED BY
Francis Josef Hickson

By MRS. ALICE P. BARNEY

Story of the Childbride, Streetwalker, Courtesan, Red Dancer, Condemned Spy
Who Set Europe Aflame

JAN. 7TH, 8TH, 9TH, 10TH, 11TH, 12TH, 13TH AND 14TH

The Great Drama
of

"O. HENRY IN PRISON"

By UPTON SINCLAIR

"BILL PORTER"

For Eight Nights

Admission $1.00
Membership

Beginning Jan. 20th

thereby find an outlet either on the stage or screen for his pieces."[4]

As her father had built an opera house for Cincinnati, she had created the National Sylvan Theatre for the nation. Now, also like her father and the opera house he built for himself in New York, Alice would open her very own theater. The Theatre Mart was housed in a Spanish-style playhouse at 605 North Juanita Avenue in an undistinguished neighborhood of small Cali-

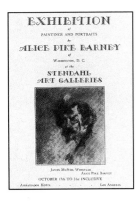

EXHIBITION

of
PAINTINGS AND PORTRAITS
by
ALICE PIKE BARNEY
of
WASHINGTON, D. C.
at the
STENDAHL
ART GALLERIES

JAMES MCNEIL WHISTLER
ALICE PIKE BARNEY

OCTOBER 17th TO 31st INCLUSIVE

AMBASSADOR HOTEL   LOS ANGELES

Top:
THEATER TICKET, 1930
Although Theatre Mart presented plays by new play-wrights, many of them such as this 1930 performance of Mata Hari were from Alice's pen.

Bottom:
CATALOG COVER, 1930
Alice's 1930 retrospective exhibition at the Stendahl Art Gallery reestablished her reputation as an artist. It included both previously shown work and new pastels created after her move to Hollywood.

fornia bungalows. In an interview with Jeannette Kuhn in *California Life,* Alice described the Mart as a "creative center for theatre people." Its purpose was to provide a means of self-expression for the artist and court recognition from commercial theater. "She believes," wrote Kuhn, "that such a mart for dramatic wares is particularly needed in Hollywood, where talent cries in vain for employment."[5]

To accomplish her goal, Alice planned for the Theatre Mart to give full-length plays by local playwrights a five-night run at the beginning of each month followed the next week by one night of one-acts. The last production of the month would be two evenings of divertissements made up of dance, pantomime, and what Alice termed "bizarre plays."

Month after month, for the next three years, Los Angeles theatergoers were invited to see original plays at the Theatre Mart, more often than not from the pen of Alice Barney. DeWitt Bodeen, who was hired as her secretary while a student at University of California, Los Angeles, remembered Alice at that time as:

A charming eccentric old lady, who wore beautiful clothes, hats, and furs that must have been fashioned when she stepped off the Ark. They were all of marvelous materials, or they had been marvelous at one time—faded silks and velvets and little velvet ribbons tied around her neck....She wore wigs; I don't know how many she had, but they were all marcelled perfectly, and she tottered along on little high heels....She loved to talk. Mrs. Barney often said she really favored Natalie, who was born before her time, but didn't miss much, it would seem....there were no barriers to her topics. She was really fun, and while she nodded through some of the musicals she sponsored at Theatre Mart...she never nodded during a play's performance.[6]

From Paris, Natalie and Laura heard reports of Alice's endeavors with increasing alarm. The words Natalie had hesitated to say to her mother in person, she now put on paper in an effort to bring Alice to her senses:

You have about three or four times the income that we have and you live less well, never spending anything on food, clothes, entertainment, or friends save to further your interest of theatrical ventures. More spending on those third-rate playwrighters, etc., hundreds and thousands for ill-spirited theatrical ventures....But consider your ingenuous treatment, your signing of plays not your own...your general scheme of material meanness to all save where your theatrical ventures are concerned, your lack of interest in our better works far superior to yours, though we are your children, critiqued by us as only vain and self centered.[7]

Alice's next letter to Natalie did not contain an apology. Instead it relayed troubling news. "Please realize," Alice wrote, "I've been very ill....I believed that I would soon die and knew that I could never travel again and could only last by keeping quiet and with great care and no excitement." The diagnosis given by her doctors was hardened arteries, two leaking heart valves, gastric trouble, and a touch of angina pectoris. "Hessie," Alice continued, "was alarmed, for she saw me in the attack."[8] She closed with the assurance that although she still felt unwell, she was on the road to recovery.

THEATRE MART, C. 1929
Theatre Mart was located at the corner of Juanita and Clinton with its main entrance on Clinton. The building, which still retains its stage, is now the site of the Los Angeles Press Club.

Opposite:
ALICE AT SEVENTY-TWO, 1929
Alice in the courtyard of Theatre Mart. She was excited about creating a new theater for Hollywood, just as her father had created an opera house for Cincinnati.

On January 10, 1931, Alice received a letter from the Theatre Mart's manager, Thomas Miller, which reported an unwelcome visit from a city building inspector and a member of the Los Angeles Fire Department. Not only was the building not zoned for a playhouse, but it did not meet fire department regulations for a performing space. Moreover, in a subsequent letter, Miller informed Alice that even with her personal financial support, the theater would be bankrupt by the end of May.

Although he knew the news was unwelcome, Miller had decided she needed to know the truth, which was that those who could best afford to support the work of the Theatre Mart ignored it. "For this," he wrote, "there may be one or more reasons, perhaps a main one being, the prevailing idea that your social and financial position does not call for co-operation or aid. Of course such ideas should have little, if anything to do with the enterprise which you have so earnestly endeavored to make a success—nevertheless we are not living in Washington, D.C., now, and people out here are altogether different, as you must know."[9]

Alice had no choice. She could not singlehandedly fight the city, mount a fundraising drive, and deal with Natalie's accusations, all at the same time. Even if her spirit were willing, her body was not. On April 28, 1931, Alice locked the doors of the Theatre Mart after the close of the evening's bill of three one-acts. Then she remembered her father. When Pike was forced to sell his New York opera house, he merely refocused his energy on something else. She would do the same. With the Theatre Mart closed, she could devote more time to her art for even though she could not see as well as she once had, it still gave her great pleasure.

The dry summer heat seemed to heal her spirits, and Alice began lecturing at various social and artistic clubs about the untapped resource for outdoor theater to be found in southern California's great gardens. "When I visit these lovely natural stage sets," Alice told her audiences, "I inquire, 'Do you give plays here?', and the answer is usually, 'No, but I have always thought I should do so.'" She challenged her listeners to think big. "I should like to see a professional theatre, like those they have during the summer in Bois at Paris and in Russia...The Bowl concerts and the Pilgrimage Play point the way to their achievement."[10]

On September 4, 1931, her ballet, *The Shepherd of Shiraz*, was presented at an afternoon gala at the Hollywood Bowl and feeling her strength returned, she decided to reopen the Theatre Mart no matter what the cost. Her play *Jimmie*, based upon her friendship with Whistler, was close to completion. She had written it especially for the well-known actor, George Arliss, who had agreed to act in the title role. Since only a few pages remained to be written, she called the papers to announce the reopening of her beloved Theatre Mart. She also looked forward to a visit from both

Laura and Natalie in November. She had no doubt she would be able to make them understand why she had decided to try one more time.

Alice rose at 6 A.M. on October 12, 1931, to meet her two dressmakers. She spent the entire morning having her dresses fitted. In the afternoon she put the finishing touches on *Jimmie*. Following a quick supper of beef broth, she was chauffeured to the McDowell Town Club for a meeting and concert. Since she had not felt too well the previous day, she chose to wear a new coat from Laura and one of the dresses whipped up by the dressmakers to raise her spirits. On her fingers were five rings and around her neck a diamond necklace that had been a gift from Albert. She entered the concert room slowly but surely. Feeling faint, she sat down on the nearest lounge to rest a minute before taking her seat, and there she died a few moments later.

Alice's body was sent to Dayton, Ohio, where it was buried according to her wishes without ceremony in Hessie's plot a short distance from Albert's grave. A simple inscription preselected by Alice was engraved on her headstone: "Alice Pike Barney, The Talented One."

Neither daughter attended the burial, but as Natalie wrote twenty years later, death did not seem to distance them from Alice, their beloved "Little One."

> Our relationship with this independent and prodigal being remains uninterrupted by death, which makes her seem even more alive than most of our still living attachments. We never had to invent qualities for her, since she really possessed them, and we never found a fault to veil in order to go on loving her. Merely to watch her creative spirit was enchantment enough, and in regarding the smallest details of her daily existence....She suffered from the heart and for and from others—and when the heart failed her, she fainted into death while listening to music, and so died as harmoniously and as simply as she had lived.[11]

XX
AFTERWORD

Named executrix of Alice's estate, Laura arrived in Washington in November 1931 where she joined William Huntington whom she had hired to help inventory the contents of Studio House. Huntington took his old room, the Whistler bedroom, and Laura occupied the rooms on the top floor. As they delved into the closets, bureaus, trunks, and boxes Alice left behind when she moved to California, they discovered how little she actually took to begin her new life.

In addition to drawers full of linens, cabinets crammed with china, and closets stuffed with decorative objects, there were over two hundred works of art and significant amounts of cash, undeposited checks, and unredeemed stock dividends. Huntington felt as if he had stumbled onto a treasure hunt. He never knew what opening one more trunk might bring. He kept his excitement to himself, however, for he learned quickly that Laura brooked no dallying or speculating. She was often abrupt and imperious, unlike Alice who had possessed a sense of humor and a flare for the dramatic.

In January 1932 Laura assembled her mother's paintings in the great studio room and invited the press, friends of her mother, and the general public for a final view of Alice's work. Hundreds of Washingtonians climbed the stairway to see Alice's paintings and pastels and to consider the accomplishments of a woman who had known George Bernard Shaw and Mrs. Patrick Campbell, Alice Roosevelt Longworth and Anna Pavlova, Mirza Abul Fazl and G. K. Chesterton, Henry Morton Stanley and James McNeill Whistler. Following the two-day exhibition, much of the work, along with selected furnishings and bibelots, was either loaned or given to various institutions such as the Los Angeles County Museum, the Dayton Art Museum, the Metropolitan Opera, the Delgado Art Museum, the Corcoran Gallery of Art, the Folger Library, the United States Capitol, Tuskeegee Institute, the University of Virginia, and the Smithsonian Institution. In addition, under the terms of Alice's will, Neighborhood House received the two buildings that had accommodated her arts and crafts classes. On December 12, 1933, Neighborhood House changed its name to Barney Neighborhood House and Social and Industrial Settlement.[1]

Laura was also faced with the task of selling three houses in the midst of a worldwide depression. No buyers could be found in spite of the best efforts of realtors in Washington and Hollywood. To solve the problem for the short run, she extended the existing lease with Harriet and Isabelle Stone on 1626 Rhode Island Avenue for their use as a private girl's school. When the school closed in 1934, 1626 Rhode Island Avenue became a boarding house, suffering the fate of similar mansions ringing Scott Circle. Washingtonians brave enough to venture into the seedy neighborhood in the 1950s knew it as the Tagodean Club with furnished rooms above. In 1962 the Barney mansion was torn down for construction of the Grammercy Inn Hotel.

Old Garden Cottage in Hollywood, California, experienced a better fate than 1626 Rhode Island Avenue, because it was situated in a stable neighborhood that improved over the years. The house was rented to a friend of Laura and Natalie's who had gone to California for his health. Because he was a French war correspondent gassed during World War I, the sisters gave him life tenancy, and not until his death in 1968 was the house was sold.

Laura soon learned, as had Alice in 1927, that Studio House was not an attractive residential property. Its idiosyncratic architecture, while artistically exciting, made it unappealing as a single-family home. Three years after Alice's death, Studio House was not only unsold, but unrented. In April 1934, Natalie wrote Laura saying:

> It annoys me each time I think of those cheeky dealers making a card house of our Little One's Studio House. Perhaps we can devise a plan to have it left to more appropriate usages. Why not a museum, free of taxes, and to contain a room of mother's best pictures, another of Romaine's [Brooks]—and another of the exceptional works Romaine has purchased by Monet, Degas, Stevens, etc. Also mother's room furnished in mother's style with her best things and another in Romaine's, who has some very good things and taste that might be an inspiration to others. But we can think this all out carefully if *en principe* we could agree in some way, and leave the marks of our epoch or influences on Washington.[2]

That fall, when Natalie and Romaine joined Laura at Studio House, a heated argument between Laura and Romaine comparing Alice and Romaine as artists, erased any chance that this proposition would work.

Not until 1936 was a tenant found for Studio House. By this time, most of the residences surrounding Sheridan Circle and those on Massachusetts Avenue as it radiated northwest and southeast from Dupont Circle had become embassies when their original owners found themselves bankrupt or short of cash to maintain them properly. From 1936 until 1950, Studio House was home to various tenants ranging from the Columbian Legation to the Peruvian embassy to a British Army officers club during World War

II to offices for the Capitol Film Libraries. Throughout this time some one hundred of Alice's pastels and paintings remained locked in a closet next to the first-floor kitchen.

Although Laura and Natalie had remained in Paris during World War I, the onset of World War II caused both sisters to move elsewhere. Natalie went to Florence, Italy, with Romaine Brooks. The widowed Laura installed herself for the duration of the war in a suite at the Wardman Towers on upper Connecticut Avenue in Washington, D.C. During those years, she not only represented the National Council of Women of the United States on its Coordinating Committee for Better Racial Understanding, but served on the Board of Trustees of the President James Monroe Foundation at Fredericksburg, Virginia, and as honorary chairman of the board of Barney Neighborhood House. She also established a portraiture prize in Alice's name for the Society of Washington Artists' annual exhibition and arranged several retrospectives of Alice's work. The first, held at Neighborhood House in 1941, was attended by First Lady Eleanor Roosevelt, who had visited Studio House in 1913 when the President was Assistant Secretary of the Navy. Another outcome of Laura's six-year stay in Washington was her increasing interest in the artistic endeavors of the Smithsonian Institution.

Throughout the majority of their adult lives, the Barney sisters lived near one another in Paris (Laura at 74 rue Raynouard and Natalie at 20 rue Jacob). Psychically, however, they were far apart. While Laura kept tight reign on the principal of their inheritance, Natalie spent her share of the interest as rapidly as possible. Where Laura sought satisfaction in intellectual pursuits and accomplishing good works, Natalie aspired to happiness by surrounding herself with stimulating people and writing pungent aphorisms. Toward the end of their lives, communication between them was primarily through letters and messages carried by mutual friends or through errands run by William Huntington.

Although both sisters lived extraordinarily rich lives, neither lived life as fully as their mother. Each seemed to take from Alice what most suited her own personality and overlooked what didn't fit. While money kept them in communication, by the end of their lives their memories of Alice seemed their only emotional link, and even there they did not always agree.

Natalie was and remains a fabled woman, subject of several biographies and noted frequently in feminist studies. Although Huntington was perceptive about why Natalie's life fascinated people, he frequently expressed puzzlement over the lack of recognition given Laura. Laura, in his opinion, was the sister who truly deserved it. She was a respected Bahai scholar and one of her books, *Some Answered Questions*, was translated into more than twenty languages. She was made a Chevalier and then an Officier of the

French Legion of Honor for her service to France during both World Wars. She served as an expert on the League of Nation's Liaison Commission of Intellectual Cooperation between the two wars. Often after listing Laura's accomplishments, Huntington would get a gleam in his eye and give a conspiratorial laugh. "Madame Barney," he would say, "was, however, a very difficult woman."

In her early seventies, Laura Barney began to focus her remaining energy on the still unresolved issue of how best to honor Alice's memory. Since the Smithsonian Institution already possessed three of her mother's paintings, in 1950 she wrote Dr. Alexander Wetmore, Secretary of the Smithsonian Institution, to offer those still retained by the estate. In 1951, along with Natalie, Laura established a memorial fund for the National Collection of Fine Arts (now the NMAA) to further appreciation of American art and for the care of her mother's paintings and drawings. During the next twenty years, the Barney sisters donated close to four hundred works of art to the NMAA. While the majority were by Alice, a significant number were by artists whose careers Alice had supported through the purchase of their work, including Henry Moser, Albert Herter, Max Weyl, Juliet Thompson, Elizabeth Nourse, and Frank Edwin Scott.

In 1960, after Laura paid Natalie the value of her share, the sisters donated Studio House to the Smithsonian Institution in both their names in Alice's memory for the Smithsonian's use as an intimate arts and cultural center. This major donation was followed in 1968 by the gift of its contents, as well as selected furnishings from Old Garden Cottage. Following Natalie's death in 1972 and Laura's in 1974, additional furnishings from their estates were installed at Studio House.

From 1960 until the house was renovated and opened to the public in 1980, Studio House was used for a variety of purposes including serving as the original headquarters for the American Association of Museums, as offices of the Smithsonian Institution's Traveling Exhibition Services, and to provide overnight accommodations for visiting dignitaries. In the late 1960s the two bedroom floors were converted into an apartment for Smithsonian scholars in residence. After its 1979 renovation, the two main floors were opened to the public for tours, special programs, and changing exhibitions. As the years passed, Studio House became by default the primary extant example of a turn-of-the-century urban studio house, as others fell to the wrecking ball or were gutted for remodeling by new owners.

More than sixty years after her death, the Sylvan Theatre is still the site of concerts and speeches at the foot of the Washington Monument on the Mall, although the name of its founder is long forgotten. Barney Neighborhood House carries on both her name and its mission as a social work agency meeting the needs of its constituents in the Mount Pleasant area of

Pages 304–305:
Lower portion of first floor
reception room, c. 1911.

Washington, D.C. A series of exhibitions presented by NMAA since 1979 has garnered greater appreciation for her art, particularly her facility with the difficult pastel medium. Theatre Mart reopened under new management, and, for the next twenty years, sold out houses saw a rousing production of the well known melodrama, *The Drunkard*. The theater is now the site of the Los Angeles Press Club. At one end of the club's large dining room is the Theatre Mart's curtained stage, which looks as if it were still awaiting the premiere of Alice's final play, *Jimmie*. That premiere did not occur until April 1985, when a fully-staged production of *Jimmie* was presented at Studio House as part of the NMAA's "An Evening At Barney Studio House" performing arts series.

In 1928 Alice filled out a questionnaire for the 1928 edition of *Outstanding Women* in which she listed what she considered her life's accomplishments.[3] Studio House and Old Garden Cottage were given solely as addresses. Although Studio House was the stage set she designed to serve the theater of her life in the nation's capital, she did not consider it her most significant venue. What was important to Alice was her work as an artist and her exhibitions; her studies with Whistler and Carolus-Duran; her participation in the Suffrage movement and the Women's Peace Party; and her affiliation with and support of Neighborhood House. Most meaningful to her, however, was her founding of two theaters: the Sylvan Theatre and the Theatre Mart. She was, after all, her father's daughter, a woman who believed in making her dreams come true.

NOTES

Abbreviations

APBS: Alice Pike Barney Scrapbooks, National Museum of American Art, Curatorial Office, Smithsonian Institution, Washington, D.C.

Four scrapbooks of newspaper and magazine clippings, programs, and tickets were donated to the National Museum of American Art. Two of them came from the Barney daughters in memory of their mother in 1968. Christian Hemmick's grandneice, Patricia Daly, donated his scrapbook. A fourth scrapbook was received from Lisette Thompson, widow of Louis B. Thompson. While the majority of its contents are related to Thompson's lifelong career in music, several pages refer to Alice.

Few of the clippings found in these scrapbooks were identified either by date or source. Although every attempt was made to find the original source, this was not always possible.

BD: Natalie Clifford Barney Archives, Bibliothèque Littéraire Jacques Doucet, Paris, France

Letters from the Natalie Barney archival collection at the Bibliothèque Doucet were transcribed orally. Punctuation and spelling may, therefore, differ from the original. The words quoted, however, are verbatim. The taped transcriptions by the author are included in the Barney papers at the National Museum of American Art.

CGA: Corcoran Gallery of Art Archives, Washington, D.C.

CHS: Cincinnati Historical Society, Cincinnati, Ohio

DCHS: Washington, D.C., Historical Society, Washington, D.C.

LPS: Lawrence Pike Scrapbook, Cincinnati Historical Society, Cincinnati, Ohio

The Lawrence Pike scrapbook was compiled over many years by Samuel N. Pike's son, Lawrence. Few, if any, of the clippings are identified by date or source. As with the contents of the Alice Pike Barney scrapbooks, every effort was made to find the original source.

NMAA: Alice Pike Barney Papers, National Museum of American Art, Curatorial Office, Smithsonian Institution, Washington, D.C.

I. Her Father's Daughter

1. William E. Huntington's remembrances of Alice Pike Barney and of his year at Studio House were obtained through a series of formal interviews and informal conversations with the author from 1965 to 1984. The most extensive interview was held on February 3, 1983. Even as he aged, his memory remained sharp and detailed. He loved nothing better than to talk about the three Barney women, whom he distinguished as Mrs. Barney (Alice), Madame Barney (Laura), and Natalie. Although he never saw Alice again after her return to California, they continued to correspond. She asked him to come to California to be her secretary following his graduation from college. Instead, in 1931, Huntington went to Europe carrying her letter of introduction to her daughters. On the return voyage he received a cablegram that Alice had died. Although Laura Barney wrote her mother that she was not particularly impressed with Mr. Huntington, she eventually hired him to manage the Barney's business affairs. He held that position for Laura and Natalie from the mid-1930s until Laura's death in 1976. Huntington died in Washington, D.C., in 1987.

2. Alice Pike Barney, *Stanley's "Lady" Alice by One Who Knew*, 1926, typescript, NMAA, Washington, D.C., p. 100. In the fall of 1926 Alice Pike Barney lived in Studio House and wrote a fictionalized third-person autobiography about her romance with Henry Morton Stanley. Writing novelistically, she took liberties with dates and events. It is unlikely that her remembrance of what was said during various conversations is a verbatim record of their content. Quotations from her autobiography are not cited.

3. 1860 Census, Dwelling 198, Family 197, Sixth Ward (Cincinnati, Hamilton County, Ohio, June 7, 1860), p. 28. Certificate of Death (City of New York, Borough of Manhattan, December 7, 1872), No. 135584. Among the various histories of Cincinnati in which Pike figured prominently are Maurice Joblin, *Cincinnati: Past and Present: or, Its Industrial History as Exhibited in the Life-labors of Its Leading Men* (Cincinnati: M. Joblin & Company, 1872); *History of Cincinnati, Ohio with Illustrations and Biographic Sketches*. Comp. by Henry A. Ford and Kate B. Ford, (Cleveland: L. A. Williams & Co., 1881); The Rev. Charles Frederick Goss, *Cincinnati, The Queen City, 1788–1912, vol. 1* (Cincinnati: S. J. Clarke Publishing Company, 1912); "Cincinnati Playhouses of Long Ago and Some of the Pioneers Who Made Them a Success," *Cincinnati Enquirer*, January 9, 1910, from Newspaper Clippings, vol. 2, collection of the Cincinnati Public Library, History Division; *The Ohio Guide*, American Guide Series, compiled by Workers of the Writers' Program of the Works Projects Administration in the State

of Ohio (New York: Oxford University Press, 1948); Alvin F. Harlow, *The Serene Cincinnatians* (New York: E. P. Dutton and Company, Inc., 1950); and Joseph E. Holliday, "Notes on Samuel N. Pike and his Opera Houses," *Bulletin of the Cincinnati Historical Society*, vol. 25, no. 3 (July 1967), pp. 163–73.

4. Michael Slater, ed., *Charles Dickens: On America and the Americans* (Austin: University of Texas Press, 1978), pp. 99, 131.

5. "Conteur" Edwin Henderson, "Pike's Opera House Fire, March 22–23, 1866," *Cincinnati Enquirer*, May 21, 1921, p. 81.

6. Holliday, p. 166. *Cincinnati Daily Commercial*, February 23, 1859, p. 1.

7. *Cincinnati Enquirer*, December 8, 1872, APBS.

8. *Cincinnati Commercial*, March 23, 1866, p. 4.

9. *Cincinnati Commercial*, March 24, 1866, p. 4.

10. *Cincinnati Commercial*, May 21, 1866, LPS.

II. New York Ventures

1. Unidentified newspaper clipping, 1867, LPS.

2. Unidentified newspaper clipping, 1867, LPS.

3. *New York Herald*, January 7, 1868, LPS.

4. Unidentified newspaper clippings, LPS.

5. Henderson, p. 81.

III. Henry Morton Stanley

1. Richard Seymour Hall, *Stanley, An Adventurer Explored* (Boston: Houghton Mifflin Company, 1975), pp. 17–21. Hall's book is currently the primary source for information concerning Henry Morton Stanley's romance with Alice Pike Barney. Hall was given total access to Stanley's papers by Richard Stanley, the explorer's grandson. Among them were letters from Alice to Stanley, the two photographs she gave him, and Stanley's diaries detailing the relationship. Several years after the book was published Stanley's papers were transferred to the Musée de l'Afrique Centrale, Tervuren, Belgium, and were unavailable during the period I researched this book. Whenever basic discrepancies exist between the two accounts (such as Alice stating that she never wrote Stanley once she left England or her lack of mention of the marriage contract), I have relied upon Hall's research.

2. *Ibid.*, pp. 18–21.

3. *Ibid.*, p. 21.

4. *Ibid.*, pp. 21–22.

5. *Ibid.*, pp. 17, 30.

6. "Stanley—His Loves, Adventures and Faith," *Cywaill yr Aclwyd*, (as cited in *The Review of Reviews*, ed. W. T. Stead, vol. 2, no. 7 (July 1890)), p. 47.

7. Hall, p. 25.

8. *Ibid.*, pp. 18, 25.

9. *Ibid.*, p. 18.

10. *Ibid.*, p. 25.

11. *Ibid.*, p. 26.

12. *Ibid.*, pp. 35, 93.

13. *Ibid.*, pp. 37–38.

IV. Marrying Albert

1. "Education of Girls in Dayton" (Dayton, Ohio: privately printed, n.d.), NMAA.

2. Unidentified newspaper clippings, APBS.

3. Hall, pp. 58–59.

4. *Ibid.*, p. 92.

5. *Ibid.*, p. 95.

6. *Ibid.*, p. 94.

7. Ellen Pike to Albert Clifford Barney, letter, May 31, 1878, NMAA.

8. Harlow, p. 282. Unidentified newspaper clippings, APBS.

9. Unidentified newspaper clipping, April 1881, LPS. Ellen Pike to Albert Barney, telegram, May 11, 1881, NMAA.

10. Natalie Clifford Barney, "Tribute to My Mother, Alice Pike Barney," typescript, 1953, NMAA.

11. Lloyd Lewis and Henry Justin Smith, *Oscar Wilde Discovers America (1882)* (New York: Harcourt, Brace and Co., 1936), pp. 388–91.

12. Natalie Barney never forgot Oscar Wilde and was a close friend of his niece, Dolly Wilde. Her epigrammatic writings closely resemble Wilde's, and she once told the writer Philippe Jullian that reading Oscar Wilde's short stories at the age of fifteen made her decide to become a writer. For an account from Natalie's perspective of her meeting with Wilde, see George Wickes, *The Amazon of Letters: The Life and Loves of Natalie Barney* (New York: Popular Library, June 1978), pp. 11–13. After Wilde's death in 1900, Natalie inscribed the following poem on the flyleaf of her copy of his *A House of Pomegranates*:

Elegy
The charm of him was like the charms of those
wild langorous flowers weary of the height
they bend from, and more weary of the bright
those twofold longings—from which longing grows
more comely at each passing passions close.

On Maidens V we weave in love's despite
Soft little songs that fall into the night
as fall the scattered petals of a rose
...Come we will sing the story of his death

We who have left unkissed his outstretched hand
And never breathed the hot impassioned breath
Of his desire...come we will proceed awhile
And with our lips remembering understand
The sad sweet wasted music of his smile.

V. Discoveries

1. Jean Chalon, *Portrait of a Seductress: The World of Natalie Barney*, trans. Carol Barko (New York: Crown Publishers, Inc., 1979), pp. 4–5. Wickes, pp. 28–29.

2. Mary Alice Heekin Burke, *Elizabeth Nourse, 1859–1938: A Salon Career* (Washington, D.C.: Smithsonian Institution Press, l983), pp. 18–24.

3. Wayne Andrews, *American Gothic: Its Origins, Its Triumphs* (New York: Random House, 1975), p. 123. Burke, pp. 20–21. Anita Ellis, "Cincinnati Art Furniture," *The Magazine Antiques*, vol. 121, no. 4 (April 1, 1982), pp. 931–3.

4. Harlow, pp. 322–4.

5. Burke, pp. 29, 204, 237.

6. Albert Clifford Barney to Ellen Miller Pike, letter, December 9, 1886, NMAA.

7. Unidentified newspaper clipping, APBS.

8. Henry Adams, *The Education of Henry Adams* (New York: The Modern Library, 1931), p. 403.

9. The painting became Natalie's favorite and she used it in 1900 as the frontispiece for her first book of poetry. Both portraits are in the collection of the NMAA.

10. Alice Barney, "An Art Student," Special Women's Edition, *The Washington Times*, July 4, 1895, p. 1.

11. Kathryn Allamong Jacob, "High Society in Washington During the Gilded Age: 'Three Distinct Aristocracies,'" (Ph.D. diss., Johns Hopkins University, 1986), pp. 260, 301, 307.

12. James B. Townsend, "The Summer Washington," *The Illustrated American*, September 7, 1885, pp. 300–302.

13. "Bar Harbor Society Studios," *Boston Sunday Globe*, undated, APBS.

14. Unidentified newspaper clipping, APBS.

15. Unidentified newspaper clipping, APBS.

16. Unidentified newspaper clipping, APBS.

VI. Society and Art

1. Constance McLaughlin Green, *Washington: A History of the Capital, 1879–1950* (New Jersey: University of Princeton Press, 1962) pp. 20–21.

2. Leila Mechlin, "Art Life in Washington," *Records of the Columbia Historical Society*, vol 24. (Washington, D.C.: Columbia Historical Society, 1921), pp. 164–78. Charles Hurd, *Washington Cavalcade* (New York: E. P. Dutton & Company, Inc., 1948), p. 159.

3. Unidentified newspaper clipping, APBS.

4. Unidentified newspaper clipping, APBS.

5. Unidentified newspaper clipping, APBS.

6. Chalon, p. 10.

7. *Ibid.*, p. 13.

8. Natalie Clifford Barney to Alice Pike Barney, letter, February 26, 1895, BD.

9. Natalie Clifford Barney to Alice Pike Barney, letter, April 2, 1895, BD.

10. Natalie Barney to Alice Pike Barney, undated letter, BD.

11. Chalon, p. 23.

12. "The Portrait Exhibition, In Excellence it Exceeds the Artists' Expectations," *Cincinnati Tribune*, May 3, 1896, APBS.

13. Chalon, pp. 18–21.

14. Wickes, p. 39.

15. Emily Clark, *Innocence Abroad* (New York: Alfred A. Knopf, 1931), p. 76.

16. Unidentifed newspaper clipping, APBS.

17. Blance V. King, "Views of Washington Water Color Club in Gallery," *Washington Post*, December 12, 1897, sec. 2, p. 6.

18. In 1894 Alice's close friend Juliet Thompson was rejected by the Society of Washington Artists. Alice was quoted in a magazine as not understanding "why it is that the Society of Washington Artists has failed to recognize, to any appreciable extent, this young woman's power....It is a shame that any work of merit should be wasted upon Washington....In New York she would take her rightful place among our foremost painters without delay and I for one, am most anxious to see her there." Unidentified magazine clipping, APBS. Thompson was elected a member the following year.

19. Mechlin, p. 164.

20. Blance V. King, "Art Exhibit—The Sketch Exhibit," *Washington Post*, January 16, 1898, sec. 1, p. 5.

21. Isabel McKenna, *Washington in the 90's* (San Francisco: Press of Overland Monthly, 1929), pp. 57–58.

22. Unidentified newspaper clipping, APBS.

23. Laura Dreyfus Barney to Albert Clifford Barney, letter, May 1898, NMAA.

24. James Henry Moser, "Art Topics," *Washington Post*, November 3, 1901, p. 28.

VII. Friendship with Whistler

1. Laura Dreyfus Barney to Alice Pike Barney, undated letter, BD.

2. Chalon, p. 25. William E. Huntington, interviews with author, 1964 to 1987. According to Huntington, after Albert's death Laura managed all the Barney business affairs for Alice and Natalie with Huntington's assistance throughout her life. She dealt with lawyers and bankers and sent Natalie her monthly allowance. She was meticulously organized, paid strict attention to detail, and had a keen business sense. Natalie, who possessed none of these attributes, was more than willing to let Laura be responsible for ensuring she could live life in her chosen style.

3. Clive Holland, "Lady Art Students in Paris," *International Studio*, November–December 1903, p. 230.

4. Barbara W. Tuchman, *The Proud Tower: A Portrait of the World Before the War, 1890–1914* (New York: The MacMillan Company, 1966), pp. 173–213.

5. Henry Adams, *Letters*, ed. Worthington Chauncey Ford, 12 vols. (Boston: Houghton Mifflin, 1930–1938), p. 151.

6. Stanley Weintraub, *Whistler, A Biography* (New York: Weybright and Talley, 1974), p. 436.

7. *Ibid.*

8. Alice Pike Barney, *Jimmie*, 1831, typescript, 1931, pp. i–iii. *Jimmie* was Alice's final play, which she wrote for the actor George Arliss. It includes a prologue and epilogue dramatizing her friendship with Whistler, which sets the scene for a one-act memory play focusing on Whistler's recollections of his early days in Paris. The play was given its premiere professional performance at Barney Studio House in 1985 as part of the Smithsonian's "An Evening at Barney Studio House" performing arts series.

9. Mary Augusta Mullikan, "Reminiscences of the Whistler Academy By An American Student," *International Studio*, vol. 34 (February 1905) ;. 237.

10. Elizabeth Robbins Pennell and Joseph Pennell, *The Life of James McNeill Whistler*, vol. 2 (London: J.B. Lippincott Company, 1908), pp. 234–35.

11. Roy McMullen, *Victorian Outsider, A Biography of J. A. M. Whistler* (New York: E. P. Dutton & Co., Inc., 1973), pp. 267–69.

12. Barney, *Jimmie*, "Prologue."

13. *Washington Times*, 1904, APBS.

14. Barney, *Jimmie*, "Epilogue."

15. McMullen, pp. 264–65.

VIII. A French Salon

1. Burke, pp. 56–60. Notably absent from Alice's salons was Elizabeth Nourse, who now lived permanently in Paris with her sister. Nourse was an expatriate, spending her summers at Saint Leger concentrating on the rural scenes of Brittany that were her specialty and winters submerged in the activities of the American Women's Art Association, which was a group of American women artists domiciled in France. Alice was not a member of the association. They remained in touch, however, and in 1898 Elizabeth gave Alice two large pastels, both of which were inscribed to Alice.

2. For an exhaustive study of the Symbolist art movement see: Robert L. Delevoy, *Symbolists and Symbolism* (New York: Rizzoli International Publications, Inc., 1978). Other detailed studies of Symbolist art or the Arts and Crafts Movement include Charles C. Eldredge, *American Imagination and Symbolist Painting* (New York: Study Center, New York University, 1979); Robert Pincus-Witten, *Occult Symbolism in France: Josephin Peladan and the Salons de la Rose-Croix* (New York: Garland Publishing, Inc., 1976); and Rowland and Betty Elzea, *The Pre-Raphaelite Era, 1848–1914: An Exhibition in Celebration of the Nation's Bicentennial, April 12–June 6, 1976* (Delaware: The Wilmington Society of the Fine Arts, 1976).

3. Delevoy, p. 12.

4. Achille Segard, "The Recent Work of Aman Jean," *International Studio*, April 1914, p. 94.

5. Francis Steegmuller, *Apollinaire, A Poet Among Painters* (New York: Farrar, Straus & Co., 1963), p. 52.

6. Wickes, p. 53. Chalon, p. 51.

7. Natalie Clifford Barney, *Quelque Portraits-Sonnets de Femmes* (Paris: Société d'Éditions Littéraries et Artistiques, Librairie Paul Ollendorff, 1900), p. 24. All translations from the chapbook are by Margaret Johnson Garrett who knew both Natalie and Laura Barney in their later years.

About Myself
Somber without worry and sad without distress,
I pity myself in vain as well as the wind
Weeping through the autumns of time,
Like an endless sigh raging without stop.

My life saddens me and luxury is a burden,
Pleasures are so old that they bite without teeth,
The brightest desires evaporate while coming to
Join the bottomless well of my sorrow.

What's wrong? I don't know, but I feel it deeply
Like the sea which searches in vain for the name
   Of its longing and of its empty fear.
   My heart is a bell with a cracked tone,
    Like the sea, it emits a muffled sob,
And moans over carrying so many tears.

8. Chalon, p. 62.
9. Natalie Clifford Barney to Albert Clifford Barney, undated letter, NMAA. A second copy of the letter is in the Natalie Barney Archives at the Bibliothèque Doucet in Paris.
10. Henri Pene du Bois, "Yankee Girl, French Poet," American Magazine, APBS.

IX. New Independence

1. *The Washington Mirror*, vol 2, no. 5 (March 31, 1900), p. 6. *The Washington Mirror*, vol. 3, no. 7 (July 14, 1900), p. 5.
2. Natalie Clifford Barney, "N. C. B. on her Mother, Alice Barney," typescript, 1953, NMAA, p. 6.
3. Jacob, pp. 280, 301, 306–307.
4. Stephen Birmingham, *"Our Crowd," The Great Jewish Families of New York* (New York: Harper & Row, 1967), pp. 257–58, 276–77.
5. Natalie Clifford Barney to Alice Pike Barney, undated letter, NMAA.
6. Alice Pike Barney to Natalie Clifford Barney, letter, January 25, 1901, BD.
7. Natalie Clifford Barney to Alice Pike Barney, undated letter, BD.
8. Alice Pike Barney to Frank McGuire, undated letter, 1901 (11027), CGA.
9. *The Washington Mirror*, vol. 7, no. 14 (August 31, 1901), p. 5.
10. Alice Pike Barney to Frank McGuire, undated letter (11027), CGA.
11. Alice Pike Barney to C. Powell Minnigerode, undated letter (11027), CGA.
12. "The Pessimist," *Washington Post*, November 17, 1901, p. 18.
13. James Henry Moser, "Art Topics," *Washington Post*, November 3, 1901, p. 28. Accompanying the painting were two lines of poetry by Natalie Barney:
    Strangely she chanted psalms from the worn book of dreams
    Whose threads are broken memories.
14. Leila Mechlin, "Art Notes," *Evening Star*, November 2, 1901, p. 26. "The Social World," *Evening Star*, November 2, 1901, p. 5.
15. James Henry Moser, "Art Topics," *Washington Post*, November 10, 1901, sec. 2, p. 28.
16. Anonymous, "Can It Be Washington Has No Artistic Instinct!" *Washington Times*, February 2, 1902, sec. 3, p. 1.

X. In the Public Eye

1. Anonymous, "Can It Be," sec. 3, p. 1.
2. A. Rosa Hausmann to Alice Pike Barney, undated letter, NMAA.
3. *The Washington Mirror*, vol. 9, no. 13 (February 22, 1902), pp. 3–5.
4. *Baltimore Times-Democrat*, March 16, 1902, APBS.
5. Unidentified newspaper clipping, APBS.
6. Alice was something of an inventor. By April 1902 she had received two patents and submitted a third. These inventions included a ceiling wardrobe on a pulley to provide extra storage in high-ceilinged bedrooms, a train parlor car that swiveled and could be adjusted in height, and an ingenious removable fastening device that connected ordinary bentwood chairs together to make a fixed row for auditorium seating.
7. *The Washington Mirror*, vol. 10, no. 5 (March 29, 1902), p. 5. In 1902 common practice was to spell Persian names phonetically. Contemporary scholarly orientalist conventions translate the name as Fadl, using Arabic transliteration.
8. *The Washington Mirror*, vol. 10, no. 10 (May 3, 1902), p.3.
9. Albert Clifford Barney to Natalie Clifford Barney, undated letter, NMAA.
10. Natalie Clifford Barney to Alice Pike Barney, undated letter, NMAA.
11. Natalie Clifford Barney to Alice Pike Barney and Laura Dreyfus Barney, letter, October 1902, BD.
12. Natalie Clifford Barney, "On Meeting Death," from "The Amazon of Letters, A World Tribute to Natalie Clifford Barney," *Adam International Review*, vol. 29, no. 299, p. 108.
13. *Ibid*.
14. "Funeral of Albert C. Barney," *Washington Post*, January 6, 1903, p. 3.

XI. Tackling Washington

1. *The Washington Mirror*, vol. 13, no. 4 (December 20, 1902), p. 3.
2. James Henry Moser, *Washington Post*, March 1, 1903, sec. 4, p. 35.
3. James Henry Moser, *Washington Post*, March 29, 1903, sec. 4, p. 44.
4. "Social and Personal; Mrs. Barney Entertains Builders of

Her Studio House. Quaint Old Custom Revived," *Washington Post*, July 6, 1903, p. 7.

5. *The Washington Mirror*, vol. 15, no. 7 (July 11, 1903), p. 4.

6. Natalie Clifford Barney to Alice Pike Barney, letter, July 31, 1903, NMAA.

7. *The Club-Fellow*, New York, February 15, 1904.

8. Anna P. Thomas, "An Artistic Home in Washington: Mrs. Alice Barney's Studio and Residence on Sheridan Circle," *Town & Country*, vol. 58, no. 47 (January 30, 1904), pp. 10–12.

9. James Henry Moser, "14th Annual Society of Washington Artists," *Washington Post*, March 20, 1904, sec. 3, p. 10.

10. Susan L. Klaus, "Barney Neighborhood House: A Stable Institution in a Changing Community," unpublished manuscript, July 1984, pp. 2–3.

11. James Henry Moser, "Art Notes," *Washington Post*, April 17, 1904, sec. 3, p. 8.

XII. Setting an Example

1. James Henry Moser, "Art and Artists," *Washington Post*, April 1, 1906, sec. 3, p. 7.

2. *Ibid*.

3. Junior League of Washington, *The City of Washington*, ed. Thomas Forneck (New York: Knopf, 1977), p. 333.

4. Suzanne Shelton, *Divine Dancer: A Biography of Ruth St. Denis* (Garden City, New York: Doubleday & Company, Inc., 1981), pp. 52–58.

5. *Ibid*., p. 58.

6. *The Club-Fellow and Washington Mirror*, May 2, 1906, vol. 7, no. 45.

7. Ruth St. Denis, *An Unfinished Life, An Autobiography* (New York: Harper & Bros. Pub., 1934), p. 75.

8. *Portraits and Sketches in Pastel*, July 3–12, 1908, Poem trans. by Susan Einbinder (The Modern Gallery, London, England), NMAA.

9. *American Art News*, vol. 7, no. 9, December 12, 1908, p. 1.

10. Alice Pike Barney to Leila Mechlin, undated letter, Archives of the Philadelphia Museum of Art.

11. Unidentified magazine clipping, APBS. The review was accompanied by a reproduction of a portrait of Laura Barney.

12. "Image in Pastel by Mrs. Barney Shown," unidentified newspaper clipping, May 11, 1909, APBS.

13. Phoebe Dwight, "Noted Charity Toiler in Hub Busy as Ever," *Boston Reveille*, October 19, 1909, APBS.

"Will Entertain Mrs. A.C. Barney," *Boston Herald*, October 18, 1909, p. 7.

XIII. Love Behind the Scenes

1. "Over the Tea Cups," *Washington Society*, ed. Hobart Brooks, vol. 1, no.1 (February 5, 1910), p. 5.

2. Isabel Anderson, *Presidents and Pies: Life in Washington 1897–1919* (New York: Houghton Mifflin Company, 1920), pp. 43–44.

3. Donald McClelland, "Edwin Scott: 1862–1929, Biographical Notes," *Paintings by Edwin Scott* (Washington, D.C.: Smithsonian Institution Press, 1970), pp. 16–20.

4. Chalon, p. 90.

5. "Why Miss Barney's Sappho Had to Move," *Dayton Journal*, November 14, 1909, sec. 2, p. 13. While it is entirely possible Natalie moved to Rue Jacob to "win back Renée Vivian" (as Shari Benstock states in *Women of the Left Bank, Paris, 1900–1940* [Austin: Univ. of Texas Press, 1986], p. 94), it is more likely that her pending eviction provided the practical impetus. See also Chalon, p. 86.

6. For a thinly disguised description of Natalie's salon see Radclyffe Hall, *The Well of Loneliness* (Paris: The Pegasus Press, 1928), pp. 405–10.

7. "Barney Statue Shocks Artistic Police Chief, *Washington Times*, October 10, 1910, p. 1.

8. "Wind Blew Covering from Barney Statue," *New York Herald*, October 11, 1910, APBS. "Statue Still Seen Despite Drapings," *Washington Times*, October 11, 1910, p. 3.

9. "Natalie Barney has Posed Only for Bust to Her Sister," *New York American*, October 13, 1910, APBS. Extant nude photographs of Natalie in the NMAA Barney archives leave no doubt that the model was Natalie. Whether the sculpture is immodest or immoral remains in the eye of the beholder. To late-twentieth century eyes, it would seem innocuous at worst.

10. "Mrs. A. C. Barney Corrects Story From Washington," *New York Herald*, October 14, 1910, APBS.

11. *The Club-Fellow and Washington Mirror*, vol. 13, no. 16 (October 19, 1910). The saga of the reclining nude refused to die. In the mid-1960s Laura Barney came to Washington to inspect the Smithsonian's selection of a new site for the statue at the rear of the Studio House garage. The occasion was captured by a Smithsonian photographer, flanked by Dr. David Scott, Director of the National Collection of Fine Arts, and Leonard Carmichael, Secretary of the

Smithsonian, as Laura ceremoniously draped it with a heavy tarp. In the mid-l970s the statue was moved into Studio House to protect it from the elements.

12. *The Club-Fellow and Washington Mirror*, March 8, 1911.

13. W. A. Hemmick to Alice Barney Hemmick, letter, March 30, 1911, NMAA.

14. Jeanette Goin to Alice Barney Hemmick, letter, August 9, 1911. Hester Talbott (Hester had remarried following Tom Negus's death) to Alice Barney Hemmick, letter, August 11, 1911, NMAA.

15. "La Vie Artistique, Des pastels et quelques toiles" unidentified French newspaper clipping, 1911, APBS.

16. Christian Hemmick to Laura Barney, undated letter, NMAA.

17. Christian Hemmick to Laura Barney, undated letter, NMAA.

18. *Washington Society*, vol. 2, no. 34 (September 23, 1911), p. 4.

XIV. The Course of True Love

1. Hurd, *Washington Cavalcade*, p. 159.

2. "Persian Priest Attracts Society Women to the Cult of Bahaism," *Washington Post*, April 26, 1912.

3. *The Club-Fellow and Washington Mirror*, vol. 14, no. 52 (June 26, 1912).

4. Alice Pike Barney Hemmick to Natalie Barney, letter, August 13, 1912, BD.

5. Kenneth W. Leish, ed., *The American Heritage History of the Presidency* (New York: American Heritage Publishing Co., Inc., 1968), p. 274.

6. "Over the Tea Cups," *Washington Society*, May 24, 1913 (vol. 5, no. 20), pp. 2–4.

7. Laura Dreyfus Barney, "From the Peace of the East to the War of the West," typescript, 1916, NMAA, p. 5.

XV. War Efforts

1. *The Club-Fellow and Washington Mirror*, vol. 16, no. 34 (February 18, 1914).

2. "Women Worth While, Their Frivolities, Interest and Hobbies," *Evening Star*, January 21, 1914, p. 11. Leila Mechlin, "News and Notes of Art and Artists," *Evening Star*, January 17, 1914, p. 7.

3. Natalie Clifford Barney to Laura Barney, letter, August 1, 1914, NMAA.

4. "Society," *Sunday Star*, August 30, 1914, sec. 7, p. 1.

5. "Women's Peace Party Opens Headquarters," *Evening Star*, February 15, 1915, p. 8.

6. "Wilson Supplies Peace Party Text," *Sunday Star*, February 21, 1915, p. 11.

7. "Mr. Roosevelt Scores Woman's Peace Party, Former President Denounces its Platform as Both 'Base and Silly'," *Evening Star*, April 17, 1915, p. 7.

8. "Society: Particularly Busy with Charity Affairs," *Sunday Star*, March. 28, 1915, sec. 7, p. 1.

9. Karla Jay, *The Amazon and the Page* (Bloomington: Indiana University Press, 1988), pp. 17–20. Florence E. Yoder, "Author of 'Opium Pipe' Describes How She Came to Write Drama," *Washington Times*, March 31, 1915, p. 10. Alice's portrait of Renée Vivien is in the Natalie Barney Archives at the Bibliothèque Doucet.

10. Florence E. Yoder, "Forty Members Quit Drama League, Back Mrs. Hemmick, Non-Endorsement of 'The Opium Pipe' Leads to Formation of New Body in Capital," *Washington Times*, May 23, 1915, p. 8.

11. "Paul Swan Wants His Art Taken Seriously: Classic Dance to Appear in *The Opium Pipe*, Tells of His Ambitions," *Evening Star*, May 10, 1915, p. 7.

12. "6,000 Persons Witness Allegory at Foot of Monument: Climax to Decoration Day," *Washington Post*, June 1, 1915, p. 3.

XVI. A Ballet for Pavlova

1. Oleg Kerensky, *Anna Pavlova* (New York: E. P. Dutton & Co., Inc., 1973), p. 111.

2. Program insert, NMAA. Alice Pike Barney, *L'École en Crinoline*, typescript, 1915, NMAA. Her narrative ballet script contains explicit stage and lighting directions, as well as suggested dance movements.

3. "Montemezzi Opera Accorded Ovation: 'The Love of Three Kings,' with Pavlowa Ballet Russe, Charms Belasco Audience," *Washington Times*, December 21, 1915, p. 5.

4. Willard Howard, "Pavlowa Gives Washington Premiere of Dance Drama by American Woman," *Oakland Tribune*, January 1, 1916, APBS.

5. Anna Pavlova, photograph inscribed to Alice Pike Barney, NMAA.

6. *The Club-Fellow and Washington Mirror*, vol. 18, no. 37 (March 9, 1916).

7. William E. Huntington, interview with author.

XVII. A National Theater

1. Louis B. Thompson, typescript, n.d., NMAA.

2. *Ibid*.

3. *Evening Star*, May 30, 1916, p. 3.

4. "Want Sylvan Theater on Monument Grounds: Mrs.

Hemmick and Mrs. Shepherd Lead Movement for Free Shakespearean Play," *Evening Star*, May 30, 1916, p. 3. "Dramatic: A Sylvan Theatre in Sight," *Washington Courier*, July 9, 1916, p. 17.

5. Thompson.

6. "Want Sylvan Theater on Monument Grounds," p. 3. "Dramatic: A Sylvan Theatre in Sight," p. 17.

7. Jean Eliot, "Jean Eliot's Letter: A Chronicle of Society," *Washington Times*, November 5, 1916, p. 6.

8. Marietta Minnigerode Andrews, *My Studio Window; Sketchs of the Pageant of Washington Life* (New York: E. P. Dutton & Company, 1928) pp. 266–67.

9. Alice Pike Barney Hemmick to Christian Hemmick, undated letter, NMAA.

10. "15,000 at Sylvan Play: Premiere on Monument Grounds Produced in Spite of Pluvius; First Drama Under Government Direction Participated in by Leaders in the Theatrical World—Society, Official-dom and Diplomats in Audience—Mrs. Hemmick is Author," *Washington Post*, June 3, 1917, p. 4.

11. "Fourth of July Celebration," program, NMAA. "Give 'Call of the Allies' at the Sylvan Theater; Washington Players Present Patriotic Pageant Before an Audience of 15,000," undated newspaper clipping, APBS.

12. Thompson.

13. *The Club-Fellow and Washington Mirror*, vol. 20, no. 5 (July 25, 1917). *The Club-Fellow and Washington Mirror*, vol. 20, no. 8 (August 18, 1917).

XVIII. The End of a Marriage

1. *The Club-Fellow and Washington Mirror*, vol. 20, no. 18 (October 24, 1917).

2. "'When a Woman Loves'; Society Play at the Grand Opera House," *Brooklyn Citizen*, December 16, 1917, APBS.

3. *The Club-Fellow and Washington Mirror*, vol. 20, no. 44 (April 24, 1918).

4. "How Mrs. Hemmick Astonished Washington Society," *Washington Post*, January 18, 1920, mag. sec., p. 1.

5. Natalie Clifford Barney to Alice Pike Barney, undated letter, BD. Laura Dreyfus Barney to Alice Pike Barney, letter, November 26, 1920, NMAA.

6. "Society Leader Discards Husband's Name; Begins New Social Campaign," *Washington Times*, November 21, 1919, p. 1.

7. "How Mrs. Hemmick Astonished Washington Society," p. 1.

8. "Hemmick Divorces Former Mrs. Barney," *New York Times*, August 29, 1920, p. 6.

9. Alice Pike Barney to Natalie Clifford Barney, undated letter, BD.

10. Alice Pike Barney to Natalie Clifford Barney, November 18, 1921, BD.

11. Alice Pike Barney, letter to Natalie Clifford Barney, November 28, 1921, BD.

12. Alice Pike Barney to Natalie Clifford Barney, undated letter, BD.

13. Alice Pike Barney to Natalie Clifford Barney, letter, January 2, 1922, BD.

14. Alice Pike Barney to Natalie Clifford Barney, undated letter, BD.

15. Alice Pike Barney to Natalie Clifford Barney, undated letter, BD.

16. Alice Pike Barney, undated typescript, NMAA.

XIX. Life in Hollywood

1. George C. Warren, "Cast Loses Fight for Hopeless Play," *San Francisco Chronicle*, February 16, 1929, p. 15.

2. Natalie Clifford Barney, "Tribute."

3. Natalie Clifford Barney, "Meeting Death," p. 107.

4. *California Graphic*, October 13, 1928, APBS.

5. Jeannette Kuhn, "Hollywood's Little Theatres," *California Life*, November 1928, p. 16.

6. DeWitt Bodeen to Mrs. Johnson Garrett, letter, March 8, 1981, NMAA.

7. Natalie Clifford Barney to Alice Pike Barney, undated letter, BD.

8. Alice Pike Barney to Natalie Clifford Barney, undated letter, BD.

9. Thomas A. Miller to Alice Pike Barney, letter, March 19, 1931, NMAA.

10. Alice Pike Barney, handwritten manuscript, undated, NMAA.

11. Natalie Clifford Barney, "Tribute."

XX. Afterword

1. Vivienne B. Hornbeck in "Background," in *The Barney Neighborhood House and Social and Industrial Settlement* (Washington, D.C.: Barney Neighborhood House, 1942), explains why Neighborhood House was renamed Barney Neighborhood House:
A name which must always be associated with the founding and early development of Neighborhood House is that of Mrs. Alice Pike Barney, who with her daughter, Laura Alice, not only gave financial assistance to the infant organization, but was the guiding spirit in the shaping of its policies. Mrs. Barney's vision of events to come and her long range planning are now being fully realized. She under-

stood what the feeling of community life meant and should be. She knew that through arts and crafts—in the full meaning of all that this implies—a healthy and enriched life could be obtained for those otherwise deprived of these opportunities. The accomplishment was to her not an abstraction but a reality because she herself was a realist, a person with a complete vision and a willingness to work for and to finance such an objective. Because of her interest in the arts and crafts and her realization of its vast possibilities, she fostered, and encouraged the work in this department which continues to be an important feature of the activities of the Settlement today.

2. Natalie Clifford Barney to Laura Dreyfus Barney, letter, April 22, 1934, NMAA.

3. Alice Pike Barney, handwritten questionnaire for *Outstanding Women*, 1928, NMAA.

EXHIBITIONS OF WORK BY ALICE PIKE BARNEY

Group Exhibtions

1889: *Salon des Beaux Arts*, Paris, France.

1893: Columbia Exposition, U.S. Pavilion, Chicago.

1896: *The Portrait Exhibition*, Cincinnati Art Museum, Cincinnati, Ohio.

Loan Exhibition of Portraits, Corcoran Gallery of Art, Washington, D.C.

1897: *Salon des Beaux Arts*, Paris.

Washington Water Color Club, Second Annual Exhibition, The Gallery, Washington, D.C.

1898: *The Sketch Exhibit*, The Gallery, Washington, D.C.

8th Annual Society of Washington Artists Exhibition, The Gallery, Washington, D.C.

Loan Exhibition, Old Corcoran Gallery [The Renwick], Washington, D.C.

1900: *Royal Academy of Arts Exhibition*, Royal Academy of Arts, London.

1902: *12th Annual Society of Washington Artists Exhibition*, Corcoran Gallery of Art, Hemicycle Room, Washington, D.C.

1903: *13th Annual Society of Washington Artists Exhibition*, Corcoran Gallery of Art, Washington, D.C.

Philadelphia Art Club Annual Exhibition of Water Colors and Pastels, Philadelphia Art Club, Philadelphia.

Richmond Art Club 8th Annual Invitational Exhibition, Richmond Art Club, Richmond, Virginia.

Loan Exhibition, Cosmos Club, Washington, D.C.

1904: *National Academy of Design Seventy-Ninth Annual Exhibition*, National Academy of Design, Vanderbilt Gallery, New York City.

14th Annual Society of Washington Artists Exhibition, Corcoran Gallery of Art, Washington, D.C.

Loan Exhibition, Corcoran Gallery of Art, Loan Exhibition Room, Washington, D.C.

Pennsylvania Academy Water-color Exhibit, Pennsylvania Academy, Philadelphia.

1905: *15th Annual Society of Washington Artists Exhibition*, Corcoran Gallery of Art, Washington, D.C.

1906: *16th Annual Society of Washington Artists Exhibition*, Corcoran Gallery of Art, Washington, D.C.

Loan Exhibition, Corcoran Gallery of Art, Loan Exhibition Room, Washington, D.C.

1911: *Etudes et Portraits au Pastel par Mme Clifford Barney de*

Washington, Galerie Devambez, Paris (catalog). Exhibition with Edwin Scott.

One-Person Exhibitions

1901: *Alice Pike Barney*, Corcoran Gallery of Art, Hemicycle Room, Washington, D.C.

1903: *Pastels by Alice Barney*, Gallery Durand-Ruel, New York City (catalog).

1908: *Portraits and Sketches in Pastel*, The Modern Gallery, London (catalog).

Pastel Studies and Portraits by Mrs. Clifford Barney of Washington, Gallerie Bernheim Jeune et Cie, Paris (catalog).

1909: *Portraits and Sketches in Pastel by Mrs. Barney of Washington*, M. Knoedler & Company, New York City (catalog).

Portraits & Sketches in Pastel By Mrs. Barney of Washington, Walter Kimball & Company, Boston (catalog).

Portraits and Sketches in Pastel By Mrs. Barney, Corcoran Gallery of Art, Washington, D.C. (catalog).

1930: *Exhibition of Paintings and Portraits by Alice Pike Barney of Washington, D.C.*, Stendahl Art Galleries, Los Angeles (catalog).

Portraits by Alice Barney, California Art Center, Eagle Rock, California. Sponsored by the Cadman Creative Club.

Posthumous Exhibitions

1932: *Paintings by Alice Pike Barney*, Studio House, Washington, D.C. Public exhibition prepared by Laura Barney.

1934: *Etudes et Portraits au Pastel par Alice Barney*, Chez Hector Brame, Paris (catalog).

1941: *Exhibition of Paintings by Alice Pike Barney*, Barney Neighborhood House, Washington, D.C.

1943: *Exhibition of Paintings by Alice Barney*, Howard University Gallery of Art, Founders Library, Washington, D.C. (catalog). Curated by Alonzo J. Aden.

1944: *An Exhibition of Paintings by Alice Barney*, Arts Club Washington, Washington, D.C. (catalog). Also exhibited: "Alice Barney" by Pierre Troubetsky and a portrait by Mike Owen, winner of the Washington Society of Artists' Alice Barney Portraiture Prize.

1945: *Paintings by Alice Pike Barney*, Clearwater Art Museum, Clearwater, Florida (brochure).

1951: *Memorial Exhibition of Oil Paintings and Pastels by Alice Pike Barney*, National Collection of Fine Arts (NCFA) Washington, D.C. (brochure).

1952: *Pastel Portraits by Alice Pike Barney*, Arts Club of Washington, Washington, D.C. (brochure). Organized by NCFA and exhibited in conjunction with 15 paintings by Edwin Scott.

Paintings by Alice Barney, Dayton Art Institute Dayton, Ohio.

Paintings by Alice Barney, Prairie View Agriculture & Mechanical College, Prairie View, Texas.

1967: *Personal Impressions by Alice Pike Barney*, NCFA, Museum of National History, Ryder Hall, Washington, D.C.

Alice Pike Barney Exhibition, Bureau of the Budget, Old Executive Office Building, Washington, D.C. Organized by NCFA.

1979: *Where Shadows Live: Alice Pike Barney and her Friends*, NCFA, Washington, D.C. (catalog by Donald B. McClelland). Co-curated by Donald B. McClelland and Jean L. Kling. The exhibit included 14 paintings by other artists, photographs, and decorative objects donated to the NCFA by Laura and Natalie Barney.

Included in *American Imagination and Symbolist Paintings*, Gray Art Gallery, New York. Curated by Charles C. Eldredge.

Alice Pike Barney and her Friends, Cosmos Club, Washington, D.C. Curated by Jean L. Kling.

1982–84: *Alice Pike Barney: Bringing Culture to a Provincial Capital*, Barney Studio House, Washington, D.C. Curated by Jean L. Kling. Didactic, multi-media exhibition: oils, pastels, photographs, decorative objects, and architectural plans.

1983–84: Included in *The Capital Image: Painters in Washington, 1800–1915*, National Museum of American Art, Washington, D.C. Curated by Andrew J. Cosentino and Henry Glassie.

1984–86: *Alice Pike Barney: Pastel Portraits from Studio House*, Barney Studio House, Washington, D.C. (catalog with introduction by Jean Kling and notes by Louise Thorlin). Curated by Jean Kling.

1986–90: *Alice Pike Barney: The Paris Years*, Barney Studio House, Washington, D.C. Curated by Jean Kling.

THEATER PIECES BY ALICE PIKE BARNEY

1897: *Vaudeville: Reveries of a Bachelor,* skits and tableaux. August 1897, Kebo Valley Club, Bar Harbor, Maine.

1898: *Tableaux for the sick and wounded in war with Spain,* tableaux. May 9, 1898, The Old Corcoran Gallery of Art [The Renwick Gallery], Washington, D.C.

1901: *St. Nicholas Kettledrum,* recitations and song. December 1901, New Willard Hotel, Ball Room, Washington, D.C.

1902: *Passing of Time,* tableaux. February 17, 1902, Chase's Theater, Washington, D.C.; March 20, 1902, Ford's Opera House, Baltimore, MD.

Tableaux for the Benefit of the Newsboys, tableaux. April 3, 1902, The New Willard Hotel, Washington, D.C.

1904: *The Dream of Queen Elizabeth* [*Queen Elizabeth's Dream*], masque. April 12, 1904, Lafayette Square Theater, Washington, D.C.; April 13, 1904, British Embassy, Washington, D.C.; April 18, 1904, Lafayette Square Theater, Washington, D.C.

1906: *Eighteenth Century Pastorale,* pantomime. May 4, 1906, "Friendship" (John R. McLean estate), Washington, D.C.; May 15, 1906, "The Oaks" (Colonel Henry F. Blount estate), Washington, D.C.

1907: *Romance of Pierrot and Pierrette,* pantomime and tableaux. February 12, 1907, The New Willard Hotel, Washington, D.C.

1909: *Tableaux to Song,* tableaux. January 30, 1909, Studio House, Washington, D.C.; December 13, 1911, March 28, 1912, Rauscher's, Washington, D.C.; Jan. 18–19, 1984, Barney Studio House, Washington, D.C.

About Thebes, musical drama. Music by Harry Wheaton Howard with incidental music by Philip Lee Scantling, Mrs. J. M. Stoddard, and Lawrence Townsend, Jr. April 19–22, 1909, Belasco Theatre, Washington, D.C.; Scenes presented December 23, 1909, Belasco Theatre, Washington, D.C.

The Bridal Veil, ballet with music from *Romeo and Juliet* by Gounoud. August 26, 1909, Building of Arts, Bar Harbor, Maine. Scenes presented December 23, 1909, Belasco Theatre, Wash-

ington, D.C. Pencil sketches of sets in script. Music performed by the Boston Symphony.

The Man in the Moon [*Luna-The Man in the Moon*], ballet and pantomime. December 20, 1909, Belasco Theatre, Washington, D.C.; Prologue, December 23, 1909, Belasco Theatre, Washington, D.C.

1910: *Tableaux of American History,* tableaux. April 7, 1910, Continental Hall, Washington, D.C.

Classic Dances, dance. April 30, 1910, Studio House, Washington, D.C.

Daphnephoria, pantomime, dance and recitations. May 23, 1910, "The Oaks" (Colonel Henry F. Blount estate), Washington, D.C. Alice Barney appeared as "Narcissus" and "The Huntress."

1912: [Mrs. Christian Hemmick] *On the Love of Echo,* Greek idyll. April 12, 1912, Belasco Theatre, Washington, D.C.

[Mrs. Christian Hemmick] *Le Reve, Dance in Crinoline,* ballet. April 12, 1912, Belasco Theatre, Washington, D.C.

[Mrs. Christian Hemmick] *Orientals,* songs and tableaux. April 12, 1912, Belasco Theatre, Washington, D.C.

1913: [Mrs. Christian Hemmick] *Some Years Hence,* play. May 20, 1913, National Theatre, Washington, D.C.

[Mrs. Christian Hemmick] *Woman,* morality play. May 20, 1913, National Theatre, Washington, D.C.; May 31, 1909, Lyric Theater, Baltimore, MD.

1914: [Mrs. Christian Hemmick] *The Mystery of the East,* mime and dance. May 8, 1914, 1626 Rhode Island Avenue, N.W., Washington, D.C.

[Mrs. Christian Hemmick] and Clarence Woods de Knight, *Power,* play. When submitted to prospective producers, the only credit given to Knight was that the play was written from papers and notes on the subject collected by Knight.

1915: [Mrs. Christian Hemmick] *Dispute of the Muses,* musical comedy, ballet and pageant. February 8–9, 1915, The New Willard Hotel, Washington, D.C.

[Mrs. Christian Hemmick] with blank verse by Hazel MacKaye, *The Awakening: War to Peace* [*Woman and War*], tableaux. February 22, 1915, New Masonic Temple, Washington, D.C.; Apr. 27, 1915, Belasco Theatre, Washington, D.C.; May 31, 1915, foot of the Washington Monument, Washington, D.C.

[Mrs. Christian Hemmick] and Mme. Laura Dreyfus Barney, *The Opium Pipe, From an Original Play of Ancient Persia,* play. April 27, 1915, Belasco Theatre, Washington, D.C.; May 10, 1915, Belasco Theatre, Washington, D.C.

[Mrs. Christian Hemmick] *L'École en Crinoline,* ballet with music by Chaminade. December 21, 1915, Belasco Theatre, Washington, D.C.; December 27–28, 1915, Lyric Theater, Baltimore, MD; January 3, 1916, 44th Street Theater, New York City; January 7, 1916, Philadelphia; January 22, 1916, Cleveland, Ohio.

1916: [Mrs. Christian Hemmick] *Pageant Egyptienne,* pageant. February 17, 1916, Beaux Arts Ball, The Willard Hotel, Washington, D.C.

[Mrs. Christian Hemmick] *Shakespeare Triumphant,* play. May 26, 1916, "The Oaks" (estate of Colonel Henry P. Blount), Washington, D.C.; May 28, 1916, Washington Monument Grounds, Washington, D.C.

[Mrs. Christian Hemmick] *Temple d'El-Kaffa,* dance-drama. November 10, 1916, Studio House, Washington, D.C. Written for Sarah Bernhardt's visit to Studio House.

[Mrs. Christian Hemmick] *Atlantis,* Symphonic ballet opera of the warfare of the elements, music composed by Louie Van Gaertner.

[Mrs. Christian Hemmick] *Moon Man,* ballet. Written for Anna Pavlova

1917: [Mrs. Christian Hemmick] *The Drama Triumphant,* masque. June 2 and July 4, 1917, National Sylvan Theatre, Washington, D.C.

[Mrs. Christian Hemmick] *The Call of the Allies,* propoganda pageant. July 4 and 13, 1917, National Sylvan Theatre, Washington, D.C.

[Mrs. Christian Hemmick] *When a Woman Loves,* play. December 17, 1917, Grand Opera House, Brooklyn, New York.

1918: [Mrs. Christian Hemmick] *The Courtesan of Rome* [*La Courtisane de Rome*], play. October 16–25, 1930, Theatre Mart, Hollywood, CA. Written for Ida Rubenstein and revised for Alla Nazimova.

[Alice Hemmick] *A Dainty Farce,* play (unfinished).

[Alice Hemmick] *A Play in One Act,* play.

1919: [Mrs. Christian Hemmick] and Natalie Barney, *The Colour of His Soul,* play. Written for a party given by Natalie in honor of the Duchese de Clermont-Tonnere.

1921: *A Botticelli,* dance.

The Brides of Venice, ballet to music of *Romeo and Juliet* by Gounoud.

Call of the Bells [*Les Cloche de Russie*], mime drama.

Challenge of Youth [*The Heart of Gold*], ballet to music of "Danse Mievire" by Armande de Polignac.

Commerage, mime ballet.

The Gold Digger [*Gold Lure*], ballet.

Gossip, mime ballet.

The Great Pearl, fantasy, mime drama to music from *Anthony & Cleopatra,* with music composed by Florent-Schmitt. Florent-Schmitt wrote the score for Ida Rubenstein's performance at the Paris Opera. Also written as a movie outline.

The Lost Cat, A Ballet of Shadows, ballet.

L'Ombrelle Volee, ballet.

The Planets, Symphonic mime with music composed by Gustuv Holst, scene and costume design renderings by Alice Barney.

Pride Has a Fall, mime ballet.

The Resourceful Rice Seller, play (Chinese comedy).

Romance en Crinoline, ballet with music composed by Eugene Goosens. Extensive rewrite of *L'École en Crinoline.*

The Scourge [*Closed Lips*], play.

The Seller of Dreams, mime ballet with music composed by Gertrude Ross.

The Stolen Sunshade, mime, drama, ballet.

1922: *About Thebes* [*Secret of the Scarab*], musical comedy revised from 1909 production, with music composed by Manlio de Veroli. Audition performance December 5, 1922, Ritz Hotel Ballroom, London.

The Lure [*The Moth and the Flame*], mime comedy with music composed by Eugene Gossens.

1923: *Driven,* play. Feb. 17–22, 1923, Belasco Theatre, Washington, D.C.

1924: *False Value,* play. May 27, 1924, Arts Club of Washington, Washington, D.C.; May 16–30, 1930, Theatre Mart, Hollywood, CA.; Feb. 16–18, 1982, Barney Studio House, Washington, D.C.; Mar. 1982, Arts Club of Washington, Washington, D.C.

Fantasie Indienne, play. May 28, 1924, "Twin Oaks," (Charles J. Bell estate), Washington, D.C. Martha S. Gielew, co-author, *Andy the Moonshiner,* play.

1925: *Atlantis,* expanded from 1916 version. Musical, mime, drama, ballet. Prologue music by Henry Cowells. Act I music composed by Florent-

Schmitt. Set design for Prologue by Alice Barney; Set Design for Act I by Clement de Swiecniski.

Luna, the Man in the Moon, musical comedy with music composed by Sol Cohen. Preview, November 22, 1925, Old Garden Cottage, Hollywood, CA.; audition, November 1, 1927, Hollywood Play House, Hollywood, CA; July 15–24, 1929, Theatre Mart, Hollywood, CA.

1926: [Mrs. Christian Hemmick] and Clarence Woods de Knight, *Passions* [*Transgressors*], play in 3 acts, 4 scenes. February15–October 28, 1926, Columbia Theater, San Francisco, CA.

Do and Bedone [*The Ermine Cloak*], mime ballet with moral, music from Grieg Concerto in A Minor opus 16 (Piano and Orchestra).

The Veil, drama, ballet with music composed by Henry Eichhaen.

The Lighthouse, play. January 24–27, 1928, Theatre Mart, Hollywood, CA. February 7–10, 1929, Hollywood Play House, Hollywood, CA. Won first prize, DC Drama League of America Playwrighting Contest, June 1927.

1927: *The Sacred Pool, An Offering of Farce and Beauty,* play and pantomime with music composed by Feodor Kolin. September 5, 1927, Old Garden Cottage, Hollywood, CA.

The Shepherd of Shiraz [*Golden Gift of the Goddess*], mime, drama, ballet. September 5, 1927, Old Garden Cottage, Hollywood, CA.; September 4, 1931, Hollywood Bowl, Hollywood, CA.

With Samuel Ross, *Fancy Women,* play. Copyright by Samuel Ross, Los Angeles, CA.

Graft, play outline.

1928: Co-author Natalie Barney, *Legitimate Lovers* [*The Colour of His Soul* or *Horace Littlefield, Esq.*], play. January 24–27, 1928, Hollywood Play House, Hollywood, CA; April 8–11, 1929, Theatre Mart, Hollywood, CA.

Is Wrong Right?, play. May 25–30, 1928, and July 1, 1928, Theatre Mart, Hollywood, CA.

The Dancer, play.

The Foreign Dancer, play. Written to be a one-reel movie staring Wanda Homeley.

His Birthday, play.

The Man in the Moon, spectacular fantastique, pantomime with music composed by Rogowski. Ballet version of 1909 play.

The Secret of the Scarab, musical comedy with music composed by Manlio di Veroli.

With James Land, *Static, A Harmonious Discord,* play.

Tom, Toms of Revenge, play.

Why One Should Send Clothes to the Laundry, skit.

1929: *The Woman Plays,* vaudeville sketches. January 15–17, 1929, Theatre Mart, Hollywood, CA.

Transgressors, [*Passions or Inheritance*], play. May 20–25, 1929, Theatre Mart, Hollywood, CA.

Moon Madness ["*Luna, the Man in the Moon*"], comedy opera with music by Sol Cohen, lyrics by William Duncan Cary and Alice Barney. October 2–November 4, 1929, Theatre Mart, Hollywood, CA; October 7–November 6, 1929, Figueroa Playhouse, Los Angeles, CA; December 9, 1929 (excerpts), Cadman Creative Club, Hollywood, CA.

The Spring Has Come, mime ballet for children with music by Fedor Kolin. Ebel Club, Hollywood, CA.

1930: *The Scar* [*The Mark of the Beast*], play. January 16–29, 1930, Theatre Mart, Hollywood, CA.

Mata-Hari [*A Spy Mata-Hari*], play. Feb. 25–28, and Mar. 1–2, 1929, Theatre Mart, Hollywood, CA.

1931: *Jimmie* [*Whistler* or *Butterfly*], play. April 17–18, 1985, Barney Studio House, Washington, D.C. Rewritten in 1931 for George Arliss as Whistler.

UNPUBLISHED FICTION BY ALICE PIKE BARNEY

Novels

The Lighthouse. NMAA, 276 pages.

The Love of Henry M. Stanley. Chapters II, III, and epilogue, NMAA, 1926, 18 pages. According to Alice's note on the cover, she had mislaid chapter I and wanted to start all over again. Written in the first person.

Joan of USA. NMAA, 269 pages.

Stanley's "Lady" Alice By One Who Knew. NMAA, 1927, 342 pages. Fictionalized autobiography written in the third person.

The Tower of Iron. NMAA, 277 pages.

Short Stories

"All's Well." NMAA, 32 pages. Written in Hollywood, CA, the preliminary title was "Ich Diem."

"The Brides of Venice, A Romance from an Historical Episode." NMAA, 50 pages. Written in Washington, D.C.

"Is Wrong Right?" NMAA, 57 pages. Written in Hollywood, CA.

"The Legend of The Great Pearl, A Fantasy." NMAA, 152 pages. Alice's handwritten note on the cover states that the story was inspired by Florent-Schmitt's score for the ballet *Anthony and Cleopatra,* danced by Ida Rubenstein in Paris.

"The Scar, Story of a Motion Picture." NMAA, 52 pages. Written in Hollywood, CA.

"The Story of Fad, a waif of Syria." NMAA, 9 pages.

SELECTED BIBLIOGRAPHY

Adams, Henry. *The Education of Henry Adams.* 1918. New York: The Modern Library, 1931.

—. *Letters.* Ed. by Worthington Chauncey Ford. Boston: Houghton Mifflin, 1930–1938.

Affairs of the Mind: The Salon in Europe and America from the Eighteenth to the Twentieth Century. Ed. by Peter Quennell. Washington, D. C.: New Republic Books, 1980.

The American Heritage History of the Presidency. Ed. by Kenneth W. Leish. New York: American Heritage Publishing Co., Inc., 1968.

Anderson, Isabel. *Presidents and Pies, Life in Washington 1897–1919.* New York: Houghton Mifflin Co., 1920.

Andrews, Marietta Minnigerode. *My Studio Window: Sketches of the Pageant of Washington Life.* New York: E. P. Dutton and Co., 1928.

Andrews, Wayne. *American Gothic: Its Origins, Its Triumphs.* New York: Random House, 1975.

Barney, Natalie Clifford. *Quelques Portraits-Sonnets de Femmes.* Paris, France: Societe de Editions Litteraries et Artistiques, Librairie Paul Ollendorff, 1900.

—. "On Meeting Death." *Adam International Review,* 29, no. 299 (1929): 104–111.

Benstock, Shari. *Women of the Left Bank: Paris, 1900–1940.* Austin, Texas: University of Texas Press, 1986.

Birmingham, Stephen. *"Our Crowd," The Great Jewish Families of New York.* New York: Harper & Row, 1967.

Breeskin, Adelyn D. *Romaine Brooks,* 2nd ed. Washington, D.C.: Smithsonian Institution Press, 1986.

Burke, Mary Alice Heekin. *Elizabeth Nourse, 1859–1938: A Salon Career.* Washington, D.C.: Smithsonian Institution Press, 1983.

Cassini, Marguerite. *Never a Dull Moment: The Memoirs of Countess Marguerite Cassini.* New York: Harper & Brothers, Pub., 1956.

Chalon, Jean. *Portrait of a Seductress: The World of Natalie Barney.* Trans. by Carol Barko. New York: Crown Publishers, Inc., 1979.

Chapon, François; Prévot, Nicole; and Sieburth, Richard. *Autour de Natalie Clifford Barney.* Paris: Bibliothèque Littéraire Jacques Doucet, 1976.

Cheny, Sheldon. *The Open-Air Theatre.* New York: Mitchell Kennerly, 1918.

Cist, Charles. *Sketches and Statistics, Cincinnati in 1859.* Cincinnati: Wm. H. Moore & Co., 1881.

Clark, Emily. *Innocence Abroad.* New York: Alfred A. Knopf, 1931.

Clark, Robert Judson, ed. *The Arts and Crafts Movement in America, 1876–1976.* Princeton, New Jersey: Princeton University Press, 1972.

Clemens, Samuel Leghorne, and Charles Dudley Warner. *The Gilded Age: A Tale of Today.* 1873. Garden City, New York: Nelson Doubleday, Inc., 1979.

Damon, Gene, and Lee Stuart. "Forgotten Lesbian Poet: Renee Vivien." In *Lesbian Lives: Biographies of Women from The Ladder.* Ed. by Barbara Grier and Reid Coletta, 290–295. Oakland, California: Diana Press, 1976.

Daniels, Jonathan. *Washington Quadrille: The Dance Beside the Documents.* Garden City, New York: Doubleday & Co., Inc., 1968.

de Chambrun, Clara Longworth. *Story of the Queen City.* New York: C. Scribner and Sons, 1939.

Delevoy, Robert L. *Symbolists and Symbolism.* New York: Rizzoli International Publications, 1978.

Dickens, Charles. *Charles Dickens, On America & the Americans.* Ed. by Michael Slater. Austin, Texas: University of Texas Press, 1978.

Eldredge, Charles C. *American Imagination and Symbolist Painting.* New York: Study Center, New York University, 1979.

Ellis, Anita. "Cincinnati Art Furniture." *The Magazine Antiques,* vol. CXXI, no. 4, April 1, 1982, 930–941.

Elzea, Rowland, and Betty Elzea. *The Pre-Raphaelite Era 1848-1914: An Exhibition in Celebration of the National Bicentennial, April 12–June 6, 1976.* Wilmington, Delaware: The Wilmington Society of the Fine Arts, 1976.

Faderman, Lillian. *Surpassing the Love of Men: Romantic Friendship and Love between Women, from the Renaissance to the Present.* New York: William Morrow and Co., Inc., 1981.

Fitch, Noel Riley. *Sylvia Beach and the Lost Generation: A History of Literary Paris in the Twenties and Thirties.* Middlesex, England: Penguin Books Ltd., 1983.

Froncek, Thomas, ed. Junior League of Washington. *The City of Washington: An Illustrated History.* New York: Knopf, 1977.

Goethe, J.W. Von. *Truth & Poetry; From My Own Life.* Translated by John Oxenford Esq. London, England: Bell & Paldy, 1872.

Goley, Mary Anne. "John White Alexander (1856–1915)." Catalogue. Washington, D.C.: National Collection of Fine Arts, Smithsonian Institution, 1976.

Goss, The Rev. Charles Frederick. Cincinnati, *The Queen City, 1788–1912.* Vol. 1. Cincinnati: S. J. Clarke Publishing Co., 1912.

Goveneur, Marian. *As I Remember: Recollections of American Society During the Nineteenth Century.* New York: D. Appleton & Co., 1911.

Green, Constance McLaughlin. *Washington: a History of the Capital, 1879– 1950.* Princeton, New Jersey: University of Princeton Press, 1962.

Hahn, Emily. *Romantic Rebels: An Informal History of Bohemianism in America.* Boston: Houghton Mifflin Co., 1967.

Hall, Richard Seymour. *Stanley: An Adventurer Explored.* Boston: Houghton Mifflin Co., 1975.

Halstead, Murat. *The Illustrious Life of William McKinley, Our Martyred President.* Chicago: Privately printed, 1901.

Harlow, Alvin F. *The Serene Cincinnatians.* New York: E. P. Dutton and Co., Inc., 1950.

Havighurst, Walter. *Ohio: A Bicentennial History.* New York: W. W. Norton & Co., Inc., 1976.

History of Cincinnati, Ohio, with Illustrations and Biographic Sketches. Comp. by Henry A. Ford and Kate B. Ford. Cleveland, Ohio: L. A. Williams & Co., 1881.

Holland, Clive. "Lady Art Students in Paris." *International Studio* vol. 21 (November–December 1903): 225–32.

Holliday, Joseph E. "Notes on Samuel N. Pike and his Opera Houses." *Bulletin of The Cincinnati Historical Society* 25, no. 3 (July 1967): 163–183.

Hurd, Charles. *Washington Cavalcade.* New York: E. P. Dutton and Co., Inc., 1948.

Jacob, Kathryn Allamong. "High Society in Washington During the Gilded Age: 'Three Distinct Aristocracies'." Baltimore: Johns Hopkins University. Ph.D. Diss., 1986.

Jay, Karla. *The Amazon and the Page: Natalie Clifford Barney and Renée Vivien.* Bloomington, Indiana: Indiana University Press, 1988.

Joblin, Maurice. *Cincinnati: Past and Present: or, Its Industrial History as Exhibited in the Life-Labors of Its Leading Men.* Cincinnati: M. Joblin & Co., 1872.

Kerensky, Oleg. *Anna Pavlova.* New York: E. P. Dutton and Co., Inc., 1973.

Kidney, Walter C. *The Architecture of Choice: Eclecticism in America 1880–1930.* New York: George Braziller, 1974.

Klaus, Susan L. "Barney Neighborhood House: A Stable Institution in a Changing Community." Unpublished manuscript, 1984.

Knepper, George W. *An Ohio Portrait.* Columbus, Ohio: Ohio Historical Society, 1976.

Kohler, Sue A. *The Commission of Fine Arts: A Brief History, 1910–1976.* Washington, D.C.: The Commission: U.S. Government Printing Office, 1977.

Kuhn, Jeannette. "Hollywood's Little Theatres." *California Life* (November 1928): 16.

Late Nineteenth Century Art: The Art, Architecture and Applied Art of the "Pompous Age". Ed. by Hans Jurgen Hansen.

Translated by Marcus Bullock. New York: McGraw Hill, 1972.

Lewis, Lloyd, and Henry Justin Smith. *Oscar Wilde Discovers America (1882)*. New York: Harcourt, Brace and Co., 1936.

Leff, Sandra. "Essay." In *John White Alexander, 1856–1915, Fin de Siecle American*. New York: Graham Gallery, 1980.

McClelland, Donald. "Edwin Scott: 1862–1929, Biographical Notes." In *Paintings by Edwin Scott from the Alice Pike Barney Memorial Collection, Smithsonian Institution*. Meriden, Connecticut: The Meriden Gravure Co. and The Stinehour Press, 1970.

McKenna, Isabel. *Washington in the 90's*. San Francisco: Press of the Overland Monthly, 1929.

McMullen, Roy. *Victorian Outsider, A Biography of J. A. M. Whistler*. New York: E. P. Dutton and Co., Inc., 1973.

Mechlin, Leila. "The Work of Wood, Donn & Deming, Washington, D.C." *The Architectural Record* 19, no. 4 (April 1906): 244–58.

—. "Art Life in Washington." *Records of the Columbia Historical Society* 24. Washington, D. C.: Columbia Historical Society: 164–78.

Mullikan, Mary Augusta. "Reminiscences of the Whistler Academy. By an American Student." *International Studio*, vol. 34 (February 1905): 237–41.

The Ohio Guide. In *American Guide Series*. Compiled by Workers of the Writers' Program of the Federal Works Projects Administration in the State of Ohio. New York: Oxford University Press, 1948.

Olszewski, George J. *History of the Mall, Washington, D. C.* Washington, D.C.: Office of History and Historic Architecture, Eastern Service Center, 1970.

Pennell, Elizabeth Robbins. *Whistler the Friend*. Philadelphia: J. B. Lippincott Co., 1930.

Pennell, Elizabeth Robbins, and Joseph Pennell. *The Life of James McNeill Whistler*. Vol. 2. London: J. B. Lippincott Co., 1908.

Pincus-Witten, Robert. *Occult Symbolism in France: Josephin Peladan and the Salons de la Rose-Croix*. New York: Garland Publishing, Inc., 1976.

Quick, Michael. *American Expatriate Painters of the Late Nineteenth Century*. Dayton, Ohio: Dayton Art Institute, 1976.

Saint-Gaudens, Homer. "John W. Alexander in the Theatre." *American Magazine of Art* 7, no. 9 (July 1916): 365–371.

Secrest, Meryle. *Between Me and Life: A Biography of Romaine Brooks*. Garden City, New York: Doubleday & Co., Inc., 1974.

Selz, Peter, and Mildred Constantine, eds. *Art Nouveau,*

Art & Design at the Turn of the Century. New York: Museum of Modern Art, 1959.

Seroff, Victor. *The Real Isadora*. New York: Avon Books, 1972.

Shelton, Suzanne. *Divine Dancer: A Biography of Ruth St. Denis*. Garden City, New York: Doubleday & Co., Inc., 1981.

Shultz, Gladys Denny. *Jenny Lind: The Swedish Nightengale*. Philadelphia: J. B. Lippincott Co., 1962.

Simon, Kate. *Fifth Avenue: A Very Social History*. New York: Harcourt Brace Jovanovich, 1978.

St. Denis, Ruth. *An Unfinished Life, An Autobiography*. New York: Harper & Brothers Publishers, 1939.

Steegmuller, Francis. *Apollinaire, A Poet Among Painters*. New York: Farrar, Straus & Co., 1963.

Stoddard, Henry L. *As I Knew Them; Presidents and Politics from Grant to Coolidge*. New York: Harper & Brothers Publishers, 1927.

Terry, Walter. *Miss Ruth, the "More Living Life" of Ruth St. Denis*. New York: Dodd, Mead & Co., 1969.

Thomas, Anna P. "An Artistic Home in Washington: Mrs. Alice Barney's Studio and Residence on Sheridan Circle." *Town & Country* 58, no. 47 (30 January 1904): 10–12.

Thompson, Paul Richard. *The Work of William Morris*. New York: The Viking Press, 1967.

Townsend, James B. "The Summer Washington." *The Illustrated American* (7 September 1985): 300–2.

Trollope, Frances Milton. *Domestic Manners of the Americans, with a History of Mrs. Trollope's Adventures in America*. 1832. Edited by Donald Smalley. New York: Alfred A. Knopf, 1949.

Tuchman, Barbara W. *The Proud Tower, A Portrait of the World Before the War, 1890–1914*. New York: The MacMillan Co., 1966.

Washburn, Wilcombe E. and Cousins, Kathryn. "The Unbuilt Capital: Lost Plans for Washington." *American Institute of Architects Journal* 67, no. 7 (June 1978): 44–45.

Watkinson, Raymond. *William Morris as Designer*. New York: Reinhold Publishing Co., 1967.

Wickes, George. *The Amazon of Letters: The Life and Loves of Natalie Barney*. New York: Popular Library, 1978.

Weintraub, Stanley. *Whistler, A Biography*. New York: Weybright and Talley, 1974.

Wiser, William. *The Crazy Years: Paris in the Twenties*. New York: Atheneum, 1983.

Zakon, Ronnie L. *The Artists and the Studio in the Eighteenth & Nineteenth Centuries*. Cleveland, Ohio: Cleveland Museum of Art, 1978.

CREDITS

Illustration Credits

Unless otherwise noted, all works of art, jewelry, and photographs are in the collection of the National Museum of American Art, Smithsonian Institution, and were the gift of Laura Dreyfus Barney and Natalie Clifford Barney in memory of their mother, Alice Pike Barney. For archival photographs, photographers or photographic studios are credited when known.

Frontispiece: Photo by Virginia Prall; p. 22: Courtesy Cincinnati Historical Society; 29: Courtesy Cincinnati Historical Society; 35: Photo by J. P. Ball; 37: Courtesy Cincinnati Historical Society; 44: Courtesy Museum of the City of New York, The Byron Collection; 45a: Courtesy Museum of the City of New York, The Byron Collection; 45b: Courtesy Museum of the City of New York, Theater Collection; 47: Photo by Sarony's; 50: Photo by Maul and Company Photographers; 68: Photo by Jessup and Appleton; 69: Photo by Jessup and Appleton; 82: Photo by Vathis; 85: Photo by Lindsey & Leighton; 89: Photo by Roseti; 90: Photo by Nadarz; 91 top and bottom: Courtesy Patricia W. Neihoff; 97: Courtesy Diplomatic Reception Rooms, United States Department of State; 98: Photo by Geo. Prince; 107: Photo by Frances Benjamin Johnston; 113: Photo by Emery; 126-7: Photo by Imbert; 135: Photo by Otto; 143: Photo by Sehab and Joaillier; 162: Photo by Gessford; 170: D.C. Building Permit #172, June 26, 1902. Courtesy National Archives; 195: Photo by Frances Benjamin Johnston; 196: Photo by Harris and Ewing; 198: Photo by Saxony; 200–201: Town & Country; 212: Photo by Virginia Prall; 214: Photo by Harris and Ewing; 216: Photo by Virginia Prall; 230: Photo by C. V. Buck, gift of Lisette Thompson and NMAA; 237: Photo by Virginia Prall; 240: Photo by Clinedinst Studio; 246: Photo by Harris and Ewing in *The Club-Fellow and Washington Mirror*; 247: Photo by E. B. Thompson; 248: Photo by Harris and Ewing, gift of Lisette Thompson; 257: Photo by C. Mishkin; 260: Photo by Harris and Ewing; 268: Photo by Geo. Prince; 269: Photo by Charlotte Fairchild; 274: Photo by Harris and Ewing; 276: Photo by L. Brun; 281: Photo by Bachrach; 286: Photo by Geo. Prince; 288: Photo by Harris and Ewing; 294: Photo by G. Edwin Williams; 297: Photo by Paralita; 298: Photo by Eddie Owens.

INDEX

JEAN L. KLING, curator of the Alice Pike Barney collection at the National Museum of American Art and Studio House, delved into Alice's private papers to offer this illuminating portrait of an American artist. In 1964 she began a thirty-year association with the NMAA's Alice Pike Barney Collection, first as registrar and then, in 1981, as curator of Studio House. Until recently, a long-time resident of Washington, D.C., she is currently living in Denver, Colorado.

WANDA M. CORN has been a professor of art history at Stanford University since 1981 and is currently the Anthony P. Meier Family Professor and Director of the Stanford Humanities Center. She lived at Studio House while a Regents Fellow at the Smithsonian in 1987 and has been an NMAA Commissioner since 1988. Her studies center on women artists and cultural leaders of the turn of the century.

DATE DUE

GAYLORD			PRINTED IN U.S.A.